An Interpretive Guide to the Personality Assessment Inventory™ (PAI®)

Leslie C. Morey, PhD

AN INTERPRETIVE GUIDE TO THE PERSONALITY ASSESSMENT INVENTORY™ (PAI®)

Leslie C. Morey, PhD

PAR®

This one is for my Dad.

Library of Congress Cataloging-in-Publication Data

Morey, Leslie Charles, 1956-
    An interpretive guide to the Personality Assessment Inventory/Leslie C. Morey
       p.   cm.
    Includes bibliographical references.
    ISBN 978-0-911907-22-3
    1. Personality Assessment Inventory.   I. Title.
    RC473.P56M67   1996
    616.89'075--dc20   96-8181
                                                       CIP

"Personality Assessment Inventory" is a trademark and "PAI" is a registered trademark owned by Psychological Assessment Resources, Inc.

PAR • 16204 N. Florida Ave. • Lutz, FL 33549 • 1.800.331.8378 • www.parinc.com

9 8 7 6 5 4 3 2 1   Reorder #RO-3341   Printed in the U.S.A.

PREFACE

The topics covered in this *Interpretive Guide* grew out of questions that frequently arose as I presented talks and workshops about using the PAI in many different settings. Participants were always interested in the latest research, conducted by myself and by others, that would help them address important issues in their assessment practice. As I began making presentations to groups who were increasingly sophisticated and experienced in using the PAI, I found it more and more difficult to provide concise answers to their questions; such complex issues required comprehensive explanations. It eventually became clear that an interpretive guide was needed to consolidate what can be determined about some of the most common concerns of the assessment practitioner and researcher who is using the PAI. This volume is an attempt to address that need.

A wealth of information about the use of the PAI has emerged since the test manual was published. Some of this information grew out of my own use of the PAI with individual clinical cases, and some was based on my work with data sets gathered by colleagues in a wide variety of settings. Over time, a number of patterns associated with various referral questions began to emerge. For example, a particular PAI configuration appeared to be common among individuals who had a history of violence, and a series of unusual profile elements tended to be seen only in situations where the motivation to deny problems was quite high. From such observations, I gradually began to articulate informal checklists, indicators to look for when considering appropriate steps to take with a particular patient. Once the lists of indicators were assembled, the next step was testing these informal observations against the assembled data—at times, I found that some element I had thought was unusual was in reality a fairly common finding among people in general. Through this process of observation and verification, my informal hunches became more explicit clinical guidelines for which norms and validity data could be provided.

At the same time, I found I was becoming more inclined to view assessment problems within a PAI framework. When participating in a discussion of a clinical case for whom no PAI results were available, I would find myself wishing for three or four specific bits of PAI profile data to address an unanswered question. When reading a research article about the description, etiology, or treatment of a particular clinical condition, I would internally translate the relevant variables into the language of the PAI scales. For example, when reading an article about the prediction of suicidal behavior, I would visualize how the author's findings would appear if mapped onto the PAI profile.

Among the most important clinical developments presented in this book are several new interpretive indices based on this process of observation and verification, using elements of the PAI profile to address specific assessment questions. These indices are derived not only from my own work, but also from groundbreaking research conducted by others since the PAI was introduced. These indices include a number of actuarial checklists that may help to identify (a) individuals who are attempting to distort their self-presentation, (b) individuals who deny substance misuse, (c) individuals at risk for suicide or for violence, and (d) individuals who may be particularly difficult to engage in therapy. These indices provide a valuable supplement to the standard PAI scales, in many cases providing alternative means of answering some of the most challenging issues in assessment.

I owe a debt of gratitude to the numerous students and PAI workshop participants whose challenging questions provided the stimulus for many of the ideas presented here. I have tried to answer their questions as completely as I can, but in many instances the answers should be considered only partial ones. The validation of a psychological test is never complete; for this reason, this book should be regarded as an "interim report" on the state of the art of PAI interpretation. Although the empirical database that serves as the foundation of this material is already substantial, I look forward to watching it grow. As the literature on the PAI continues to increase, subsequent editions of this book will encompass these new developments. Hopefully, the book will serve as a catalyst for such developments, as there are as many hypotheses remaining to be tested as there are clients in need of assessment. I encourage all readers to contribute to the examination of these hypotheses and to let me know about interesting results so that these new findings can be incorporated into later editions of this *Interpretive Guide*.

L. Morey
Cambridge, Massachusetts

TABLE OF CONTENTS

LIST OF TABLES

LIST OF FIGURES

CHAPTER 1
GENERAL INTRODUCTION AND OVERVIEW

The *Personality Assessment Inventory* (PAI; Morey, 1991) is a self-administered, objective test of personality and psychopathology designed to provide information on critical client variables in professional settings. From its inception, the PAI was developed to provide measures of constructs that are central in treatment planning, implementation, and evaluation. Although it was introduced fairly recently, the PAI already has generated considerable attention from clinicians and researchers, and the test has been described as a "substantial improvement from a psychometric perspective over the existing standard in the area" (Helmes, 1993, p. 417) and as "one of the most exciting new personality tests" (Schlosser, 1992, p. 12). The various applications of the test have generated findings that are important considerations in the interpretation of the test. The purpose of this interpretive guide is to integrate this recent work, and in doing so, to provide specific interpretive information about the use of the PAI in addressing questions central to the clinician and the researcher. This chapter will provide a summary of basic psychometric information about the test, including reliability and validity studies. Subsequent chapters will be devoted to the use of the PAI in addressing specific clinical issues.

The PAI: Rationale and Development

The development of the PAI was based upon a construct validation framework that emphasized a rational as well as quantitative method of scale development. This framework placed a strong emphasis on a theoretically informed approach to the development and selection of items and on the assessment of their stability and correlates. The theoretical articulation of the constructs to be measured was assumed to be critical, because this articulation had to serve as a guide to the content of information sampled and to the subsequent assessment of content validity. In this process, both the conceptual nature and empirical adequacy of the items played an important role in their inclusion in the final version of the inventory. The development of the test went through four iterations in a sequential construct validation strategy similar to that described by Loevinger (1957) and Jackson (1971), although a number of item parameters were considered in addition to those described by these authors. Of paramount importance in the development of the test was the assumption that no single quantitative item parameter should be used as the sole criterion for item selection. An overreliance on a single parameter in item selection typically leads to a scale with one desirable psychometric property and numerous undesirable ones.

As an example, each PAI scale was constructed to include items addressing the full range of severity of the construct, including both its milder as well as most severe forms. Such coverage would not be possible if a single item selection criterion was applied; "milder" items would be most effective in distinguishing clinical subjects from normal respondents, while items reflecting more severe pathology would be more useful in discriminating among different clinical groups. Also, item-total correlations for such different items would be expected to vary as a composition of the sample, due to restriction of range considerations; milder items would display higher biserial correlations in a community sample, whereas more severe items would do so in an inpatient psychiatric sample. Thus, items selected according to a single criterion (e.g., discrimination between groups or item-total correlation) are doomed to provide limited coverage of the full range of symptomatology and/or severity of a clinical construct. The PAI sought to include items that struck a balance between different desirable item parameters, including content coverage as well as empirical characteristics, so that the scales could be useful across a number of different applications.

The clinical syndromes assessed by the PAI were selected on the basis of two criteria: the stability of their importance within the nosology of mental disorder, and their significance in contemporary diagnostic practice. These criteria were assessed through a review of the historical and contemporary literature as well as through a survey of practicing diagnosticians. In generating items for these syndromes, the literature on each clinical syndrome was examined to identify those components most central to the definition of the disorder, and items were written directed at providing an assessment of each component of the syndrome in question.

The test itself contains 344 items that are answered on a four-alternative scale, with the anchors *Totally False, Slightly True, Mainly True*, and *Very True*. Each response is weighted according to the intensity of the feature that the different alternatives represent. Thus, a client who answers *Very True* to the item "Sometimes I think I'm worthless" adds 3 points to his or her raw score on the Depression scale, whereas a client who responds *Slightly True* to the same item adds only 1 point. The use of this four-alternative scaling is justified psychometrically in that it allows a scale to capture more true variance per item, meaning that even scales of modest length can achieve satisfactory reliability. It is also justified clinically, because sometimes even a *Slightly True* response to some constructs (e.g., as suicidal ideation) may merit clinical attention. Furthermore, clients themselves often express dissatisfaction with forced choice alternatives, expressing the belief that the true state of affairs lies somewhere "in the middle" of the two extremes presented.

The 344 items of the PAI comprise 22 nonoverlapping full scales: 4 validity, 11 clinical, 5 treatment consideration, and 2 interpersonal scales. Ten of the full scales contain conceptually derived subscales that were designed into the test to facilitate interpretation and coverage of the full breadth of complex clinical constructs. A brief description of the PAI full scales is provided in Table 1-1; Table 1-2 presents a description of the PAI subscales.

Table 1-1
PAI Full Scales and Their Descriptions

Scale (designation)	Description
Validity Scales	
Inconsistency (*ICN*)	Determines if client is answering consistently throughout inventory. Each pair consists of highly correlated (positively or negatively) items.
Infrequency (*INF*)	Determines if client is responding carelessly or randomly. Items are neutral with respect to psychopathology and have extremely high or low endorsement rates.
Negative Impression (*NIM*)	Suggests an exaggerated unfavorable impression or malingering. Items have relatively low endorsement rates among respondents in clinical settings.
Positive Impression (*PIM*)	Suggests the presentation of a very favorable impression or reluctance to admit minor flaws.
Clinical Scales	
Somatic Complaints (*SOM*)	Focuses on preoccupation with health matters and somatic complaints associated with somatization and conversion disorders.
Anxiety (*ANX*)	Focuses on phenomenology and observable signs of anxiety with an emphasis on assessment across different response modalities.
Anxiety-Related Disorders (*ARD*)	Focuses on symptoms and behaviors related to specific anxiety disorders, particularly phobias, traumatic stress, and obsessive-compulsive symptoms.
Depression (*DEP*)	Focuses on symptoms and phenomenology of depressive disorders.

(continued)

Table 1-1 (continued)
PAI Full Scales and Their Descriptions

Scale (designation)	Description
Clinical Scales (continued)	
Mania (*MAN*)	Focuses on affective, cognitive, and behavioral symptoms of mania and hypomania.
Paranoia (*PAR*)	Focuses on symptoms of paranoid disorders and more enduring characteristics of paranoid personality.
Schizophrenia (*SCZ*)	Focuses on symptoms relevant to the broad spectrum of schizophrenic disorders.
Borderline Features (*BOR*)	Focuses on attributes indicative of a borderline level of personality functioning, including unstable and fluctuating interpersonal relations, impulsivity, affective lability and instability, and uncontrolled anger.
Antisocial Features (*ANT*)	Focuses on history of illegal acts and authority problems, egocentrism, lack of empathy and loyalty, instability, and excitement-seeking.
Alcohol Problems (*ALC*)	Focuses on problematic consequences of alcohol use and features of alcohol dependence.
Drug Problems (*DRG*)	Focuses on problematic consequences of drug use (both prescription and illicit) and features of drug dependence.
Treatment Scales	
Aggression (*AGG*)	Focuses on characteristics and attitudes related to anger, assertiveness, hostility, and aggression.
Suicidal Ideation (*SUI*)	Focuses on suicidal ideation, ranging from hopelessness to thoughts and plans for the suicidal act.
Stress (*STR*)	Measures the impact of recent stressors in major life areas.
Nonsupport (*NON*)	Measures a lack of perceived social support, considering both the level and quality of available support.
Treatment Rejection (*RXR*)	Focuses on attributes and attitudes theoretically predictive of interest and motivation in making personal changes of a psychological or emotional nature.
Interpersonal Scales	
Dominance (*DOM*)	Assesses the extent to which a person is controlling and independent in personal relationships. A bipolar dimension with a dominant style at the high end and a submissive style at the low end.
Warmth (*WRM*)	Assesses the extent to which a person is interested in supportive and empathic personal relationships. A bipolar dimension with a warm, outgoing style at the high end and a cold, rejecting style at the low end.

Table 1-2
PAI Subscales and Their Descriptions

Subscale (designation)	Description
Somatic Complaints	
Conversion (*SOM-C*)	Focuses on symptoms associated with conversion disorder, particularly sensory or motor dysfunctions.
Somatization (*SOM-S*)	Focuses on the frequent occurrence of various common physical symptoms and vague complaints of ill health and fatigue.
Health Concerns (*SOM-H*)	Focuses on a preoccupation with health status and physical problems.
Anxiety	
Cognitive (*ANX-C*)	Focuses on ruminative worry and concern about current issues that result in impaired concentration and attention.
Affective (*ANX-A*)	Focuses on the experience of tension, difficulty in relaxing, and the presence of fatigue as a result of high perceived stress.
Physiological (*ANX-P*)	Focuses on overt physical signs of tension and stress, such as sweaty palms, trembling hands, complaints of irregular heartbeats, and shortness of breath.
Anxiety-Related Disorders	
Obsessive-Compulsive (*ARD-O*)	Focuses on intrusive thoughts or behaviors, rigidity, indecision, perfectionism, and affective constriction.
Phobias (*ARD-P*)	Focuses on common phobic fears, such as social situations, public transportation, heights, enclosed spaces, or other specific objects.
Traumatic Stress (*ARD-T*)	Focuses on the experience of traumatic events that cause continuing distress and that are experienced as having left the client changed or damaged in some fundamental way.
Depression	
Cognitive (*DEP-C*)	Focuses on thoughts of worthlessness, hopelessness, and personal failure, as well as indecisiveness and difficulties in concentration.
Affective (*DEP-A*)	Focuses on feeling of sadness, loss of interest in normal activities, and anhedonia.
Physiological (*DEP-P*)	Focuses on level of physical functioning, activity, and energy, including disturbance in sleep pattern and changes in appetite and/or weight loss.
Mania	
Activity Level (*MAN-A*)	Focuses on overinvolvement in a wide variety of activities in a somewhat disorganized manner and the experience of accelerated thought processes and behavior.
Grandiosity (*MAN-G*)	Focuses on inflated self-esteem, expansiveness, and the belief that one has special and unique skills or talents.

(continued)

Table 1-2 (continued)
PAI Subscales and Their Descriptions

Subscale (designation)	Description
Mania (continued)	
Irritability (*MAN-I*)	Focuses on the presence of strained relationships due to the respondent's frustration with the inability or unwillingness of others to keep up with their plans, demands, and possibly unrealistic ideas.
Paranoia	
Hypervigilance (*PAR-H*)	Focuses on suspiciousness and the tendency to monitor the environment for real or imagined slights by others.
Persecution (*PAR-P*)	Focuses on the belief that one has been treated inequitably and that there is a concerted effort among others to undermine one's interests.
Resentment (*PAR-R*)	Focuses on a bitterness and cynicism in interpersonal relationships, and a tendency to hold grudges and externalize blame for any misfortunes.
Schizophrenia	
Psychotic Experiences (*SCZ-P*)	Focuses on the experience of unusual perceptions and sensations, magical thinking, and/or other unusual ideas that may involve delusional beliefs.
Social Detachment (*SCZ-S*)	Focuses on social isolation, discomfort and awkwardness in social interactions.
Thought Disorder (*SCZ-T*)	Focuses on confusion, concentration problems, and disorganization of thought processes.
Borderline Features	
Affective Instability (*BOR-A*)	Focuses on emotional responsiveness, rapid mood changes, and poor emotional control.
Identity Problems (*BOR-I*)	Focuses on uncertainty about major life issues and feelings of emptiness, unfulfillment, and an absence of purpose.
Negative Relationships (*BOR-N*)	Focuses on a history of ambivalent, intense relationships in which one has felt exploited and betrayed.
Self-Harm (*BOR-S*)	Focuses on impulsivity in areas that have high potential for negative consequences.
Antisocial Features	
Antisocial Behaviors (*ANT-A*)	Focuses on a history of antisocial acts and involvement in illegal activities.
Egocentricity (*ANT-E*)	Focuses on a lack of empathy or remorse and a generally exploitive approach to interpersonal relationships.
Stimulus-Seeking (*ANT-S*)	Focuses on a craving for excitement and sensation, a low tolerance for boredom, and a tendency to be reckless and risk-taking.

(continued)

Table 1-2 (continued)
PAI Subscales and Their Descriptions

Subscale (designation)	Description
Aggression	
Aggressive Attitude (*AGG-A*)	Focuses on hostility, poor control over anger expression, and a belief in the instrumental utility of aggression.
Verbal Aggression (*AGG-V*)	Focuses on verbal expressions of anger ranging from assertiveness to abusiveness, and a readiness to express anger to others.
Physical Aggression (*AGG-P*)	Focuses on a tendency to physical displays of anger, including damage to property, physical fights, and threats of violence.

Normative Data

The PAI was developed and standardized for use in the clinical assessment of individuals in the age range of 18 through adulthood. The initial reading level analyses of the PAI test items indicated that reading ability at the fourth-grade level was necessary to complete the inventory. Subsequent studies of this issue (e.g., Schinka & Borum, 1993) have supported the conclusion that the PAI items are written at a grade equivalent lower than estimates for comparable instruments.

PAI scale and subscale raw scores are transformed to *T* scores in order to provide interpretation relative to a standardization sample of 1,000 community-dwelling adults. This sample was carefully selected to match 1995 U.S. census projections on the basis of gender, race, and age; the educational level of the standardization sample was selected to be representative given the required fourth-grade reading level. The only stipulation for inclusion in the standardization sample (other than stratification fit) was that the respondent had to endorse more than 90% of PAI items (i.e., no more than 33 items could be left blank). No other restrictions based upon PAI data were applied in creating the census-matched standardization sample.

The PAI *T* scores are calibrated to have a mean of 50 and a standard deviation of 10, using a standard linear transformation from the community sample norms. Thus, a *T*-score value greater than 50 lies above the mean in comparison to the scores of respondents in the standardization sample. Roughly 84% of nonclinical respondents will have a *T* score below 60 (i.e., 1 *SD* above the mean) on most scales, whereas 98% of nonclinical respondents will have scores below 70 (i.e., 2 *SD* above the mean). Thus, a *T* score at or above 70 represents a pronounced deviation from the typical responses of adults living in the community.

For each scale and subscale, the *T* scores were linearly transformed from the means and standard deviations derived from the census-matched standardization sample. Unlike many other similar instruments, the PAI does not calculate *T* scores differently for men and women; instead, the same (combined) norms are used for both genders. This is because separate norms distort natural epidemiological differences between genders. For example, women are less likely than men to receive a diagnosis of antisocial personality, and this is reflected in lower mean scores for women on the Antisocial Features (*ANT*) scale. A separate normative procedure for men and women would result in similar numbers of each gender scoring in the clinically significant range, a result that does not reflect the established gender ratio for this disorder. The PAI development included several procedures designed to eliminate items that might be biased due to demographic features (e.g., race, gender, or age), and items that displayed any signs of being interpreted differently as a function of these features were eliminated in the course of selecting the final test items. As it turns out, with relatively few exceptions, differences as a function of demography were negligible in the community sample. Table 1-3 lists all PAI variables for which any of three demographic variables (i.e., race, gender, or age) accounted for more than 5% of the variance in the PAI score and the resulting effect (in terms of *T*-score units) of that variable.

Table 1-3
Summary of Significant Gender, Race, and
Age Influences on PAI Scale Scores

PAI Scale	Demographic influences		Primary subscales affected
PAR	Non-White:	+ 6T	PAR-H
	18-29 years:	+ 5T	PAR-P
	60+ years:	− 4T	PAR-R
BOR	18-29 years:	+ 6T	BOR-I
	60+ years:	− 4T	BOR-I
ANT	Male:	+ 3T	ANT-A
	18-29 years:	+ 7T	ANT-S
	60+ years:	− 4T	ANT-A
AGG	18-29 years:	+ 5T	AGG-V
	60+ years:	− 4T	AGG-P
STR	18-29 years:	+ 4T	(no subscales)
	60+ years:	− 4T	

T scores are derived from a representative community sample; therefore, they provide a useful means for determining whether certain problems are clinically significant, because relatively few normal adults will obtain markedly elevated scores. However, other comparisons are often of equal importance in clinical decision-making. For example, nearly all patients report depression at their initial evaluation; the question confronting the clinician considering a diagnosis of major depression is one of *relative* severity of symptomatology. Knowing that an individual's score on the PAI Depression scale is elevated in comparison to the standardization sample is of value, but a comparison of the elevation relative to a clinical sample may be more critical in forming diagnostic hypotheses.

To facilitate these comparisons, the PAI profile form (shown in Figure 1-1) also indicates the *T* scores that correspond to marked elevations when referenced against a representative *clinical* sample. The profile "skyline" indicates the score for each scale and subscale that represents the raw score that is 2 standard deviations above the mean for a clinical sample of 1,246 patients selected from a wide variety of different professional settings. Thus, roughly 98% of clinical patients will obtain scores below the skyline on the profile form. Therefore, scores above this

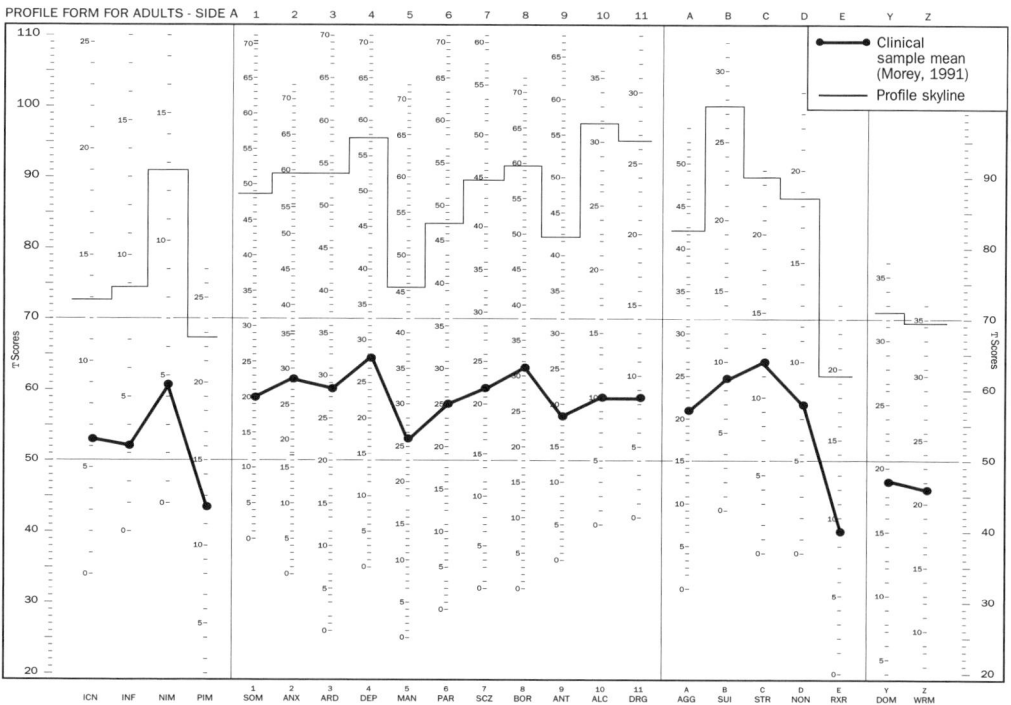

Figure 1-1. Mean PAI *T* scores for a clinical sample of adults (*N* = 1,246) and the skyline at 2 *SD* above the mean in that clinical sample.

skyline represent a marked elevation of scores relative to those of *patients in clinical settings*. Thus, interpretation of PAI profiles can be accomplished in comparison to both normal and clinical samples.

The *PAI Professional Manual* (Morey, 1991) provides normative transformations for a number of different comparisons. The appendices provide *T*-score transformations referenced against the clinical sample and a large sample of college students (*N* = 1,051), as well as for various demographic subgroups of the community standardization sample. Although the differences between different demographic groups were generally quite small, there are occasions where it may be useful to make comparisons with reference to particular groups. The raw score means and standard deviations needed to convert raw scores to *T* scores with reference to normative data provided by particular groups (men, women, Blacks, and respondents over age 60) are provided in the manual for this purpose. However, for most clinical and research applications, the use of the *T* scores derived from the full normative data is strongly recommended, because this sample was both large and representative of the general population.

Reliability of the PAI

The reliability of the PAI has been examined in a number of different studies that have examined the internal consistency, test-retest reliability, and configural stability of the instrument.

The internal consistency of the PAI has been examined in a number of different populations (Alterman et al., 1995; Boyle & Lennon, 1994; Morey, 1991; Rogers, Flores, Ustad, & Sewell, 1995; Schinka, 1995). This has involved the use of coefficient alpha (Cronbach, 1951), which can be interpreted as an estimate of the mean of all possible split-half combinations of items. The internal consistency alphas for the PAI full scales are satisfactory; in the *PAI Professional Manual*, Morey reports median alphas for the full scales of .81, .82, and .86 for normative, college, and clinical samples, respectively. As expected, the scales tend to appear more internally consistent in more heterogeneous samples. Alterman et al. found a median alpha of .78 in a sample of methadone maintenance patients; Schinka found a median alpha of .86 for full scales and .77 for the subscales in an alcoholic sample. Boyle and Lennon (1994) reported a median alpha of .84 in a mixed clinical–normal sample. Internal consistency estimates for the *ICN* and *INF* scales are consistently lower than those for other scales, because these scales do not measure theoretical constructs; instead, they measure the care with which the respondent completed the test. Lower alphas for such scales would be anticipated, as carelessness might vary within a given sitting (e.g., a respondent might complete the first half of the test accurately, but complete the last half haphazardly).

The lowest internal consistency estimates for the PAI reported in the literature were obtained using the Spanish version of the instrument (Rogers et al., 1995), where an average alpha of .63 was obtained. Rogers and colleagues concluded that the internal consistency of the treatment consideration scales seemed to be most affected by the translation of the test. Examination of internal consistency estimates for the PAI full scales for groups defined by various demographic characteristics (Morey, 1991) does suggest that there is little variability in internal consistency (i.e., median scale alphas) as a function of race (i.e., Whites = .77, non-Whites = .78), gender (i.e., men = .79, women = .75), or age (i.e., under 40 years = .79, 40 years and over = .75).

The temporal stability of PAI scales has been examined by administering the test to respondents on two different occasions (Boyle & Lennon, 1994; Morey, 1991; Rogers et al., 1995). For the standardization studies, median test-retest reliability over a 4-week interval for the 11 full clinical scales was .86 (Morey, 1991), leading to standard error of measurement estimates for these scales on the order of 3 to 4 *T*-score points, with 95% confidence intervals of ±6 to 8 *T*-score points. Examination of the mean absolute *T*-score change values for scales also revealed that the absolute changes over time were quite small, on the order of 2 to 3 *T*-score points for most of the full scales (Morey, 1991). Boyle and Lennon (1994) reported a median test-retest reliability of .73 in their normal sample over 28 days. Rogers et al. (1995) found an average stability of .71 for the Spanish version of the PAI, administered over a 2-week interval.

Because multiple-scale inventories are often interpreted configurally, additional questions concerning the stability of configurations on the 11 PAI clinical scales are necessary. One such analysis (Morey, 1991) examined the inverse (or Q-type) correlation between each respondent's test and retest profiles. Correlations were obtained for each of the 155 respondents in the full retest sample, and a distribution of these within-subject profile correlations was obtained. Conducted in this manner, the median correlation over time of the clinical scale configuration was .83, indicating a substantial degree of stability in profile configurations over time.

Validity of the PAI

The validation of measures of clinical constructs is a process that requires accumulation of data concerning convergent and discriminant validity correlates. In Morey's (1991) examination of PAI validity, a number of the best available clinical indicators were administered concurrently to various samples to determine their convergence with corresponding PAI scales. Furthermore, diagnostic and other clinical judgments concerning clinical behaviors (as rated by the treating clinician) were also examined to determine whether their PAI correlates were consistent with hypothesized relationships. Finally, a number of simulation studies were performed to determine the efficacy of the PAI validity scales in identifying response sets. To date, a number of studies have been conducted examining correlates of various PAI scales; in the *PAI Professional Manual*, Morey provides information about correlations of individual scales with over 50 concurrent indices of psychopathology. Noteworthy findings from these studies are described in the following paragraphs.

The PAI validity scales were developed to provide an assessment of the potential influence of certain response tendencies on PAI test performance. Two of these scales, Inconsistency (*ICN*) and Infrequency (*INF*), were developed to assess deviations from conscientious responding, whereas the other two validity scales, Negative Impression (*NIM*) and Positive Impression (*PIM*), were developed to provide an assessment of efforts at impression management by the respondent.

To model the performance of respondents completing the PAI in a random fashion, computer-generated profiles were created by generating random responses to individual PAI items and then scoring all scales according to their normal scoring algorithms. A total of 1,000 simulated protocols were generated for this analysis. Comparison of profiles derived from normal respondents, clinical respondents, and the random response simulations demonstrated a clear separation between scores of actual respondents and scores from the random simulations; 99.4% of these random profiles were identified as such by either *ICN* or *INF* (Morey, 1991).

To model the performance of respondents attempting to manage their impressions in either a positive or negative direction, studies have been performed (Morey, 1991) in which respondents were instructed to simulate such response styles. Comparisons of profiles for normal respondents, clinical respondents, and the corresponding response style simulation groups demonstrated a clear separation between scores for the actual respondents and scores for the simulated response groups. Respondents scoring above the critical level of *NIM* were 14.7 times more likely to be a member of the malingering group than of the clinical sample, whereas respondents scoring above threshold on *PIM* were 13.9 times more likely to be from the positive dissimulation sample than from a community sample. Subsequent studies generally support the ability of these scales to distinguish simulators from actual protocols under a variety of response set conditions (e.g., Cashel, Rogers, Sewell, & Martin-Cannici, 1995; Rogers, Ornduff, & Sewell, 1993). Results of these studies are reviewed in greater detail in chapters 4 and 5.

In addition to such simulation studies, a number of correlational studies have been performed to determine the convergent and discriminant validity of the PAI validity scales as measured against other commonly used measures of similar constructs (Ban, Fjetland, Kutcher, & Morey, 1993; Costa & McCrae, 1992; Morey, 1991). For example, *NIM* correlated significantly ($r = .54$) with the Minnesota Multiphasic Personality Inventory (MMPI; Hathaway & McKinley, 1967) *F* scale; *PIM* was associated with the Marlowe-Crowne (Crowne & Marlowe, 1957) Social Desirability scale ($r = .56$) as well as with the MMPI *K* ($r = .47$) and *L* ($r = .41$) scales (Morey, 1991). PAI scales *INF* and *ICN* displayed negligible correlations with any measures, an expected result as these scales were designed as relatively pure indicators of measurement error.

The clinical scales of the PAI were assembled to provide information about critical diagnostic features of 11 important clinical constructs. A number of different validity indicators have been used to provide information on the convergent and discriminant validity of the PAI clinical scales; these indicators can be divided into measures of "neurotic features," "psychotic features," and "behavior disorder features." Within the neurotic spectrum, correlations with the NEO Personality Inventory (NEO-PI; Costa & McCrae, 1985), the MMPI clinical and research scales (Hathaway & McKinley, 1967; Morey, Waugh, & Blashfield, 1985; Wiggins, 1966), and several specialized assessment instruments have been examined. These specialized instruments include the following: the Wahler Physical Symptoms Inventory (Wahler Inventory; Wahler, 1983), a broad measure of somatic complaints; the Beck Depression Inventory (BDI; Beck & Steer, 1987), the Beck Anxiety Inventory (BAI; Beck & Steer, 1990) and the Beck Hopelessness Scale (BHS; Beck & Steer, 1988), three widely used and well-validated measures of negative affect; the Hamilton Rating Scale for Depression (HAM-D: Hamilton, 1960), perhaps the most widely used measure of outcome in treatment studies of depression; the State-Trait Anxiety Inventory (STAI; Spielberger, 1983), a widely used measure that distinguishes between the situational and more enduring elements of anxiety; the Fear Survey Schedule (FSS; Wolpe & Lang, 1964), a comprehensive assessment of common fears; the Maudsley Obsessive-Compulsive Inventory (Maudsley Inventory; Rachman & Hodgson, 1980), a measure of severe obsessional ideation and contamination fears; and the Mississippi Scale for Combat-Related Posttraumatic Stress Disorder (Mississippi PTSD; Keane, Caddell, & Taylor, 1988).

Correlations between each of the full scale scores for the four PAI neurotic cluster scales and the validation measures described above follow hypothesized patterns, demonstrating strong associations with other measures of neuroticism (Costa & McCrae, 1992; Montag & Levin, 1994; Morey, 1991). The strongest correlates for Somatic Complaints (*SOM*) were found with the Wiggins Health Concerns ($r = .80$) and Organic Problems ($r = .82$) content scales, the Wahler Inventory ($r = .72$), and the MMPI Hypochondriasis ($r = .60$) scale. Each of these measures is a fairly straightforward assessment of complaints regarding physical functioning, so this pattern of correlations is consistent with expectations. The *SOM* scale also displays small-to-moderate relationships with measures of distress, such as anxiety or depression. The *SOM* scale is generally the highest point of the PAI profile in a general medical population, although, even in such populations, the average score is typically below 70*T* (Osborne, 1994).

The Anxiety (*ANX*) scale demonstrated substantial correlations with a number of measures of negative affect, including the NEO-PI Neuroticism ($r = .76$) and Anxiety ($r = .76$), the STAI Trait Anxiety Inventory ($r = .73$), and the Wiggins Depression content ($r = .76$) scales. This finding is consistent with research results highlighting the prominent role of anxiety in many mental disorders; such a pattern should be anticipated, as *ANX* was intended to be a general measure of anxiety rather than a specific diagnostic indicator. In contrast, the Anxiety-Related Disorders (*ARD*) scale was designed to provide content relevant to more specific diagnostic differentiations; hence, the pattern of correlations tends to be more specific than that observed with *ANX*. The largest correlation for *ARD* was with the Mississippi PTSD scale ($r = .81$), and the second largest involved the FSS ($r = .66$); each of these scales directly parallels a disorder for which *ARD* was designed to provide coverage. The *ARD* scale has also been found to correlate with the probability of getting nightmares ($r = .46$), with *ARD-T* ($r = .51$), in particular, being associated with night terrors (Greenstein, 1993). The *ARD* scale (particularly *ARD-T*) also has been found to differentiate between women psychiatric patients who were victims of childhood abuse and women patients who did not experience such abuse (Cherepon & Prinzhorn, 1994).

The Depression (*DEP*) scale demonstrates its highest correlations with various well validated indicators of depression, such as the BDI ($r = .81$), the HAM-D ($r = .78$), and the Wiggins Depression content scale ($r = .81$). This is consistent with expectations, because these measures are widely used in the assessment of depression and related symptomatology. Other noteworthy correlates of the Depression scale include the MMPI *D* scale ($r = .66$), the Wiggins Poor Morale scale ($r = .74$), the NEO-PI Neuroticism ($r = .69$) and Depression ($r = .70$) scales, and the Beck Hopelessness scale ($r = .67$).

In addition, correlations with a number of other measures of related constructs can provide information relevant to the convergent and discriminant validity of the PAI "psychotic cluster" scales. For example, the MMPI, the NEO-PI, the Interpersonal Adjective Scale (IAS-R; Trapnell & Wiggins, 1990) and the clinician-rated Brief Psychiatric Rating Scale (BPRS; Overall & Gorham, 1962) include scales that capture the cognitive and interpersonal abnormalities that characterize these disorders. Correlations between each the three PAI psychotic spectrum scales and these validation measures generally follow the expected pattern (Ban et al., 1993; Costa & McCrae, 1992; Morey, 1991). The Mania (*MAN*) scale has demonstrated its strongest correlations with Wiggins Hypomania ($r = .63$), Psychoticism ($r = .58$), and Hostility ($r = .55$) content scales; with the BPRS clinical ratings of Grandiosity ($r = .48$) and Conceptual Disorganization ($r = .40$); and with the MMPI *Ma* scale ($r = .53$). The Paranoia (*PAR*) scale demonstrated its largest correlations with the MMPI Paranoid personality disorder scale ($r = .70$), the Wiggins Psychoticism scale ($r = .60$), and various measures of hostility such as the Wiggins Hostility content scale ($r = .54$) and the NEO-PI Hostility facet scale ($r = .55$). A moderate correlation with the MMPI *Pa* scale was also observed ($r = .45$). The Schizophrenia (*SCZ*) scale has been found to correlate with the Wiggins Psychoticism content scale ($r = .76$) and the MMPI Schizotypal ($r = .67$) and Paranoid ($r = .66$) personality disorder scales. The *SCZ* scale was also positively correlated with the MMPI *Sc* scale ($r = .55$) and negatively associated with indices of sociability and social effectiveness such as the NEO-PI Agreeableness ($r = -.49$) and Gregariousness ($r = -.57$) scales. This pattern indicates that scores on the *SCZ* scale reflect disruptions in both the cognitive (e.g., delusions, hallucinations) and the interpersonal (e.g., limited social competence) realms of functioning. Finally, the *SCZ* scale has been found to distinguish schizophrenic patients from controls (Boyle & Lennon, 1994). In that study the schizophrenic sample did not differ significantly from a sample of alcoholics on *SCZ* scores, although the article suggested that many of the alcoholic patients completed the PAI during detoxification, which might complicate differential diagnosis based solely upon *SCZ* scores.

Information on the convergent and discriminant validity of the PAI scales in the behavior disorders cluster is also available. In addition to the NEO-PI, the IAS-R, and the MMPI, the PAI scales have been correlated with a number of specialized assessment instruments, including the Bell Object Relations Inventory (Bell Inventory; Bell, Billington, & Becker, 1985), a multifactorial questionnaire constructed to measure a variety of interpersonal attitudes and beliefs indicative of early pathological object relations thought to be at the core of the borderline syndrome

(Bell, Billington, Cicchetti, & Gibbons, 1988); the Michigan Alcoholism Screening Test (MAST; Selzer, 1971), a widely used and well validated measure of problem behaviors associated with drinking; the Drug Abuse Screening Test (DAST; Skinner, 1982), a measure, patterned after the MAST, that assesses the consequences of drug abuse; and the Self-Report Psychopathy test designed by Hare (1985) to assess his model of psychopathy.

Correlations between scores for the four PAI behavior disorder cluster scales and these validation measures follow expected patterns (Costa & McCrae, 1992; Kurtz, Morey, & Tomarken, 1993; Morey, 1991). The strongest correlates of the Borderline Features (BOR) scale are the MMPI Borderline personality disorder scale (r = .77), the NEO-PI Neuroticism scale (r = .67), and several different measures of hostility, such as the NEO-PI Hostility facet (r = .70). The BOR scale also displayed substantial correlations with the Bell Inventory Insecure Attachment scale (r = .63), the NEO-PI Impulsiveness facet (r = .52), and the Wiggins Family Problems (r = .63) and Psychoticism (r = .63) content scales. This pattern of anger, impulsiveness, and interpersonal clashes is consistent with the core features of the borderline syndrome. Other studies have supported the validity and utility of this scale in a variety of clinical contexts. The BOR scale in isolation has been found to distinguish borderline patients from unscreened controls with an 80% hit rate; it successfully identified 91% of these respondents as part of a discriminant function (Bell-Pringle, 1994). Classifications based on the BOR scale have been validated in a variety of domains related to borderline functioning, including depression, personality traits, coping, Axis I disorders, and interpersonal problems (Trull, 1995). These BOR scale classifications were also found to be predictive of 2-year outcome on academic indices in college students, even controlling for academic potential and diagnoses of substance abuse (Trull, Useda, Conforti, & Doan, 1995).

The PAI Antisocial Features (ANT) scale demonstrated its largest correlations with the Hare Psychopathy Scale (r = .82) and the MMPI Antisocial personality disorder scale (r = .77). Other correlates included the Wiggins Hostility (r = .57) and Family Problems (r = .52) content scales, the NEO-PI Excitement Seeking facet (r = .56), and the IAS-R cold interpersonal octant (r = .45). This pattern suggests that the ANT scale addresses the personality, interpersonal, and behavioral elements of psychopathy. The correlation with the MMPI Pd scale is positive, but not impressive (r = .34), suggesting that the two scales represent the core features of the disorder somewhat differently. The PAI Alcohol Problems (ALC) and Drug Problems (DRG) scales each demonstrate a similar pattern of correlates: strong correlations with corresponding measures of substance abuse and moderate associations with indicators of antisocial personality. ALC yields a correlation of .89 with the MAST, whereas *DRG* correlates .69 with the DAST. The *ALC* scale has been found to differentiate patients in an alcohol rehabilitation clinic from both patients with schizophrenia and normal controls (Boyle & Lennon, 1994). The *DRG* scale has also been found to successfully discriminate drug abusers and methadone maintenance patients from general clinical and community samples (Alterman et al., 1995).

The treatment consideration scales of the PAI were assembled to provide indicators of potential complications in treatment that would not necessarily be apparent from diagnostic information. There are five of these scales: two indicators of potential for harm to self or others, two measures of the respondent's environmental circumstances, and one indicator of the respondent's motivation for treatment. These scales have been compared to a number of measures of related constructs. In addition to the NEO-PI, the IAS-R, and the MMPI, the scales have been correlated with a number of specialized assessment instruments. The BDI, BAI, and BHS provide convergent correlates for suicidal ideation. Also, the Suicide Probability Scale (SPS; Cull & Gill, 1982) serves as a concurrent indicator of suicide potential. The SPS has four subscales that assess hopelessness, suicidal ideation, negative self-evaluation, and hostility, in addition to yielding a total score for suicide probability. The State-Trait Anger Expression Inventory (STAXI; Spielberger, 1988) provides a marker for aggression that is broken down into six scales and two subscales. The Perceived Social Support scales (Procidano & Heller, 1983) provide an assessment of the subjective impact of supportive transactions between the respondent and his or her social support system; two separate scales assess support provided by the respondent's family and the respondent's friends. Finally, the Schedule of Recent Events (SRE; Holmes & Rahe, 1967) is a unit-scoring adaptation of the widely used Holmes and Rahe (1967) checklist of recent stressors, where respondents are asked to indicate major life changes that have taken place during the 12 months prior to evaluation.

Correlations between the PAI treatment consideration scales and such validation measures provide support for the construct validity of these PAI scales (Costa & McCrae, 1992; Morey, 1991). Substantial correlations have been identified between the Aggression (*AGG*) scale and the NEO-PI Hostility ($r = .83$) and STAXI Trait Anger ($r = .75$) scales. The *AGG* scale also was negatively correlated with the STAXI Anger Control scale ($r = -.57$). The Suicidal Ideation (*SUI*) scale was most positively correlated with the BHS ($r = .64$), the BDI ($r = .61$), the Suicidal Ideation ($r = .56$) and Total Score ($r = .40$) of the SPS; it also was found to be negatively correlated with the measures of perceived social support. As expected, the Non-support (*NON*) scale was found to be highly (and inversely) correlated with the social support measures: $-.67$ with PSS-Family and $-.63$ with PSS-Friends. *NON* also was moderately associated with numerous measures of distress and tension. The Stress (STR) scale displayed its largest correlations with the SRE ($r = .50$) and also was associated with various indices of depression and poor morale. Finally, the Treatment Rejection (RXR) scale was found to be negatively associated with Wiggins Poor Morale ($r = -.78$) and the NEO-PI Vulnerability ($r = -.54$) scales, consistent with the idea that distress can serve as a motivator for treatment. The Treatment Rejection scale has been shown to be positively associated with indices of social support ($r = .26$ to $.49$), suggesting that people are less likely to be motivated for treatment if they have an intact and available support system as an alternative.

The interpersonal scales of the PAI were designed to provide an assessment of the interpersonal style of respondents along two dimensions: (a) a warmly affiliative versus a cold rejecting axis, and (b) a dominating and controlling versus a meekly submissive style. These axes provide a useful way of conceptualizing variation in normal personality as well as in many different mental disorders, and persons at the extremes of these dimensions may present with a variety of disorders. The *PAI Professional Manual* (Morey, 1991) describes a number of studies indicating that diagnostic groups differ on these dimensions; for example, spouse-abusers are relatively high on the Dominance (DOM) scale, whereas schizophrenics are low on the Warmth (WRM) scale. Correlations with related measures also provide support for the construct validity of these scales. For example, the correlations with the IAS-R vector scores are consistent with expectations, with PAI *DOM* associated with the IAS-R Dominance vector ($r = .61$) and PAI *WRM* associated with the IAS-R Love vector ($r = .65$). The NEO-PI Extroversion scale roughly bisects the high *DOM*/high *WRM* quadrant, as it is moderately positively correlated with both scales; this finding is consistent with previous research (Trapnell & Wiggins, 1990). The *WRM* scale was also correlated with the NEO-PI Gregariousness scale ($r = .46$), whereas *DOM* was associated with the NEO Assertiveness facet ($r = .71$).

In summary, the PAI scales have been found to associate in theoretically concordant ways with most major instruments for the assessment of diagnosis and treatment efficacy. Strategies for the interpretation of the PAI profile and its use in treatment planning and evaluation are presented in following sections.

Basic Interpretive Strategy

Because the development of the PAI emphasized the importance of both convergent and discriminant validity of the instrument, the interpretation of PAI protocols is relatively straightforward. For example, scales were designed to be generally pure measures of the specific constructs; thus, an elevation on the *DEP* scale may be interpreted as indicating that the respondent reports a number of experiences consistent with the symptomatology of clinical depression. Interpretive hypotheses may be generated at four different levels: the *item* level, the *subscale* level, the *full scale* level, and the *configuration* level.

Interpretation of PAI responses at the item level are meaningful because the content of each item was assumed to be critical in determining its relevance for the assessment of the construct. For example, each item was reviewed by a panel of experts to ensure that its content was directly relevant to the specific clinical construct. As a result, a review of item content can provide specific information about the nature of the difficulties experienced by the respondent. In addition, 27 PAI items were identified as "critical items" based on two criteria: (a) importance of their content as an indicator of potential crisis situations, and (b) very low endorsement rates in normal individuals. Endorsement of any of these items should be followed by more detailed questioning that can clarify the nature and severity of these concerns.

The PAI subscales were constructed as an aid in isolating the core elements of the different clinical constructs measured by the instrument. These subscales can serve to clarify the meaning of full scale elevations, and may be used configurally in diagnostic decision-making. For example, many patients typically come to clinical settings with marked distress and dysphoria; this often leads to elevations on most unidimensional depression scales. However, unless other manifestations of the syndrome are present, this does not necessarily indicate that Major Depressive Disorder is the likely diagnosis. In the absence of features such as vegetative signs, lowered self-esteem, and negative expectancies, the diagnosis may not be warranted even with a prominent elevation on a unidimensional depression scale. On the PAI, such a pattern would lead to an elevation on *DEP-A*, representing the dysphoria and distress, but no elevations on *DEP-P* (the vegetative signs) and *DEP-C* (the cognitive signs). As a result, an overall elevation on *DEP* in this instance would not be interpreted as diagnostic of major depression because of the lack of supporting data from the subscale configuration.

Interpretation of PAI full scale scores is aided by comparison to two referents: expected scores in the community and expected scores in clinical patients. As described earlier, the PAI profile form (Figure 1-1) provides a skyline marking an elevation of 2 standard deviations with respect to the clinical sample. The similarity of expected scores for these two populations varies a great deal across scales. For example, the interpersonal scales *DOM* and *WRM* have distributions that are quite similar in both community and clinical samples; thus, marked elevations (or very low scores) are noteworthy regardless of the nature of the client. On the other hand, the *RXR* scale (which was designed to identify risk for early treatment termination) has a markedly different distribution in clinical and community samples. A majority of clinical respondents who are currently in treatment obtain scores that are considerably lower than those of community respondents, who are typically not in psychological treatment and have little interest in it. Thus, a *T* score of 50 on *RXR* in a client presenting for psychotherapy, although "average" for a community sample, is actually considerably above the expected score for respondents in clinical settings. In this instance, the *RXR* score should be interpreted as indicating potentially significant resistance to change for this client. In contrast, an *RXR* score of 50*T* in an individual who was administered the PAI for personnel selection purposes would be unremarkable. In these two examples, the differences in the assessment question leads to differences in the interpretation of the information yielded by a normative transformation.

The broadest level of PAI interpretation involves the analysis of scale configuration. Traditionally, the premise behind multidimensional inventories such as the PAI has been that the *combination* of information provided by the multiple scales is greater than any of its parts; hence, most previous research focused on the profile yielded by such an inventory, rather than any single scale elevations. There are a variety of ways to examine profile configuration; to date, there have been five research approaches to studying the configural use of PAI profile data. These approaches include the use of mean profiles, profile codetypes, cluster profiles, actuarial functions, and conceptually driven configural decision rules. These differing approaches can be applied to different issues in decision-making, including diagnostic (e.g., Is this a schizophrenic patient or a depressed patient?), intervention (e.g., Does this patient require inpatient treatment?), or protocol-related (e.g., Is this a valid PAI protocol?) issues. Each of these approaches will be discussed throughout this guide in the context of these different types of decisions.

The following chapters will focus on the four different interpretive levels in an effort to resolve certain dilemmas the test user may face in interpreting the PAI. The initial focus is on understanding the composition and interpretation of the individual scales; this is followed by a discussion of the meaning of different two-point combinations of scales (codetypes). The remainder of this interpretive guide explores specific issues commonly encountered in PAI interpretation: Is this patient malingering or defensive? What diagnoses should be considered? What is the person's characteristic view of self and of others? What initial steps should be considered in planning treatment? In all cases, the available data are used to address these questions, but, as is the case with any assessment instrument, many questions require further study. It is hoped that current and future PAI users can help to fill the gaps in this literature, so that subsequent editions of this guide can incorporate the advances made possible by such work.

CHAPTER 2
INTERPRETING PAI CLINICAL SCALE ELEVATIONS

The starting point in interpreting the PAI lies at the level of the individual scales that were developed to measure the specific construct implied by the scale name. Each scale on the test was designed to measure the major facets of a different clinical construct, as determined by current theoretical and empirical work on those constructs. Most of the clinical scales offer subscales. Therefore, configural interpretation of the test is possible even at the level of the individual scales, because two identical elevations on a particular scale may be interpreted quite differently depending on the configuration of the subscales. The following sections describe the logic underlying the PAI clinical scales and the interpretations of different ranges and configurations of scores on each scale.

Somatic Complaints (*SOM*)

The Somatic Complaints scale is precisely what the scale name suggests: the items reflect complaints and concerns about physical functioning and health matters in general. Interpretively, there are many things that the *SOM* scale should not be expected to do. In isolation, *SOM* cannot distinguish between *functional* and *organic* somatic features. It is not a neuropsychological assessment instrument, and it certainly is not sufficient evidence for establishing a diagnosis of a physical condition. However, the scale is useful for assessing the extent to which physical conditions are a central concern in an individual's life. It is important to recognize that people with very similar physical conditions can differ drastically in their reactions to the condition. For example, one person faced with a crippling chronic condition might react stoically, successfully adapting to any impairment and, perhaps, refusing to acknowledge the limitations imposed by his or her health. Another person, faced with the same condition, might ruminate bitterly about these limitations, complaining endlessly about physical problems and, perhaps, even using the problems as a means of controlling other people. There are valid physical problems in both situations, but the psychological reaction to the problems is quite different. The *SOM* scale provides information about the latter, but it should not be used in isolation to determine the former.

The *Diagnostic and Statistical Manual of Mental Disorders* (*DSM-IV*; American Psychiatric Association, 1994) classification system groups a variety of syndromes under the concept of Somatoform Disorder; all involve physical symptoms suggestive of some organic disorder, but one for which there are no known physiologic mechanisms. The constructs included in this group of disorders (e.g., conversion hysteria and hypochondriasis) have had a variety of clinical meanings over the years; for this reason, it is difficult to evaluate the results of diagnostic research that has accumulated on this topic. One of the central distinctions drawn in recent years has been between individuals who present with multiple, relatively minor physiologic symptoms and individuals who complain of major disability of some sensory or motor function. In the *DSM* manual, the former individuals are referred to as having Somatization Disorder, whereas the latter are typically diagnosed with Conversion Disorder. This distinction can be traced back to the early studies of Briquet (1859), who found that most patients with "hysteria" displayed few of the symptoms thought to be pathognomonic of the disorder. More recently, the symptomatic approach of Briquet has been applied to contemporary diagnoses, with research suggesting that "Briquet's syndrome" (or Somatization Disorder, as it is now called) reflects a distinct diagnostic entity from the traditional construct of conversion hysteria (Guze, Woodruff, & Clayton, 1971). Both disorders are viewed as distinct from Hypochondriasis, which, in contemporary diagnostic practice, refers to a preoccupation with the fear or belief of having a disease.

The PAI *SOM* scale was designed to provide a differential assessment of some of these components of somatoform disorders. The three subscales of *SOM* reflect different facets of somatic complaints frequently associated with psychological conditions. Although two of the subscale names reflect this association, one should not assume that an elevation on one of these scales indicates that the *diagnosis* is present, as for each of those diagnoses the presumption is made that organic factors have been ruled out. Rather, elevation indicates that the respondent is reporting symptoms consistent with these disorders. To support such caution in interpretation, the *SOM* scale is generally the highest point of the PAI profile in a general clinical population, although, even in such populations, the average score is typically below 70T (Osborne, 1994). Perhaps more than on any other scale, the primary question about discriminant validity (i.e., whether these might be valid physical problems) lies outside of the domains measured by the PAI.

SOM-C: Conversion

The Conversion subscale includes items corresponding to the dramatic physiological symptoms that have been found to be prevalent in conversion disorders (Watson & Buranen, 1979). As it turns out, most of these symptoms involve unusual sensory-motor problems: impairments in perception (e.g., vision or hearing problems, numbness) or motor problems (e.g., paralysis). The mean raw score in the normative sample on the Conversion subscale was very low, indicating that, for the most part, these symptoms are quite unusual in the general population. Although such symptoms may be rare, there are some populations in which these symptoms are more common, because there are a variety of physical conditions that result in sensory-motor problems. For example, people with multiple sclerosis, stroke victims, and those with other neurological disorders all may have sensory-motor problems. It has been observed that the *SOM-C* subscale is probably the most sensitive scale on the PAI to various forms of Central Nervous System (CNS) impairment. One diagnostic group that frequently obtains elevations on *SOM-C* are chronic alcoholics who are beginning to experience some neuropsychological compromise associated with their drinking. Often, clinicians will use indicators on self-report personality inventories to distinguish a conversion reaction from a "genuine" organic problem or to distinguish functional from organic pain, but, in actuality, this diagnostic distinction should never be based solely on the results of such tests. In such instances, a thorough medical evaluation is recommended.

Thus, an elevated score on *SOM-C* indicates a report of problems in physical functioning due to symptoms often associated with conversion disorders, such as sensory or motor dysfunctions. Such problems are likely to be unusual ones, rather than a more severe form of more common problems such as headaches or dizziness. Perhaps consistent with the notion of *la belle indifference*, the *SOM-C* scale is relatively uncorrelated with other indicators of distress; thus, an isolated elevation does not necessarily signify that the reported symptoms are of great concern to the respondent (cf. the score on *DEP* and the *SOM-H* subscale for such distress or preoccupation). Marked elevations could be a sign of (a) a debilitating physical illness leading to marked sensorimotor impairment, (b) a rather dramatic conversion reaction, or (c) severe hypochondriasis or, perhaps, even somatic delusions. More moderate elevations would be expected in a person with a more circumscribed sensory or motor impairment, such as those associated with mild cerebrovascular infarcts. Because of the rarity of these somatic signs in the general population, *SOM-C* has a rather "hard floor," and it is not possible to obtain extremely low scores.

Individuals with *SOM-C* elevations are likely to report that their daily functioning has been compromised by one or more serious and rather unusual physical problems. Although they may feel that their health is good in general, if the other *SOM* subscales are not elevated, they will feel that the health problems that they do have are complex and difficult to treat successfully. Physical complaints are likely to focus on symptoms of distress in neurological and musculoskeletal systems, and may involve features often associated with conversion disorders, such as unusual sensory or motor dysfunctions. As scores become extreme (i.e., ≥ 95T), the possibility of somatic delusions should also be considered.

SOM-S: Somatization

The Somatization subscale inquires about routine physical complaints, such as headaches, back problems, pain, or gastrointestinal ailments; these complaints are diagnostic by virtue of their frequency rather than their presence. In comparison to SOM-C, the Somatization subscale consists of complaints that are more vague and diffuse, not localized in any one organ system. There are two components to elevations on the subscale, one element involving the physical symptoms (which can include a general lethargy and malaise), and a second element relating to a more general complaintiveness and dissatisfaction. The SOM-S subscale yields substantial correlations with measures of both psychological and physical distress; individuals with SOM-S elevations are likely to have a litany of physical complaints that they will share with anyone who will listen.

Individuals with SOM-S elevations will report that their daily functioning has been compromised by numerous and varied physical problems. They will report particular problems with the frequent occurrence of various minor physical symptoms and vague complaints of ill health and fatigue, often accompanied by unhappiness and bitterness about their health. This pattern of symptoms is often consistent with a somatization disorder.

SOM-H: Health Concerns

The Health Concerns subscale indicates a preoccupation with health and physical functioning. Items on this subscale are related to the self-perceived complexity of the individual's health problems and the intensity of the individual's efforts to ameliorate these problems. The SOM-H subscale is a measure of focus rather than of severity; a general medical population has a very wide distribution, and individuals with serious health problems can still obtain low scores on this subscale. Such people will tend to strike others as quite stoic about their problems, whereas individuals with SOM-H elevations will tend to focus a great deal on their health issues.

Individuals with elevations on SOM-H are likely to report that their daily functioning has been compromised by numerous and varied physical problems. If the other subscales are not elevated, such individuals may appear to be relatively healthy to other observers, but they will see themselves as having a history of complex medical problems. They will tend to feel that their health is not as good as that of their age peers, who may view such individuals as rather hypochondriacal. There are likely to be continuous concerns with health status and physical problems, and the poor health may be a major component of the self-image, with such individuals accustomed to being in the patient role.

SOM Full Scale Interpretation

As the sum of these three elements, the full scale of *SOM* reflects the degree of concern about physical functioning and health matters and the extent of perceived impairment arising from somatic symptoms. Average scores on *SOM* (i.e., < 60T) reflect a person with few bodily complaints. Such individuals are typically seen as optimistic, alert, and effective. Scores between 60T and 70T indicate some concern about health functioning and will not be uncommon in older respondents or in medical patients with relatively specific organic symptoms. Scores above 70T suggest significant concerns about somatic functioning and probable impairment arising from somatic symptoms. Such a person will feel that his or her health is not as good as that of age peers and is likely to believe that the health problems are complex and difficult to treat successfully. For such people, social interactions and conversations are likely to focus often on their health problems, and self-image may be largely influenced by the belief that they are handicapped by poor health. Individuals scoring in this range may be seen as unhappy, complaining, and pessimistic. They may be using somatic complaints to control others in a passive-aggressive manner.

SOM scores that are markedly elevated (i.e., > 87T) are unusual even in clinical samples; such scores suggest a ruminative preoccupation with physical functioning and health matters and severe impairment arising from somatic symptoms. In that range, the somatic complaints are likely to be chronic and accompanied by fatigue and weakness that render the individual incapable of performing even minimal role expectations. Such scores require elevations on all three subscales, reflecting a large number of somatic complaints affecting most organ systems, including the neurological, gastrointestinal, and musculoskeletal systems. Scores in this range will reflect a diagnosable somatoform disorder in most instances. These patients may be resistant to psychological explanations for problems and may be poor candidates for psychotherapy, particularly if there are few accompanying indications of psychological distress.

SOM Subscale Configurations

The following sections describe some of the implications of particular combinations of elevations on *SOM* subscales.

SOM-C high, SOM-S high, SOM-H high

Individuals with this subscale pattern will report that their daily functioning has been compromised by numerous and varied physical problems. They feel that their health is not as good as that of their age peers and are likely to believe that their health problems are complex and difficult to treat successfully. Physical complaints are likely to include symptoms of distress in several biological systems, including the neurological, gastrointestinal, and musculoskeletal systems. The pattern indicates the report of unusual sensorimotor symptoms as well as severe manifestations of more ordinary complaints, such as headaches or pains. Such individuals are likely to be continuously concerned with their health status and physical problems, and social interactions and conversations will tend to focus on their health problems. The self-image may be largely influenced by a belief that they are handicapped by poor health, and such individuals may be quite accustomed to being in the patient role.

SOM-C high, SOM-S high, SOM-H average

This subscale pattern is rather unusual, as it represents a report of numerous and varied physical problems but relatively little focus on these problems. The physical complaints are likely to include symptoms of distress in several biological systems, including the neurological, gastrointestinal, and musculoskeletal systems. The item endorsement pattern indicates the report of symptoms consistent with both conversion and somatization disorders. The lower scores on SOM-H suggest less complaintiveness than is typical of individuals with SOM-S elevations.

SOM-C high, SOM-S average, SOM-H high

Individuals with this subscale pattern will report that their daily functioning is impeded by unusual physical problems. They feel that their health is not as good as that of their age peers and are likely to believe that their health problems are particularly challenging and treatment resistant. Physical complaints are likely to focus on symptoms of distress across varied physical systems, particularly neurological and musculoskeletal systems; these involve features often associated with conversion disorders, such as unusual sensory or motor dysfunctions. Such people tend to be continuously concerned with their health status and physical problems, and there may be underlying concerns about the ability of the medical system to treat these problems effectively.

SOM-C average, SOM-S high, SOM-H high

People displaying this pattern are likely to report that they cannot function normally due to various physical problems. They feel that their health is not as good as that of others, reporting that their health problems are complicated and difficult to treat successfully. They report particular problems with the frequent occurrence of various minor physical symptoms (e.g., headaches, pain, or gastrointestinal problems) and vague complaints of ill health and fatigue. Health status and physical problems are likely to be continuous concerns, and social interactions and conversations will tend to focus on health problems. Marked dissatisfaction with the quality and effectiveness of the care they have received is also likely.

Anxiety (ANX)

Anxiety is a prominent part of many of the major syndromes of mental disorder. Unfortunately, with respect to measurement it also represents one of the most elusive psychological constructs. An important conceptualization by Lang (1971) addressed some of these measurement difficulties by portraying anxiety as comprised of three components: "cognitive" (in a person's thoughts), "somatic" (involving physiological reactions), and "behavioral" (observed in a person's actions). Lang viewed each of these three components as related but independent modes of the expression of anxiety; as such, the comprehensive assessment of anxiety involved the measurement of each individual component. Lang included the subjective feeling of anxiety as part of the cognitive component of anxiety, but more recent efforts (Zajonc, 1980) have distinguished between the affective and cognitive experiences of emotion. Koksal and Power (1990) demonstrated that the cognitive and affective components of anxiety were clearly related but could be reliably differentiated by self-report methods and suggested that a comprehensive assessment of anxiety includes an assessment of four systems: affective, cognitive, behavioral, and somatic.

The *ANX* scale of the PAI was designed to assess three of these components of anxiety; the behavioral component of anxiety was not included as a subscale. Specific behaviors often serve as the basis of making differential diagnostic decisions; for example, avoidance behavior is a critical component of the definition of a phobia, whereas ritualistic behavior is a critical sign of Obsessive-Compulsive Disorder. Thus, in the PAI, these specific behaviors were assessed in the context of a scale (*ARD*) pertaining to specific anxiety-related disorders, as described in a later section. This exclusion makes the scale a more general, nonspecific index of anxiety that does not have specific ties to a particular diagnostic construct. Rather, it relates broadly to the experience of anxiety and to how it is typically expressed.

ANX-C: Cognitive

The Cognitive subscale of *ANX* includes items that tap an expectation of harm, ruminative worry, and cognitive beliefs of the type described by Beck and Emery

(1979) within the context of cognitive therapy of anxiety disorders. This cognitive component involves a ruminative form of anxiety expression; people operating in this mode of expression tend to dwell on events, running them over and over in their minds. This is an internalizing approach to anxiety; such people tend to be vigilant to the experience of anxiety, rather than repressing it, and these feelings of being ill at ease will tend to have an ideational target or source. This mode of anxiety expression also tends to have strong trait aspects, meaning that it is both a characteristic style of dealing with anxiety and an indication of current distress.

Elevated scores on *ANX-C* indicate worry and concern about current issues to a degree that may impair the person's ability to concentrate and attend. Such people are likely to be overly concerned about issues and events over which they have no control. As scores exceed 85*T*, the worry and negative expectations are likely to be debilitating, and the possibility of intrusive obsessions should be investigated.

ANX-A: Affective

The Affective subscale includes items that measure the feelings of tension, apprehension, and nervousness that are characteristic of anxiety. This anxiety tends to be free-floating rather than attached to specific objects or events. Also, the anxiety reflected in this subscale tends to be rather persistent and trait-like; it reflects a dispositionally low threshold for the experience of events as alarming. High scorers on this scale experience a great deal of tension, have difficulty relaxing, and tend to be easily fatigued as a result of constant apprehension and high perceived stress. Elevations on this subscale in the absence of elevations on the remaining *ANX* subscales are suggestive of generalized anxiety rather than more specific fears.

ANX-P: Physiological

The Physiological subscale of *ANX* includes items that assess the somatic expression of anxiety, such as racing heart, sweaty palms, rapid breathing, and dizziness. This subscale has a fairly different pattern of relationships to other constructs than *ANX-C* and *ANX-A*. For example, *ANX-P* correlates most highly with the state component (as opposed to the trait component) of the STAI. However, this may, in part, be due to the nature of that instrument, as many of its "state" items are physiological in nature, and mode of anxiety expression may be confounded with duration of anxiety on the STAI (Spielberger, 1983).

Another distinction of *ANX-P* is that it is associated much less with indicators of depression and much more with physical symptom expression, as compared to *ANX-C* or *ANX-A*. This distinction captures the difference between somatization and ideation. *ANX-P* correlates most highly with the expression of physical symptomatology. People with this pattern may not psychologically experience themselves as anxious, but they show physiological signs that most people associate with anxiety. This suggests a repressive style of dealing with stress; the person may notice overt physical signs such as sweaty palms and shortness of breath, and still not recognize these as signs of anxiety and stress.

ANX Full Scale Interpretation

As mentioned earlier, the full scale score of *ANX* is a nonspecific indicator of the degree of tension and negative affect experienced by the respondent. Average scores on *ANX* (i.e., < 60*T*) reflect a person with few complaints of anxiety or tension. Such individuals are typically seen as calm, optimistic, and effective in dealing with stress. Very low scores (i.e., < 40*T*) are indicative of a person reporting fearlessness, and it is possible that this represents a reckless lack of prudence in certain situations. Scores between 60*T* and 70*T* are indicative of a person who may be experiencing some stress and who is worried, sensitive, and emotional. Scores above 70*T* suggest significant anxiety and tension. With scores in this range, the respondent is probably tense much of the time and ruminative about anticipated misfortune. These individuals may be seen as high strung, nervous, timid, and dependent. With scores above 70*T*, at least one *ANX* subscale is likely to be elevated and such elevations should be examined to determine the typical modality in which anxiety is expressed.

ANX scores that are markedly elevated (i.e., > 90*T*) will likely have elevations on all three subscales, reflecting a generalized impairment associated with anxiety. Such a person's life will be seriously constricted, and the individual may not be able to meet even minimal role expectations without feeling overwhelmed. Mild stressors are likely to precipitate a crisis, and this repeating pattern of crises may present difficulties for psychotherapy despite the motivating nature of the individual's distress. Scores in this range will reflect a diagnosable anxiety disorder in most instances; scores on *ARD* may suggest a specific focus for the fears, or a lack of elevation on *ARD* may suggest that the anxiety is free-floating and generalized.

ANX Subscale Configurations

The following sections describe some of the implications of elevations on two or more *ANX* subscales.

ANX-C high, ANX-A high, ANX-P high

Individuals who have all three subscales elevated are likely to be plagued by worry to a degree that interferes with their ability to concentrate, attend, and manage stressful periods in their lives. Anxiety is experienced in all modalities, ideationally as well as physically. Such people will ruminate about issues and events of seemingly minor significance and over which they have no control. There is likely to be prominent motor tension, little capacity to relax, and a general fatigue and malaise as a result of high perceived stress.

ANX-C high, ANX-A high, ANX-P average

This pattern suggests an ideational and sensitized approach to anxiety. The tendency to dwell on decisions and issues most likely interferes with their ability to concentrate and focus on matters at hand. The respondent's level of tension and difficulties in relaxing are probably readily apparent to others, who are likely to perceive the respondent as worrying needlessly and excessively about most matters.

ANX-C high, ANX-A average, ANX-P high

This is an unusual configuration in that the person does not report a strong subjective experience of tension or major difficulties in relaxing, yet there appears to be considerable worry and tension surrounding specific events or issues, and overt physical signs of tension and stress (e.g., sweaty palms, trembling hands, complaints of irregular heartbeats, and shortness of breath) are also present. Such a pattern suggests some denial or lack of recognition of the degree to which generalized stress is affecting the person's functioning.

ANX-C average, ANX-A high, ANX-P high

The primary manifestations of the respondent's anxiety appear to be in the affective and physiological areas. Such people feel quite tense much of the time, have difficulty relaxing, and are likely to experience considerable fatigue and malaise as a result of high perceived stress levels. There may be a tendency to try to handle stress by simply not thinking about the stressful issues, as ideation does not appear to be a prominent component of the anxiety, but it is apparent that it is being expressed in other ways, particularly in somatic form.

Anxiety-Related Disorders (*ARD*)

Anxiety is typically a feature in most clinical disorders, and, as such, an anxiety scale such as *ANX* is of limited use in identifying specific disorders in which anxiety may be prominent. The behavioral expression of anxiety, however, varies across different disorders, and, as such, these different diagnostic syndromes are typically defined by characteristic behaviors. The *ARD* scale assesses phenomena central to three important anxiety-related disorders that, in conjunction with marked anxiety as measured by *ANX*, can serve as a more specific indicator of these disorders.

ARD-O: Obsessive-Compulsive

The Obsessive-Compulsive subscale includes items related to both the symptomatic features of the disorder (e.g., fears of contamination and performance of rituals) and the personality elements of the disorder (e.g., perfectionism and hyper-attentiveness to detail). In *DSM-IV* terms, these two components represent both Axis I (clinical syndrome) and Axis II (personality trait) aspects of the disorder. The Axis I component involves intrusive, recurrent thoughts, images, or behaviors; the literature suggests a number of common themes to these thoughts, such as fears of contamination leading to characteristic avoidance behaviors (e.g., hand-washing). The Axis II component involves a personality style that is rigid, dogmatic, and affectively constricted. For example, if you were to visit the house of an obsessional individual and pick up an object, the Axis I obsessional would be concerned that you left germs on the object, whereas the Axis II obsessional would be concerned that you did not return the object to its proper place. Although these are fairly different responses to the situation, both are represented on *ARD-O*.

The correlational pattern of *ARD-O* suggests that the Axis II manifestations are most heavily represented, as the scale is less correlated with traditional markers of anxiety and neuroticism than other *ARD* subscales. This pattern suggests that high scorers are using obsessional tactics to try to control anxiety (i.e., control through order and predictability). The relatively lower associations with *ANX*, for example, point out that there are a number of individuals who are successful in these efforts (i.e., they have little subjective experience of anxiety). Thus, with *ARD-O* elevated and the full-scale of *ANX* low, this suggests that the obsessional tactics are reasonably effective. However, this control of anxiety may be achieved at a cost; other aspects of the test may reveal pronounced interpersonal problems (e.g., low *WRM*, *SCZ-S*, *BOR-N*) associated with the individual's rigidity and need for control. However, as both *ANX* and *ARD-O* elevate, this is a sign that the obsessional tactics are failing to control the anxiety.

By comparison to most other clinical subscales, elevations on *ARD-O* are less frequent in clinical samples. This suggests that these behaviors and defenses are more unusual in clinical samples, as compared to the straightforward experience of anxiety. Thus, relatively moderate elevations (i.e., 55*T* to 65*T*) are interpretively significant in the clinical settings. Such people may be seen by others as being ruminating, detail-oriented, conforming, and somewhat rigid in attitudes and behavior. Scores ranging from 65*T* to 75*T* suggest a fairly rigid individual who follows his or her own guidelines for personal conduct in an inflexible and unyielding manner. Such people ruminate about matters to the degree that they often have difficulty in making decisions and in perceiving the larger significance of decisions they do make. Changes in routine, unexpected events, and contradictory information are likely to generate untoward stress, and such individuals will be particularly wary of situations with strong affective demands. Scores at or above 75*T* indicate marked rigidity and significant ruminative concerns; intrusive thoughts are likely to be present. Such people may fear their own impulses and doubt their own ability to control them. They are likely to be extremely indecisive, and obsessional defenses are probably failing to control marked anxiety.

ARD-P: Phobias

The Phobias subscale assesses several of the more common phobic fears, including heights, enclosed places, public transportation, and social exhibition. These fears were selected based on commonality of reporting in the research literature—commonality within clinical, rather than research, settings. For example, snake and insect phobias are frequent objects of study in research laboratories, yet they constitute a fairly minor proportion of presenting complaints in anxiety disorder clinics. Given the prevalence of social phobias, these items are heavily represented on the scale, and elevations may indicate marked social anxiety. The *ARD-P* subscale correlates well with most other indicators of phobic fears as well as with indicators of more general anxiety.

The *ARD-P* scale is interesting in that it also has interpretive significance at very low scores, as the scale has a rather soft floor. Raw scores of 0 or 1 place a person at roughly 35*T*; such scores are typically obtained in people who regard themselves as fearless, unafraid of anything, even at times when fear is merited. In such people, there is a possibility of recklessness because they are not likely to be inhibited by appropriate caution; such scores are sometimes obtained in psychopathic individuals. Scores in the range from 60*T* to 70*T* suggest the possibility of specific fears, but avoidance behaviors are not likely to be severe and probably will not preclude a relatively successful level of daily functioning. As scores elevate above 70*T*, phobic behaviors are likely to interfere in some significant way, and such people will tend to monitor their environment in an effort to avoid contact with the feared object or situation. Marked elevations indicate the likelihood of multiple phobias or a more pervasive phobia, such as agoraphobia, as opposed to a simple, more circumscribed phobia.

ARD-T: Traumatic Stress

The Traumatic Stress subscale concerns phenomena related to reactions to traumatic stressors, including nightmares, sudden anxiety reactions, and feelings of being irreversibly changed by a traumatic event. Items were not written to detail the nature of the traumatic event; such events might include combat experiences, rape or abuse, or some other highly stressful experience. Positive responses to the items indicate that (a) some terrible event or events happened to this person, and (b) these events changed the person for the worse in some way.

In light of significant elevations on this subscale, the precise nature of the event can be determined through a follow-up inquiry. The test score can serve as a useful means of broaching a topic that an individual may not be willing to disclose during an intake interview. The PAI assessment provides an opportunity to divulge discomforting information. The information is divulged in a "safe" forum, as it is simply a check mark on a piece of paper; however, including it with the rest of the items also acknowledges to the respondent that these are important issues and that it is acceptable to discuss such issues in the context of a professional assessment. Because this scale is commonly elevated in clinical samples, it is often an entry to further discussion while providing the client with feedback on test results. For example, one might say, "I notice your score is very high on the traumatic stress scale; this usually occurs with people who have had something very bad happen to them that really changed their life, that really affected them in a negative way. What do you think about that?" Although this interpretation is rather unexceptional given the content of the items, clients are often impressed by the extent to which they differ from others in this regard. In addition, the acknowledgment that the clinician understands that these are particularly important issues for the client is generally reassuring and increases the client's confidence in the clinician.

One aspect of *ARD-T* that merits mention is that it is quite frequently elevated in clinical settings; the average score for clinical respondents is 64*T*, which approaches the 90th percentile for the general population. It should be recognized that individuals in treatment settings tend to have very high rates of traumatic events; prevalence of a history of physical and/or sexual abuse has been estimated as high as 70-80% in some settings. However, the frequency of this elevation also should serve as a caution against an indeterminate use of this scale as an indication of posttraumatic stress disorder (PTSD), which tends to have a characteristic profile that includes other features as well as *ARD-T* elevations (see chapter 6). PTSD is a syndrome that is not limited to the particular feature identified by *ARD-T*, although the scale is certainly a beginning point in the identification of this syndrome.

Scores in the moderately elevated range on *ARD-T* (i.e., 65*T* to 75*T*) suggest that the respondent has likely experienced a disturbing traumatic event in the past, an event that continues to be a source of distress and to produce recurrent episodes of anxiety. Although the item content of the PAI does not address specific causes of traumatic stress, possible traumatic events involve victimization (e.g., rape, abuse), combat experiences, life-threatening accidents, and natural disasters. As scores become increasingly elevated, preoccupation with the trauma increases, and scores above 90T indicate that the trauma (single or multiple) is the overriding focus of the person's life and that individual views himself or herself as having been severely damaged, perhaps irreparably, by the experience.

ARD Full Scale Interpretation

The full scale of *ARD* is perhaps the most difficult to interpret on the inventory, due to its composition of three fairly diverse conditions. In general, it is a measure of the extent of behavioral expression of anxiety. Average scores on *ARD* (i.e., < 60T) reflect a person who reports little distress across many situations. Such individuals are typically seen as secure, adaptable, and calm under fire. Scores between 60T and 70T reflect a person who occasionally experiences, or experiences only to a mild degree, maladaptive behavior patterns aimed at controlling anxiety. Such people will have some specific fears or worries and also may have little self-confidence. Scores above 70T suggest impairment associated with fears surrounding a particular situation; specific subscale elevations should reveal more precisely the nature of these fears. Such individuals may be seen as insecure and self-doubting, ruminative, and particularly uncomfortable in social situations.

ARD scores that are markedly elevated (i.e., > 90T) are likely to have elevations on all three subscales, reflecting multiple anxiety disorder diagnoses and broad impairment associated with anxiety. These individuals are in severe psychological turmoil; they are faced with constant rumination and often are guilt ridden over past transgressions, whether real or imagined. A number of maladaptive behavior patterns aimed at controlling anxiety are probably present, but these patterns are having little effect in preventing anxiety from intruding into experience and functioning.

ARD Subscale Configurations

The following sections describe some of the implications when two or more *ARD* subscales are elevated in combination.

ARD-O high, ARD-P high, ARD-T high

This pattern reveals that the respondent is likely to have significant symptoms and behaviors related to anxiety in a variety of domains, including phobic avoidance, obsessive rumination, and troublesome thoughts related to a traumatic event. The resulting avoidance behaviors are likely to interfere with social role functioning in some significant way; such people tend to monitor their environment constantly in a vigilant manner in an effort to avoid contact with particular situations, particularly those that evoke a disturbing traumatic event in the past. Although phobic fears are likely, such people are more likely to have multiple phobias or a more debilitating phobia, such as agoraphobia, than to suffer from a simple phobia.

There appears to be an attempt, apparently unsuccessful, to control these anxieties through rigidity and affective constriction. Such people are often seen by others as being perfectionistic and overly anxious about trifles. They are likely to set and follow their personal guidelines for conduct in an inflexible and unyielding manner, but they pay for this lack of flexibility by ruminating about matters (both past and present) to the degree that decisions cannot be made. Predictability is very important for such people, and changes in routine, unexpected life events, and contradictory information are likely to overtax the person's efforts at control. They also may fear their own impulses and doubt their ability to control them.

ARD-O high, ARD-P high, ARD-T average

This subscale pattern suggests a fearful individual who attempts to manage anxiety through rigid planning and tries to avoid affective arousal. However, anxiety and avoidance behaviors are likely to be interfering in some significant way in the individual's life, and it is probable that such individuals monitor their surroundings closely to avoid unexpected disruptions in routine. Such people tend to fear novel situations and will avoid risk-taking as much as possible. This pattern, particularly with a concomitant elevation on *DOM*, suggests a person who manages this fear of novelty through a rigid and inflexible need for control. However, this need for control is complicated by the tendency to constantly ruminate about decisions and about the unexpected consequences of any decisions that are made. Changes in routine, unexpected events, and contradictory information are likely to be particularly difficult to handle.

ARD-O high, ARD-P average, ARD-T high

This pattern of responses suggests an individual who ruminatively dwells on past events in his or her life. Such people attempt to manage the discomfort generated by these past events through affective constriction and by organizing their lives in an inflexible and unyielding manner. Although these strategies may help in managing anxiety, they fill the person with doubt and, hence, such individuals will have difficulty in making personal decisions and in perceiving the larger consequences of decisions they do make. Such people may particularly fear their own impulses and doubt their ability to control them should their rigid efforts at self-control fail.

ARD-O average, ARD-P high, ARD-T high

This subscale pattern reflects individuals who have experienced a disturbing traumatic event in the past, an event that continues to serve as a source of marked distress and to produce recurrent episodes of anxiety. Such people tend to vigilantly monitor their environment in an effort to avoid situations reminiscent of past stressful events; avoidance behaviors related to these fears are likely to be sufficiently severe to interfere with social role functioning. Interpersonal withdrawal in close relationships is likely (look for low scores on *WRM*), and multiple phobias or a more distressing phobia, such as agoraphobia, may be present.

Depression (*DEP*)

The measurement of depression has perhaps received more research attention than any other construct in mental disorders. There are a host of widely used instruments for assessing depression, including the self-report Beck Depression Inventory, the Zung (1965) Depression Scale, and MMPI *D* scale, as well as observer rating scales such as the Hamilton Rating Scale for Depression (HAM-D; Hamilton, 1960). Despite the fact that these scales are widely used and tend to be positively correlated, each has somewhat different characteristics (Lambert, Hatch, Kingston, & Edwards, 1986). For example, the BDI is based on the cognitive features of depression, such as beliefs about helplessness and negative expectations about the future (e.g., Louks, Hayne, & Smith, 1989). In contrast, the HAM-D addresses vegetative signs of depression more heavily than the BDI; as a result, the two instruments have substantially different factor structures (Favarelli, Albanesi, & Poli, 1986). However, both instruments share the characteristic of having very low mean scores and little variance in normal samples. In contrast, the MMPI *D* scale has a relatively "soft floor" with greater variability among normal respondents; thus, it may be more useful for the assessment of depressive features within the milder ranges (Hollon & Mandel, 1979). However, the MMPI items emphasize affective features such as unhappiness and psychological discomfort, with limited assessment of either the cognitive or the physiological features of depression.

The *DEP* scale of the PAI was assembled to provide an equal weighting among the major components of the depressive syndrome and still provide items that would prove useful across the full range of severity of symptomatology. The clinical syndrome of depression is typically found to have three components: an affective component, characterized by unhappy and apathetic mood; a cognitive component, marked by negative expectancies; and a physiological component, where sleep and appetite disturbances and low energy are prominent (e.g., Moran & Lambert, 1983). Thus, three *DEP* subscales were designed: Cognitive, to tap negative expectancies, helplessness, and cognitive errors of the type described by Beck (e.g., 1967) within the context of his theory of depression; Physiological, to assess the vegetative and somatic features (e.g., disturbances in sleep, appetite, and sexual drive) that are commonly found in depressed patients; and Affective, to measure the unhappiness, dysphoria, and apathy that are universally identified with this population.

DEP-C: Cognitive

The Cognitive component of depression involves expectancies or beliefs regarding one's inadequacy, powerlessness, or helplessness in dealing with the demands of the environment. According to Beck (1967, 1976) and other cognitively-oriented theorists such as Abramson, Seligman, and Teasdale (1978), the root of depressive symptomatology lies in these beliefs. Individuals with this cognitive style tend to globally attribute negative events in their lives to their own incompetence or inadequacy, whereas any positive events are minimized or attributed to some external source (e.g., good luck, assistance from others, etc.). Beck notes a number of other characteristics of the depressive cognitive style, including (a) a tendency to think in dichotomies, with events viewed as extremes (good or bad, black or white); (b) making self-referential assumptions, such as believing everyone notices if one makes a small mistake; and (c) selective abstraction of negative events.

The *DEP-C* scale, by tapping such cognitions, reflects an important component of self-esteem involving a sense of personal competence or self-efficacy. Individuals with *DEP-C* elevations are likely to report feeling worthless, hopeless, and as having failed at most important life tasks. They are likely to be quite pessimistic and to have very little self-confidence. Concentration problems and indecisiveness are also likely to be present. Conversely, people with very low scores on *DEP-C* (i.e., < 40T) report that their abilities have few limits; such a pattern could reflect grandiosity or narcissism.

DEP-A: Affective

The affective component of depression refers to the experience of feeling distressed, unhappy, sad, blue, and down in the dumps. Elevations on *DEP-A* suggest sadness, a loss of interest in normal activities, and a loss of sense of pleasure in things that were previously enjoyed. This scale is probably one of the most direct measures of overall life satisfaction on the PAI. Thus, as a relatively pure measure of distress, *DEP-A* can be considered a positive prognostic indicator, as it reflects a dissatisfaction with current circumstances, and the distress can serve as a motivator for change.

DEP-P: Physiological

The *DEP-P* subscale involves what are called the vegetative signs of depression: sleep problems, appetite problems, lack of interest, and lack of drive. Of the three *DEP* subscales, *DEP-P* demonstrates the largest correlation with the Hamilton Rating Scale (HAM-D) for Depression ($r = .75$). This is informative in that the HAM-D is the most widely used measure of depressive symptomatology in psychopharmacological trials of antidepressant medication; these medications tend to be particularly effective in treating vegetative signs of depression. Therefore, the *DEP-P* scale may be useful in identifying target symptoms that may be amenable to treatment with such medications.

Elevations on *DEP-P* suggest that the respondent has experienced a change in level of physical functioning. Such people are likely to show a disturbance in sleep pattern, a decrease in energy and level of sexual interest, and a loss of appetite and/or weight loss. Motor slowing also may be present.

DEP Full Scale Interpretation

As the sum of the three subscales, the *DEP* full scale score indicates the broad spectrum of diagnostic depressive symptomatology. Because all three components are involved in the *DSM* definition of a disorder, the full scale can be useful in diagnostic decision-making. Average scores on *DEP* (i.e., < 60T) reflect a person with few complaints about unhappiness or distress. Such individuals are typically seen as stable, self-confident, active, and relaxed. Scores between 60T and 70T are indicative of a person who may be unhappy and who is sensitive, pessimistic, and self-doubting. Scores above 70T suggest prominent unhappiness and dysphoria. With scores in this range, the respondent is probably despondent much of the time and withdrawing from activities he or she previously enjoyed. These individuals may be seen as guilt-ridden, moody, and dissatisfied. With scores above 70T, at least one subscale is likely to be elevated, and these scores should be examined to determine the typical modality in which the depression is manifest. As scores become elevated above 80T, there is an increasing likelihood of a diagnosis of Major Depressive Disorder.

DEP scores that are markedly elevated (i.e., > 95T) are likely to have elevations on all three subscales, often reflecting a diagnosis of Major Depressive Disorder. These individuals feel hopeless, discouraged, and useless. They are socially withdrawn and feel misunderstood by others. Typically, there is little motivation to pursue interests and little energy with which to do so. Suicidal ideation is not uncommon with scores in this range, and particular attention should be given to *SUI* elevations when *DEP* is markedly elevated.

DEP Subscale Configurations

The following sections describe some of the implications of different combinations of elevations on the three *DEP* subscales.

DEP-C high, DEP-A high, DEP-P high

With all three subscales elevated, the respondent is quite likely to meet the diagnostic criteria for a major depressive episode. Plagued by thoughts of worthlessness and hopelessness, such individuals are preoccupied with feelings of sadness, a loss of interest in normal activities, and a loss of sense of pleasure in things that were previously enjoyed. They are likely to show a disturbance in sleep pattern, a decrease in level of energy and sexual interest, and a loss of appetite and/or weight loss. Psychomotor slowing or retardation might also be expected.

DEP-C high, DEP-A high, DEP-P average

This subscale pattern reflects an individual who is plagued by ruminative thoughts of worthlessness and personal failure. Such people admit openly to feelings of sadness, a loss of interest in normal activities, and a loss of the sense of pleasure in things that were previously enjoyed, and they blame themselves for feeling this way. However, the absence of physiological signs of depression suggests that the complete spectrum of depressive symptomatology is not present, and the person may not meet diagnostic criteria for a major depressive episode. This pattern is common in more chronic dysphoric conditions, such as those seen with dysthymic disorder or with certain personality disorders.

DEP-C high, DEP-A average, DEP-P high

An individual with this unusual subscale pattern reports markedly low self-esteem and numerous physiological signs of depression, yet he or she is not admitting to feeling unhappy or distressed. This suggests that the individual might not recognize the aforementioned symptoms as signs of dysphoria and stress or might be repressing the experience of unhappiness to some extent. Alternatively, the person may not be willing to admit to personal unhappiness, viewing it as a sign of weakness. Regardless, it is likely that the person is unhappy at some level and will be vulnerable to future episodes of depression during times of stress.

DEP-C average, DEP-A high, DEP-P high

Although such people do not appear to feel hopeless and their self-esteem is largely intact, they are manifesting affective and physiological signs of depression. Such a pattern would appear to contraindicate a more cognitively-based intervention for the depression and, instead, may underscore the importance of managing the physical symptoms, perhaps with antidepressant medication. The relatively lower score on *DEP-C* suggests that external circumstances, rather than internal shortcomings, may be blamed for the person's current unhappiness.

Mania (*MAN*)

By definition, mania is a disorder with a fluctuating presentation of symptomatology, and this fluctuation presents a measurement challenge for traditional assessment methods. Within a particular manic episode, symptoms can vary widely; for example, mood can be alternatively elevated, irritable, or depressed within a brief time span. Over the past few decades, an empirical literature has emerged that documents the symptomatic complexity of patients presenting during a manic episode. Goodwin and Jamison (1990), in a comprehensive description of the manic-depressive syndrome, reviewed the results of a number of these studies of symptomatology in an attempt to identify the most salient diagnostic features of mania. They divided symptoms into four broad areas: (a) mood, (b) cognitive, (c) activity and behavior, and (d) psychotic symptoms. By collapsing results across several studies, Goodwin and Jamison were able to calculate a weighted mean representing the diagnostic sensitivity of different signs and symptoms within each of the four areas. With respect to mood symptoms, the most commonly observed were irritability (80% of patients), followed by depression (72%), and euphoria (71%); among cognitive symptoms, grandiosity (78%), racing thoughts (71%), and poor concentration (71%) were most common; and among behavioral symptoms, hyperactivity (87%), typically involving pressured speech (98%), and decreased sleep (81%) were often observed. However, psychotic symptoms such as delusions (48%) or hallucinations (15%) were much less frequently observed.

The *MAN* scale of the PAI was designed to assess prototypic signs of a manic episode. Consistent with the findings of Goodwin and Jamison (1990), disruptions in mood, cognition, and behavior were each assessed via different subscales; because of the low sensitivity of psychotic symptomatology and because such symptoms are often of limited utility in making a differential diagnosis from other psychotic disorders (Carlson & Goodwin, 1973), assessment of psychotic features received relatively little weight in the final scale. Thus, three *MAN* subscales were designed: Activity Level, with items addressing pressured speech, decreased sleep, increased motor activity, and extravagance; Grandiosity, including inflated self-esteem, overvalued ideas, and interpersonal overconfidence; and Irritability, particularly involving impatience and demandingness with others.

MAN-A: Activity Level

The primary feature of manic behavior is that it is elevated; individuals in a manic episode engage in more behaviors than most people. The activity level is heightened with respect to ideational as well as behavioral activity, so ideas flow as rapidly as behaviors (i.e., flight of ideas). However, this increase in *quantity* of behavior is accompanied by a decrease in *quality*; both the ideation and the overt activity become pressured and disorganized. Thus, high scorers on the scale are not merely involved in many activities; instead, they are overinvolved and ineffective at managing all of their commitments.

The *MAN-A* subscale has one of the "softest floors" of the PAI clinical scales, meaning that it is possible to obtain very low scores. Scores in this range (i.e., < 30T) represent very low activity levels and marked apathy and indifference that often characterize severely depressed individuals. Scores in the moderate range (i.e., 55T to 65T) suggest an activity level somewhat higher than normal; in the upper end of this range, the person may be overcommitted to a wide variety of activities, but not necessarily in a disorganized fashion. Scores between 65T and 75T represent an activity level that is perceptibly high to most observers. Such people tend to be involved in a wide variety of activities in a somewhat disorganized manner and to experience accelerated thought processes. As scores exceed 75T, this acceleration renders the person confused and difficult to understand; scores in this range are unusual, as such people often have difficulty focusing their attention for the time required to complete the PAI.

MAN-G: Grandiosity

The grandiosity component of mania involves an overevaluated self-image, an overestimation of one's talents and capabilities. Hence, *MAN-G* items inquire about the person's self-evaluation of many talents and abilities. Grandiose individuals tend to believe they are good at almost anything, and, thus, they obtain elevated scores. In milder forms, this may merely reflect an optimism and an unwillingness to be hampered by one's limitations. In more extreme forms, this represents an incapacity to recognize one's limitations and an inability to think clearly about one's own capabilities.

The *MAN-G* subscale, like *MAN-A*, is interpretively useful at the lower end. Because the scale has a major component of self-evaluation, it can be useful in identifying persons with low self-esteem who are not necessarily depressed. Very low scores on *MAN-G* can render an individual vulnerable to depression, as such people tend to feel rather inadequate and to be unwilling to accept or acknowledge their own positive aspects. Conversely, when *DEP* is elevated and *MAN-G* is not suppressed, this may indicate that blame for the current circumstances is being externalized. Thus, for example, a paranoid individual may be pessimistic about his or her ability to deal with external forces, yet the self-esteem will remain intact. So, although they may have an elevated *DEP-C*, suggesting that they doubt their ability to succeed against external forces, their self-esteem is unimpaired because they simply project the blame outward. Thus, even more than *DEP-C*, the *MAN-G* score may reflect the extent to which a low self-concept has been internalized.

Scores on *MAN-G* that are in the moderately elevated range (i.e., 60*T* to 70*T*) represent an optimistic and, perhaps, driven type of individual. Content of thought is likely to be marked by an element of expansiveness and self-confidence, with a focus on strategies for success or achievement. Toward the upper end of this range, the possibility of inflated self-esteem increases. As scores exceed 70*T*, the likelihood of grandiosity must be considered, as scores in this range are unusual in clinical settings. Such elements may range from beliefs of having exceptionally high levels of common skills to beliefs that border on delusional in terms of having special and unique talents that will lead to fame and fortune. Others may view such people as self-centered and narcissistic.

MAN-I: Irritability

Although elevated mood is one of the more striking affective features of mania, it is actually not as characteristic of mania as might be expected. More typical of manic affect is volatility; the mood can change rather abruptly, particularly in response to frustration. Thus, *MAN-I* items tap a frustration-responsive irritability that is typical of manic patients. There tend to be two aspects to these items, one involving a certain degree of ambition and the other involving low frustration tolerance. It is this combination of features that makes the scale reasonably specific, rather than a more general marker of trait hostility, a characteristic that may be more directly addressed by some of the *PAR* subscales.

Low scores on *MAN-I* (i.e., ≤ 40*T*) reflect an individual who portrays himself or herself as very patient and rather immune to frustrations. Milder elevations (i.e., 60*T* to 70*T*) suggest a person who is impatient, and individuals with scores in the upper end of this range may be seen by others as demanding. Such people may have difficulty with others who do not cooperate with them or who do not keep up with their plans and schedule of activities. As scores exceed 70*T*, relationships with others are probably under stress due to the demanding presentation of the respondent. Such people are easily frustrated by lack of ability or cooperation in other people, and these other people will tend to be blamed for the respondent's failures and to be accused of attempting to thwart the respondent's possibly unrealistic plans for success and achievement. With scores above 80T, the person is quite volatile in response to frustration, and his or her judgment in such situations may be poor. The quality of mood state in such people can change very rapidly, and they are prone to lash out at people they view as the source of their frustrations.

MAN Full Scale Interpretation

Elevations on the full scale of *MAN* tend to be rarer in clinical settings than any of the other clinical scales of the PAI. Indeed, the average scores for clinical and community respondents are nearly identical, which is certainly not the case with any other PAI clinical scale. As such, the "psychological threshold" for identifying *MAN* scores as problematic should be lowered in most clinical settings.

Average scores on *MAN* (i.e., < 55T) reflect a person with few features of mania or hypomania. Although depressed individuals are rarely grandiose and do not have heightened activity levels, they are often quite irritable; hence, depression will not invariably be associated with very low *MAN* scores. Scores between 55T and 65T are indicative of a person who may be seen as active, outgoing, ambitious, and self-confident; however, toward the upper end of this range such individuals also may be rather impatient, hostile and quick-tempered. Scores in the 65T to 75T range are associated with increasing restlessness, impulsivity, and high energy levels. Other people are likely to perceive such individuals as unsympathetic and hot-headed.

MAN scores that are markedly elevated (i.e., > 75T) are typically associated with disorders such as mania, hypomania, or cyclothymia. These individuals take on more than they can handle and react in a hostile manner to suggestions that they reduce their activities. They are typically quite impulsive and have little ability to delay gratification; their lack of judgment in such situations is likely to lead to significant impairment in role functioning. They may be experience flights of ideas, and their grandiosity may be delusional in proportion. Their interactions with others are likely to be problematic, as their self-importance, hostility, and narcissism impede their ability to be empathic in relationships.

MAN Subscale Configurations

The following sections describe some of the implications of different combinations of evaluations on the three *MAN* subscales. Because *MAN* subscale elevations tend to be unusual in clinical settings, subscale scores greater than 65T should be considered "high" in interpreting configurations using the following paragraphs.

MAN-A high, MAN-G high, MAN-I high

This pattern of subscale scores suggests a clinical picture with numerous elements of mania. Such people will have an activity level that is perceptibly high to most observers. They are probably involved in these activities in an overcommitted and disorganized manner, and they may experience their thought processes as being accelerated, although they may not recognize the extent of their disorganization. In part, they are active in many areas because they feel that they have special talents in many areas; content of thought is likely to be marked by overvalued ideas, inflated self-esteem, or grandiosity. They may believe that they have exceptionally high levels of common skills, and they possibly harbor delusional beliefs of having special and unique talents that will lead to fame and fortune. Relationships with others are probably under stress, due to a frustration with the inability or unwillingness of these other people to keep up with overvalued plans and possibly unrealistic ideas. At its extreme, this irritability may result in accusations that significant others are attempting to thwart these plans for success and achievement, particularly when there is an accompanying elevation on *PAR*.

MAN-A high, MAN-G high, MAN-I average

This pattern of responses represents a very active person who is probably involved in his or her activities in an enthusiastic, overcommitted, and disorganized manner. The significance or importance of these activities may be overvalued, as may the person's self-perception of his or her talents and abilities. The lack of any elevation of *MAN-I* is a favorable sign (i.e., it suggests greater perseverance in these behaviors than might be found otherwise), and this increases the possibility that some of the individual's energy and enthusiasm can be translated into effective action.

MAN-A high, MAN-G average, MAN-I high

This pattern suggests that the clinical picture is characterized by heightened energy levels and irritability. This combination suggests a great emphasis on action and activity, perhaps at the expense of relationships and feelings. Other people probably view the respondent as driven, impatient, and demanding, and the respondent is easily frustrated by any inability or unwillingness of these other people to keep up with the agenda and accompanying (possibly unrealistic) expectations. At its extreme, this irritability may result in resentment that significant others are attempting to thwart the respondent's plans for success and achievement.

MAN-A average, MAN-G high, MAN-I high

This pattern of scores suggests an individual with inflated self-esteem and overvalued ideas, who has little tolerance for others who fail to recognize his or her special talents and unique abilities. Others are likely to view the respondent as demanding, impatient, and arrogant. The self-esteem may be particularly vulnerable to insult (particularly if *BOR-I* is elevated), and, when it is threatened, such individuals may lash out in frustration at those around them. Relationships with others are probably strained, as such people will repeatedly clash with anyone who differs from them or their agenda. However, they probably do not view themselves as hostile, but rather as acting in a manner merited by the strength and importance of their ideas and convictions.

Paranoia (*PAR*)

As is the case with anxiety in milder conditions, symptoms of paranoia are found in a variety of diverse and more severe psychopathologic conditions. The manifestations can range from characterological suspiciousness (e.g., that found in Paranoid Personality Disorder) to the frank persecutory delusions that characterize paranoid psychosis. However, paranoid symptoms are not specific to these syndromes; these beliefs are often encountered in schizophrenia, mania, other personality disorders such as antisocial and borderline personality, and certain organic conditions. Regardless of the nature of the primary diagnosis, paranoid symptoms present a difficult assessment challenge because the respondent is, by definition, defensive and suspicious of diagnostic and treatment efforts. In identifying the relevant components of the paranoia construct for the PAI, a decision was made to place an emphasis on the phenomenology of the disorder, rather than on the more overt symptomatology, in an effort to reduce the impact of defensiveness on scale performance.

The *PAR* scale was designed to identify the personological elements of paranoia, as well as the more symptomatic elements. One of the three *PAR* subscales, Persecution (*PAR-P*), includes items consistent with the typical delusional beliefs associated with severe paranoia. The items for the remaining two subscales were written to capture the experience of the paranoid in a manner that might be less affected by the typically guarded posture of the paranoid respondent. The Hypervigilance (*PAR-H*) subscale indicates an attitude of preparedness, sensitivity, and wariness in interactions with others. The Resentment (*PAR-R*) subscale involves somewhat bitter and envious feelings toward others, along with a sense of being treated unfairly by others.

PAR-H: *Hypervigilance*

The paranoid individual carries the predisposition to distrust people that he or she does not know well. As a result, such individuals tend to be vigilant and guarded in their interactions with others, looking for warning signs that the person with whom they are dealing is not completely trustworthy. This tendency is more of an interpersonal set, a way of relating to others, than it is a specific belief; therefore, elevations should not be interpreted as indicative of a delusional system. Rather, there is a wariness in interactions with others and a reluctance to let one's guard down in relationships.

PAR-H has a reasonably soft floor and very low scores are possible. When scores below 40T are obtained, this suggests a person who reports being exceedingly trusting and open in relationships. If this self-report is accurate, such people are vulnerable to interpersonal exploitation, particularly if *DOM* is low. However, such scores may also be obtained by individuals who are motivated to appear as trusting. Moderate elevations (i.e., 60T to 70T) suggest individuals who are pragmatic and skeptical in relationships with others; such people may be difficult to know well and may keep casual acquaintances at arm's length. Scores above 70T indicate a person who spends a great deal of time monitoring the environment for evidence that others are not trustworthy and may be trying to harm or discredit the individual in some way. Others will view such people as hypersensitive and easily insulted in their interactions. Such people will question and mistrust the motives of those around them as a matter of course, despite the nature or history of the relationships. As a result, working relationships with others are likely to be strained and may require an unusual degree of support and assistance in order to succeed.

PAR-P: Persecution

The items on the Persecution subscale directly address beliefs that others are attempting to obstruct or impede the respondent's efforts. These beliefs can range from mild feelings of jealousy to delusional beliefs of conspiracy and intrigue. Of the three *PAR* subscales, *PAR-P* is most closely tied to Axis I manifestations of delusional disorders involving paranoia.

Because item content on *PAR-P* is unusual, raw scores tend to be low in the general population and the standard deviation tends to be small. Hence, the scale can elevate rapidly even if relatively few items are answered in the positive direction. Elevated scores suggest an individual who is quick to feel that he or she is being treated inequitably and easily believes that there is a concerted effort among others to undermine his or her best interests. Working and social relationships are likely to be very strained, despite any efforts by others to demonstrate support and assistance. As scores increase above 85T, the possibility of delusional beliefs should be investigated, particularly if *SCZ-P* is also elevated.

PAR-R: Resentment

The third *PAR* subscale captures the hostility and bitterness of the paranoid character, the tendency to approach life with a "chip on the shoulder." The obstructions provided by others (reflected in the scores on the other subscales) are a source of lingering resentment for such individuals. These people feel that they have not treated fairly in life, and they nurse grudges against all who have transgressed against them in the past. Blame for any failure is projected outwards, and forgiveness from the respondent is not likely. Indeed, "getting even" with the objects of this resentment may be a major preoccupation for such people.

Scores on *PAR-R* that are moderately elevated (i.e., 60T to 70T) suggest a sensitive person who is easily insulted or slighted and responds by holding grudges toward the offending party. As scores elevate above 70T, the respondents are increasingly inclined to attribute their misfortunes to the neglect of others and to discredit the successes of others as being the result of luck or favoritism. They are likely to be envious of others and disinclined to assist others in achieving their goals and successes. As scores exceed 80T, the person may dwell on past slights by others and may be preoccupied with evening the score. Examination of scores on *DOM* and *AGG* may suggest whether this hostility is likely to be expressed directly or in more passive-aggressive form.

PAR Full Scale Elevations

The *PAR* scale measures the characteristic phenomenology of the paranoid individual with respect to both symptomatology and personality elements. The item content addresses a vigilance in monitoring the environment for potential harm, a tendency to be resentful and to hold grudges, and a readiness to spot inequities in the way the respondent has been treated by others. At the full scale level, *PAR* represents a direct measure of interpersonal mistrust and hostility.

Average scores on *PAR* (i.e., < 60T) reflect a person who reports being open and forgiving in relationships with others. Scores between 60T and 70T are indicative of a person who may be seen as sensitive, tough-minded, and skeptical. Toward the upper end of this range, individuals may also be rather wary and cautious in their interpersonal relationships. With scores above 70T, the person is likely to be overtly suspicious and hostile. Such a person tends to be distrustful of close interpersonal relationships and probably has few close friends.

PAR scores that are markedly elevated (i.e., > 84T) are typically associated with paranoia of potentially delusional proportions. These individuals are bitter and resentful of the the way they have been treated by others, and they expect that others will attempt to exploit them. Any close relationships that may exist are probably troubled by jealousy and accusations. Ideas of reference and delusions of persecution or grandiosity are not uncommon when scores are in this range.

PAR Subscale Configurations

The following sections describe some of the implications of different combinations of elevations on the three *PAR* subscales.

PAR-H high, PAR-P high, PAR-R high

This pattern suggests a hypersensitive and hypervigilant individual who often questions and mistrusts the motives of others. Such people are extremely touchy in interactions with others and tend to harbor strong feelings of resentment as a result of perceived slights and insults. When circumstances fail to go their way, they are quick to feel that they are being treated inequitably and often holds grudges against others, even if the perceived affront is unintentional. Consistent with the constellation of hypervigilance, suspiciousness, and resentment, such people are seen by others as being quite hostile. Working relationships with others are likely to be very strained, despite any efforts by others to demonstrate support, reassurance, and assistance.

PAR-H high, PAR-P high, PAR-R average

This type of individual feels that he or she has been taken advantage of in the past and is on guard to prevent similar circumstances from happening again. Such individuals approach relationships in a hypervigilant fashion and easily mistrust the motives of others. They are very sensitive to any perceived affronts and will withdrawal quickly from individuals who are perceived as anything less than totally supportive. Casual relationships are likely to be quite distant and strained, and even efforts by others to demonstrate support and assistance may be viewed with skepticism by the respondent.

PAR-H high, PAR-P average, PAR-R high

This patterns suggests a characterologically suspicious individual who is predisposed to question and mistrust the motives of others. Such people are vigilant to any signs that they are being treated unfairly, and they will harbor strong and lingering feelings of resentment following any perceived slights and insults. Although they may not view themselves as unduly suspicious, others are likely to see such people as hostile and unforgiving. Establishing close relationships with such people tends to be quite difficult because of the lack of trust and the suspicion of any efforts to render assistance.

PAR-H average, PAR-P high, PAR-R high

This pattern suggests a person who feels that life has treated him or her unfairly. Such people are bitter about their perceived mistreatment, and they feel they have been victimized in some manner through the neglect or active interference of others. They tend to be envious of others and to denigrate their accomplishments, and they are not likely to support or cooperate with the efforts of others. They are very slow to forgive transgressions and may ruminate about past slights and insults at the hands of others. Such people are prone to attribute the causes for any untoward circumstances externally, and they often feel as if they have very little control over the outcomes in their lives, seeing themselves as the pawn of various malevolent forces. They place a very high premium on loyalty in the people around them, but their high expectations in this regard are often impossible to meet.

Schizophrenia (SCZ)

Schizophrenia is one of the most heterogeneous of all clinical syndromes, and this heterogeneity poses a number of problems for assessment. Historically, there have been many schemes for subtyping schizophrenia, with the number of subtypes ranging from the three originally described by Kraepelin (i.e., paranoid, catatonic, hebephrenic) to the dozens of subtypes described by Leonhard (e.g., Ban, 1982). The distinction between "positive" and "negative" symptoms in schizophrenia has received considerable research support in recent years. Positive symptoms involve the presence of features that are normally *not* present in individuals; they include phenomena such as hallucinations, delusions, and bizarre behavior. Negative symptoms represent the absence of features that normally *are* present in individuals, such as social behavior and affective responsiveness (Andraesen, 1985). The clinical import of the distinction can be found in a wide variety of areas; for example, patients with predominantly negative symptoms often show little response to neuroleptic medication and have poorer prognoses (Angrist, Rotrosen, & Gershon, 1980).

However, thought disorder is an important diagnostic feature of schizophrenia that does not fit neatly into the positive–negative distinction. Some features of thought disorder (e.g., tangential speech) are considered positive symptoms, whereas others (e.g., thought blocking, attentional problems) are sometimes characterized as negative symptoms. Confirmatory factor analyses have demonstrated that features of thought disorder tend not to group well with either symptom group (Lenzenweger, Dworkin, & Wethington, 1980), and some analyses have suggested that thought disorder should be considered a third, relatively independent pattern of impairment in schizophrenia.

The *SCZ* scale of the PAI was designed to assess these three aspects of schizophrenia. Positive symptoms, negative symptoms, and thought disorder were each assessed via different subscales. The Psychotic Experiences subscale emphasizes the positive symptoms of schizophrenia, such as delusions and hallucinations, that are central to the *DSM* definition of the disorder. The Social Detachment subscale focuses on the most characteristic negative symptom of schizophrenia, social withdrawal and poor rapport. Finally, the Thought Disorder subscale includes items assessing experiences such as thought blocking, confusion, distractibility, and concentration problems.

SCZ-P: Psychotic Experiences

Positive symptoms of schizophrenia involve delusions and hallucinations, as well as characteristic bizarre thought content. The positive symptoms tend to have a rather distinct course, with episodic exacerbations and often complete remissions, and persons with predominantly positive symptomatology do not tend to demonstrate intellectual impairments. These symptoms also tend to respond favorably to antipsychotic medications.

The *SCZ-P* items tap various positive symptoms of schizophrenia that vary in severity from unusual perceptions and magical thinking to the characteristic first-rank psychotic symptoms of schizophrenia. In keeping with efforts to maintain discriminant validity, the features are designed to be relatively specific to schizophrenia rather than more broadly defined, nonspecific symptoms that might be found in other syndromes (e.g., delusions of grandeur or nihilistic delusions). Scores that are moderately elevated (i.e., $60T$ to $70T$) suggest that the respondent may entertain some ideas that others tend to find unconventional or unusual; toward the upper end of this range, the person may strike others as peculiar and eccentric. Scores above $70T$ indicate the experience of unusual perceptual or sensory events and/or unusual ideas that may involve delusional beliefs. Scores exceeding $85T$ are often associated with an active psychotic episode, with poor judgment and breakdown in reality testing as hallmark features; full blown hallucinations or delusions are probable.

SCZ-S: Social Detachment

The negative symptoms of schizophrenia involve behavioral deficits such as poor interpersonal rapport, flattening of affect, and poverty of communication. Such individuals are apathetically indifferent to others, usually speaking to others only when necessary and avoiding interpersonal contact whenever possible. In schizophrenia, the course of these negative symptoms tends to be enduring, as opposed to episodic, and they are less responsive than positive symptoms to pharmacologic interventions. This pattern of behaviors is also consistent with the features of schizoid personality, which may simply be an alternative name for the same phenomenon.

The *SCZ-S* items focus upon the features of social disinterest and lack of affective responsivity. Moderate scores (i.e., 60T to 70T) suggest a quiet, impassive individual who exhibits little interest in the lives of other people. Toward the upper end of this range, scores may indicate a lack of ability to interpret the normal nuances of interpersonal behavior that provide the meaning to personal relationships. Scores above 70T reflect a person who neither desires nor enjoys close relationships; social isolation and detachment may serve to decrease the sense of discomfort fostered by interpersonal contact. Their lack of interest in others is mirrored in a lack of self-interest; they are generally indifferent to how others view them and are disinterested in introspection. They are made particularly uncomfortable by strong emotions, which they themselves tend not to experience and which they do not understand in others.

SCZ-T: Thought Disorder

Schizophrenia is characterized by disruptions in thought process that do not seem to covary with either positive or negative symptoms. At the extreme, a thought disorder can render the patient incoherent and unable to string together an intelligible sentence. In its milder forms, difficulties in concentration, decision-making, and memory will occur. It should be recognized that these milder features tend to be nonspecific, associated with severe affective disorders in particular. Thus, *SCZ-T* elevations are commonly observed in severe major depression, without accompanying elevations on *SCZ-P*.

The *SCZ-T* items sample across the range of clarity and freedom from confusion in thought processes. Moderate elevations (i.e., 60T to 70T) suggest problems in concentration and decision-making; such scores would not be unexpected among depressed or anxious individuals. However, toward the upper end of this range, there will be increasing likelihood of confusion and perplexity in addition to the more benign cognitive inefficiencies. Scores above 70T reflect a loosening of associations and increased difficulties in self-expression and communication. However, in the absence of a clinical elevation of the full *SCZ* scale, this finding can reflect various causes other than schizophrenic disorder. Severe depression or mania, the sequelae of brain injury or disease, the effects of medication, and the consequences of drug or alcohol abuse should all be explored as potential causes of elevations on this subscale.

SCZ Full Scale Elevations

The *SCZ* scale was designed to measure a number of the different facets of schizophrenia; this multifaceted approach is necessary, because the disorder is one of the most heterogeneous of all clinical groups. Hence, elevations on the full scale could result from a number of causes: unusual beliefs and perceptions; poor social competence and social anhedonia; or inefficiency and disturbances in attention, concentration, and associational processes. Average scores on *SCZ* (i.e., < 60*T*) reflect a person who reports being effective in social relationships and has no trouble with attention or concentration problems. Scores between 60*T* and 70*T* are indicative of a person who may be seen as withdrawn, aloof, and unconventional. Toward the upper end of this range, individuals may be quite cautious and hostile in their few interpersonal relationships. With scores above 70*T*, the person is likely to be isolated and to feel misunderstood and alienated from others. Some difficulties in thinking, concentration, and decision-making are probable with scores in this range. Specific subscale elevations may reveal the presence of unusual perceptions or beliefs that may be psychotic in nature.

SCZ scores that are markedly elevated (i.e., > 90*T*) are typically associated with an active schizophrenic episode. These individuals are confused, withdrawn, suspicious, and tend to have poor judgment and reality testing. Prominent psychotic symptomatology is likely with scores in this range, and specific elevations on other scales may be helpful in identifying the precise nature of such symptoms. For example, concomitant elevations on *PAR* may indicate the presence of delusions of persecution. With increasing *T*-score elevations, delusions of thought broadcasting, thought insertion, thought withdrawal, and thought control become more likely. These individuals may require referral to evaluate the need for psychotropic medications.

SCZ Subscale Configurations

The following sections describe some of the implications of different combinations of elevations on the three *SCZ* subscales.

SCZ-P high, SCZ-S high, SCZ-T high

This pattern indicates prominent features from across the schizophrenic spectrum. It is likely that the respondent experiences unusual perceptual events or full-blown hallucinations as well as unusual ideas that may include magical thinking or delusional beliefs. However, because such people are quiet and avoid interactions with others, this unusual thought content may not be readily apparent. Such people are likely to be socially isolated, with few interpersonal relationships that could be described as being close and warm. In addition to having limited social skills, the person's thought processes are likely to be marked by confusion, distractibility, and difficulties in concentration; such individuals may experience their thoughts as blocked, withdrawn, or somehow influenced by others.

SCZ-P high, SCZ-S high, SCZ-T average

This pattern represents a person who reports unusual thought content with no disruptions in thought process. The thought content may involve unusual perceptual or sensory events (perhaps including full-blown hallucinations) and/or as unusual ideas that may include magical thinking or delusional beliefs. If *PAR-P* is markedly elevated, these ideas may involve persecutory beliefs that may be part of a well integrated delusional system. Such a finding would also explain the person's presentation as being a socially isolated individual with few, if any, close relationships.

SCZ-P high, SCZ-S average, SCZ-T high

This pattern suggests an individual presenting with acute psychotic symptomatology, involving unusual perceptual or sensory events (perhaps including full-blown hallucinations) as well as unusual ideas that may include magical thinking or delusional beliefs. The person's thought processes are likely to be marked by confusion, distractibility, and difficulties in concentration, and he or she may experience thoughts as being blocked, withdrawn, or somehow influenced by others. The relative absence of negative symptoms may be a favorable prognostic sign for eventual remission of these symptoms.

SCZ-P average, SCZ-S high, SCZ-T high

This pattern suggests a socially isolated individual who has few interpersonal relationships that could be described as being close and warm. Such people tend to have limited social skills, with particular difficulty in interpreting the normal nuances of interpersonal behavior that provide the meaning to personal relationships. Generally apathetic and disinterested in other people and their emotional state, such individuals may withdraw from social interaction to decrease the sense of confusion fostered by interpersonal contact. Thought processes are likely to be inefficient and marked by distractibility and concentration problems. Such individuals are likely to have difficulty communicating effectively, and others who succeed in getting to know them (probably a difficult task) may see them as strange and peculiar.

Borderline Features (*BOR*)

The *BOR* scale assesses a number of elements related to severe personality disorder; although all of these elements are part of the borderline syndrome, individually they are also common to numerous other disorders. This scale is the only PAI scale that has four subscales, largely due to the complexity of the construct as it has been represented in the literature. Part of the reason for this complexity is that this is inherently a more nebulous construct than some that have been recognized for a much longer time (e.g., depression or schizophrenia). The borderline concept has always been thought of as reflecting a "boundary," presumably representing some border, but the nature of the border has never been exactly clear. Initially, borderline personality represented the border of analyzability (i.e., patients who were marginally able to be treated with psychoanalysis). Over time, this came to be synonymous with the boundary between neurosis and psychosis, with a neurotic level of adaptation presumably reflecting problems in the Oedipal stage characterized primarily by difficulties with anxiety, and with psychosis reflecting more primitive issues involving breaks with reality. In this framework, borderline individuals fell somewhere in the middle. It was thought that much of the time the borderline individual superficially would appear to be at a neurotic level of adaptation, but that, under stress, and particularly in more unstructured situations, such individuals would deteriorate and appear psychotic.

The actual incorporation of borderline personality into the diagnostic literature occurred in the *DSM-III* (1980). The formulation of the current construct grew out of work conducted by Robert Spitzer, the chair of the *DSM-III* Task Force, who identified two types of individuals who were being identified as borderline: One type who appeared to lie at the boundary of psychosis or the boundary of schizophrenia and another type who were affectively and behaviorally unstable and erratic. The "unstable" variant was eventually renamed "borderline"; the other type was named Schizotypal Personality Disorder and was considered to represent a schizophrenia spectrum disorder. The resulting borderline criteria, reflecting an erratic and inconsistent group of individuals, were quite factorially complex, but subsumed personality features useful in understanding a variety of different and severe personality disorders.

Over the years, a number of investigators have examined the borderline construct using factor-analytic or cluster-analytic studies (e.g., Grinker, Werble, & Drye,1968; Hurt & Clarkin,1990; Morey, 1989). These studies have provided convergence in identifying the major facets of the borderline construct, and each facet represents a theoretically important etiological mechanism. The four *BOR* subscales of the PAI were designed to reflect these facets.

BOR-A: Affective Instability

Individuals with borderline personality present with emotions that fluctuate impressively, leading some theorists to propose that the disorder may represent a variant of bipolar affective disorder (e.g., Akiskal, Yerevanian, & Davis, 1985). However, the mood changes in borderline patients tend to differ in many ways from the mood changes in bipolar patients. First, the mood changes in borderline individuals are not regular. Instead, they tend to be very sudden, without any rhythmicity. Also, borderline patients rarely, if ever, return to a period of normal affect; there are few days where there is not some dramatic affective change in such individuals. Furthermore, studies of family histories yield smaller estimates of relatedness between the disorders than would be expected if borderline was a bipolar spectrum disorder.

Nonetheless, affective instability in the form of sudden emotional change is one of the hallmark characteristics of borderline personality. These affects are not a polarity between happiness and sadness, however. Rather, for borderline patients affective instability involves a propensity to rapidly become anxious, angry, depressed, or irritable. The *BOR-A* subscale reflects this rapidity of mood shift. Elevations could, for example, represent an individual with a bad temper (which can be confirmed by an examination of the *AGG-A* subscale), or it might indicate a person who becomes anxious easily (a conclusion that might be supported from inspecting the *ANX-A* or *ARD-P* subscales). The unique contribution of the *BOR-A* subscale is in ascertaining the suddenness of the affective change.

Thus, high scorers on *BOR-A* are highly responsive emotionally, typically manifesting rapid and extreme mood swings, rather than the more cyclic mood changes seen in affective disorders. In the highest ranges (i.e., roughly > 80*T*) all affects are likely to be involved, including episodes of poorly controlled anger. In the range from 70*T* to 80*T*, a propensity to experience a particular negative affect may be responsible, and investigation of other scales may determine whether anxiety (*ANX-A* or *ARD-P*), depression (*DEP-A*), or anger (*AGG-A*) is the typical response. On the other hand, unusually low scores (i.e., < 40*T*) reflect individuals who describe themselves as fairly unresponsive emotionally and who may appear to others as affectively constricted.

BOR-I: Identity Problems

Theoretically, the notion of issues surrounding identity are central to Kernberg's (1975) view of borderline personality. Kernberg describes this facet as "identity diffusion," meaning that borderline patients have a difficult time maintaining a constant representation of who they are, where they are headed in life, and what they value. As a result of this diffuse sense of self, such individuals tend to rely on others to help them formulate an identity, thus defining themselves primarily in relationship to other people. Theoretically, this involves a developmental failure to establish an autonomous identity independent of the primary caregivers, leading to similar difficulties in adulthood. In a sense, this involves being dependent upon others, as illustrated in *DSM* criteria such as "fears of abandonment." Although there is certainly substantial diagnostic overlap between borderline and dependent personality disorder (Morey, 1988), there is a qualitative difference in the nature of these behaviors. Borderline individuals do not really want the assistance of others to make sure that they perform their jobs effectively or make good decisions; rather, they have a profound *need* for others to help them define for themselves who they are. In the absence of these important others, borderline individuals may initiate very desperate and frantic efforts to try to reestablish this needed contact, not out of fear that they will be unable to do their jobs effectively, but because they are afraid they will cease to exist.

Because borderline individuals may desperately cling to the people who are most important and central to defining them, it is at times assumed that this represents a form of "over-idealization" of others; indeed, this notion is incorporated into the *DSM* criteria. However, to some extent this description misinterprets the behavior of the borderline individual, confusing a profound need for others with an idealization of those others. Many times, this need will not necessarily be manifest in idealization; in fact, borderline individuals are likely to have constant conflicts with the people closest to them. Nonetheless, even through this conflict with important others, the borderline individual can continue to maintain an identity as an extension of these others, as a spouse, a friend, an offspring, or even as an enemy. It is the urgent necessity of these relationships, rather than their idealized quality, that is characteristic of the borderline individual.

One implication of the problems in identity and sense of self reflected by *BOR-I* is that the self-concept is unstable and inconsistent. At any particular moment, a borderline individual may have an overriding life ambition that he or she can describe with great earnestness, but by the next week, the ambitions are likely to be totally different. No matter how deep an attachment to some particular course of action may appear, within a short period of time a design of equal intensity may emerge in an entirely different direction. Individuals with elevations on *BOR-I* are likely to be prone to these sudden shifts in ambitions and goals.

In sum, scores above *70T* represent uncertainty about major life issues and difficulties in developing and maintaining a sense of purpose. Such uncertainty is more common in younger adults, and *BOR-I* is correlated with age: The average score for persons 18 to 29 years of age is 55*T*, whereas it is 46*T* for those above age 60. Nonetheless, scores above 70*T* are reflective of identity issues beyond what is expected during adulthood, regardless of age. With more extreme scores (i.e., > 80*T*) this may involve quite sudden and unpredictable reversals in life plans and directions; more modest elevations suggest feelings of emptiness, lack of fulfillment, and boredom. Elevations also suggest a fair degree of anxiety around identity issues and disruption or dysfunction within the family of origin is a possibility to be explored. Scores at the low end of *BOR-I* (i.e., < 45*T*) suggest a more stable and fixed self-concept. In many cases, this represents a strength, but it can also involve a therapeutic challenge if there are strongly fixed negative elements to the person's identity.

BOR-N: Negative Relationships

The concept of "negative relationships" involves the interpersonal presentation of borderline personality: a tendency to repeatedly become involved in relationships that are very intense and chaotic. High scores on *BOR-N* are an indication that the person's closest attachment relationships are likely to be stormy; these relationships might include one's family, spouse or partner, or therapist. Part of the storminess revolves around the borderline individual's experience that important other people have not met his or her needs. They approach such relationships with a great deal of longing and hope (which may be where the supposed "idealization" originates); invariably, however, the borderline individual eventually comes away feeling not just disappointed, but betrayed and exploited. To some extent, this stems from the general affective reactivity of the borderline personality described earlier (i.e., a fairly small slight can generate a very catastrophic response). However, the research literature indicates that borderline patients have extremely high rates of physical and sexual abuse during childhood (Herman, Perry, & Van der Kolk, 1989). With this background, it is easy to understand the borderline individual's fear that the people who are closest are likely to exploit him or her. The *BOR-N* items tap this perception of betrayal in past relationships, as well as a distrust and pessimism surrounding future relationships.

Considered in isolation, the *BOR-N* scale reflects a history of involvement in ambivalent, intense, and unstable relationships. At extreme scores (i.e., > 80*T*), the person is quite bitter and resentful about the way past relationships have gone, feeling betrayed by the people who were once closest and preoccupied with fears of abandonment or rejection by those who are currently important to him or her. Scores between 70*T* and 80*T* suggest numerous problems and failures in past attachment relationships, although intense feelings of past exploitation are less likely in this range than in higher scores.

The concept of "ambivalence" is often raised in discussions of borderline personality, usually in reference to the putative defense of "splitting." In splitting, the person is presumably unable to integrate the positive and negative elements of another person, and this results in alternating periods of extreme idealization and devaluation of important others. However, as discussed in relation to *BOR-I*, the ambivalence that seems more central to the borderline personality is not one between good and bad, but one between need and fear. The *BOR-I* and *BOR-N* scales together capture this latter, fundamental ambivalence in borderline individuals: the profound need for others in order to establish who they themselves are, a tremendous distrust of these critically important people, and an expectation that they are going to be exploited or abused. Obviously, a person entering a relationship with this set of expectations is likely to experience problems, both in nonclinical interpersonal relationships and in therapeutic ones. If both *BOR-I* and *BOR-N* are elevated upon entering therapy, the treating clinician is likely to be taken aback by both the intensity of the client's need for the therapist and his or her readiness to perceive in the clinician signs of rejection, disinterest, or abuse, including any efforts the therapist might make to set limits on the relationship.

BOR-S: Self-Harm

The final borderline subscale reflects a tendency to act impulsively without much attention to the consequences of those acts. Such acts will thus be viewed by others as self-damaging or self-destructive (e.g., substance abuse, sexual recklessness, or quitting a job suddenly with no future job prospects). *BOR-S* is sometimes mistaken for a direct indicator of suicidal behaviors or self-mutilation. Although a person with a high score on *BOR-S* would be expected to more at risk for such behaviors than someone with a low score, the scale is more directly reflective of impulsivity than of either suicide risk or self-mutilation. Although a sample of self-mutilators did yield elevated *BOR-S* scores (Morey, 1991), not all elevations on *BOR-S* will involve self-mutilation. Similarly, whereas persons currently on suicide precautions scored above the mean on *BOR-S*, their average scores were only around 60*T* (Morey, 1991). Because many completed suicides are quite premeditated and are not impulsive acts, *BOR-S* is probably neither sensitive nor specific if used in isolation as a suicide indicator.

Extreme elevations on *BOR-S* (e.g., above 85*T*) reflect hazardous levels of impulsivity and recklessness. These individuals are impulsive in areas that have high potential for negative consequences (e.g., spending money, sex, substance abuse). Such behavior has typically interfered repeatedly with effective social or occupational performance, or both. High scorers may also be at increased risk for self-mutilation and suicidal behavior, and accompanying *SUI* elevations may indicate a risk for impulsive suicide gestures.

BOR Full Scale Interpretation

The configuration of the *BOR* subscales is critical in assigning *DSM*-based diagnoses of borderline personality; if three or four of the subscales are elevated, the person is likely to meet the criteria for the disorder. However, a similar conclusion should not be drawn from elevations of the full scale. The full scale score is probably better considered in line with Kernberg's (1975) view of borderline personality as a level of personality organization or adaptation that ranges somewhere between neurosis and psychosis. Thus, low scorers will tend to be fairly healthy with respect to personality issues, whereas high scorers will present with fairly primitive concerns, perhaps across many different variants of personality disorder as they are categorized in the *DSM* manuals. Diagnostically, if the full *BOR* scale is elevated, it is a sign of problems in the personality realm, whereas the configuration of the subscales can confirm whether the problems are classically borderline (i.e., elevations on three or four subscales) or circumscribed problems associated with other issues (e.g., *BOR-N* reflecting relationship problems stemming from posttraumatic stress disorder).

Average scores on *BOR* (i.e., < 60T) reflect a person who reports being emotionally stable and who also has stable relationships. Scores between 60T and 70T are indicative of a person who may be seen as moody, sensitive, and having some uncertainty about life goals; scores in this range are not uncommon in young adults. Toward the upper end of this range, individuals may be increasingly angry and dissatisfied with their interpersonal relationships. Individuals with scores above 70T are likely to be impulsive and emotionally labile; they tend to feel misunderstood by others (who often perceive them as egocentric) and find it difficult to sustain close relationships. They tend to be angry and suspicious and, at the same time, anxious and needy, making them quite ambivalent about interactions with others. However, scores in this range do not necessarily suggest a diagnosis of borderline personality disorder unless there are prominent elevations on each of the four *BOR* subscales, because individual features are common to other disorders.

BOR scores that are markedly elevated (i.e., > 90T) are typically associated with personality functioning within the borderline range. These individuals typically present in a state of crisis, often regarding difficulties in their relationships. With elevations in this range, respondents are invariably hostile and feel angry and betrayed by the people around them. Symptomatically, they often report being very depressed and anxious in response to their circumstances. They are impulsive and will act in ways that appear to others to be quite self-destructive; for example, they seem to sabotage their own best intentions with acting-out behaviors. These behaviors can include alcohol or drug abuse, suicidal gestures, or aggressive outbursts; scores on *ALC*, *DRG*, *SUI* and *AGG* should be consulted to identify potential problem areas of this type.

BOR Subscale Configurations

The following sections describe the implications of particular combinations where two or more *BOR* subscales are elevated together.

BOR-A high, BOR-I high, BOR-N high, BOR-S high

This pattern of scale elevations suggests difficulties in numerous areas: emotional instability, volatile interpersonal relationships, anger, identity disturbance, and impulsivity. The respondent is likely to be quite emotionally labile, manifesting fairly rapid and extreme mood swings, and, in particular, is probably quick to display intense and poorly controlled anger. There is also uncertainty about major life issues, with little sense of direction or purpose in life. A history of involvement in intense and volatile relationships is likely, as well as preoccupations with fears of being abandoned or rejected by those important to the respondent. The individual's response to these perceived interpersonal rejections is likely to involve impulsive acts that are likely to be self-harmful or self-destructive (e.g., spending money, sex, substance abuse). This pattern of behaviors is consistent with a diagnosis of Borderline Personality Disorder.

BOR-A high, BOR-I high, BOR-N high, BOR-S average

This subscale configuration suggests difficulties with emotional instability, volatile interpersonal relationships, underlying anger, and identity issues. Such individuals are likely to be quite emotionally labile, manifesting fairly rapid and extreme mood swings and reactive anger. There is likely to be much uncertainty and ambivalence surrounding major life issues, goals, values, and close relationships. These latter relationships are likely to be intense and volatile, with ruminative fears of abandonment, rejection, or exploitation. The comparatively lower score on *BOR-S* is a positive sign in that it suggests that, although such people may respond dramatically to affectively arousing situations, this response does not typically involve self-destructive impulsive acts.

BOR-A high, BOR-I high, BOR-N average, BOR-S high

This pattern suggests difficulties with emotional instability, anger, identity disturbance, and impulsivity. Such individuals are likely to be quite emotionally labile, manifesting fairly rapid and extreme mood swings; in particular, they tend to experience episodes of poorly controlled anger. There also appears to be uncertainty about major life issues and little sense of direction or purpose in life at this time. They are also quite impulsive and prone to behaviors that are likely to be self-harmful or self-destructive (e.g., spending money, sex, substance abuse); there also may be increased risk for self-mutilation or suicidal behavior, and scores on *SUI* should be examined. The relatively lower score on *BOR-N* suggests that these individuals may be devoting considerable efforts to maintaining their relationships in the face of their anger and impulsivity; they may experience considerable guilt following impulsive or angry acts, and their contrition may serve to sustain relationships that would otherwise crumble.

BOR-A high, BOR-I average, BOR-N high, BOR-S high

This configuration of *BOR* subscales suggests difficulties in emotional control, volatile interpersonal relationships, and notable impulsivity. Such individuals are likely to be quite emotionally labile, manifesting fairly rapid and extreme mood swings and, in particular, episodes of poorly controlled anger during which they lash out at the persons closest to them. It is likely that, as a result, they have a history of involvement in intense and volatile relationships that may lead to a preoccupation with fears of being abandoned or rejected by important others. They also are likely to be impulsive in other areas, prone to behaviors that are likely to be self-harmful or self-destructive (e.g., spending money, sex, substance abuse); they may also be at increased risk for self-mutilation or suicidal behavior, and the score on *SUI* should be examined. The comparative lack of elevation on *BOR-I* may suggest that this is a relatively fixed (as opposed to a reactive) pattern of behavior and, thus, may be quite difficult to change.

BOR-A average, BOR-I high, BOR-N high, BOR-S high

This pattern suggests a history of involvement in volatile interpersonal relationships, a poorly formed personal identity, and noteworthy impulsivity. The history of relationship problems may have left such individuals preoccupied with consistent fears of being abandoned or rejected by those around them. Such preoccupations are worsened by an uncertainty about major life issues and a lack of sense of direction or purpose indicated by the elevation on *BOR-I*; such individuals are not certain what to do without important others to guide them. The pattern also includes marked impulsivity, suggesting a tendency to display behaviors likely to be self-harmful or self-destructive (e.g., spending money, sex, substance abuse). These behaviors are likely to be most prominent following disruptions or crises in close interpersonal relationships and may reflect "acting-out" as a way of warding off the experience of unpleasant affects.

BOR-A high, BOR-I high, BOR-N average, BOR-S average

This configuration suggests that issues of affect control and identity formation are important personality problems for such individuals. They are likely to be quite emotionally labile, manifesting fairly rapid and extreme mood swings; in particular, their anger may be poorly controlled. There is also an uncertainty about major life issues, and their sense of direction or purpose in life probably vacillates in relation to their mood. The comparative lack of impulsivity or severe interpersonal disruption may indicate that much of their anger is directed internally, rather than impulsively expressed toward the people around them.

BOR-A high, BOR-I average, BOR-N high, BOR-S average

This subscale configuration suggests that the person is likely to be quite emotionally labile and moody, with anger management likely to be an issue. This emotionality and hostility probably have contributed to an apparent history of involvement in stormy and volatile relationships. The comparative lack of impulsivity may suggest that, during most normal situations, a fair amount of effort to control emotions is being expended. However, during times of stress, particularly during heated interpersonal conflict, the person is likely to react with sudden emotional outbursts.

BOR-A average, BOR-I high, BOR-N high, BOR-S average

This configuration represents the BOR "splitting" duo of interpersonal need (represented by BOR-I) and interpersonal conflict and distrust (represented by BOR-N). There is uncertainty about major life issues and a lack of direction or purpose in life. This uncertainty is likely to extend to the arena of interpersonal relationships, as such individuals may have a very unstable sense of what they desire from these interactions. As a result, a history of involvement in intense, needy, and short-lived relationships is likely, and they tend to be preoccupied with consistent fears of being abandoned or rejected in these relationships. As a result, they are quick to perceive in others any sign of real or imagined rejection, disinterest, or abuse, often including any efforts another person might make to put limits on the relationship.

BOR-A high, BOR-I average, BOR-N average, BOR-S high

This pattern indicates emotional lability, with fairly rapid and extreme mood swings and, in particular, episodes of poorly controlled and impulsively expressed anger. However, rather than being directed at others, the anger may be self-directed, resulting in behaviors likely to be self-harmful or self-destructive (e.g., irresponsible spending, sex, substance abuse). Any angry gestures that are outwardly directed may be followed by considerable guilt, and their contrition may serve to sustain relationships that would otherwise suffer. Such individuals may be at increased risk for self-mutilation or suicidal behavior during times of affective turmoil, and the score on *SUI* should be examined.

BOR-A average, BOR-I high, BOR-N average, BOR-S high

This configuration indicates pronounced uncertainty about major life issues and a lack of direction or purpose in life as it currently stands. This is likely to be exacerbated by impulsivity, such that frequent and impulsive changes of direction in vocational interests, hobbies, religion, or other social roles may be the norm. There may also be some more overtly self-harmful or self-destructive behaviors (e.g., spending money, sex, substance abuse).

BOR-A average, BOR-I average, BOR-N high, BOR-S high

This subscale pattern suggests a history of involvement in intense and short-lived relationships. These relationships may be impulsively ended, or they may dissolve due to the respondent's tendency to engage in behaviors likely to be self-harmful or self-destructive (e.g., spending money, sex, substance abuse). This pattern makes such individuals pessimistic about relationships, and they may be preoccupied with fears or expectations of being abandoned or rejected. The pattern of impulsivity and volatile relationships may place such individuals at increased risk for self-mutilation or suicidal behavior, particularly during times of marked conflict in relationships, and scores on *SUI* should be examined.

Antisocial Features (*ANT*)

The *ANT* scale is the second of the two scales (*BOR* being the other) that specifically assess character pathology. These two constructs were selected for the PAI because, together, they account for nearly all empirical research that has been conducted on personality disorders. However, it is important to note that the representation of antisocial personality on *ANT* departs more than the *BOR* scale from the *DSM* conceptualization of the disorder.

The history of this construct is an interesting one. The origins of the concept of Antisocial Personality Disorder are generally traced back to Pinel's notion of *manie sans delire* (madness without delirium) described at the turn of the 19th century. This concept was one of the first to describe a mental disorder that did not include a defect in reasoning; for this reason, Pinel's concept has been described as the forerunner of all modern theory on personality disorders (Mack, 1975). Gradually the concept acquired an element of defects in morality, and it eventually evolved into a notion resembling one of the "born criminal"; Koch (1891) selected

Table 2-1
Cleckley's (1941) 16 Diagnostic Indicators of Psychopathy

1. Superficial charm and good "intelligence"
2. Absence of delusions and other signs of irrational thinking
3. Absence of "nervousness" or psychoneurotic manifestations
4. Unreliability
5. Untruthfulness and insincerity
6. Lack of remorse or shame
7. Inadequately motivated antisocial behavior
8. Poor judgment and failure to learn by experience
9. Pathologic egocentricity and incapacity for love
10. General poverty in major affective reactions
11. Specific loss of insight
12. Unresponsiveness in general interpersonal relations
13. Fantastic and inviting behavior with drink and sometimes without
14. Suicide rarely carried out
15. Sex life impersonal, trivial, and poorly integrated
16. Failure to follow any life plan

the term *psychopathic inferiority* for this condition to emphasize its purported con-stitutional basis, and this term served as the foundation of the term "psychopath."

Perhaps the most influential development in the evolution of this concept was the publication of *The Mask of Sanity* by Cleckley (1941). This book made explicit the personological features that set the psychopathic personality apart from crim-inality. Among the features Cleckley stressed as pathognomonic of this personality constellation were a lack of guilt, a general absence of anxiety or depression, and a seeming inability to learn from experience. For assistance in diagnosis, Cleckley described 16 signs that have become firmly embedded in the clinical lore sur-rounding this syndrome; these 16 features are presented in Table 2-1.

The *DSM-III* (1980) conceptualization of Antisocial Personality Disorder rep-resented a substantial departure from the notion of psychopathy. The *DSM-III* def-inition was based extensively on a history of delinquent or antisocial behavior, in contrast to the personality elements described by Cleckley and others. To a large extent, these behaviors were derived from the well known study by Robins (1966), which attempted to establish the adolescent antecedents of antisocial behavior in adults. However, these criteria seem to tap a somewhat different population than did the older "psychopathic personality" concept.

One difficulty with the representation of this construct in the *DSM-III* (1980) and its successors is that, in failing to include the more personological elements of the construct, it misses critical motivational differences for antisocial behavior. Some have criticized the *DSM* definition as being practically synonymous with criminal behavior; for example, at least half (if not more) of inmates will meet such criteria for the disorder (Hart & Hare, 1989). Others have expressed the concern that the *DSM* focus on delinquent behaviors leads to an overapplication of the diagnosis to lower socioeconomic groups, missing "white-collar" variants of the disorder. Finally, there is some support for the conclusion that the concept of psychopathy may be more valid than the *DSM* representation of this disorder. For example, some studies (e.g., Hart, Kropp, & Hare, 1988; Serin, Peters, & Barbaree, 1990) indicate psychopathy ratings are more useful than the *DSM* concept of antisocial personality in predicting recidivism in prisoners.

Hare's approach (Hare et al., 1988) to the representation of psychopathy has been found to have two different components or factors. One of these is a behavioral component that involves a variety of antisocial acts; this factor corresponds reasonably closely to the *DSM-III* (1980) conceptualization. However, the second factor involves a component of psychopathy that incorporates personality traits, such as tendencies to be unempathic, callous, or egocentric. The inclusion of such traits in the conceptualization of the disorder increases predictive validity; for this reason, the PAI was constructed to assess each of these facets. The final version of the *ANT* scale included a total of three facets, one (*ANT-A*) assessing antisocial behaviors, and the remaining two (*ANT-E*, *ANT-S*) tapping antisocial traits.

ANT-A: Antisocial Behaviors

The items comprising the *ANT-A* subscale inquire about antisocial acts during both adolescence and adulthood. High scorers are likely to have manifested a conduct disorder during adolescence, and during adulthood they may have been involved in illegal occupations or engaged in criminal acts involving theft, destruction of property, and physical aggression toward others. This subscale of *ANT* is the one that corresponds most closely to the more behavioral *DSM-III* (1980) and *DSM-III-R* (1987) definition of the disorder, as it reflects an individual who commits antisocial acts. The subscale in isolation does not, however, indicate psychological attributes underlying these acts. Such behaviors could arise from impulsivity, from egocentricity or entitlement, from environmental presses, or from anger-management problems. Inspection of other PAI scales and subscales can shed light on each of these potential sources.

Scores above 70T on *ANT-A* reflect a history of difficulties with both authority and social convention. A pattern of antisocial behavior was probably first evident in adolescence, and, with scores in this range, it is likely that the pattern has continued into adulthood. Scores in the moderate range (i.e., 60 to 69T) may be more likely than more elevated scores to reflect historical problems. However, because many of the questions on the subscale are historical in nature, a past history of such acts can lead to elevations that may not reflect current functioning. For example, the item "I've done some things that weren't exactly legal" might be referring to behaviors that occurred 30 years earlier. Scores that are very low (i.e., ≤ 40T) could indicate a very conforming, perhaps moralistic individual, or perhaps, a person motivated to deny any history of mischievous behavior whatsoever.

ANT-E: Egocentricity

The items comprising the ANT-E subscale tap a callousness and lack of empathy in interactions with others. It is this personological component that is probably closest to the classic definition of the "psychopath," yet, in isolation, this scale does not imply psychopathy. Instead, it suggests a certain self-centeredness that also could be suggestive of a histrionic or narcissistic personality pattern. However, in combination with acting-out behavior (ANT-A) and anger-management problems (AGG), the likelihood of psychopathy as opposed to other issues increases considerably. It should also be recognized that higher scores are obtained in younger people; the average score for individuals 18 to 29 years of age is 56T.

High scorers on ANT-E (i.e., ≥ 70T) tend to be seen as egocentric, with little regard for others or for the opinions of the society around them. In their desire to satisfy their own goals and impulses, they may take advantage of others, even those who are closest to them. They feel little responsibility for the welfare of others and have little loyalty to their acquaintances. Such individuals would be expected to place little importance in their social role obligations (e.g., as a spouse, parent, or employee). Although they may describe feelings of guilt over past transgressions, they are not likely to feel much remorse of any lasting nature, as their inflated sense of self and their feelings of entitlement would make them unlikely to believe that they were in the wrong. Such people may be perceived by others as hostile, but, aside from irritability, there may be little affective involvement in their interactions with others. More marked anger and hostility, if present, will be identified by elevations on AGG and PAR, rather than on ANT-E.

Moderate elevations on ANT-E (i.e., 60T to 69T) suggest a person who tends to be self-centered and pragmatic in interactions with others. Such people feel relatively little social anxiety or guilt, and, therefore, they may be quite effective in superficial social contacts. However, long-lasting relationships may be less successful, as these individuals rarely will place others' needs before their own. In contrast, scores that are very low (i.e., ≤ 40*T*) suggest a person who may repeatedly place others' needs first and, as such, have difficulty getting his or her own needs met. In combination with below-average scores on *MAN-G*, this suggests a humility that is driven by low self-esteem.

ANT-S: Stimulus Seeking

The *ANT-S* items tap a personality component associated with a willingness to take risks and a desire for novelty. Although individuals with antisocial personality score considerably above the average on most sensation-seeking scales, this trait is certainly not specific to this diagnostic group, nor is it in isolation a pathological, or even an undesirable, characteristic. However, in combination with other traits (e.g., lack of empathy, poor impulse control, or anger management problems), this characteristic can lead to a variety of problem behaviors, because the inhibiting effects of anxiety are minimized. Thus, in relation to other PAI scales, *ANT-S* has a disinhibition component that might heighten the impact of elevations beyond what might be expected otherwise. As is true of the other *ANT* subscales, *ANT-S* scores tend to be higher in younger individuals (i.e., the average score is 56*T* in 18- to 29-year-olds), perhaps lending empirical support to the notion of "the recklessness of youth."

High scorers on *ANT-S* (i.e., ≥ 70*T*) are likely to manifest behavior that is reckless and potentially dangerous to themselves and/or those around them. They crave novelty and stimulation; easily bored by routine and convention, they may act impulsively in an effort to stir up excitement. Their desire for new experiences may lead to periods of nomadic wandering and make any long-term commitments unlikely. They also tend to be less anxious than most people, even in situations where anxiety should be expected. More moderate elevations (i.e., 60*T* to 69*T*) suggest a more controlled, but still potentially reckless, individual. In this range, however, the trait may not have led to difficulties. However, accompanying elevations on *ANT-A*, *AGG*, *BOR-S*, *ALC*, or *DRG* are all signs that novelty is being sought in self-destructive, acting-out ways.

Very low scores on *ANT-S* (i.e., ≤ 40*T*) suggest a person who is very timid and avoidant of novelty. These people are likely to feel uneasy over disruptions in routine, and *ARD-P* should be examined for the possibility of phobic avoidance behaviors.

ANT Full Scale Interpretation

At the full scale level, the *ANT* scale provides an assessment of personality and behavioral features relevant to the constructs of antisocial personality and psychopathy. As noted earlier, *ANT* item content ranges from indicators of egocentricity, adventuresomeness, and poor empathy to items addressing antisocial attitudes and behaviors; as a result, individuals with average-to-moderate eleva-tions can have quite different constellations of features. It is the conjunction of ele-vations on the three subscales that is suggestive of the psychopath; however, a per-son with antisocial behaviors, but without psychopathic personality features, may achieve a full scale elevation on *ANT* solely through the elevated *ANT-A*.

Average scores on *ANT* (i.e., < 60*T*) reflect individuals who report being con-siderate and warm in their relationships with others; these individuals also typi-cally exhibit reasonable control over impulses and behavior. Scores between 60*T* and 70*T* are indicative of individuals who may be seen as somewhat impulsive and risk-taking; scores in this range are fairly common in young adults, particularly in young men (i.e., the average *T* score for such a group approaches 60*T*). Toward the upper end of this range, individuals may be increasingly self-centered, disinhib-ited, skeptical of other's intentions, and unsentimental in their interpersonal rela-tionships. With scores above 70*T*, the respondent is likely to be impulsive and hostile, and there may be a history of reckless or antisocial acts. Such individuals may be seen by others as callous in their relationships, and long-lasting friendships tend to be the exception to the rule.

When *ANT* scores are markedly elevated (i.e., > 82*T*) individuals typically dis-play the prominent features of antisocial personality disorder. They are likely to be unreliable and irresponsible and probably have had little sustained success in either social or occupational realms. They tend to have a coldly pragmatic approach to relationships and will exploit such interactions to suit their own needs. Such people tend to be impulsive in their approach to life and have a his-tory of conflicts with authority figures.

ANT Subscale Configurations

The following sections describe the implications of particular combinations where two or more *ANT* subscales are elevated simultaneously.

ANT-A high, ANT-E high, ANT-S high

This triumvirate represents the pattern associated with the classic formulation of the psychopath. There is a history of antisocial behavior that likely began dur-ing adolescence, and, given the personality attributes of egocentricity and sensa-tion seeking, this pattern has probably persisted to the present time. Such people tend to have little regard for others or for the opinions of society. In order to sat-isfy their own impulses, they will take advantage of others, and there is likely to be little sense of loyalty, even to those who are closest to them. Such people approach life in a reckless manner, entertaining risks that are poorly motivated and potentially dangerous to themselves and to those around them. Social-role responsibilities are likely to be neglected in favor of pursuing novelty and excitement; old occupations and old relationships lose their appeal quickly for such individuals. Although feelings of guilt over past transgressions may be reported, it is unlikely that there is real remorse of any lasting nature.

ANT-A high, ANT-E high, ANT-S average

This subscale pattern suggests a history of antisocial behavior reflecting more of a callous disregard for others than a desire for excitement. Conduct problems probably date back to adolescence, and are most likely to represent a pattern of illegal occupations or acts motivated by personal gain. Such acts may involve planful exploitation, rather than impulsive acting-out, particularly if *BOR-S* reveals no elevation. People with this pattern are likely to be egocentric, with little regard for others or for the opinions or conventions of the society. Substantial feelings of loyalty or remorse are unlikely, and responsibility for the history of behavioral difficulties is likely to be projected outward, especially with above-average scores on *PAR-R*.

ANT-A high, ANT-E average, ANT-S high

This pattern suggests a history of impulsive and poorly motivated antisocial acts and behaviors, likely beginning with a conduct disorder during adolescence. Such people display reckless and risky behaviors that are potentially dangerous to themselves and to those around them. Some of these behaviors may have involved destruction of property, and physical aggression toward others may have been part of the picture (i.e., inspect for elevated scores on *AGG-P*). As many of the acts may have been impulsive, rather than premeditated, respondents may experience genuine remorse for their behavior, but feel unable to control or prevent repeat occurrences.

ANT-A average, ANT-E high, ANT-S high

This pattern suggests an individual who may appear successful and effective, but who is ultimately likely to be self-centered and irresponsible in dealing with social and vocational obligations. Although the individual may be able to conform to social convention in order to avoid negative consequences, this pattern reflects a lack of empathy or respect for others. In their desire to satisfy their own impulses or needs, such people may exploit others, regardless of the closeness of the relationship. For this reason, relationships with others are predictably short lived due to the predatory and manipulative behavior that characterizes such people. Although guilt over past transgressions may be professed, it is unlikely that there is remorse of any lasting nature. Dangerous risks may be taken, resulting from the desire for personal gain as well as the sheer excitement of the danger, and such people may not hesitate to expose others to similar risks.

Substance Abuse Scales

The PAI includes two scales pertinent to substance abuse, one measuring alcohol problems (ALC) and one related to drug use and abuse (DRG). Alcohol and drug problems are common among patients with mental disorders, but, at times, these problems are overlooked when more dramatic psychological problems are evident. The frequency of such problems merited the inclusion of this scale within a broad-band diagnostic instrument. As is true of the other clinical scales, items for ALC and DRG vary along a continuum of severity. The measurement model for ALC and DRG was patterned after the approach taken by Edwards and Gross (1976), who emphasized two facets of alcohol problems: core features of alcohol dependence, such as withdrawal symptoms and loss of control over drinking, and alcohol-related disabilities, such as social or legal consequences of drinking. Subsequent work (e.g., Edwards, Arif, & Hodgson, 1982) suggested that a similar pattern could be found in the drug abuse area. Because of the high interrelationship between dependence and disability, ALC and DRG were designed as unitary scales without subscales; however, this is not meant to imply that alcohol-related problems are either unitary or homogeneous. The ALC and DRG scale items were written to identify the presence and severity of alcohol and drug-related problems. Once such a problem has been identified, a more specialized assessment device (i.e., one predicated on the assumption that the respondent has problems with substance abuse) may be used to further pinpoint the nature and pattern of alcohol or substance use.

The ALC and DRG scales share certain features that are critical in evaluating respondents' scores on these scales. First, a good deal of the information gathered on these scales is historical (i.e., inquiries are made about events that may have happened in the past). These historical items reflect major milestones or major markers that exist in the development of a substance abuse behavior pattern (e.g., Jellinek, 1960), and it is these markers that are critical in assigning diagnoses under most widely used diagnostic systems, including the DSM. As such, ALC or DRG, or both, can be elevated in people who have had a substance abuse problem in the past, but who are not currently drinking or using drugs. An individual who has a current substance abuse problem will tend to have scores that are quite elevated. However, it is certainly possible for a person to score in the vicinity of 70T on either scale largely through historical information. A "recovering" alcoholic who has been abstinent for 10 years still might obtain an elevated score on ALC if, for example, he or she has lost jobs or has experienced withdrawal symptoms during past episodes of heavy drinking. Thus, moderate elevations on these scales should be followed up with some inquiry about current or recent substance consumption patterns.

In rare instances, respondents may refuse to answer *ALC* items and, particularly, *DRG* items, claiming the items are not relevant because they do not use alcohol or drugs. This has been most commonly observed in individuals who approach the test in a suspicious or legalistic manner; for instance, such responses are sometimes found in preemployment screening applications of the test. For example, such people will not answer an item such as, "My drug use has never caused problems for me," because they feel this would be admitting to using drugs. In such instances, it is recommended that the respondent be asked to consider all types of drugs, not just illegal or street drugs: prescription medication, over the counter preparations, and so forth. A refusal to respond to these items is most likely not to indicate hidden substance abuse; rather, it suggests that the test is being approached in a very careful and guarded manner, and this may be of use in evaluating the test results.

Examining Substance Abuse Denial

A feature shared by the *ALC* and *DRG* scales is that both address substance use and problems directly related to substance use. In other words, the item content is not subtle; hence, the scales are susceptible to denial, a problem of concern to many professionals in the substance abuse field. This direct method of inquiry is potentially problematic in a population noted for denial and dishonesty, and a number of writers have questioned the validity of such self-reports (Fuller, Lee, & Gordis, 1988). However, the general results of studies support the direct questioning method used in the PAI. For example, Sobell and Sobell (1975) found that the self-report of alcoholics about information (later verified through contact with agencies such as the FBI, the Department of Motor Vehicles, and state and county hospitals) was quite accurate, and that overestimates of problems by the patients were more frequent than underestimates. Another study of this issue (Hesselbrock et al., 1983) found that self-reported drinking estimates were supported by collateral informants and also were good predictors of post-discharge drinking. Furthermore, strategies that rely on a covert assessment of substance abuse tend to have dubious validity. Physiological markers of alcoholism (e.g., use of various liver function tests) generally have much lower sensitivity and specificity than self-report measures (Bernadt et al., 1982; Skinner et al., 1986). Indirect psychological markers of substance abuse have also been of limited utility. For example, the MacAndrew scale (1965), which was designed to covertly identify alcohol use from the MMPI item pool, has been found to correctly identify only 25% of alcoholics in inpatient treatment programs (Colligan et al., 1990). Given such findings, the direct content-based approach was taken in the PAI. However, if a person is motivated to deny substance use or the problems associated with such use, this will affect scores on these scales. It is easy to imagine why, in certain contexts, someone would deny use of illegal drugs, and the test user must be aware of this potential factor.

To some extent, the problems in identifying denial of alcohol and/or drug abuse are similar to those of defensiveness in general. As such, the general strategies for identifying defensive responding on the PAI (described in chapter 5) can be useful within the specific domain of substance use. For example, Fals-Stewart (1996) evaluated the ability of the *PIM* score to identify individuals attempting to deny substance abuse problems. He compared patients receiving treatment for drug abuse and normal controls with two "questionable responding" groups, one a group of drug abuse patients instructed to respond defensively, the second a group of respondents receiving the PAI as part of a forensic assessment, who were referred by the criminal justice system and who had positive urinalysis testing for recent drug ingestion but had denied drug use during the past 6 months. Fals-Stewart (1996) found that the optimal cutting score for *PIM* ($T > 56$) described in the *PAI Professional Manual* (Morey, 1991) successfully identified 88% of the individuals in the "questionable responding" groups while incorrectly identifying 20% of controls (both patients and nonclinical respondents) as "questionable." In other words, individuals motivated to deny substance abuse problems were more than four times as likely to score above 56*T* on *PIM* than individuals without such motivation. This result demonstrates that *PIM* is a useful starting point in evaluating substance abuse denial; chapter 5 provides a more detailed discussion of this scale and other strategies for identifying general defensiveness that may also be of use in identifying such individuals.

However, individuals may be specifically motivated to deny alcohol or drug abuse (for example, in the context of pre-employment screening) although not necessarily being defensive in describing other domains of their lives. Such individuals will tend to obtain very low raw scores on *ALC* and *DRG* (e.g., 0 or 1), reporting that they are teetotalers, that they neither drink nor use drugs of any sort. Although persons motivated to deny substance use will obtain scores in this range, so will large numbers of adults in the community, and thus, in most instances, such low scores are accurate reflections of their use of substances. However, these low scores should be regarded with some suspicion if the person has other characteristics that would lead one to expect the person to have at least experimented with alcohol or controlled substances. Although this approach has limitations (e.g., witness the limited efficacy of the MacAndrew scale), to a certain extent these characteristics may be inferred from PAI scale scores. In particular, five scales demonstrate substantial correlations with both *ALC* and *DRG*; these scales are *BOR-S* (indicating impulsivity), *ANT-S* (sensation-seeking), *ANT-A* (history of antisocial behavior), *ANT-E* (interpersonal callousness), and *AGG-P* (history of physical aggression). If these five scales are elevated, one would expect *ALC* or *DRG*, or both, to also be elevated, as such behaviors are part of this constellation. These features represent a personality style that is particularly prone to use of alcohol or other substances, and *ALC* and *DRG* scores that are markedly low in such individuals are rare.

To systematize this possibility, simple linear regression estimates of predicted scores on *ALC* and *DRG* using the sum of *T* scores from these five scales were derived from the clinical normative data (*n* = 1,246). The following regression equations were obtained:

Estimated *ALC T* score = [0.162184 **x** (sum of *BOR-S, ANT-A, ANT-E, ANT-S, AGG-P*)] + 14.39

Estimated *DRG T* score = [0.199293 **x** (sum of *BOR-S, ANT-A, ANT-E, ANT-S, AGG-P*)] + 3.07

For convenience, the predicted estimates for *ALC* and *DRG* scores based upon the sum of these five scales are presented in Table 2-2; this sum correlates at .46 with the *ALC* scale and .59 with the *DRG* scale. Obtained scores on the substance abuse scales that are markedly lower than the estimates provided in Table 2-2 raise the possibility that some denial of substance problems may be operating. For example, Figure 2-1 presents the mean PAI profiles of the two "questionable responding" groups from the study by Fals-Stewart (1996)[1] described earlier. There were two such groups in that study. One was a "forensic" group consisting of 59 individuals referred for evaluation by the criminal justice system; these individuals (a) reported no illicit drug use or alcohol abuse during the 6 months prior to the evaluation; (b) expressly refused treatment for substance abuse; and (c) tested positive on urine assays or breath tests conducted at the time of evaluation, suggesting that one or more psychoactive substances had been recently ingested. The second group was a "positive dissimulation" group of 59 patients in treatment for substance abuse problems who had been instructed to deny substance abuse problems in responding to the PAI. A variety of scenarios were presented to these patients, such as child custody evaluation, applying for a job, avoiding unwanted

---

[1]The author would like to thank Dr. W. Fals-Stewart (personal communication) for providing the complete PAI means for all scales from the Fals-Stewart (1996) article.

Table 2-2
Predicted *ALC* and *DRG* Scores From the Sum of
BOR-S*, *ANT-A*, *ANT-E*, *ANT-S*, and *AGG-P

Sum of 5 predictor scales (*T* scores)	Expected *ALC* *T* score	Expected *DRG* *T* score
0	14	3
25	18	8
50	22	13
75	27	18
100	31	23
125	35	28
150	39	33
175	43	38
200	47	43
225	51	48
250	55	53
275	59	58
300	63	63
325	67	68
350	71	73
375	75	78
400	79	83
425	83	88
450	87	93
475	91	98
500	95	103

substance abuse treatment, or undergoing a court-ordered presentencing evaluation. The "positive dissimulation" patients were offered movie passes if they could avoid detection as having engaged in positive dissimulation and of having problems with substance use.

The characteristics of the profiles in Figure 2-1 confirm many of the observations noted in the preceding paragraphs. For example, the *PIM* elevation in these groups should immediately raise questions of defensiveness. Also, as will be seen in chapter 5, the prominent *RXR* scores seen in these profiles are also an indicator of generally defensive responding. More specifically, however, this figure demonstrates that the five substance predictor scales all display some relative elevations in these groups. Table 2-3 provides a summary of the actual and estimated *ALC*

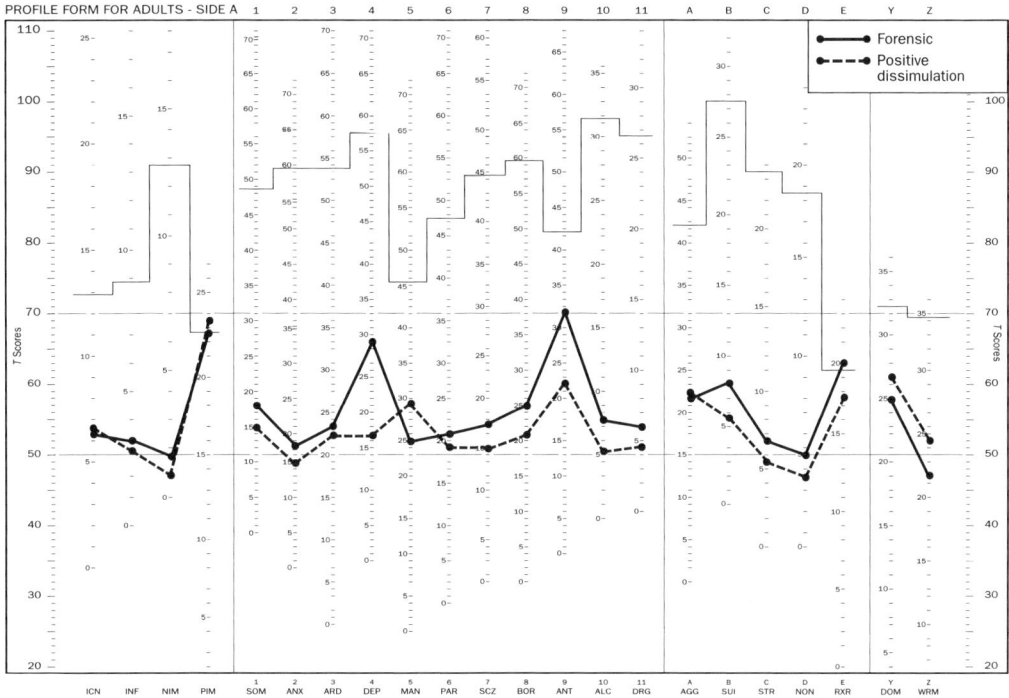

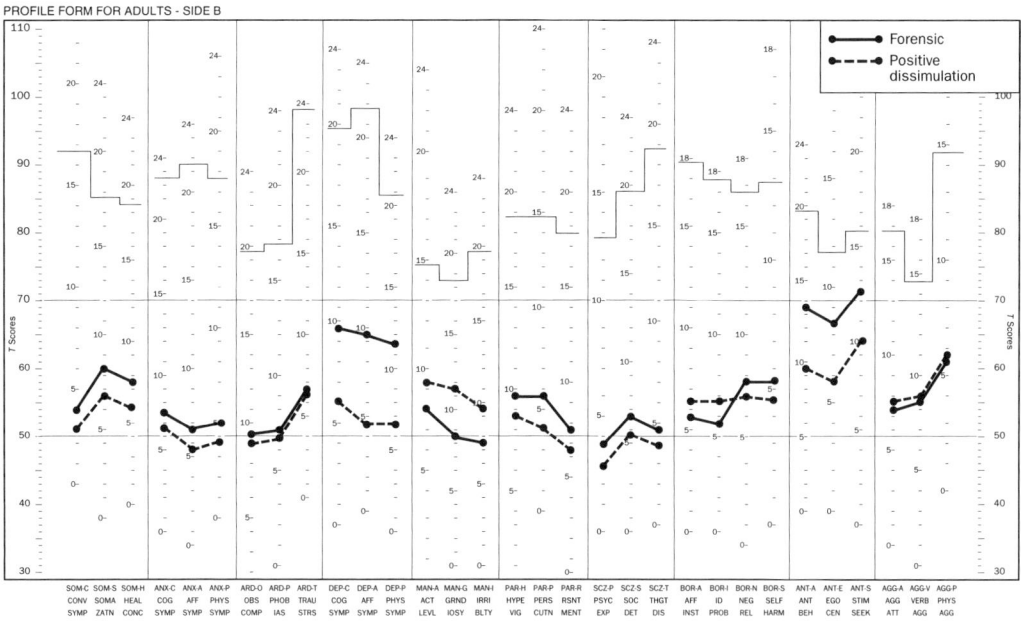

Figure 2-1. Mean profiles for groups denying substance abuse problems, adapted from Fals-Stewart (1996).

Table 2-3
Observed and Estimated *ALC* and *DRG* Scores for
Groups From the Fals-Stewart (1996) Study

Group	N	Sum of mean scores for *BOR-S, ANT-A, ANT-E, ANT-S, AGG-P*	Est *ALC* *T* score	Obs *ALC* *T* score	Est *DRG* *T* score	Obs *DRG* *T* score
Forensic	59	324.8	67	55	68	54
Positive dissimulation	59	299.3	63	50	63	51
Substance abuse patients	59	349.2	71	74	73	85

Note. Est = Estimated; Obs = Observed.

and *DRG* scores for these two groups, as well as for the "standard instruction" substance abuse treatment group from the Fals-Stewart (1996) study, using the regression estimates described earlier. For both of the "questionable responding" groups, the estimated scores on the substance abuse scales exceeded the observed scores by a considerable margin. The group of substance abuse patients who completed the test under standard instructions obtained *ALC* and *DRG* scores equal to or above their predicted scores.

The results of these analyses support the conclusion that in instances where the estimated substance abuse score from Table 2-2 exceeds the observed score by 10*T* or more, there is reason to suspect that some denial of substance use may be operating. When this occurs, discussing substance use with some type of collateral informant (e.g., a spouse or family member) might be worthwhile. It should be recognized that any indirect method of ascertaining substance abuse has limited ability to circumvent denial issues, and asking directly about use of substances is the most straightforward and most accurate means of obtaining such information in most cases. Nonetheless, there are situations that provide powerful motivation to deny such problems, as in forensic situations, custody evaluations, or pre-employment screenings. In such circumstances, an overall evaluation of of the profile for defensiveness (as discussed in chapter 5) followed by a specific evaluation of the possibility of substance abuse denial (as described earlier) should be conducted.

Alcohol Problems (ALC)

The *ALC* scale provides an assessment of behaviors and consequences related to alcohol use, abuse, and dependence. The item content ranges from statements of total abstinence through frequent use to the severe consequences of drinking, loss of control, and alcohol-related cravings. Questions inquire directly about the use of alcohol; thus, prominent denial of alcohol problems can suppress scores on the scale. If *ALC* raw scores are very low and there are elevated scores on the five predictor scales mentioned earlier, some follow-up inquiry about alcohol use might be appropriate. However, in general, direct inquiry about alcohol use will usually provide more accurate data than making inferences from indirect sources of information.

Average scores on *ALC* (i.e., < 60*T*) reflect a person who reports a moderate alcohol intake and few adverse consequences related to drinking. Scores between 60*T* and 70*T* are indicative of a person who may drink regularly and who may have experienced some adverse consequences as a result. Toward the upper end of this range, there is increasing likelihood that alcohol has caused or is causing problems for the person. With scores above 70*T*, the respondent is likely to meet criteria for alcohol abuse. Such a score indicates that use of alcohol has had a negative impact on the respondent's life. Alcohol-related problems are likely, including difficulties in interpersonal relationships, difficulties on the job, and possible health complications; the respondent's current functioning is probably compromised.

ALC scores that are markedly elevated (i.e., above 84*T*, which is the average score for individuals in alcoholism treatment centers), are typically associated with severe alcohol dependence. Such a score indicates that alcohol use has resulted in a number of adverse consequences for the individual. Numerous alcohol-related problems are likely, including difficulties in interpersonal relationships, difficulties on the job, and possible health complications. Such individuals are likely to be unable to cut down on their drinking despite repeated attempts at sobriety. They typically feel quite guilty about their drinking, but report little ability to control the effect it has on their lives. They probably have a history of social and occupational failures that were related to drinking and have had episodes when they were intoxicated for prolonged periods. Blackouts and physiological signs of dependence and withdrawal are probable with scores in this range.

Drug Problems (DRG)

The *DRG* scale provides an assessment of behaviors and consequences related to drug use, abuse, and dependence. The item content ranges from statements of total abstinence through frequent use to the severe consequences of drug use. Questions inquire directly about the use of drugs (both prescription and illicit); thus, prominent denial of drug use can suppress scores on the scale. As with *ALC*, if *DRG* raw scores are very low and there are elevated scores on the five predictor scales described earlier, some follow-up inquiry about drug use might be appropriate. However, in general, direct inquiry about a history of drug use will usually provide reasonably accurate data in the absence of strong situational pressures (e.g., in forensic settings or pre-employment screenings) to deny drug use.

Average scores on *DRG* (i.e., < 60*T*) reflect a person who reports using drugs infrequently, if at all. Scores between 60*T* and 70*T* are indicative of a person who may use drugs on a fairly regular basis and who may have experienced some adverse consequences as a result. Toward the upper end of this range there is increasing likelihood that drug use has caused, or is causing, problems for the person. With scores above 70*T*, the respondent is likely to meet criteria for drug abuse. It is likely that drug use has caused difficulties in interpersonal relationships or in work performance, and the individual's current functioning is probably compromised.

DRG scores that are markedly elevated (i.e., > 80*T*, which is the average score for individuals in treatment for drug abuse) are typically associated with drug dependence. Such individuals are likely to be unable to cut down on drug use despite repeated attempts and have little ability to control the effect that the desire for drugs has on their lives. They probably have a history of social and occupational failures related to drug use. Depending on the primary substance of abuse, physiological signs of dependence and withdrawal are probable with scores in this range.

CHAPTER 3
TWO-POINT CODETYPES IN PROFILE INTERPRETATION

The use of two-point codes in profile interpretation has become somewhat of a tradition in the assessment field. Although two-point codes provide a starting point for the configural interpretation of the PAI profile, it is important to note that such a code provides a severely limited summary of the information contained in the profile. First, the two-point code obviously ignores the wealth of information provided by the other test scales. Second, because of the subscale structure of the PAI scales, meaningful differences on even the two scales that comprise the code can be observed between individuals who have identical codes. Finally, the reliability of the small differences that can determine a two-point code on any psychological instrument is often suspect. For example, consider a profile where *DEP* is at 85*T*, *ANX* is at 82*T*, and *BOR* is at 81*T*. Although this is nominally a *DEP-ANX* two-point code, the difference between *ANX* and *BOR* is considerably less than one standard error of measurement, and that difference is not interpretively significant. Yet, the *DEP-BOR* codetype has different implications than the *DEP-ANX* codetype. Given these limitations, it is best to (a) consider the following descriptions of codetypes as a rough beginning to interpretation, and (b) examine *all* relevant descriptions (e.g., *DEP-ANX*, *DEP-BOR*, *ANX-BOR* in the present example) when scales determining the codetype fall within one standard error of each other.

The following sections describe the major features and interpretive significance of the 55 possible PAI two-point codes. Inclusion in one of these codetypes is based upon the two highest scores on the 11 PAI clinical scales, with each of the 2 scales involving scores of at least 70*T*. No distinction is provided in these sections with respect to order of the scales within the code: For example, the *DEP-ANX* codetype applies to all profiles for which *DEP* and *ANX* have the two highest clinical scale scores, regardless of which is higher, with both at least 70*T*. Reported frequencies and diagnostic correlates of these profiles were derived from Appendix A of the *PAI Professional Manual* (Morey, 1991).

SOM-ANX

This pattern suggests a person who is reporting marked distress, with particular concerns about physical functioning. Such individuals see their lives as severely disrupted by a variety of physical problems, some of which may be stress-related. These problems render them tense, unhappy, and probably impaired in their ability both to concentrate on and to perform important life tasks. The somatic concerns may have led to friction in close relationships, and other people often perceive these individuals as complaining and demanding. Secondary elevations on *ARD* and *DEP* are often observed with this codetype, and the level of *STR* can be informative in ascertaining the degree of life disruption associated with the somatic concerns. This is a relatively common profile configuration, observed in 1.1% of clinical respondents. Common diagnostic correlates include somatoform disorders, posttraumatic stress, adjustment reactions, and major depression. Interestingly, this codetype also is observed disproportionately in schizophrenia, perhaps reflecting the onset of somatic delusions.

SOM-ARD

This configuration of the clinical scales suggests a person who has ruminative concerns about physical functioning. Such people see their lives as disrupted by a variety of physical problems, some of which may be related to marked stressors; an inspection of the relative elevations of *ARD-T* and *STR* may reveal whether such stressors involve recent or more long-term events. These problems have left them tense and worried, and this may have led to disruption in close relationships. Secondary elevations on *ANX* and *DEP* are often observed with this codetype; elevations in other areas, however, are unusual. This pattern, observed in 0.9% of clinical respondents, tends to be seen more often in anxiety disorders (including posttraumatic stress) than in more purely somatoform disorders.

SOM-DEP

This configuration of the clinical scales suggests a person who is reporting significant distress, with particular concerns about physical functioning. Such people see their lives as severely disrupted by a variety of physical problems. These problems have left them unhappy, with little energy or enthusiasm for concentrating on important life tasks and little hope for improvement in the future. Performance in important social roles has probably suffered as a result, and lack of success in these roles will serve as an additional source of stress. Secondary elevations on *ANX* are frequent, and *SUI* is often elevated; this pattern suggests that some probe of suicidal ideation is merited when the *SOM-DEP* codetype is observed. This is a relatively common profile, observed in 2.8% of clinical respondents. Common diagnostic correlates include somatoform disorders, organic mental disorders, and major depression.

SOM-MAN

This configuration of the clinical scales is rather unusual, as it suggests a person who is reporting significant problems in physical functioning accompanied by heightened activity levels and irritability. The somatic concerns and emotionally labile style are likely to have led to some friction in close relationships, and others may see such people as complaining and demanding. Secondary elevations on *ARD*, *BOR*, and *STR* are often observed with this codetype, suggesting that both situational and characterological factors should be considered in evaluating the somatic concerns. Inspection of *DRG* also is warranted, as abuse of prescription drugs may be a risk for this type of individual. This is a relatively uncommon pattern, seen in only 0.2% of clinical respondents. This pattern was observed with some frequency in patients diagnosed with Schizoaffective Disorder.

SOM-PAR

This configuration of the clinical scales is unusual. It suggests a person with prominent hostility and suspiciousness who is also reporting significant problems in physical functioning. Such respondents perceive others as unsympathetic to their somatic concerns and unsupportive of their perceived limitations. Their hostility has probably led to some friction in close relationships: other people may see them as complaining and demanding, but the respondents probably attribute the source of these conflicts to the way that they are treated by others. If presenting for treatment, they are unlikely to be receptive to examining any psychological factors that might be associated with their physical complaints, and they probably will be resistant to psychological interventions. Secondary elevations on *NON* are often observed with this codetype, underscoring the resentment they experience toward the perceived lack of support they receive from family and friends regarding their health concerns. This is a rare configuration, with only 0.1% of patients in the clinical standardization sample displaying this pattern. Among these patients, individuals with organic mental disorders were disproportionately represented.

SOM-SCZ

This configuration of the clinical scales suggests a person with significant thinking and concentration problems accompanied by marked concerns about health and physical functioning. The somatic complaints may be highly unusual, and, in some circumstances, can involve somatic delusions. The reported combination of physical limitations and social discomfort severely limits the extent of their social interactions; whatever few close relationships there are may revolve around somatic preoccupations. Secondary elevations on *DEP* are often observed with this codetype, as are pronounced elevations on *NIM*, suggesting that the possibility of symptom exaggeration should be evaluated. This pattern was observed in 0.6% of clinical respondents. Common diagnostic correlates include schizophrenia and bipolar disorder, manic episode.

SOM-BOR

This pattern on the clinical scales suggests a person reporting significant problems in physical functioning who is also hostile and emotionally labile. Such people are likely to harbor some bitterness toward important others, who may be viewed as unsympathetic to the respondents' somatic concerns and unsupportive of their perceived limitations. This hostility and emotionality has probably been the source of friction in close relationships; others are likely to see such people as complaining and demanding, and these others may view the somatic complaints as a manipulative means through which the respondent can control the relationship. Secondary elevations on *DEP* and *SUI* often are observed with this codetype, underscoring the distress of such people; the intensity of associated bitterness and anger is often revealed with elevations on *PAR* and *AGG*. This is a relatively rare profile, observed in 0.3% of clinical respondents. Common diagnostic correlates include somatoform disorders, posttraumatic stress, and antisocial personality.

SOM-ANT

This configuration of the clinical scales is quite unusual. It suggests a person who is self-centered and preoccupied with his or her somatic problems to the exclusion of concern or caring for other people. Others are likely to view such people as complaining, self-centered, and demanding, and these others may view the somatic complaints as a manipulative means through which the respondent can control the relationship. If in treatment, such clients tend to be very difficult to work with, as they are typically unreceptive to examining psychological factors associated with their physical complaints and resistant to psychological interventions. *ALC*, and particularly *DRG*, should be examined to determine whether substance abuse may be contributing to the health issues, or, alternatively, the health issues may serve as a means to obtain prescription medication. This is a very uncommon profile pattern, as it was never obtained in the clinical standardization sample.

SOM-ALC

This configuration of the clinical scales suggests a person with a history of drinking problems who is experiencing a number of physiological difficulties that may be partially related to the drinking. These somatic problems might involve withdrawal symptoms, or they might be medical complications of alcohol abuse (e.g., problems associated with the central nervous system sequelae of alcoholism). The combination of alcohol use and physical symptomatology is probably causing severe disruptions in relationships and work, and these difficulties are most likely serving as additional sources of stress; secondary elevations on *STR* are often observed with this codetype. Seen in 1.3% of clinical respondents, the most common diagnostic correlates include alcohol dependence and organic mental disorders.

SOM-DRG

This configuration of the clinical scales suggests a person with a history of drug abuse who is experiencing a number of physiological problems that may be partially related to the use of drugs. These somatic problems might involve withdrawal symptoms, or they might be medical complications of drug abuse. The combination of substance use and physical symptomatology is probably causing severe disruptions in social-role functioning, and these difficulties typically will serve as additional sources of stress. Secondary elevations on *DEP* and *BOR* are often observed with this codetype; elevations on *ANT* and *BOR* may raise the possibility that the person is at risk for abusing prescription medication associated with the somatic condition. This profile is observed in 0.6% of clinical respondents, with somatoform disorders predominating.

ANX-ARD

This clinical scale configuration suggests a person with marked anxiety and tension. Such people may be particularly uneasy and ruminative about their personal relationships, some of which are probably not going well; these relationships may be an important source of current distress, and such people tend to respond to their circumstances by becoming socially withdrawn or passively dependent. The disruptions in their lives often leave them questioning their goals and priorities and tense and fearful about what the future may hold. Secondary elevations on *DEP* and *SUI* are often observed with this codetype and are prominent as the distress becomes more debilitating. This is a fairly common profile, observed in 1.9% of clinical respondents. Common diagnostic correlates include various types of anxiety disorders as well as major depression.

ANX-DEP

This configuration of the clinical scales suggests a person with significant unhappiness, moodiness, and tension. Although such people are quite distressed and acutely aware of their need for help, their low energy level, passivity, and withdrawal may make them difficult to engage in treatment. Typically, self-esteem is quite low, and they view themselves as ineffectual and powerless to change their life direction. Often accompanied by elevations on *STR*, life disruptions can leave such people uncertain about goals and priorities and tense and pessimistic about what the future may hold. They are likely to have difficulties in concentrating and making decisions, and the combination of hopelessness, agitation, confusion, and stress apparent in these scores may place such people at increased risk for self-harm; secondary elevations on *SUI* are often observed with this codetype. This pattern is observed in 1.3% of clinical respondents, and it is associated with diagnoses of Dysthymic Disorder, Major Depressive Disorder, and Borderline Personality Disorder.

ANX-MAN

This is an unusual configuration of the clinical scales. It suggests a person who is agitated, irritable, and affectively labile. Such people may have a high activity level that has left them stretched thin and thus hindered in their ability to perform any of their roles effectively. The resulting strain has left the respondent tense and feeling overwhelmed by self-imposed demands. Close relationships may have suffered particular strain from the moody and often demanding presentation characteristic of these individuals. Secondary elevations on *BOR* and *STR* often are observed with this codetype. *DOM* also is often elevated, indicative of the respondent's strong need for control; anxiety is likely to ensue when this control must be relinquished. This is an uncommon profile pattern, observed in only 0.2% of clinical respondents.

ANX-PAR

This is a relatively unusual configuration of the clinical scales, suggesting a person with prominent hostility and suspiciousness who is also acutely anxious, sensitive, and tense. These individuals tend to demonstrate heightened sensitivity in social interactions that probably serves as a formidable obstacle to the development of close relationships. Although such people may harbor considerable anger and resentment, the degree of anxiety may lessen the likelihood that this anger is expressed directly. Secondary elevations on *ARD* and *BOR* are often observed with this codetype. *SUI* can be quite elevated in these individuals, and any such ideation should be carefully evaluated given the extent of the hostility and anxiety suggested by the profile. This pattern is uncommon, observed in 0.1% of clinical respondents.

ANX-SCZ

This configuration of the clinical scales suggests a person with significant thinking and concentration problems, accompanied by prominent agitation and distress. Such individuals are likely to be withdrawn and isolated, with few if any close interpersonal relationships, and may become quite anxious and threatened by such relationships. Social judgment is probably fairly poor, and such people tend to have marked difficulty in making decisions, even about matters of little apparent significance. Secondary elevations on *DEP* are often observed with this codetype, which further underscores the extent of the distress and cognitive inefficiency. Seen in 0.9% of clinical respondents, this pattern is most frequently associated with diagnoses of Schizoaffective Disorder, Schizophrenia, and Posttraumatic Stress Disorder.

ANX-BOR

This configuration of the clinical scales suggests a person who is tense, angry, unhappy, and emotionally labile. Such people often present in a state of crisis and marked distress that may be associated with difficulties or rejection (perceived or actual) in interpersonal relationships. This may be part of a more general pattern of anxious ambivalence in close relationships, marked by bitterness and resentment on the one hand, and by dependency and marked anxiety about possible rejection on the other. Secondary elevations are often observed on *DEP* (suggesting the primacy of the distress) and *AGG* (when present pointing to significant underlying anger). This profile is observed in 0.9% of clinical respondents. Common diagnostic correlates include borderline personality and somatoform disorders.

ANX-ANT

This configuration of the clinical scales is quite unusual. It suggests a person who is impulsive and self-centered, yet is experiencing considerable anxiety and tension. Because these two personality elements are so inversely correlated, such respondents are likely to fluctuate between these disparate elements, with periods of impulsive acting-out followed by worry and anxiety regarding the consequences of their impulsive behavior. They may view themselves as incapable of controlling their reactions to stressful circumstances; however, this pattern of impulsivity will tend to recur and lead others to doubt the sincerity of their concern and desire to alter their behavior. This pattern was never observed in the clinical standardization sample.

ANX-ALC

This configuration of the clinical scales suggests a person with a history of drinking problems who is experiencing prominent anxiety. The anxiety and alcohol use may be related in a number of different ways; for example, alcohol use may be serving a functional role of tension reduction. The person is also likely to be anxious and guilty about the impairment in social role performance that has resulted from drinking; the alcohol use is probably causing severe disruptions in relationships and work, with these difficulties serving as additional sources of stress and, perhaps, further aggravating the drinking problems. Secondary elevations on *STR* are often observed with this codetype, further supporting the possibility that alcohol is serving a stress-reduction function. This profile pattern, observed in 1.0% of clinical respondents, is associated with diagnoses of Alcohol Dependence, Major Depressive Disorder, and Dysthymic Disorder.

ANX-DRG

This clinical scale configuration suggests a person with a history of substance-abuse problems who is experiencing prominent anxiety. This anxiety and the substance use may be related in a number of different ways: for example, the drug use may be serving a functional role of tension reduction, or the impairments associated with the drug use may be heightening subjective distress. Such people tend to be anxious and guilty about these impairments in social-role performance, including relationships and work; such difficulties serve as additional sources of stress and, perhaps, further aggravate the tendency to abuse drugs. Secondary elevations on *DEP* and *SUI* are often observed with this codetype. Also, it is not uncommon to see *RXR* in a range that suggests limited motivation for treatment, perhaps associated with a reliance on drugs to solve the individual's problems. This profile configuration, observed in 1.0% of clinical respondents, is actually relatively uncommon in substance-abusing samples, but it is seen with some frequency in individuals who have psychotic symptoms.

ARD-DEP

This configuration of the clinical scales suggests a person with significant tension, unhappiness, and pessimism. Although such people are quite distressed and acutely aware of their need for help, their low energy level, tension, and withdrawal may make them difficult to engage in treatment. Various stressors, both past and present, have adversely affected self-esteem, and they tend to view themselves as ineffectual and powerless to change their life direction. The life disruptions have left them feeling uncertain about goals and priorities, and tense and pessimistic about what the future may hold. They are likely to have difficulties in concentrating and in making decisions, and the combination of hopelessness, anxiety, and stress apparent in these scores places a person at increased risk for self-harm. Secondary elevations on *ANX* and *SUI* are often observed with this codetype. This is a relatively common profile, observed in 2.5% of clinical respondents. Common diagnostic correlates include posttraumatic stress and other anxiety disorders, major depression and dysthymic disorder, borderline personality, and schizoaffective disorder.

ARD-MAN

This combination of the clinical scales is quite unusual. It suggests a person who is fearful, irritable, and affectively labile. Such people may see themselves as overextended and vulnerable, with goals and expectations that are beyond their capacity, leaving them stretched thin and hindering their ability to perform any roles effectively. The resulting strain has probably left the respondent tense and feeling overwhelmed by these demands. Close relationships may have suffered particular strain from the moody and often demanding presentation of the respondent. This profile pattern is quite rare, and it was never observed in the clinical standardization sample.

ARD-PAR

This is an unusual configuration of the clinical scales; it suggests a person with prominent hostility and suspiciousness who is acutely tense, fearful, and hypersensitive. The respondent's heightened sensitivity in social interactions probably serves as a formidable obstacle to the development of close relationships, and those relationships that are established are probably a source of ruminative worry. Although the pattern hints at considerable anger and resentment, the degree of anxiety concerning social interaction may lessen the likelihood that this anger is directly expressed. Secondary elevations on *BOR* are often observed with this codetype, as are elevations on *NIM*, raising the question of symptom exaggeration. This is a rare profile, observed in only 0.1% of clinical respondents.

ARD-SCZ

This configuration of the clinical scales suggests a person with significant problems in thinking and concentration, accompanied by prominent distress and ruminative worry. Such respondents are likely to be withdrawn and isolated, feeling estranged from others. As a result, they probably have few, if any, close interpersonal relationships, and they tend to become quite anxious and threatened by such relationships. Their social judgment tends to be fairly poor, and they are often confused about their goals and pessimistic about what the future may hold. Secondary elevations on *SUI* are often observed with this codetype, and the combination of marked anxiety and clouded judgment heightens concerns in this area. This profile is seen in 0.4% of clinical respondents, with diagnoses of Posttraumatic Stress Disorder and Bipolar Disorder disproportionately represented.

ARD-BOR

This pattern suggests a person who is uncomfortable, impulsive, angry, and resentful. People with this type of profile often are presenting in a state of crisis and marked distress. Such crises often are associated with difficulties or rejection (perceived or actual) in interpersonal relationships; these respondents often feel betrayed or abandoned by others who are close to them. This may be part of a more general pattern of anxious ambivalence in close relationships, marked by bitterness and resentment, on the one hand, and by dependency and anxiety about possible rejection on the other. Various stressors, both past and present, may have both contributed to and maintained this pattern of interpersonal turmoil; *ARD-T* and *STR* may yield information about the relative importance of recent, as opposed to more distant, stressors. Regardless of the temporal progression, the disruptions in their lives leave such people uncertain about goals and priorities, and tense and cynical about future prospects. Secondary elevations on *DEP* and *SUI* are often observed with this codetype, which is obtained in 1.6% of clinical respondents. Common diagnostic correlates include borderline personality, major depression, and dysthymic disorder.

ARD-ANT

This configuration of the clinical scales is unusual. It suggests a person who is anxious, tense, and ruminative, combined with impulsivity and the potential for acting-out behaviors. Such people are likely to fluctuate between these seemingly disparate personality elements, with periods of impulsive acts followed by worry and rumination regarding the consequences of their behavior. They may view themselves as victims of their impulsivity, incapable of controlling their reactions to stressful circumstances. However, this pattern of impulsivity will tend to recur, and it may lead others to conclude that they are hostile and to doubt the sincerity of any expressed concern and desire to alter their behavior. Secondary elevations on *MAN* and *PAR* are often observed with this codetype. This is a rare profile, observed in 0.1% of clinical respondents.

ARD-ALC

This configuration of the clinical scales suggests a person with a history of drinking problems who is experiencing prominent stress and anxiety. The anxiety and alcohol use may be related in a number of different ways. Alcohol use could be serving a functional role of reducing tension, as it may be seen as relieving the impact of stressors past and present. The respondent is likely to ruminate about life circumstances, and the urge to drink may be at the center of many of these ruminations. Such individuals are likely to be quite anxious and guilty about the impairment in social-role performance that has resulted from their drinking; the alcohol use is probably causing severe disruptions in relationships and work, with these difficulties serving as additional sources of stress and perhaps further aggravating the drinking problems. Secondary elevations on *BOR* and *DEP* are commonly seen with this codetype. This profile, observed in 0.6% of clinical respondents, is most commonly associated with a diagnosis of Alcohol Abuse or Alcohol Dependence.

ARD-DRG

This configuration of the clinical scales suggests a person with a history of substance abuse problems who is experiencing prominent stress and anxiety. The anxiety and drug use may be related in a number of different ways: for example, the use of drugs could be serving a functional role of reducing tension, and the person may use it to relieve the impact of past and present stressors. Such people tend to ruminate about life circumstances, and the desire and craving for drugs may be at the center of these ruminations. They tend to be quite anxious and guilty about the impairment in social-role performance that has resulted from the substance abuse; the drug use is probably causing severe disruptions in their relationships and work, with these difficulties serving as additional sources of stress and, perhaps, further aggravating the drug problems. Secondary elevations on *BOR* and *ANT* are often observed with this codetype, suggesting characterological problems. This is a relatively uncommon profile, observed in 0.2% of clinical respondents. Common diagnostic correlates include substance abuse, major depression, and acting-out personality disorders (e.g., borderline and antisocial).

DEP-MAN

This configuration of the clinical scales is quite unusual, as it suggests a person who is experiencing severe distress, irritability, and unhappiness, as well as periods of heightened activity and energy. Typically, people with this pattern fluctuate between these disparate mood states, with periods of dysphoria followed by episodes of elevated mood. Hypomanic features may be masking a severe depression that may not be apparent from overt behaviors. Such people tend to be rather preoccupied and self-absorbed by their mood state and to be regarded by others as irritable and, perhaps, self-centered. Even individuals with marked mood swings tend not to obtain this profile; instead, whatever mood state they are currently experiencing tends to dominate the profile configuration. This pattern was never observed in the clinical standardization sample.

DEP-PAR

This configuration of the clinical scales suggests a person with prominent depression and hostility. People displaying such a pattern may be experiencing an embittered pessimism, attributing many of the negative circumstances occurring in their lives to the shortcomings of others, and they see little hope that they can change these circumstances. Their heightened sensitivity in social interactions has most likely led to significant withdrawal, and it probably serves as a formidable obstacle to the development of close and trusting relationships. Although such people appear to harbor considerable anger and resentment, this anger is as much directed at themselves as it is directed at others. Profiles with this configuration often have a number of secondary elevations, both on the neurotic side of the spectrum (e.g., *ANX, SOM, ARD*) and on the more impaired side (e.g., *SCZ, BOR, SUI*). Elevations on *NON* are also observed with this codetype, and this underscores the degree of resentment directed at significant others. This profile was observed in 0.9% of clinical respondents. Common diagnostic correlates include schizoaffective disorder, major depression, and posttraumatic stress disorder.

DEP-SCZ

This configuration of the clinical scales suggests a person with significant problems in thinking and concentration problems, accompanied by prominent distress and dysphoria. Such people are likely to be quite withdrawn and isolated, feeling estranged from the people around them. These current difficulties have probably placed a strain on the few close interpersonal relationships that the person does have. Such people see little hope that their circumstances will improve to any significant degree, and this hopelessness and pessimism, combined with the likelihood of impaired judgment, may place them at increased risk for self-harm; secondary elevations on *SUI* are often observed with this codetype. This configuration is reasonably common in clinical settings and was observed in 2.4% of respondents in the clinical standardization sample. Common diagnostic correlates include schizoaffective disorder, posttraumatic stress or other severe anxiety disorders, borderline personality, major depression, and schizophrenia.

DEP-BOR

This pattern suggests a person who is unhappy, emotionally labile, and probably quite angry at some level. Clients with such profiles are typically presenting in a state of crisis with marked distress and depression. The current distress may be associated with difficulties or rejection, perceived or actual, in interpersonal relationships. Individuals with such profiles often feel betrayed or abandoned by those close to them, and this compounds their feelings of helplessness and hopelessness. For the respondent, this may be part of a more general pattern of anxious ambivalence in close relationships, marked by bitterness and resentment on the one hand, and by dependency and anxiety about possible rejection on the other. The underlying anger can cause such people to lash out impulsively at those closest to them; however, the anger seems as much self-directed as it is directed at others. Life disruptions leave these individuals quite uncertain and ambivalent about goals and priorities and tense and pessimistic about what the future may hold. The combination of hopelessness, resentment, and impulsivity may place such people at increased risk for self-harm, and *SUI* and *STR* are typically elevated with this codetype. This is a relatively common profile, observed in 2.5% of clinical respondents. Common diagnostic correlates include borderline personality, major depression, and adjustment disorders.

DEP-ANT

This configuration of the clinical scales is rather unusual. It suggests a person who is dysphoric and pessimistic, combined with impulsivity and the potential for acting-out behaviors. Such people are likely to fluctuate between these seemingly disparate personality elements, with periods of impulsive acts followed by worry and guilt regarding the consequences of their behavior. They may see themselves as incapable of controlling their acting-out behavior, viewing it as a reaction to stressful external circumstances. However, this pattern of impulsivity will tend to recur, and it may lead others to view them as hostile and unreliable and to doubt the sincerity of any displayed remorse or stated desire to alter their behavior. Typically, this configuration has few other neurotic elements, suggesting that most of the distress arises from external, rather than internal, precipitants; secondary elevations on *PAR* are also common, indicating an outward projection of blame for current sources of stress. This is an unusual profile type, observed in only 0.2% of clinical respondents.

DEP-ALC

This configuration of the clinical scales suggests a person with a history of drinking problems who is quite unhappy and pessimistic. For such individuals, alcohol problems probably have led to severe impairment in the ability to maintain their social-role expectations, and this behavior has most likely alienated many of the people who were once central in their lives. Such setbacks have probably led to significant guilt and rumination about their life circumstances, and the urge to drink may be at the center of many of these ruminations. The depression and the alcohol use may be related in a number of different ways: for example, the depression could be driving the alcohol use, or it could be a consequence of the social disruption associated with alcohol use. Regardless of whether the depression is primary or secondary, the respondent may well be desperate for help, but cynical about the prospects for change or improvement. Secondary elevations on *SUI* are often observed with this codetype and, when present, heighten concerns about the possibility of self-harm, given the potential for disinhibition associated with alcohol use. Observed in 1.7% of clinical respondents, this configuration is commonly associated with diagnoses of Alcohol Dependence, Major Depressive Disorder, and Posttraumatic Stress Disorder.

DEP-DRG

This configuration of the clinical scales suggests a person with a history of substance-abuse problems who is quite unhappy and pessimistic. The drug use has probably led to severe impairment in the ability to maintain social-role expectations concerning relationships and employment, and the drug-related behaviors have likely alienated many of the people who were once close to the respondent. The configuration indicates significant guilt and distress about current life circumstances. The depression and drug use may be related in a number of different ways: for example, the depression could be driving the use of drugs, or it could be a consequence of the disruption associated with substance abuse. Regardless of whether the depression is primary or secondary, it has probably left the person quite pessimistic about the prospects for change or improvement. Secondary elevations on *SUI* are often observed with this codetype, and this should be monitored closely, given the potential for disinhibition associated with drug misuse. This configuration is found in 1.0% of clinical respondents, and is commonly associated with diagnoses of Borderline Personality, Major Depressive Disorder, and disorders involving drug abuse and/or dependence.

MAN-PAR

This combination of clinical scales is rather rare. It suggests a person with expansive mood and heightened activity accompanied by prominent hostility and irritability. Such people tend to see themselves as having had their plans thwarted by the neglect or obstruction of others; however, they are probably more impeded by an activity level that includes self-expectations that are beyond their actual capacity. The sensitivity in social interactions and perhaps unrealistic self-appraisal probably serve as formidable obstacles to the development of close relationships, and those close relationships that are established have most likely suffered particular strain from their moody and often demanding presentation. The combination of impulsivity, resentment, and high energy levels could cause such individuals to lash out impulsively at those whom they feel have slighted them in some way. Secondary elevations on *NON* are often observed with this codetype, perhaps pointing to the potentially unrealistic demands that such individuals place on others. This is an uncommon profile, observed in only 0.1% of clinical respondents.

MAN-SCZ

This configuration of the clinical scales suggests a person with significant problems in thinking and concentration, accompanied by heightened activity levels and irritable and expansive mood. Such people are likely to be agitated and confused, feeling both irritated with and estranged from the people around them. Their social judgment is probably quite poor, and those close relationships that have been maintained are probably strained by their moody, disorganized, and often demanding style of relating to others. Secondary elevations on *STR* and, occasionally, *SOM* may be seen with this codetype. This is a relatively uncommon profile pattern, observed in only 0.1% of clinical respondents.

MAN-BOR

This pattern on the clinical scales suggests a person with very labile mood, impulsivity, and heightened activity levels, accompanied by prominent hostility and irritability. For such people, interpersonal relationships are likely to be fairly stormy, and even those close relationships that have been maintained have most likely suffered particular strain from their moody, unpredictable, and often demanding presentation. The combination of impulsivity, resentment, and high energy levels could cause such people to overreact to minor events and to be at risk for lashing out impulsively at those closest to them. These same traits also place the respondent at increased risk for acting-out behaviors. Secondary elevations on *NON* are often observed with this codetype; elevations on *DOM* can reveal very strong needs for control in relationships that are seldom met. Observed in 0.5% of clinical respondents, this configuration appears to be more strongly related to bipolar disorder than to borderline personality.

MAN-ANT

This configuration of the clinical scales suggests a person who is impulsive, hostile, impatient, and unempathic. Interpersonal relationships are likely to be fairly stormy and rather short-lived; even those close relationships that are maintained most likely will have suffered strain from their hostile, self-centered, and often demanding presentation. The combination of impulsivity, resentment, and high energy levels could cause such people to have little consideration for the needs of others and to lash out impulsively at those around them when crossed. These same traits also place such people at increased risk for acting-out behaviors, and it is likely that these behaviors have led to impairment in their ability to maintain social-role expectations in both formal (e.g., work) and informal settings. Secondary elevations on *STR* are common; elevations on *AGG* also are frequent and, when present in the context of this codetype, represent a particular concern. This is not a particularly common configuration, seen in 0.4% of clinical respondents, but observed with some frequency in individuals with bipolar disorder, antisocial personality, and drug abuse or dependence.

MAN-ALC

This configuration of the clinical scales suggests a person with a history of drinking problems who is emotionally labile and impulsive. The alcohol problems have likely led to fairly severe impairment in their ability to maintain social role expectations, and their general recklessness has probably alienated their friends and family. Such people are likely to be particularly disinhibited under the influence of alcohol and to display exceptionally poor judgment and demonstrate other acting-out behaviors while intoxicated. It is also unlikely that there is much lasting remorse associated with any such behaviors. Secondary elevations on *STR* and *AGG* often are observed with this codetype. This is a relatively rare profile, observed in only 0.1% of clinical respondents, and it is unusual to find this profile in the absence of alcohol dependence.

MAN-DRG

This clinical scale configuration suggests an emotionally labile and impulsive person with a history of substance abuse problems. The drug problems probably have led to fairly severe impairment in the ability to maintain social role expectations, and their generally reckless approach to life has probably alienated many of the people around them. They are likely to be particularly disinhibited under the influence of drugs and may display markedly poor judgment and demonstrate other acting-out behaviors while intoxicated. Secondary elevations on *ANT* and *NON* are often observed with this codetype, indicating the externalization of blame for the respondent's current difficulties. This profile type is uncommon, observed in only 0.1% of clinical respondents.

PAR-SCZ

This configuration of the clinical scales suggests a person with significant problems in thinking and concentration, accompanied by prominent hostility, resentment, and suspiciousness. Sensitivity in social interactions probably serves as a formidable obstacle to the development of close relationships, and, thus, they are likely to be cautious, withdrawn, and isolated, feeling both estranged from and mistreated by the people around them. Their judgment is probably fairly poor, and they are likely to be chronically tense and apprehensive about what the future may hold. If such a person presents for treatment, establishing a therapeutic relationship may be challenging because such people tend to become quite anxious and threatened by the offer of a close interpersonal relationship. Secondary elevations on *NIM* are often observed with this codetype, raising the possibility that symptom exaggeration may be driving up the scores on *PAR* and *SCZ*. This is a relatively common profile in inpatient settings, observed in 2.4% of respondents in the clinical standardization sample. Common diagnostic correlates include schizophrenia, schizoaffective disorder, antisocial personality, and drug dependence.

PAR-BOR

This configuration of the clinical scales represents a person who is angry, resentful, impulsive, and emotionally labile. Such people are likely to be extremely sensitive in social interactions and very quick to perceive rejection, real or imagined, by others; they are likely to feel that they are repeatedly betrayed by those close to them. This is likely to be part of a more general pattern of chronic maladjustment in social relationships, marked by anxious ambivalence between bitterness and resentment, on the one hand, and by dependency and fear of possible rejection on the other. The bitterness is likely to surface readily, and they may react impulsively when they feel others have slighted them in some way. The combination of impulsivity, anger, and dysphoria could place the respondent at increased risk for self-harm or acting-out behaviors. Secondary elevations on *AGG* and *DEP* are often observed with this codetype, and, when present, may indicate that angry outbursts tend to be followed by rumination over the interpersonal consequences of these outbursts. This profile, observed in 0.4% of clinical respondents, is more typically observed in antisocial personality disorder than in borderline personality.

PAR-ANT

This configuration of the clinical scales suggests a person who is impulsive, hostile, bitter, and unempathic. Interpersonal relationships are likely to be short-lived and to be characterized by marked conflict; even those close relationships that are maintained most likely will have suffered strain from an irritable and self-centered style. The combination of impulsivity, egocentricity, and anger could cause such individuals to lash out angrily at those who are perceived as having impeded them in some way. These same traits also place them at increased risk for acting-out behaviors, and it is likely that these behaviors have led to marked impairment in the respondent's capacity to work effectively with others. Secondary elevations on *AGG* and *SUI* often are observed with this codetype, and these elevations heighten concerns about managing these individuals in treatment. This profile is seen in 0.4% of clinical respondents and is found with relative frequency among individuals with a diagnosis of Antisocial Personality Disorder.

PAR-ALC

This configuration of the clinical scales suggests a person with a history of drinking problems who is embittered and angry. A general sensitivity and hostility in social interactions probably serve as formidable obstacles to the development of close relationships, and, thus, such people are likely to be withdrawn and isolated. Alcohol may be playing a functional role in helping them withdraw from such relationships or in reducing the anxiety and threat that they pose. The respondents are likely to ruminate about their life circumstances, but they may not fully acknowledge the severity of their drinking problems. It is likely that there is significant impairment in social-role performance that has resulted from drinking; however, such people are more likely to attribute such problems to external factors than to admit the connection to their drinking. This is a relatively rare profile configuration, observed in 0.2% of clinical respondents, and it is most commonly seen with diagnoses of drug dependence or Antisocial Personality Disorder, or both.

PAR-DRG

This pattern on the clinical scales suggests a person with a history of substance-abuse problems who is embittered, suspicious, and angry. Sensitivity and hostility in social interactions probably serves as a formidable obstacle to the development of close relationships, and, thus, such individuals are likely to be withdrawn and isolated. The drugs may be playing a functional role in helping them withdraw from such relationships or in reducing the anxiety and threat that they pose, but the drug use may also be contributing to the suspicion and mistrust with which they view others. The respondent is likely to ruminate about life circumstances, and the urge and craving for drugs may be at the center of many of these ruminations. It is likely that there is significant impairment in social role performance that has resulted from the substance abuse; however, the respondent is more likely to attribute such problems to external factors than to admit the connection to drug use. Secondary elevations on *BOR* and *STR* are often observed with this codetype. This pattern is found in 0.3% of clinical patients and is most commonly associated with diagnoses involving abuse and/or dependence on substances.

SCZ-BOR

This configuration of the clinical scales suggests a person who is confused, emotionally labile, and angry. The respondent is reporting marked interpersonal dysfunction and significant problems in thinking and concentration; it is possible that bitterness and constant preoccupations with relationships impairs their ability to think clearly. Individuals with this profile are typically presenting in a state of crisis and marked distress, often related to interpersonal disruption. During such crisis periods, the respondents may experience brief episodes during which judgment and reality testing deteriorates markedly. Because of their unhappiness, resentment, impulsivity, and poor judgment, these individuals may be at increased risk for self-harm or acting-out behaviors. Secondary elevations on *DEP* and *AGG* are often observed with this codetype, and the relative positioning of these latter scales may reveal whether anger will be directed outward or inward. This profile, observed in 0.6% of clinical respondents, is particularly associated with diagnoses of Bipolar Disorder and Posttraumatic Stress Disorder.

SCZ-ANT

This combination of clinical scales is quite unusual. It suggests a person with significant problems in thinking and concentration, accompanied by impulsivity and the potential for acting-out behaviors. Given such a pattern, social judgment is probably quite poor, and those few social relationships that have been maintained are probably strained by an unempathic and self-centered approach. The combination of impulsivity and poor judgment contributes to a propensity for antisocial behaviors, and such people may view themselves as incapable of controlling these behaviors, seeing them as reactions to external circumstances. This is a rare configuration, and none of the patients in the clinical standardization sample demonstrated this pattern.

SCZ-ALC

This configuration of the clinical scales suggests a person with a history of drinking problems who is confused and socially isolated. A general discomfort in social interactions probably serves as a formidable obstacle to the development of close relationships, and, thus, such people are likely to be withdrawn and isolated and to feel estranged from the people around them. Alcohol may be playing a functional role in helping them distance themselves from such relationships or in reducing the anxiety and threat posed by such relationships. Their judgment is probably fairly poor, and they are generally both apprehensive about what the future may hold and cynical about the prospects for change. Secondary elevations on *NIM* are often observed with this codetype, raising the possibility that symptom exaggeration may be contributing to the *SCZ* elevation. This codetype is not uncommon, as it is seen in 1.0% of clinical respondents. Alcohol dependence is the most common diagnostic correlate of this pattern.

SCZ-DRG

This clinical scale configuration suggests a person with a history of substance-abuse problems who is confused and socially isolated. Discomfort in social interactions probably impedes the development of close relationships, and, thus, such individuals are likely to be withdrawn and isolated and to feel estranged from the people around them. Drugs may be playing a functional role in helping them withdraw from such relationships or in reducing the anxiety and threat posed by such relationships, but the mistrust and exploitativeness that characterizes this lifestyle is likely to simply exacerbate such problems. In most areas, their judgment is probably fairly poor, and they are likely to be pessimistic and cynical about long-term plans for change. Secondary elevations on *BOR* and *SUI* are often observed with this codetype and, when present, heighten concerns about the individual's capacity for self-destruction. This profile, observed in 0.6% of clinical respondents, is seen with relative frequency in individuals with drug dependence, as well as with antisocial personality.

BOR-ANT

This configuration of the clinical scales suggests a person who is impulsive, emotionally labile, and unempathic. For such people, interpersonal relationships are likely to be short-lived and to be characterized by marked conflict; even those close relationships that have been maintained most likely will have suffered strain from their hostile, self-centered, and perhaps manipulative style. The combination of impulsivity, egocentricity, and anger could cause them to lash out at those whom they feel have slighted them in some way. These same traits also place them at increased risk for acting-out behaviors, and it is likely that these behaviors have led to severe impairment in their ability to maintain employment. They may view themselves as incapable of controlling such acting-out behavior, seeing themselves as victims of unfair and stressful circumstances. However, this pattern of impulsivity will tend to be recurrent, leading others to view them as irresponsible and unreliable and to doubt the sincerity of any remorse or desire to alter their behavior. Secondary elevations on *AGG* and *SUI* are often observed with this codetype and, when present, may point to a worrisome state intensification of the characterological issues. This profile, observed in 0.9% of clinical respondents, is particularly common in borderline personality, but also is seen with antisocial personality.

BOR-ALC

This configuration of the clinical scales suggests a person with a history of drinking problems who is impulsive and affectively labile. Drinking may be part of a more general pattern of self-destructive behavior. Interpersonal relationships are likely to be volatile and to be characterized by marked conflict; even those close relationships that have been maintained will have suffered some strain from an impulsive, unpredictable, and probably hostile style of interaction. These relationships likely will have deteriorated even further as a consequence of the drinking. Such people are likely to be particularly disinhibited under the influence of alcohol, and they may display remarkably poor judgment and demonstrate other acting-out behaviors while intoxicated, perhaps blaming the alcohol for their own unacceptable behavior. Secondary elevations on *STR* and low scores on *RXR* are often observed with this codetype and, when present, suggest a desperate recognition of the need for help. This is a relatively common profile, observed in 1.3%

of clinical respondents. Common diagnostic correlates include alcohol dependence, and antisocial as well as borderline personality.

BOR-DRG

This configuration of the clinical scales suggests a person with a history of substance-abuse problems who is impulsive and affectively labile. The drug use may be part of a more general pattern of self-destructive behavior, and it probably exacerbates an already erratic approach to life. Interpersonal relationships are likely to be volatile and to be characterized by marked conflict; even those close relationships that have been maintained will have suffered some strain from the unpredictable and hostile style of interaction. These relationships likely will have deteriorated even further as a consequence of the drug abuse. Such people are likely to be particularly disinhibited under the influence of drugs, and they will tend to display particularly poor judgment and to demonstrate other acting-out behaviors while intoxicated. Secondary elevations on *AGG* are often observed with this codetype. This profile, observed in 1.1% of clinical respondents, is most commonly associated with drug abuse and/or dependence diagnoses and Borderline Personality.

ANT-ALC

This configuration of the clinical scales suggests a person with a history of acting-out behavior, most notably in the area of alcohol abuse, but probably involving other behaviors as well. The impulsivity and drinking problems likely have led to severe impairment in the ability to maintain social-role expectations, and their reckless approach to life has probably alienated most of the people who were once close to them. Generally impulsive and thrill-seeking, the alcohol use probably further impairs their already suspect judgment. Interpersonal relationships are likely to be volatile and short-lived; even those relationships that have been maintained will have suffered some strain from the egocentricity and from the consequences of drinking. Secondary elevations on *DRG* often are observed with this codetype, and very low raw scores on this scale may reflect denial. This profile, observed in 0.7% of clinical respondents, is observed frequently among polysubstance abusers.

ANT-DRG

This configuration of the clinical scales suggests a person with a history of acting-out behavior, most notably in the area of substance abuse, but probably involving other behaviors as well. Impulsivity and drug use have likely led to severe impairment in their ability to maintain stable employment; their reckless-ness has probably alienated most of their family and friends. Generally impulsive and thrill-seeking, the use of drugs is likely to further impair their already suspect judgment. Interpersonal relationships are likely to be superficial, volatile, and short-lived; even those relationships that have been maintained will have suffered some strain from the respondents' egocentricity and from the consequences of their drug use. Secondary elevations on *AGG* are often observed with this codetype and, when present, suggest one possible result of the disinhibition associated with drug use. This is a relatively common profile, observed in 2.1% of clinical respon-dents. This pattern is common in groups with drug dependence diagnoses, Bor-derline Personality, or both.

ALC-DRG

This pattern on the clinical scales suggests a person with a history of polysub-stance abuse, including alcohol as well as other drugs. When disinhibited by the substance use, other acting-out behaviors may become apparent as well. The substance abuse is probably causing severe disruptions in social relationships and work performance, with these difficulties serving as additional sources of stress and, perhaps, further aggravating the tendency to drink and use drugs. Secondary elevations on *STR* are often observed with this codetype. This profile pattern is quite common, observed in 9.0% of clinical respondents, and it characterizes roughly one fourth of the individuals in alcohol or drug treatment. Other common diagnostic correlates include antisocial personality and bipolar disorder.

CHAPTER 4
NEGATIVE DISTORTION: RANDOM RESPONDING AND MALINGERING

One of the difficulties that have beset the field of psychological assessment since its inception concerns the accuracy of self-reported information as an indication of psychological status. Myriad reasons have been offered as to why self-report might be distorted. One source of distortion may arise from an intention to deceive the recipient of the information; such examinees may attempt to distort their responses in order to appear either better adjusted or more poorly adjusted than is actually the case. A second source of distortion may arise from limited insight or self-deception. Such examinees may genuinely believe that they are doing quite well or quite poorly, but this belief might be at odds with the impressions of objective observers. A third source of distortion might arise from carelessness or indifference in taking a test; examinees who answer questions with little reflection (or even randomly) may yield results that do not accurately mirror their experiences.

Such concerns have led many test developers to create scales that provide measures of these sources of distortion. The PAI offers four *validity* scales that are designed to provide an assessment of factors that could distort the results of a self-report questionnaire, as well as indices constructed to supplement these scales. Elevated scores on any of these scales suggests that other scales should be viewed with caution and that any interpretation of results should be tentative. In general, if a subject obtains a score that is more than 2 standard deviations above the mean of the representative *clinical* sample on any of these scales or indices, the profile is likely to be seriously distorted by some test-taking response style. This result casts serious doubt on all other information derived from the test, and, under such conditions, the need to consider the PAI protocol in light of information derived from other sources becomes particularly critical.

The specific distortions to be considered in this chapter involve those that might lead the interpreter to draw a more negative conclusion from the data than might otherwise be warranted. Two particular sources of such distortion will be considered: first, test protocols that were completed carelessly, randomly, or idiosyncratically by the respondent; and, second, the effect of efforts to malinger or simulate mental disorder.

Detecting Careless or Idiosyncratic Responding

When clinical scales are elevated on a self-report test, several reasons for this elevation must be considered. One possibility involves careless responding, where the person answers the items more or less randomly because of confusion, disinterest, resistance, or clerical errors in test-taking or scoring. Because many items on the PAI reflect severe psychopathology and have very low endorsement rates, such individuals will obtain marked elevations (i.e., many of these items will be endorsed). Two of the PAI validity scales were designed to identify this source of distortion.

Infrequency (INF)

The *INF* scale is useful in the identification of people who complete the PAI in an atypical way because of carelessness, confusion, reading difficulties, or other sources of random responding. The scale consists of items that were designed to be answered similarly by all respondents, regardless of clinical status; half of these items are expected to be answered *Totally False* (e.g., "My favorite poet is Raymond Kertezc."), whereas the other half should be answered *Very True* (e.g., "Most people would rather win than lose."). The *INF* items are placed evenly throughout the PAI to identify potentially problematic responding at any point within the test-taking. There is no thematic connection between the content of different items on the scale. The items were selected on the basis of very low endorsement frequencies in both normal and clinical respondents; this contrasts with scales such as the MMPI *F* scale, where items were selected on the basis of infrequency in the normative sample. Such scales often yield elevations in clinical samples. This is because the item content is confounded with psychopathological symptoms that are infrequent in normative samples, but may reflect valid responding in a clinical respondent.

INF scale items were written to provide item content that would be infrequent, yet would not sound bizarre (e.g., "I have never seen a building."). For example, one question asks if the respondent's two favorite hobbies are archery and stamp collecting. Interest in these hobbies actually turns out to be inversely related, and, as such, there are few people for whom both these hobbies are primary interests. However, the combination is not implausible; it is merely uncommon. Because each individual item on the scale is uncommon, an individual who endorses more than a few of these items is a unique individual indeed.

The Infrequency scale is primarily a measure of carelessness in responding. However, there is another potential element underlying *INF* elevations, reflecting a tendency to answer the PAI items in a very idiosyncratic way. A quick inquiry about *INF* items can easily distinguish between these two sources of elevation. Individuals who respond idiosyncratically to the inventory will have an explanation for their endorsement, albeit an explanation that suggests that the test items may have been interpreted in an unusual way. Because such people are not approaching the test in the way that most people do, the results of the self-report test should not be interpreted as if they were. For example, one respondent who obtained an *INF* score of 85T was questioned about his responses, and his comments were revealing about the nature of the elevation. For the item "My favorite sporting event on television is the high jump," he answered *Very True*. He was asked about the source of this interest and whether he had been a high-jumper in high school. He responded that he didn't think he had actually ever seen the high jump on television, but he said, "Well, I really like to watch sports on TV, and I think that is a big part of my personality, so I wanted to make sure that you knew that, and I didn't see any other opportunity to tell you that on here, so I was going to tell you with that item." This response reveals both that the respondent was trying to answer the test honestly, and that he was probably not being careless. However, if a person makes idiosyncratic inferences about items that do not reflect the actual content of the item, or if he or she begins to respond to items figuratively rather than literally, the results will not be interpretable in any straightforward way.

The distribution of *INF* is similar for both normal and clinical respondents; both distributions are quite dissimilar from the distribution derived by simulating random responding. Generally, low scores (i.e., < 60T) suggest that the respondent did attend appropriately to item content in responding to the PAI items. Moderate elevations (i.e., 60T to 75T) indicate some unusual responses to *INF* items, and, at the higher end of this range, one should consider potential sources such as reading difficulties, random responding, confusion, errors in scoring, idiosyncratic item interpretation, or failure to follow the test instructions. Any interpretive hypotheses based on the PAI should be reviewed with caution if *INF* is in this range, and some inquiry about *INF* responses would be useful *before* clinical scale results are interpreted.

High scores on *INF* (i.e., ≥ 75T) suggest that the respondent did not attend appropriately to item content in responding to the PAI items; a completely random completion of the PAI would result in an average *INF* score of 86*T*. There are several potential reasons for scores in this range, including reading difficulties, random responding, confusion, errors in scoring, or failure to follow the test instructions. Regardless of the cause, however, the test results are best assumed to be invalid and no clinical interpretation of the PAI is recommended. However, an examination of specific *INF* items may yield useful information. For example, if the endorsed *INF* items are all from the second half of the test, the subject may have completed the initial half of the instrument appropriately and may have begun responding haphazardly at a later point. In this instance, score estimates for most PAI scales may be extrapolated from the responses to the first 160 items, as described in chapter 11 of the *PAI Professional Manual* (Morey, 1991).

Inconsistency (ICN)

The *ICN* scale is an empirically derived scale that reflects the consistency with which the respondent completed items with similar content. The scale is comprised of 10 pairs of items with related content; 5 of these pairs should be answered similarly and 5 of the pairs are psychologically opposite. The items on *ICN* were the pairs that were empirically found to be the most similar during the development of the PAI. Although each pair of items is similar in content, the pairs differ from one another; thus, the scale does not reflect any particular construct other than response consistency.

Because *ICN* theoretically reflects measurement error, it tends to have low correlations with most other measures. The largest correlation of *ICN* appears to be with the Marlowe-Crowne (1957) Social Desirability scale ($r = -.24$). Although low, this correlation is informative, as it suggests that people who tend to respond in a socially desirable direction also tend to answer questions consistently. Thus, if social desirability is considered to have any sort of an impression-management component, a person trying to manage his or her self-presentation appears to do so with some care. This suggests that *ICN* elevations are probably not the result of efforts at impression management, although, at times, such scales are interpreted in this manner (i.e., people who tell an inconsistent story are not telling the truth). However, if someone is consciously trying to distort in a given direction, *ICN* often does not elevate at all. Rather, *ICN* is much more likely to reflect carelessness or confusion in responding.

One commonly observed problem that can cause elevations on *ICN* is a failure to attend to negated items (i.e., item statements that contain the word *not*). Although there are relatively few such items on the PAI, these items are overrepresented on *ICN* to examine how such items were interpreted. Respondents who are not attending closely may misinterpret the question that reads, "I have no trouble falling asleep," instead reading it as, "I have trouble falling asleep." This pattern alerts the interpreter that the respondent may not have been reading the items carefully when completing the inventory.

The distribution of *ICN* is fairly similar for both normal and clinical respondents, although clinical respondents tend to score slightly higher (i.e., respond slightly less consistently) than normal respondents. The distributions from clinical and normal respondents are quite dissimilar from that derived by simulating random responding. Generally, low scores on *ICN* (i.e., < 64*T*) suggest that the respondent did respond consistently and probably attended appropriately to item content in responding to the PAI items. Moderate elevations (i.e., 64*T* to 73*T*) indicate some inconsistency in responses to similar items, which could arise from a variety of sources ranging from carelessness or confusion to attempts at impression management. Interpretive hypotheses based on other PAI scales should be reviewed with caution if *ICN* is in this range.

High scores on *ICN* (i.e., ≥ 73*T*) suggest that the respondent did not attend consistently or appropriately to item content in responding to the PAI items; a completely random completion of the PAI would result in an average *ICN* score of approximately 73*T*. There are several potential reasons for scores in this range, including carelessness, reading difficulties, confusion, errors in scoring, or failure to follow the test instructions. Regardless of the cause, however, the test results are best assumed to be invalid, and no clinical interpretation of the PAI is recommended when *ICN* scores are in this range.

Random Responding: Scale Configuration

The mean profile for a group of 1,000 protocols that were generated using random-responding simulations is presented in Figure 4-1. The most prominent characteristic of this profile is that both *INF* and *ICN* fall above the thresholds for profile validity described in previous sections. This result is quite rare in actual protocols; only 0.2% of respondents in both the community and clinical normative samples had both *INF* and *ICN* above the recommended cutoffs. The *NIM* scale is also elevated in this profile, although not to the extent that occurs in malingering simulation samples. In general, if both *INF* and *NIM* are elevated and the scores are comparable (i.e., within 10*T* of one another), then random responding is suggested. Malingered protocols tend to lead to profiles where *NIM* greatly exceeds *INF*, typically by 20*T* or more.

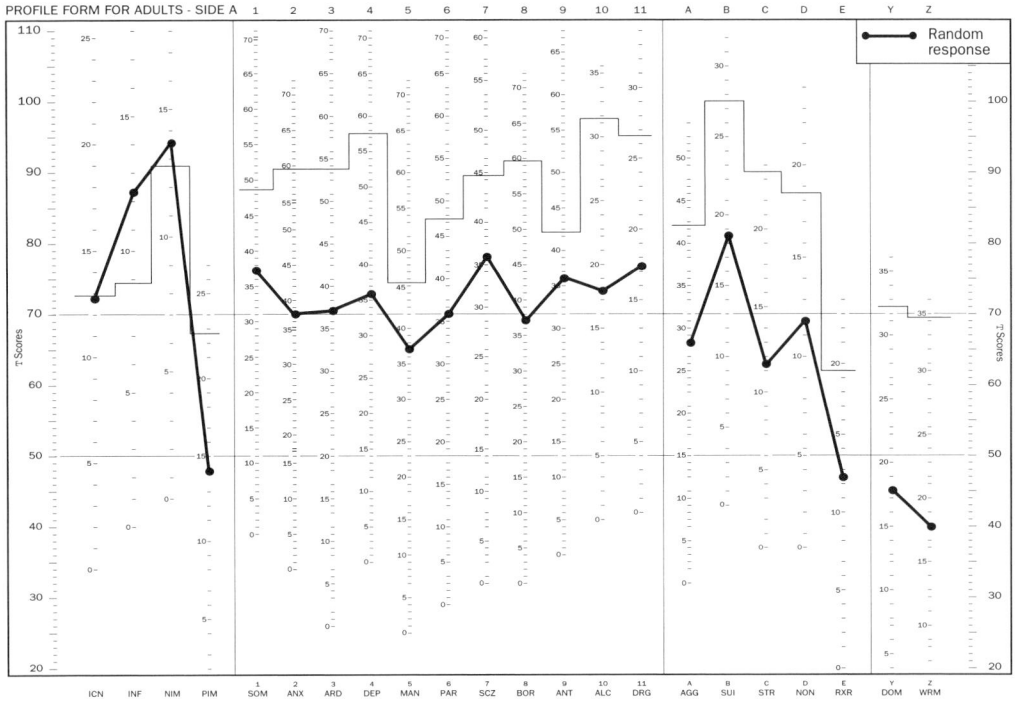

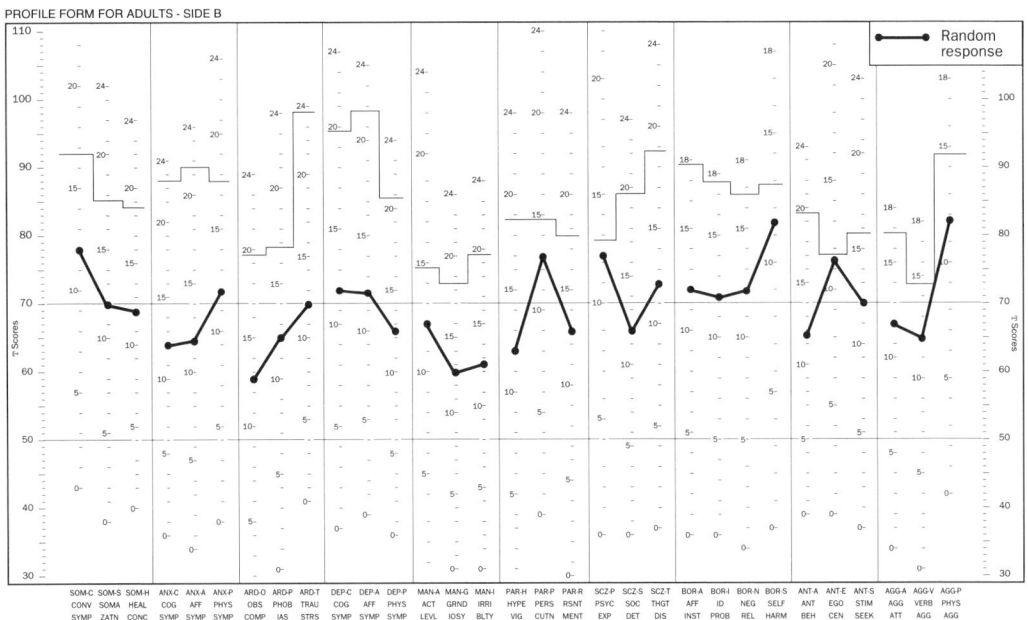

Figure 4-1. PAI profile for 1,000 protocols (Morey, 1991) using random-responding simulations.

Because random responding will include many positive responses to unusual items, the overall profile is elevated. However, these elevations are not as marked as tends to be seen in malingered protocols; for example, fewer than half of the subscales are elevated above 70T in the random response profile. Another note-worthy feature of the random response profile is the lack of differentiation among the clinical scales, with most falling between 65T and 75T. Because of the empha-sis on discriminant validity in the construction of the PAI, a relatively "flat" profile in the elevated range tends to be usual, as it involves clinical features that are not commonly seen in the same person (e.g., anxiety and antisocial features, or depression and increased self-esteem). In general, malingered profiles tend to be more elevated than random profiles, because responses are consistently patho-logical, rather than randomly either pathological or healthy. However, the malin-gered profile also has sharper differentiations, with some scales (e.g., *SCZ*) likely to be markedly elevated and others (e.g., *MAN*) to be influenced less consistently when pathology is simulated.

Detecting Malingering

Negative Impression (NIM)

Generally, the starting point in the evaluation of malingering is the *NIM* scale, although it must be emphasized that *NIM* is not a malingering scale. The *NIM* scale was designed to alert the interpreter to the possibility that the test results may por-tray a more negative impression of the individual than might otherwise be mer-ited. In other words, the self-report of a high scorer on *NIM* is probably more pathological than an objective observer would report. The items were selected on the basis of low endorsement frequencies in both normal and clinical respondents, although *NIM* items are endorsed with greater frequency in clinical patients than in normal adults. Individuals with clear-cut and severe emotional problems can and will obtain elevated scores on *NIM*, and more disturbed populations obtain higher scores than those who are less impaired. For example, the mean for the out-patient mental health patients in the PAI clinical normative sample on *NIM* was 59T (i.e., nearly 1 *SD* above the mean of the community sample), whereas the cor-responding value for inpatients was 65T (i.e., 1.5 *SD* above the community mean).

If *NIM* is a measure of a response style, rather than a measure of psycho-pathology, why should there be such a relationship between psychopathology and *NIM* elevations? The answer lies in the association between certain forms of mental disorder and the characteristic perceptual and cognitive features that can lead to negative response styles. Several different types of mental disorders lead individuals to perceive themselves, other people, or situations in a more negative manner than might be warranted in the eyes of an objective observer. A depressed patient views himself or herself as worthless, incompetent, and inadequate, whereas others may view the patient as capable and highly effective. Interpersonal relationships that appear solid to others may be suspect in the mind of the paranoid individual. A situation that may appear relatively benign to the clinician may be perceived as an insurmountable crisis by the borderline patient. In these cases, patients are likely to portray themselves or their circumstances, or both, in a more negative manner than appears objectively warranted. However, these individuals are not malingering; in fact, they do have significant, and perhaps quite severe, forms of mental disorder. Nonetheless, in interpreting the PAI profile, the clinician must be cognizant of the influence of these perceptual styles on the obtained pattern of responses.

The *NIM* scale includes two types of items: some present an exaggerated or distorted impression of the self and the present circumstances, and some represent extremely bizarre and unlikely symptoms. Each of these tendencies may cause distortion of a self-report in a negative direction. Individuals who tend to exaggerate the negative aspects of their lives can provide self-reports that appear quite pathological. However, this tendency does not necessarily reflect malingering, which is a conscious attempt to simulate psychopathology. Rather, this response style can actually represent a prominent component of many psychopathological syndromes. For example, depression, which is a prominent affect in the majority of clinical respondents, lends a negative coloration to most events and circumstances. People who are depressed often can find the grey cloud around every silver lining. A depressed person may describe his or her childhood in very bleak terms, yet the same person might report a happy childhood following the remission of the depressive episode. In fact, both the *DEP* scale and the clinical diagnosis of major depression are positively correlated with *NIM*. This does not mean that people who are depressed are malingering. Rather, it may mean that, when such people are asked questions about negative events in their lives, they tend to magnify the negative, and, given the opportunity to describe their circumstances, they tend to portray them very bleakly. Hence, it becomes an issue of discriminant validity. However, this does not mean that *NIM* is a depression scale, either; depressed people may score very high on *NIM*, whereas others can score quite low. The *NIM* scale can reveal the degree to which this negative perceptual style is operating within the profile of a particular depressed individual and how much distortion may be resulting from this style. At times, there may be so much distortion that the test results are rendered invalid, although this does not mean that the person was malingering. Rather, the test is invalid in the sense that there are serious distortions, and extreme caution must be exercised in interpreting the test results at face value. Nonetheless, the result may accurately depict the way such individuals feel about themselves and their circumstances.

A second example of the operation of cognitive style as an influence on self-report may be found in borderline personality. Individuals with Borderline Personality Disorder tend to have an extremely negative evaluation of everything in their environment that is not uniformly positive, whereas depression leads to negative *self*-evaluations. This tendency is sometimes referred to as splitting, where self and others are divided into good and bad, with no middle ground; but the true split is between what the individual perceives as uniformly positive and everything else, which is evaluated in an intensely negative manner. Because self-report tests such as the PAI repeatedly ask for an evaluation of present life circumstances, operation of this cognitive style can lead to distorted test results that portray events as much more negative than they would seem to an objective observer.

It is true, however, that all patient groups score considerably lower on *NIM* than research respondents instructed to simulate the responses of a mentally disordered patient, and, as such, the scale serves as a useful beginning point in the detection of malingering. This is because another group of *NIM* items is more closely related to malingering. These items were written to sound as if they represented pathological symptoms, but they were, in fact, extremely rare or nonexistent in clinical populations. The item content is varied, but the items share the feature that they are dramatic sounding and play to stereotypes of mental disorder. In fact, a few of the items are dissociative in nature, and it has been observed that individuals with severe dissociative disorders sometimes obtain marked elevations on *NIM*. Idiosyncratic responses to item content also can result in *NIM* elevations, although in these instances *INF* also tends to be elevated. Regardless of the context, some inquiry about the nature of positive responses to these *NIM* items is merited.

Generally, low scores (i.e., < 73*T*) on *NIM* suggest that there is little distortion in a negative direction on the clinical scales; the respondent probably did not attempt to present a more negative impression than the clinical picture would warrant. Moderate elevations (i.e., 73*T* to 84*T*) suggest an element of exaggeration of complaints and problems. Any interpretive hypotheses based on clinical scale elevations should be considered with caution, because there is some possibility that the hypotheses will overrepresent the extent and degree of significant test findings. The likelihood of distortion increases in the range from 84*T* to 92*T*. Elevations in this range may be indicative of a "cry for help" or an extremely negative evaluation of both self and life; some deliberate distortion of the clinical picture also may be present. The cutoff of 84T has been found to optimally discriminate malingerers from actual patients when the a priori probability of malingering is 50%.

High scores on NIM (i.e., ≥ 92T) suggest that the respondent attempted to portray himself or herself in an especially negative manner. The item content suggests the strong possibility of careless responding, extremely negative self-presentation, or malingering; research respondents who were instructed to malinger obtained an average NIM score of 117T; a completely random completion of the PAI would result in an average NIM score of 96T. Regardless of the cause, however, the test results are best assumed to be invalid, and no clinical interpretation of other PAI scales is recommended when scores are in this range.

The utility of NIM as an indicator of malingering has been explored in a number of research studies. The PAI Professional Manual(Morey, 1991) details the results of studies where college students were instructed to simulate the responses of an individual with a severe mental disorder. The distributions of actual clinical respondents and these malingerers crossed at a score of 84T; this cutoff yielded a sensitivity of 88.6% in the identification of malingering, with a specificity of 89.8% among true clinical respondents. The 2 clinical standard deviation cutoff of 92T resulted in a sensitivity of 86.5% and a specificity of 94.1%.

A sophisticated study of malingering was performed by Rogers, Ornduff, and Sewell (1993), who examined the effectiveness of the NIM scale in identifying both naive and sophisticated simulators (advanced graduate students in clinical and counseling psychology) who were given a financial incentive to avoid detection as malingerers. Rogers et al. found that the recommended NIM scale cutoff successfully identified 90.9% of respondents attempting to feign schizophrenia, 55.9% of respondents simulating depression, and 38.7% of respondents simulating an anxiety disorder. In contrast, only 2.5% of control respondents were identified as simulators. Interestingly, there was no effect of subject sophistication; the scale was equally effective in identifying both naive and sophisticated malingerers. Rogers et al. concluded from these results that the NIM scale is most effective in identifying the malingering of more severe mental disorders.

Gaies (1993) conducted a similar study of malingering, focusing on the feigning of clinical depression. Gaies compared four groups of women: an "informed malingering" group who were instructed to malinger depression, and who were given detailed information about the diagnosis of depression; a "naive malingering" group who were asked to simulate depression but were given no information about the disorder; a "depression" group consisting of outpatients being treated for depression who obtained Beck Depression Inventory scores above 14 and MMPI-2 Scale 2 scores above 64T; and a "control" group of college students responding to the PAI in standard fashion. Average scores on *NIM* were 92*T* for the informed malingerers and 81*T* for the naive malingerers. Sensitivity and specificity results for particular *NIM* cutoffs were not reported. However, these results are similar to those of Rogers et al. (1993) in suggesting that respondents attempting to simulate milder forms of mental disorder (in this case, depression) will obtain more "moderate" elevations on *NIM*, (i.e., scores of around 85*T*) as opposed to the scores of 110*T* that are typical with the simulation of psychosis.

Rogers, Sewell, Morey, and Ustad (in press) investigated the effectiveness of *NIM* in detecting individuals feigning three specific disorders: schizophrenia, major depression, and generalized anxiety disorder. This study compared naive simulators (undergraduates with minimal preparation) with sophisticated simulators (doctoral psychology students with one week of preparation and coaching) and actual clinical respondents diagnosed with the three disorders in question. Although the naive simulators obtained *NIM* scores that were quite elevated (*M* = 84*T*), the scores of the sophisticated simulators (*M* = 69*T*) differed only slightly from those of the bona fide clinical respondents (*M* = 63*T*). In this particular mix of respondents, the optimal *NIM* cutting score was 77*T*, which was reasonably effective in identifying the naive simulators (69% for malingered schizophrenia, 82% for depression, 45% for anxiety) but less effective with the sophisticated simulators (55% for feigned schizophrenia, 19% for depression, 0% for generalized anxiety). In contrast to the Rogers et al. (1993) study, this study found that sophisticated participants were considerably more effective in avoiding detection by the *NIM* scale, with one potential source of the difference involving the use of specific preparation in the Rogers et al. (in press) study. These results suggest that the utility of *NIM* as a measure of malingering is affected by preparation and coaching for the evaluation.

In summary, the *NIM* scale has a place in the assessment of malingering on the PAI, but it also has limitations. It appears to work best with efforts to simulate severe forms of mental disorder; where milder forms of disorder are falsified, it is less effective. In addition to limitations associated with the *type* of mental disorder malingered, the *NIM* scale has limited utility as a specific indicator of malingering. This is because *NIM* was designed as a general measure of a response style, that would lead the clinician to form a more negative impression than might be objectively warranted; it is not a malingering scale per se.

Malingering Responding: Scale Configuration

The mean profiles for malingered mental disorder from Morey (1991) and malingered depression, both naive and informed (Gaies, 1993), are presented in Figure 4-2. The most prominent characteristic of the profile from Morey (1991) is

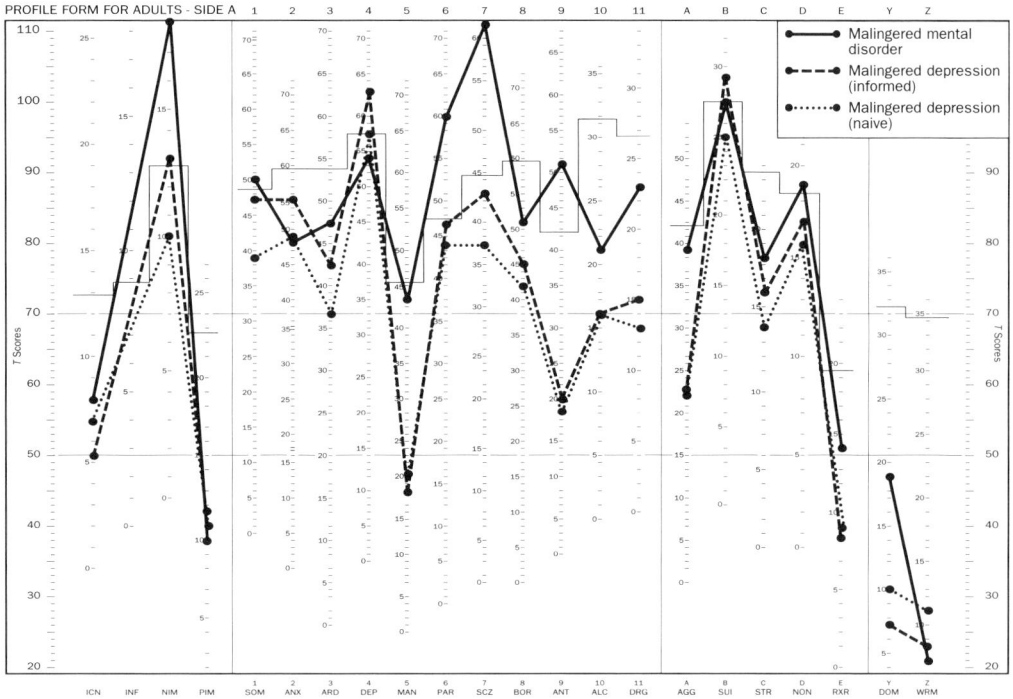

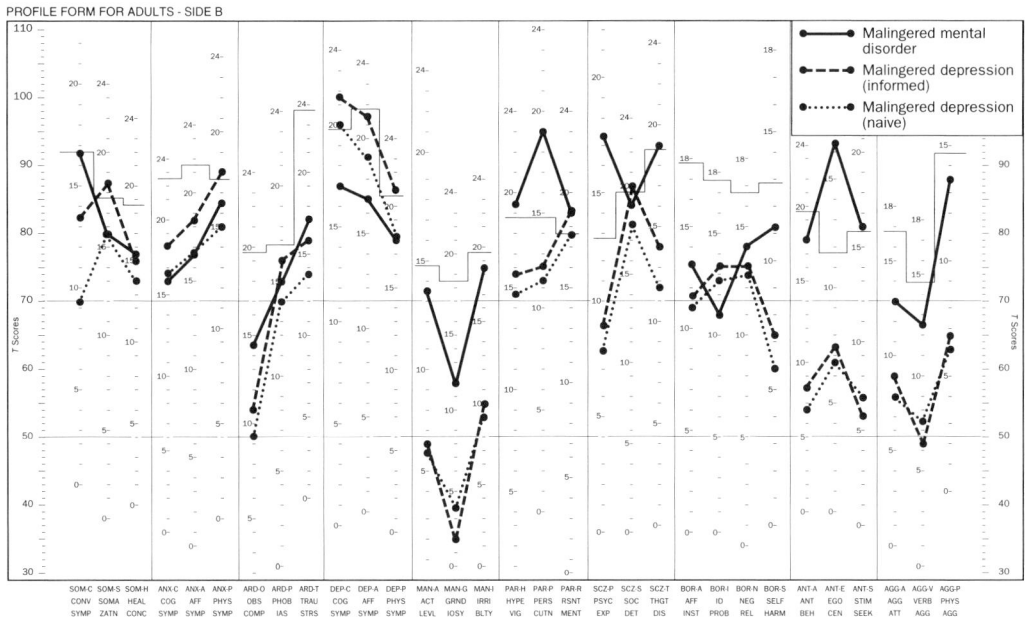

Figure 4-2. PAI profiles for malingered mental disorder (Morey, 1991) and malingered depression, informed and naive (Gaies, 1993).

obviously the extreme elevation on *NIM*, which falls far above the thresholds for profile validity described in previous sections. The Gaies profiles both demonstrate *NIM* elevations, although, in the simulation of depression, *NIM* appears to be a less prominent part of the profile. On the validity scales, *INF* also tends to be elevated in these samples; this combined elevation of *INF* and *NIM* is quite rare in actual protocols, with scores above the recommended cutoffs on both scales occurring in only 0.2% of respondents in both the community and clinical normative samples. Although the random-responding profile shown in Figure 4-1 also had both of these scales elevated, there are differences in the configuration of the two scales. Malingered protocols tend to lead to profiles where *NIM* greatly exceeds *INF*, typically by 20*T* or more; when scores on the two scales are comparable (i.e., within 10*T* of one another), random responding is suggested.

The malingered profiles also tend to be quite elevated, with many clinical scales above 70*T*. Although profiles from random responding also can be elevated, the malingered profiles tend to have sharper differentiations than randomly produced profiles, with some scales (e.g., *SCZ*) likely to elevate markedly, and others (e.g., *MAN*) influenced less consistently when pathology is simulated. Nonetheless, there are a variety of profile elements on the clinical scales that are inconsistent with those generated even in severe mental disorder. For example, it is very unusual to have both *DEP* and *MAN* scores above 70*T*, but this pattern was seen in the simulation of severe mental disorder (Morey, 1991); even bipolar patients rarely obtain these elevations simultaneously. Also, the *RXR* score tends to be rather high for profiles with this degree of pathology; as will be discussed later, this probably results from inaccurate lay stereotypes of individuals with a severe mental disorder.

An actuarial use of PAI profile information for detecting malingering was provided in a study by Rogers et al. (in press) described in the previous section. This study constructed a discriminant function that was designed to distinguish the profiles of bona fide patients from those simulating such patients (including both their naive and sophisticated simulator groups). This study found that the resulting function was considerably more accurate than the *NIM* scale in isolation in identifying the feigned disorders. The discriminant function loadings are presented in Table 4-1; to obtain the function score, each weight is multiplied by the *T* score for the corresponding PAI scale and the resulting numbers are summed (including a value for a constant). Rogers et al. evaluated the effectiveness of a cutting score of .12368 for this function; scores above this value were predicted to be feigned, whereas scores below this value were predicted to be bona fide cases. The function was found to have a sensitivity of 87% in identifying feigned disorder and a 96% specificity; in cross-validation, the sensitivity for malingering identification was

Table 4-1
Discriminant Function Weights Used in Computation of the
Discriminant Function for the Assessment of Malingering

Scale	Weight
ICN	+ .01718613
INF	+ .01976398
SOM-C	− .03403340
SOM-H	+ .02824221
ANX-A	− .04109886
ANX-P	+ .05324155
ARD-O	− .01773748
ARD-P	+ .02758030
ARD-T	− .01741280
DEP-C	+ .04121700
PAR-H	+ .01603311
PAR-R	+ .01554190
SCZ-P	+ .01775538
SCZ-T	− .02750892
BOR-I	− .02909405
BOR-N	+ .03675012
BOR-S	− .01793721
ANT-E	+ .02152554
STR	− .01917862
RXR	+ .02103711
Constant	− 6.60458400

Note. Material in this table was adapted from "Detection of Feigned Mental Disorders on the Personality Assessment Inventory: A Discriminant Analysis," by R. Rogers, K. W. Sewell, L. C. Morey, and K. L. Ustad, in press.

found to be 80% and the specificity was 81%. These results suggest that this function, which uses information from 20 different PAI scale and subscale scores, can successfully identify over 80% of individuals attempting to simulate a wide array of emotional disorders, ranging from mild (e.g., generalized anxiety) to severe (e.g., schizophrenia) pathology.

To investigate the generalizability of this function and to obtain an estimate of expected distributions when the function scores are calculated, Table 4-2 presents descriptive statistics for the results of the function when applied to various samples from the *PAI Professional Manual* (Morey, 1991). This Table reveals that the only group to obtain a mean score above the cutoff recommended by Rogers et al.

Table 4-2
Descriptive Statistics for the Rogers Discriminant Function (RDF)
for Relevant Samples From the *PAI Professional Manual*

Sample type	N	M	SD
Community sample	1,000	−1.00	1.08
Clinical sample	1,246	−1.15	1.17
Student sample, "fake bad" responding	44	2.27	1.16
Student sample, "fake good" responding	45	−1.15	0.72

(in press) was the "fake bad" or malingering group; all other groups obtained values that were 2 to 3 standard deviations below this group. It is interesting to note that the community and clinical samples obtain very similar scores on this function, even though they tend to obtain dissimilar values on other validity indicators such as *NIM*. Such a result suggests that this function may be useful in identifying malingering in a variety of assessment contexts, including both clinical and community settings. To assist in interpreting the results of the Rogers et al. Discriminant Function (RDF), Table 4-3 lists *T*-score equivalents for different values of the function as applied to the community norms presented in Table 4-2. Using the results presented in Table 4-2, it appears that individuals instructed to simulate the responses of patients with severe mental disorders typically obtain scores of around 80*T*; the empirically based cutoff recommended by Rogers et al. corresponds to a value of roughly 60*T*. Thus, scores at or above 60*T* suggest the possibility of efforts to feign mental disorder, whereas scores at or above 70*T* on the RDF index are indicative of overt attempts at malingering.

The Appendix provides a variety of correlates for RDF scores; some of the most informative of these correlates are presented in Table 4-4. This table reveals that the RDF score is positively but weakly related to most other indicators of negative distortion; correlations are minimal with *NIM* and with the MMPI *F* scale, and somewhat higher with the Malingering Index (to be discussed in the following section). Within the realm of clinical constructs, the RDF is most associated with *PAR-R* of the PAI scales and subscales, and with *Si* on the MMPI. On other indicators, State Anxiety from the STAI (Spielberger, 1983) is among the largest correlates. In summary, the RDF appears to be tapping an element of negative distortion that is largely independent of most other indicators of profile validity, providing the potential for a separate evaluation of validity concerns. In part, this independence is achieved through the inclusion of suppressor variables in the function that serve to remove the overall level of pathology manifest in the profile to a

Table 4-3
T-Score Conversions for Rogers Discriminant Function (RDF)
Scores, Standardized Against the PAI Normative Sample

Function result	T-score equivalent	Function result	T-score equivalent
−5.00	13	0.25	62
−4.75	15	0.50	64
−4.50	18	0.75	66
−4.24	20	1.00	69
−4.00	22	1.25	71
−3.75	25	1.50	73
−3.50	27	1.75	75
−3.25	29	2.00	78
−3.00	31	2.25	80
−2.75	36	2.50	82
−2.50	36	2.75	85
−2.25	38	3.00	87
−2.00	41	3.25	89
−1.75	43	3.50	92
−1.50	45	3.75	94
−1.25	48	4.00	96
−1.00	50	4.25	99
−0.75	52	4.50	101
−0.50	55	4.75	103
−0.25	57	5.00	106
0.00	59		

considerable degree, reducing correlations with validity indicators that are associated with global psychopathology. Evidence of this can be seen in Table 4-2, which demonstrates that the clinical and community normative samples have similar scores on the RDF despite marked differences in the overall elevation of the profiles in these samples. To the extent that the RDF is related to specific forms of psychopathology, it is modestly related to a hostile and anxious withdrawal from others.

The PAI Malingering Index (MAL)

The need for a specific indicator of malingering more specific than NIM led to the development of the Malingering Index (Morey, 1993). The Malingering Index (MAL) is comprised of eight configural features of the PAI profile that tend to be observed much more frequently in the profiles of respondents simulating mental disorder (particularly severe mental disorders) than in actual clinical patients.

Table 4-4
Selected Correlates of the Rogers Discriminant Function (RDF) Score

Variable description	Correlation with RDF score
PAI *INF*	.37
PAI *NIM*	.09
PAI Malingering Index	.26
MMPI *F*	.13
PAI *PAR-R*	.43
MMPI *Si*	.31
State-Trait Anxiety Scale, State Anxiety	.39

Note. MMPI = Minnesota Multiphasic Personality Inventory.

Table 4-5
Prevalence of Features of the PAI Malingering Index (MAL) in Community, Clinical, and Simulating Samples

Index item	Item weight	Community[a] M	Clinical[b] M	Fake bad[c] M	Fake good[d] M
1. *NIM* ≥ 110*T*	1	.00	.01	.64	.00
2. *NIM* minus *INF* ≥ 20*T*	1	.04	.19	.73	.00
3. *INF* minus *ICN* ≥ 15*T*	1	.08	.08	.61	.37
4. *PAR-P* minus *PAR-H* ≥ 15*T*	1	.05	.07	.43	.00
5. *PAR-P* minus *PAR-R* ≥ 15*T*	1	.05	.09	.39	.00
6. *MAN-I* minus *MAN-G* ≥ 15*T*	1	.09	.23	.52	.00
7. *DEP* ≥ 85*T* and *RXR* ≥ 45*T*	1	.00	.01	.36	.00
8. *ANT-E* minus *ANT-A* ≥ 10*T*	1	.15	.12	.73	.35
Total *M*		.46	.80	4.41	.72
Total *SD*		.74	.98	1.80	.73

[a]*N* = 1,505. [b]*N* = 1,246. [c]*n* = 44. [d]*n* = 45.

Table 4-5 presents these eight features and the proportions of individuals manifesting the features in four samples: the community and the clinical normative samples, and samples of college students instructed to "simulate a major mental disorder" (fake bad) or to "present your best possible front" (fake good). This table reveals that each feature was observed with far greater frequency in the "fake bad" group than in actual clinical or community samples.

The computation and significance of the eight Malingering Index (MAL) items are as follows:

1. *NIM ≥ 110T (1 point)*. As mentioned previously, NIM represents the starting point for the assessment of malingering, although its limits for this use have been described. Nonetheless, although elevations on NIM are not uncommon in clinical samples, extreme elevations (i.e., ≥ 110T) are very uncommon in samples of respondents completing the test under standard instructions. In contrast, elevations in this range are the rule rather than the exception for respondents instructed to simulate disorders; in fact, the average NIM score for such respondents is typically above 110T. Although only 1% of respondents in the clinical normative sample and *none* of the respondents in the community normative sample obtained scores of 110T or greater, a full 64% of "fake bad" respondents did so. Thus, any *NIM T* score at or above 110T adds 1 point to the Malingering Index.

2. *NIM minus INF ≥ 20T (1 point)*. Both NIM and INF are validity scales with extremely small means and standard deviations in the community normative sample; as such, endorsing only a few items on each of these scales can lead to elevations. This means that, statistically, the two scales are quite similar and that, on each scale, item endorsements are infrequent. The only difference lies in the content of the scales; although the content of INF items is unusual (e.g., having your favorite sporting event be the high jump), it does not necessarily appear to be pathological, even to the lay person. In contrast, many NIM items were selected specifically because they address lay stereotypes of mental disorder in a dramatic and overt way. Therefore, individuals attempting to simulate mental disorder are much more likely to endorse the pathological-sounding NIM items than the unusual, but relatively benign, INF items. A difference of at least 20 *T*-score points in favor of NIM is typical in such individuals. The *T* score of NIM is at least 20 points higher than that of INF in 73% of "fake bad" respondents, but this difference occurs in only 19% of clinical patients and less than 5% of community respondents. A difference of 20 points or more in this direction adds 1 point to the Malingering Index.

3. *INF minus ICN ≥ 15T (1 point)*. Although the content of INF items is less pathological than that of NIM items, the former are sufficiently unusual sounding to sometimes be misinterpreted as indicators of mental disorder by respondents attempting to simulate psychopathology. For example, the item "Most people look forward to a trip to the dentist" is generally recognized as a false statement by most test-takers. However, respondents attempting to simulate severe disorders may misinterpret this item as measuring insight and perceptual accuracy and give a *Very True* response. As such, INF elevations in malingering samples, although

nowhere near as prominent as *NIM* elevations, are commonly obtained. In contrast, the *ICN* scale, which, like *INF*, was designed to identify carelessness or random responding, is rarely elevated in simulation studies. This is most likely because an individual who is motivated to simulate a mental disorder will be careful and consistent in responding to questions; the PAI profile elevations that result are not from carelessness, but rather a careful attempt to manipulate self-presentation. As a result, *INF* scores are typically more than 15 *T*-score points higher than *ICN* scores in such samples. A difference of this magnitude is found in 61% of "fake bad" respondents, but in only 8% of the clinical and community normative respondents. A difference of 15 *T*-score points or more in favor of *INF* adds 1 point to the Malingering Index.

4. *PAR-P minus PAR-H ≥ 15T (1 point); 5. PAR-P minus PAR-R ≥ 15T (1 point).* Both of these indicators are obtained by examining the configuration of subscales on the *PAR* scale. The item content of the three subscales of *PAR* is fairly different, with *PAR-P* comprised largely of items tapping paranoid psychotic content (e.g., ideas of reference, or delusions of persecution), whereas *PAR-R* and *PAR-H* assess more personological or cognitive features of paranoia (e.g., hostility, resentment, and wariness). The latter two aspects of the syndrome are more commonly encountered in the general population (as witnessed by their relatively high mean score in comparison to *PAR-P*) and, thus, do not seem as overtly pathological to a lay population. Nonetheless, these elements are invariably part of the paranoid syndrome, and these scales should be elevated in any full-blown delusional episode of the sort that might lead to an elevation on *PAR-P*. Most individuals who have a smattering of knowledge about psychopathology can recognize persecutory symptoms as evidence of paranoia, but they understand little else about the disorder. Thus, lay respondents instructed to simulate psychosis do not recognize vigilance and resentment as being central to a paranoid psychosis, and they rarely provide scores on either *PAR-H* or *PAR-R* that approach that of *PAR-P*. Differences of 15 points between these scales are obtained roughly 40% of the time in simulation samples, but less than 10% of the time in actual clinical respondents. For either comparison, a difference of 15 *T*-score points or more in favor of *PAR-P* adds 1 point each to the Malingering Index (MAL).

6. *MAN-I minus MAN-G ≥ 15T (1 point).* The items of the *MAN-I* scale address a ready irritability that arises out of a low tolerance for frustration and an impatience with interference from others. Implicit in these frustrations is a fundamental belief in the importance and significance of the respondent's own plans, and, as such, there is an underlying grandiosity typically associated with this irritability. However, to the lay observer, these two components seem quite unrelated;

whereas *MAN-I* items suggest marked problems with other people and are interpreted as a negative attribute, *MAN-G* items denote positive self-esteem and do not overtly appear to be indicative of psychopathology. Thus, in malingering simulation samples, these scales often are found to be inversely correlated, whereas, in clinical samples, they are positively associated. Over one half of simulation respondents will obtain a 15-point differential in favor of *MAN-I*, whereas less than a quarter of clinical respondents will display this pattern. Hence, a difference of 15 *T*-score points, with *MAN-I* larger than *MAN-G*, adds 1 point to the Malingering Index (MAL).

7. *DEP ≥ 85T and RXR ≥ 45T (1 point).* One of the most prominent lay stereotypes of mental disorders is that individuals suffering from such disorders all lack insight into the nature and severity of their condition. These beliefs can be found in expressions such as, "The first step to being normal is knowing that you are crazy." These stereotypes often lead lay observers to underestimate the marked distress and motivation for change that characterize most forms of mental disorder. On the PAI, it is very uncommon to find respondents who report both a significant degree of distress (as indicated by elevations on *DEP*) and little motivation to change (as indicated by scores on *RXR* approximating those obtained from non-patients). In actual clinical samples, these two scales display a strong inverse relationship, and elevations on *DEP* are typically associated with very low (i.e., ≤ 35*T*) scores on *RXR*. Scores at or above 45*T* on *RXR* are almost never associated with *DEP* scores of 85*T* or above in true patients. However, in simulation samples, *RXR* is often found to be close to 50*T*, even in the presence of indicators of marked distress; more than a third of such patients meet this MAL item. Thus, a score at or above 45*T* on *RXR* coupled with a *DEP* score of 85*T* or above adds 1 point to the Malingering Index (MAL).

8. *ANT-E minus ANT-A ≥ 10T (1 point).* As noted previously with the scales assessing mania and paranoia, lay observers often recognize certain dramatic or prominent elements of syndromes of mental disorders without understanding other facets of these syndromes that invariably are associated with these elements. This tendency also appears to occur in the consideration of the different facets of antisocial personality. Here, the unempathic and amoral elements of antisocial personality strike lay observers as severely pathological; in fact, the majority of such observers appear to attribute such characteristics to all patients with severe mental disorder. Thus, when such lay persons attempt to simulate severe psychopathology, they invariably obtain marked elevations on *ANT-E*. Apparently however, the antisocial behaviors that are actually the invariable sequelae of this character style are not part of the stereotype of mental disorder; scores on *ANT-A*

in such samples are often within normal limits. In simulation samples, 73% of malingerers obtain *ANT-E* scores that are 10 or more *T*-score points above the *ANT-A* score, whereas only 12% of true clinical respondents yield this differential. When observed, this difference adds 1 point to the Malingering Index (MAL).

Factors Underlying Malingering Index (MAL) Items. In order to further facilitate interpretation of the Malingering Index, the eight items of the index were factor analyzed (principal components analysis followed by varimax rotation) using data obtained from both the community and clinical normative samples. In both samples, two factors could be extracted, and the loadings were quite similar in both samples. The first factor involves an endorsement of severe and rather unusual psychotic symptoms, without the marked anxiety and wariness in dealing with the environment that typically accompany these symptoms. Malingering Index (MAL) Items 4, 5 and, to a lesser extent, 1 are included on this factor. Prototypic of individuals endorsing such items would be a person who believes that others are plotting against him or her (as indicated by *PAR-P*), yet who professes to experience relatively little anger, anxiety, or resentment that this is occurring. The second factor involves a tendency to portray oneself (i.e., a very low *MAN-G*) and one's environment (i.e., a very high *NIM*) in a very negative light, accentuating the negative and minimizing the positive elements of each. Malingering Index (MAL) Items 1, 2, and 6 demonstrated substantial loadings on this factor. Prototypic of such individuals would be those who reflexively deprecate all elements of their experience, including their experience of themselves.

PAI Malingering Index (MAL) Interpretation

Table 4-5 reveals that the average score for a malingering sample on the Malingering Index was 4.41 items, compared to a mean of 0.80 for the clinical standardization sample and 0.46 for the community normative sample. Transformation of Malingering Index items to *T* scores, based on the means and standard deviations of both the community standardization sample and the clinical standardization sample, are listed for convenience in Table 4-6. This table reveals that the malingering sample obtained a score that was more than 5 standard deviations above the mean of the community sample; this score was also more than 3 standard deviations above the mean for the clinical sample. The latter is probably the better referent, as malingering involves the distinction between actual and feigned disorders, rather than a comparison to community normal respondents. Thus, using a 2 standard deviation referent against the clinical sample, MAL scores of 3 or above should raise questions of malingering; scores of 5 or more are highly unusual in clinical samples, and they tend to occur only when severe mental disorder is being feigned.

Table 4-6
T-Score Equivalents for the PAI Malingering Index (MAL)
Standardized Against Community and Clinical Normative Samples

MAL score	*T*-score equivalent, community[a] norms	*T*-score equivalent, clinical[b] norms
0	44	42
1	57	52
2	71	62
3	84	72
4	98	83
5	111	93
6	125	103
7	138	113
8	151	123

[a]$N = 1,000.$ [b]$N = 1,246.$

The Gaies (1993) study of the malingering of depression (described earlier in this chapter) provides additional support for the utility of the Malingering Index. Using a cutoff of 3 or greater as an indicator of malingering, Gaies found a sensitivity of 56.6% for identifying the informed malingerers and 34.2% for identifying the naive malingerers. Specificity of the index in a sample of patients who were actually depressed was 89.3%, whereas normal controls demonstrated a specificity of 100%. Similar to the results obtained using *NIM*, it appears that the sensitivity of the Malingering Index will decline somewhat when milder forms of psychopathology (e.g., depression or anxiety) are being simulated. In settings where the malingering of such disorders is a concern, adjustments to the Index cutoff may be needed to optimize the utility of decisions.

The Appendix provides a variety of correlates for the Malingering Index (MAL), of which selected results are presented in Table 4-7. This table reveals that the Malingering Index is moderately related to *NIM* (which should be expected, as *NIM* elevations comprise part of the Index) and also somewhat related to the MMPI *F* scale. Within the realm of clinical constructs, the MAL is most associated with *PAR-P* of the PAI scales and subscales, and with *Pa* on the MMPI, confirming that dramatic paranoid psychotic features are most likely to lead to Index elevations. On other indicators, an Antisocial presentation on diagnostic interview is among the largest correlates of this Index. In summary, the Malingering Index appears to be tapping an element of negative distortion related to an atypical presentation of severe mental disorder, particularly that of paranoid psychosis. In

Table 4-7
Selected Correlates of the PAI Malingering Index (MAL) Total Score

Variable description	Correlation with MAL score
PAI *INF*	.00
PAI *NIM*	.61
PAI *PIM*	−.39
MMPI *F*	.39
PAI *PAR-P*	.65
MMPI *Pa*	.38
Diagnostic Interview for Personality Disorder, Antisocial diagnosis	.42

Note. MMPI = Minnesota Multiphasic Personality Inventory.

combination with other features such as *NIM* and the RDF score, the Malingering Index can help identify profiles that suggest overt attempts at the feigning of mental disorder.

CHAPTER 5
IDENTIFYING DEFENSIVENESS ON THE PAI

The stigma of mental illness and the limitations of psychological insight in most people can give rise to an underreporting of clinical problems that can potentially distort the accuracy of self-reported information. The distorting factors can be quite diverse. They may result from personality traits or from situational influences on a respondent; they may involve intentional distortion or a genuine lack of insight; and they may involve selective defensiveness about some problem areas (e.g., substance abuse) but not about others (e.g., depression). For this reason, the PAI does not include any "correction" factors of the sort employed by other inventories; these corrections invariably fail to enhance validity, mainly due to the use of one omnibus correction that cannot discriminate among such varied influences on defensiveness. Nonetheless, it is clear that the assessment of such potential distortions is an important part of interpreting any self-report instrument, and identifying such distortions has arguably been the most difficult assessment task for researchers and clinicians. Most procedures that have been developed to identify defensiveness show large overlap with normal functioning, leading some investigators to speculate about widespread "illusory mental health" (Shedler, Mayman, & Manis, 1993) when assessments are based upon self-reports.

Detecting generally defensive response patterns with the PAI may be accomplished through the use of a number of strategies, including the *PIM* scale and profile configuration information such as that used in the Defensiveness Index; specific denial of substance abuse problems is discussed in chapter 2. Each strategy provides information useful in assessing profile validity, but none is infallible; the identification of defensiveness continues to be one of the most difficult challenges to self-report psychological assessment. As with any assessment, all sources of information should be considered. The supplementation of PAI profile information with concurrent reports from family members, peers, documents or records, and other psychological and/or laboratory testing is recommended when situational factors raise the a priori probability of underreporting of clinical problems. Such situations can include, but are not limited to the following: preemployment screenings, fitness for duty evaluations, child custody suits, criminal dispositions, and involuntary hospitalization or treatment decisions.

Positive Impression (*PIM*)

The content of *PIM* scale items involves the presentation of a very favorable impression or the denial of relatively minor faults. The items were selected by examining the distributions of scores for normal respondents, patients, and research respondents responding to the PAI under positive-impression-enhancement instructional sets. The items were selected on the basis of low endorsement frequencies in both normal and clinical respondents; however, *PIM* items are endorsed with greater frequency in normal adults than in clinical patients. Marked elevations in clinical respondents are particularly rare and, hence, are interpretively significant if obtained. Both patients and normal respondents score considerably lower than research respondents completing the PAI under a positive impression enhancement instructional set.

For the most part, *PIM* items offer the opportunity for individuals to say something negative about themselves. Hence, elevated scores indicate that respondents do not take many opportunities to say negative things about themselves. There are a number of reasons why individuals might not report negative characteristics. One possibility is that they have no negative characteristics, or, at least, they have fewer of these than most people. A second possibility is that they are not telling the truth, that they are trying to deceive the recipient of the test results into believing that they have more positive features than they really do. A third possibility is that they simply are not aware of certain faults that they may have, that they lack insight into some of their personal shortcomings. In either of the latter two instances, the results of a self-report test will lead one to form a more positive impression of the respondent's life circumstances and psychological adjustment than would probably be merited in the opinion of an independent observer. It is these latter two characteristics that *PIM* was designed to measure.

It should be recognized that the tendency for favorable self-presentation is actually fairly common in the normal population. Typically, most clinically derived cutting scores on indices of social desirability will end up identifying 30% to 40% of the general population as "faking good." Such results underscore the difficulty of distinguishing defensive responding from normality with respect to clinical instruments. A number of instruments have used scales similar to *PIM* to "correct" other scales on the test for defensive responding, as if such scales tapped pure suppressor variables, but the PAI makes no such correction for a number of reasons. First, using a single scale to correct numerous other scales lessens the discriminant validity of those other scales by forcing them to intercorrelate artifactually. A second reason involves the mistaken assumption that social desirability is a suppressor variable; this is not the case, because it actually does correlate with clinical criteria in most instances. In other words, most forms of mental disorder involve symptoms that are not socially desirable. For example, hallucinations or drinking problems simply are not desirable characteristics, and people who have such problems often say negative things about themselves because they are true, not just because they are more willing to admit to them. Thus, attempts to remove "social desirability" from clinical scale scores will remove criterion-related variance and, hence, lower validity.

A third problem with defensiveness "corrections" is that this construct has strong situational influences on it. Although people certainly may be defensive in responding to self-report inventories, there are a variety of reasons why they are defensive and an equal variety of reasons why some particular scales might be affected and other scales might not. If an individual is acutely paranoid and does not want the examiner to know this, the biggest effect is likely to be on *PAR*. If an individual is using drugs, but is trying to hide this, the effect will be observed on *DRG*. A person masking depression may have lowered effects on *DEP* and, perhaps, inflated scores on *MAN*. To be useful, any correction to such scores should be made based on the nature of the individual and the type of problems he or she has and on whatever operations of denial and defensiveness are taking place. Application of a single correction to multiple scales by treating the characteristic as a trait is doomed to failure, because these influences are not cross-situationally consistent. This does not mean that scales such as *PIM* are unimportant; it simply means that such corrections must be made integratively by the test interpreter who has access to all situational and contextual information.

The original decision points for interpreting *PIM* scores were based on the performance of respondents who were attempting to manage their impression in a positive direction. The point of rarity between the impression management sample (i.e., "fake good") and the community normative sample can be used as a cutting score, above which a person's scores are more similar to those of simulated respondents than to those of typical respondents. This point of rarity was 18 or above (57*T*) on *PIM*. Application of this rule resulted in a sensitivity in the identification of positive dissimulation of 82%, and a specificity with respect to normal respondents of 70%. Interestingly, a study by Cashel, Rogers, Sewell, and Martin-Cannici (1995) also identified 57*T* as their optimal cutting score, which yielded sensitivity and specificity rates of 48% and 81%, respectively. Cashel et al. (1995) further found that scores below 43*T* could be used with very high specificity (i.e., virtually no respondents attempting to manage their impression obtained scores below that value on *PIM*). Finally, Fals-Stewart (1996), in a study of defensive responding and denial among drug abusers (described in more detail in chapter 2), found that the 57*T* cutting score on *PIM* had a sensitivity of 88% and a specificity of 80% in identifying substance-abusing individuals motivated to avoid detection by the PAI.

Thus, low scores on *PIM* (i.e., < 44*T*) are strongly indicative of honest responding. Generally, scores between 44*T* and 56*T* suggest that the respondent did not attempt to present an unrealistically favorable impression in completing the test, although scores in the upper end of this range tend to be unusual in clinical settings. Moderate elevations (i.e., 57*T* to 67*T*) suggest that the examinee responded in a manner to portray himself or herself as relatively free of the common shortcomings to which most individuals will admit. With *PIM* in this range, the accuracy of interpretations based on the PAI clinical scales profile may be distorted, and interpretive hypotheses should be reviewed with caution. It is likely that the PAI profile will underrepresent the extent and degree of significant test findings.

Another method of identifying problematic protocols uses cutting scores derived from the distributions of clinical respondents. Use of the reference data from clinical respondents is particularly relevant for the impression management scales, as normal respondents and clinical respondents tend to differ in this regard. For *PIM*, a raw score of 23 or above (68*T*) corresponds to a score that is more than 2 standard deviations above the mean for clinical respondents. Applying this more conservative decision rule results in decisions that are more specific to attempts at impression management than those provided by the empirical cutoffs. In other words, relatively few actual protocols are identified as invalid using the 2-standard deviation clinical norms cutoff; the specificity rates for this cutoff are 95% or greater, although the sensitivity in identifying dissimulated protocols falls to 52% (Morey, 1991), and sensitivity drops to 17% when respondents are coached regarding believability of results (Cashel et al., 1995). Thus, such high scores on *PIM* (i.e., ≥ 68*T*) suggest that the respondent attempted to portray himself or herself as exceptionally free of the common shortcomings to which most individuals will admit. When scores in this range are obtained, the validity of the PAI clinical scale profile is seriously questioned, and no clinical interpretation of other PAI scales is recommended. However, such scores are usually rare, and concerns about defensiveness should be raised at even lower scores, as noted earlier.

Defensive Responding Profile Configuration

The *PAI Professional Manual* (Morey, 1991) described the results of a study of 45 college students who were instructed to respond as if they were taking the PAI to qualify for a desired job and they wanted to appear psychologically fit for this job. The mean profile for this group of respondents is presented in Figure 5-1. The scores for this sample were extremely suppressed, with nearly all scores below 50T. Only five scales demonstrated scores above 60T: *PIM, MAN, RXR*, and the two interpersonal scales, *DOM* and *WRM*. This basic portrayal is of an individual with above-average self-esteem and energy who is interested and effective in interpersonal relationships and good at controlling these relationships. Such individuals admit to no problems in functioning and would adamantly resist the notion that some aspect of their lives could be changed for the better. Not only are there no signs of any personal weaknesses, but the individuals surrounding the person are also described as exceptionally efficient and supportive, as evidenced by the suppressed score on *NON*. Similar trends can be found in "fake good" profiles reported in a detailed study of defensive responding on the PAI conducted by Cashel, Rogers, Sewell, and Martin-Cannici (1995). Cashel et al. instructed two types of respondents (i.e., college students and prison inmates) to answer the PAI in a way that would portray them in the best possible manner, but stressed the believability of the resulting profile. The mean profiles for the offender and student groups (collapsed across order of taking the test) also are presented in Figure 5-1. Again, the same five scales reveal elevations, and *NON* is again one of the lowest scales. Also, it is important to note that for all three samples *ICN* scores are quite low, demonstrating that intentional distortion of PAI responses in a positive direction is more likely to suppress *ICN* than to lead to elevations on this scale.

Cashel et al. (1995) also constructed a discriminant function that was designed to distinguish optimally between defensive and honest responding. The authors found that this function was more accurate in identifying dissimulated responding than either the *PIM* score in isolation or the score on the Defensiveness Index, or DEF (described later). The Cashel et al. Discriminant Function (CDF) demonstrated sensitivities ranging from 79% to 87% in identifying falsified profiles, with specificity of 88%. This discriminant function, calculated by multiplying PAI *T* scores by a weighting factor, is as follows:

$$CDF = 1.67(BOR) + .97(PIM) + .72(MAN) + .60(RXR) - .52(ALC) - .68(STR)$$

Because these standardized discriminant function coefficients are calibrated to the means and standard deviations of their particular samples, interpretation of the number resulting from this formula is not straightforward in other settings. To assist researchers and clinicians in using and interpreting the results of this formula, the formula was applied to the normative community sample of the PAI, resulting in a mean value of 138.14 and a standard deviation of 14.91 for this composite. To give some idea how different groups score on this composite, Table 5-1 presents results from a number of different samples.

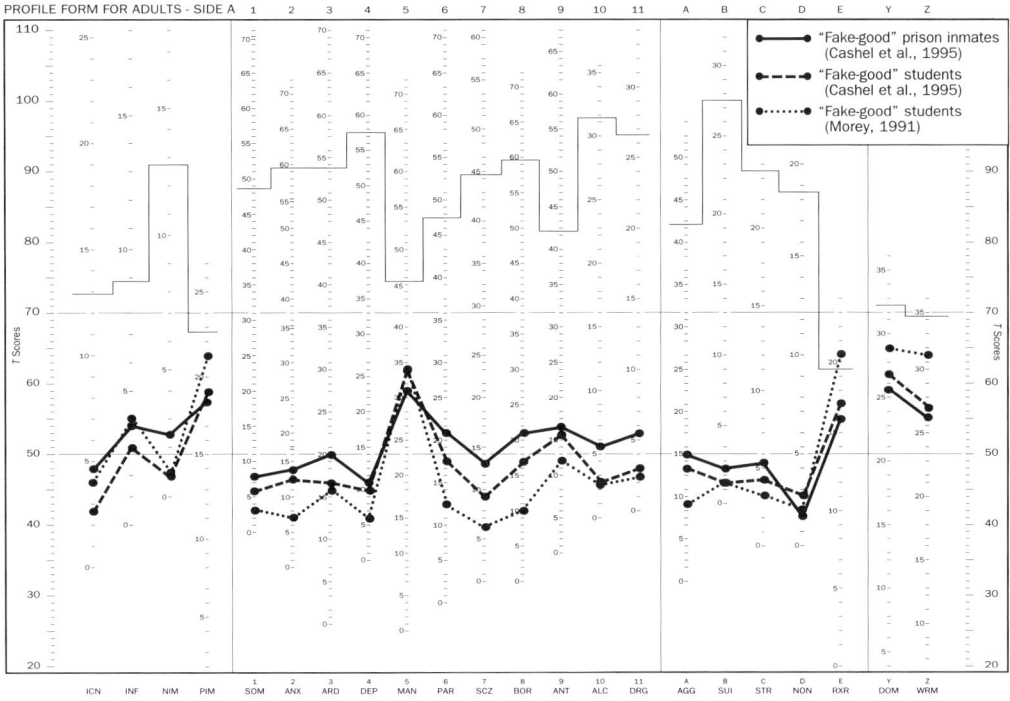

Figure 5-1. Mean "Fake-good" PAI profiles for prison inmates and students.

Table 5-1 reveals that all of the dissimulating groups obtained scores on the discriminant function that were over 1 standard deviation above the mean of the normative sample. It is also interesting to notice that the "fake good" samples obtained scores that were quite similar, even though the profiles portrayed in Figure 5-1 show considerable differences in the configurations from the different settings.

Table 5-1
Discriminant Function Means for Honest and Dissimulating Groups

Sample type	N	M	SD
Community sample[a]	1,000	138.14	14.91
Clinical sample[a]	1,246	135.28	18.79
Offender sample, honest responding[b]	45	135.11	—
Student sample, honest responding[b]	38	144.66	—
Student sample, fake good responding[a]	45	161.41	20.30
Offender sample, fake good responding[b]	45	157.04	—
Student sample, fake good responding[b]	38	161.60	—

Note. The discriminant function formula was developed by Cashel et al., 1995.
[a]From the *PAI Professional Manual* (Morey, 1991). [b]From (Cashel et al., 1995). Standard deviations were not provided.

Table 5-2
T-Score Conversions for Cashel Discriminant Function (CDF)[a]
Results Standardized Against the PAI Normative Sample

Function result	*T*-score equivalent	Function result	*T*-score equivalent
75	8	132	46
78	10	135	48
81	12	138	50
84	14	141	52
87	16	144	54
90	18	147	56
93	20	150	58
96	22	153	60
99	24	156	62
102	26	159	64
105	28	162	66
108	30	165	68
111	32	168	70
114	34	171	72
117	36	174	74
120	38	177	76
123	40	180	78
126	42	183	80
129	44	186	82

[a]Cashel et al. (1995).

This suggests that the function proposed by Cashel et al. (1995) may be useful in detecting defensiveness in a wide variety of different settings. To assist in interpreting the result of the function, Table 5-2 lists *T*-score equivalents for different values of the function. From the results presented in Table 5-1, it appears that groups instructed to "fake good" typically yield mean scores in the range from 65*T* to 70*T* on this composite; scores above 70*T* thus suggest the operation of overt efforts at positive impression management.

The Appendix provides a variety of correlates for the Cashel Discriminant Function (CDF; Cashel et al., 1995), of which selected results are presented in Table 5-3. This table reveals that the CDF score is relatively independent of most other indicators of defensiveness; the correlation with *PIM* is close to zero and the association with the MMPI *K* scale is negative (−.29). Interestingly, the association of the CDF score with *NIM* was greater than that with *PIM*. More consistent with

Table 5-3
Selected Correlates of the Cashel Discriminant Function (CDF) Score

Variable description	Correlation with CDF score
PAI *PIM*	.06
MMPI *K*	−.29
Marlowe-Crowne Social Desirability Scale	.27
PAI Defensiveness Index (*DEF*)	.32
PAI *NIM*	.26
PAI *MAN*	.40
PAI *ALC*	−.52
Wiggins MMPI Hypomania	.61
Wiggins MMPI Psychoticism	.63
PAI *SCZ-P*	.18

Note. MMPI = Minnesota Multiphasic Personality Inventory.

expectations, positive but modest associations were noted with the DEF, the PAI Defensiveness Index (to be discussed in the following section) and the Marlowe-Crowne (Crowne & Marlowe, 1964) Social Desirability Scale. Within the realm of clinical constructs, the Cashel Discriminant Function is most associated with indicators of mania and hypomania, such as *MAN* and the Wiggins (1966) *HYP* MMPI content scale. For the PAI *MAN* scale, the association with the full scale score was larger than for any of the individual subscales; of the three subscales, *MAN-G* was least associated with the CDF score, despite being greatly influenced in most response set studies. The CDF score was also fairly highly correlated with the Wiggins Psychoticism content scale, a puzzling finding, as it displayed minimal relationships with other indicators of psychotic features, such as the PAI *SCZ-P* subscale.

In summary, the Cashel (Cashel et al., 1995) Discriminant Function (CDF) score appears to be tapping an element of positive dissimulation that is largely independent of most other indicators of profile validity, providing the potential for a supplemental evaluation of validity concerns. This independence is achieved through the inclusion of suppressor variables in the function that serve to remove the overall level of pathology manifest in the profile to a considerable degree, reducing correlations with defensiveness indicators that are associated more globally with social desirability. Evidence of this characteristic can be seen in Table 5-1, which demonstrates that the clinical and community normative samples have similar CDF scores despite marked differences in the overall elevation (and hence, social desirability) of the profiles in these samples. To the extent that the CDF score is related to specific forms of psychopathology, it appears to be related to a hypomanic and disorganized manner. In combination with other features such as *PIM* and the Defensiveness Index (DEF), the CDF score can help identify profiles that suggest overt attempts at favorable impression management.

The PAI Defensiveness Index (DEF)

To further supplement the tools for identifying defensive responding, a set of indicators known as the PAI Defensiveness Index (Morey, 1993) was developed. The Defensiveness Index (DEF) is comprised of eight configural features of the PAI profile that tend to be observed much more frequently in the profiles of respondents instructed to present a positive impression than in actual normal or clinical respondents. One of the items, involving the *PIM* scale, is double-weighted if it exceeds the 50*T* threshold; all other items are worth 1 point, if present. Table 5-4 presents these eight features and the proportions of individuals manifesting the features in four samples: the community and the clinical normative samples, and samples of college students instructed to "simulate a major mental disorder" ("fake bad") or to "present your best possible front" ("fake good"). This table reveals that each feature was observed with far greater frequency in the "fake good" group than in actual clinical or community samples.

The computation and significance of the eight DEF items is as follows:

1. PIM ≥ 50T (2 points) or PIM ≥ 45T to 49T (1 point). The most obvious place to begin a search for defensive responding on the PAI is with the *PIM* scale, because the scale was constructed for this purpose. The first item on the Defensiveness Index (DEF) reflects elevations on *PIM* that are atypical in clinical populations; it is quite unusual for individuals in clinical settings to obtain scores above 50*T*, and even scores of 45*T* are uncommon among this group. This item is weighted 2 points for *PIM* scores at or above 50*T*, and 1 point for a score between 45*T* and 49*T*. Obviously, elevations in this range are common in the general population, as about one half of such respondents would be expected to score above the mean of 50*T*. However, the mean scores presented in Table 5-4 reveal that nearly all respondents instructed to "fake good" score above 50*T*, because the mean on this item is 1.95 out of a possible 2.0 for this group. Thus, this DEF item appears to be a useful indicator, but, in isolation, it is not sufficient evidence of defensiveness, because many normal respondents also will be positive for this item.

Table 5-4
Prevalence of Features of the PAI Defensiveness Index (DEF) in Community, Clinical, and Simulating Samples

DEF Index item	Item weight	Community[a] M	Clinical[b] M	Fake bad[c] M	Fake Good[d] M
1. *PIM* ≥ 50*T*	2				
or 45*T* to 49*T*	1	1.24	.79	.41	1.95
2. *RXR* ≥ 45*T*	1	.70	.32	.61	.90
3. *ANT-E* minus *ANT-A* ≥ 10*T*	1	.15	.12	.73	.35
4. *ANT-S* minus *ANT-A* ≥ 10*T*	1	.03	.03	.07	.19
5. *MAN-G* minus *MAN-I* ≥ 10*T*	1	.19	.16	.11	.77
6. *ARD-O* minus *ANX-A* ≥ 10*T*	1	.23	.12	.07	.74
7. *DOM* minus *AGG-V* ≥ 15*T*	1	.10	.07	.02	.65
8. *MAN-A* minus *STR* ≥ 10*T*	1	.19	.05	.11	.67
Total *M*		2.81	1.66	2.13	6.23
Total *SD*		1.52	1.54	1.45	1.82

[a]$N = 1,000.$ [b]$N = 1,246.$ [c]$n = 44.$ [d]$n = 45.$

2. RXR ≥ 45T (1 point). The *RXR* scale (described in more detail in chapter 10) was designed to identify openness to psychological treatment. As should be expected, most adults in the community tend to score higher than is typical for clinical respondents, indicating that individuals in clinical settings (and, hence, probably in treatment) acknowledge a greater need for treatment than individuals in the community (and, hence, probably not in treatment). However, it should be recognized that the typical adult in the community obtains scores that suggest some openness to the idea of changes in his or her life and a willingness to accept responsibility for the direction such changes need to take. People who respond to the PAI in a defensive fashion demonstrate a rigidity and opposition to psychological change that often result in some elevation in scores on *RXR*. In many ways, the *RXR* scale is a more subtle indicator of defensiveness than *PIM*. Defensive responding drives *RXR* up, and even fairly sophisticated individuals instructed to "fake good" often do not recognize that their responses are rather rigid and unwilling to consider the possibility of personal change. *RXR* elevations suggest that such individuals believe nothing about themselves needs to change. On *PIM*, guarded respondents may be willing to admit to a few faults, yet on *RXR* they often deny any need to change those faults, indicating they are fine precisely as they are.

The threshold for this item in the Defensiveness Index is set at 45*T*, which may initially seem quite low given that it is below the mean of the normative sample.

However, such elevations tend to be rare in clinical samples; more than two thirds of respondents in clinical settings obtain scores below 45T. In contrast, only 9% of individuals taking the PAI under "fake good" or dissimulation responding instructions obtain *RXR* scores below 45T. Thus, this criterion is particularly effective in the identification of defensive responding in clinical settings.

3. ANT-E minus ANT-A ≥ 10T (1 point). ANT-E scores that are markedly elevated reflect unempathic and amoral elements of antisocial personality that strike even lay observers as severely pathological personality features. However, in its milder forms, this construct seems much less negative to the general public. In fact, it represents a certain mental toughness and a self-reliance that are valued aspects in this culture. However, the troublesome behaviors associated with *ANT-A* do not have this evaluative complexity; they are unambiguously undesirable, and individuals instructed to make a positive impression yield raw scores close to zero on this subscale. People instructed to answer the test defensively often are willing to admit that they look out for themselves, yet they will deny the possibility that this tendency has ever created the types of problems for them that are typically associated with this attitude. This is a fairly curious configural item, in that it is rarely obtained unless the person is attempting to impression-manage in either a positive *or* a negative direction. When respondents distort in a positive direction, the configuration is *ANT-E* moderate, *ANT-A* very low; when distorting in a negative direction, the configuration becomes *ANT-E* very high, and *ANT-A* more moderate. Thus, this item has the peculiar distinction of being on both the Defensiveness Index (DEF) *and* the Malingering Index (MAL).

4. ANT-S minus ANT-A ≥ 10T (1 point). The rationale behind this item is similar to that for Item 3: certain personality traits tend to lead to an increased risk for behavioral problems. *ANT-S*, which reflects a craving for novelty and excitement, is one of these traits. A person who is constantly seeking new sensory experiences and challenges is more likely to have experienced some behavioral problems (as reflected by *ANT-A*) than a person who responds anxiously to novel situations, and, in fact, the *ANT-S* and *ANT-A* scales correlate at .53 in the general population. The 10-point discrepancy described in this item is almost never found in an actual clinical community sample; being a risk-taker tends to lead to trouble, and the two scales tend to elevate together. When there is a discrepancy with the stimulus-seeking scale being higher, it is generally an indication that the person desires to make a favorable impression on the recipient of the test results.

5. MAN-G minus MAN-I ≥ 10T (1 point). The fifth item of the Defensiveness Index (DEF) involves a comparison between the grandiosity and irritability components of the *MAN* scale. Individuals attempting to manage a positive impression show a large difference on these two subscales; 77% of "fake good" respondents show this 10-point split in favor of *MAN-G*, whereas only 19% of normal respondents do so. This configuration involves saying a number of positive things about oneself without admitting to the downside of these positive statements. The prototype of this combination would be an individual who claims to have both the "genius of Einstein" and the "patience of Job." However, as self-esteem increases, one's patience with others who are perceived as less capable often decreases. When less capable people get in one's way, the natural response is one of frustration, but the low desirability valence of frustration suppresses this score in respondents attempting to "fake good." The 10-point split described in this item tends to be quite infrequent in any other population.

6. *ARD-O minus ANX-A ≥ 10T (1 point)*. The sixth item of the Defensiveness Index (DEF) represents a difference in portrayed levels of obsessionality and anxiety. At the extreme, the Obsessive-Compulsive subscale of *ARD* can reflect rigidity and perfectionism, but, in the moderate range, it represents a certain number of desirable characteristics: concern with order, high standards for oneself and others, and careful control over emotions. Often the motivating force to maintain that level of order and that level of affective constraint is to avoid the experience of anxiety; when these strategies are working reasonably well (i.e., for most of the general population) the *T*-scores for the two scales will be comparable. However, individuals instructed to "fake good" will portray themselves as exceptionally orderly without any accompanying anxiety; they place a premium on control, but the loss of this control does not concern them in the least. Among such respondents, 74% report this level of discrepancy between their need to maintain order and anxiety around order, whereas only 23% of normal respondents demonstrate a comparable split.

7. *DOM minus AGG-V ≥ 15T (1 point)*. The seventh item of the Defensiveness Index (DEF) involves a 15-point discrepancy between reported levels of dominance and the tendency to express anger verbally. The *DOM* scale often is elevated in dissimulation samples, as it represents the ability to assume leadership roles effectively. A person demonstrating this difference between *DOM* and *AGG-V* is describing himself or herself as very effective in controlling other people without ever having to raise his or her voice; they are such natural leaders that others will follow their commands without any need for assertiveness on their part. This quite desirable, but unlikely, combination of features appears six to seven times more frequently in individuals "faking good" than it does in the general population.

8. *MAN-A minus STR ≥ 10T (1 point)*. The last DEF item involves a person reporting very high activity levels without any stress associated with this level of

involvement. People with this pattern describe being involved in numerous important activities, yet being able to function in an effective and controlled way amid all this commotion. This configuration is three to four times more likely to occur in "fake good" samples than in the general population; the appearance of this discrepancy in a clinical population is also quite unusual.

Structure of Defensiveness Index (DEF) items. The Defensiveness Index can be treated as an eight-item scale with a factor structure. A standard principal components extraction with varimax rotation factor analysis, performed using the data from both clinical and community respondents, yielded three highly converging factors across the two samples. The first factor, which includes sizable loadings on DEF Items 1, 2, and 5, involves a refusal to admit that any aspects of life are less than optimal or to acknowledge negative elements about oneself. The second factor involves Items 6, 7, and, to a lesser extent, 5. In each of these items, the positive aspects of a personality trait are emphasized, and the negative aspects are minimized; there is a tendency to deny that some positive characteristics often can have negative consequences in certain contexts. Thus, these items suggest that there is a denial of the internal consequences of the respondents' personality style; high standards can lead to anxiety, and capability can lead to impatience, yet not for these respondents. The third component, involving Items 3, 4, and 8, reflect individuals who are more oriented to denying that some of their behaviors have external consequences, ones that adversely affect other people. The problems being denied here tend to be ones in the societal realm, whereas the second factor involves more internal repercussions.

Defensiveness Index (DEF) Interpretation

As can be seen in Table 5-4, the average score for a "fake good" sample on the Defensiveness Index (DEF) was 6.23, as compared to 2.81 for these features in the normative community sample. Transformation of Defensiveness Index scores to *T* scores based on the mean and standard deviation of this normative sample are listed for convenience in Table 5-5; this table reveals that the "fake good" sample obtained a score that was more than 2 standard deviations above the mean of the community sample. However, a comparable sample obtained by Cashel et al. (1995) obtained a mean score of only 4.27 on the Defensiveness Index, a value that lies roughly 1 standard deviation above the norm. The results of the Cashel et al. study raise questions about the sensitivity of the Index in samples coached for "believability" in being defensive and raise the possibility that the Defensiveness Index may be a better *inclusion* sign for defensiveness than it is as an *exclusion* sign. Thus, respondents with score of six or greater on the Index are most likely defensive;

Table 5-5
_T_-Score Equivalents for the PAI Defensiveness Index (DEF)
Standardized Against a Community Normative Sample

DEF score	_T_-score equivalent
0	32
1	38
2	45
3	51
4	58
5	64
6	71
7	78
8	84
9	91

Note. N = 1,000.

however, defensive people may not score high on DEF, and scores within normal limits should not be considered to rule out the possibility of a dissimulated protocol. Nonetheless, the Defensiveness Index has promise and merits further study as a tool for addressing this most difficult of assessment issues.

The Appendix details numerous correlates for the Defensiveness Index, of which selected results are presented in Table 5-6. This table reveals that the Defensiveness Index (DEF) is positively correlated with other indicators of defensiveness and/or socially desirable responding. DEF correlates moderately with _PIM_, which should be expected, as _PIM_ elevations comprise part of the Defensiveness Index. However, the correlation with the MMPI _L_ scale is nearly identical to that found with _PIM_, which provides an independent verification of the positive dissimulation content of the Defensiveness Index items. Within the realm of clinical constructs, DEF is negatively associated with depressed mood as rated by an independent observer on the Brief Psychiatric Rating Scale (BPRS; Overall & Gorham, 1962). This finding is interesting, because it may suggest that the self-portrayal of positive mental health reflected in the DEF items can be convincing to others. The Defensiveness Index also displays a strong negative relationship with somatic complaints, indicating that respondents with elevated DEF scores are as unlikely to complain about their physical health as they are to complain about their mental health. In summary, the Defensiveness Index appears to be tapping an element of positive dissimulation related to a presentation of various unlikely virtues. In combination with other features such as _PIM_ and the CDF (Cashel et al., 1995) score,

Table 5-6
Selected Correlates of the PAI
Defensiveness Index (DEF) Total Score

Variable description	Correlation with DEF score
PAI *PIM*	.56
MMPI *L*	.55
MMPI *K*	.25
Marlowe-Crowne Social Desirability Scale	.28
CDF score (community sample)	.32
PAI *NIM*	−.18
PAI *MAN-G*	.52
PAI *RXR*	.52
Brief Psychiatric Rating Scale, Depressed Mood (BPRS)	−.49
Wahler Physical Symptoms Inventory	−.79

Note. MMPI = Minnesota Multiphasic Personality Inventory.

the Defensiveness Index can help with the particularly difficult challenge of identifying profiles resulting from overt attempts at positive impression management.

CHAPTER 6
USE OF THE PAI IN DIAGNOSIS

There are a variety of ways to use the PAI in deriving diagnostic hypotheses, all of which rely on the configuration of the PAI profile. The profile configuration represents the highest interpretive level of the instrument, and traditionally, the premise behind multidimensional inventories such as the PAI has been that the *combination* of information provided by the multiple scales is greater than any of its parts. The following sections discuss some of the major diagnostic classes of mental disorder and aspects of the PAI profile configuration that are useful for assigning such diagnoses. The sections discuss hypotheses drawn from three primary sources of information: (a) mean profiles; (b) actuarial functions; and (c) configural decision rules. For example, with respect to mean profiles, the PAI manual presents the average profiles derived from 24 different groups isolated on the basis of a particular diagnosis. The following sections describe these profiles and, where available, present similar information from other studies. However, mean diagnostic profiles are limited in the context of interpreting the PAI, because they do not represent a "prototypic" profile for a diagnosis; rather, they present the "lowest common denominator" for the diagnosis. Because of the extensive comorbidity among emotional disorders and variations in diagnostic practice among clinicians, the resulting mean profile for a given diagnosis may not fully capture the elements of the PAI that most reflect that disorder. Thus, the mean profile is only a beginning point in understanding the relationship between diagnoses and profile configurations.

Various analyses have also been conducted to identify actuarial decision rules for diagnostic assignment. In one example of such efforts, LOGIT analyses (Finney, 1971) were performed to construct models of diagnostic decisions provided by clinicians on patients who completed the PAI. These LOGIT functions were incorporated into the PAI Software System (Morey, 1991) in an attempt to realize the promise of computerized actuarial interpretation, and these functions are discussed in the sections of this chapter where such analyses have been performed. In these functions, the probability that a person carries the given diagnosis is estimated by solving the function provided and including that value in the following formula:

$$\text{Probability of diagnosis} = \frac{\exp[2(x_{dx}-5)]}{1+\exp[2(x_{dx}-5)]}$$

where x_{dx} is the result of the function described for the diagnosis and exp is the exponential of the bracketed expression. However, only diagnoses with adequate numbers of respondents (at least five for each predictor variable) were investigated using LOGIT analyses, and the calculations are sufficiently complex to hinder use of such functions in routine clinical contexts other than their incorporation into the interpretation software. Nonetheless, the composition of such functions is often informative in illustrating important points about the diagnosis and its PAI profile. One important aspect of these functions is that they involve contrasts between a particular diagnostic group and the clinical respondents as a whole (rather than comparing the group to normal controls). Thus, the parameters of these functions can be useful guides to discriminating among different clinical groups, facilitating the discriminant validity of any resulting diagnoses.

Finally, *DSM*-based configural rules also have been developed for a number of the *DSM-IV* (APA, 1994) diagnostic categories; these rules were designed to match the *DSM-IV* criteria with corresponding constructs on the PAI and also were incorporated into the interpretation software. The primary scales used in these rules are described in the text and summarized in tables for each of the following major diagnostic categories. It should be recognized that these decision rules were based on trends in the standardization samples of the PAI, and there is a clear need for cross-validational research. However, these rules are in keeping with the nature of the symptomatology specified in the *DSM-IV* and, as such, they provide a useful starting point in identifying particular disorders.

Depression and Related Disorders

In thinking about depression, the obvious place to begin diagnostic consideration is the *DEP* scale, which is described in detail in chapter 2. A diagnosis of depression in the absence of some elevation on *DEP* is unlikely, unless defensiveness is distorting the profile. However, there are a number of different disorders in which depression is a core element, and examination of profile configurations can help to sort out these different diagnostic possibilities. For example, Figure 6-1 presents the mean profiles (originally presented in the *PAI Professional Manual* [Morey, 1991]) for three disorders in which depressed affect is prominent: Adjustment Disorder, Dysthymic Disorder, and Major Depressive Disorder. The figure demonstrates that the mean profiles for the three disorders are similarly shaped, but there are interesting configural differences between them. The following paragraphs offer suggestions for the identification of these three diagnostic groups.

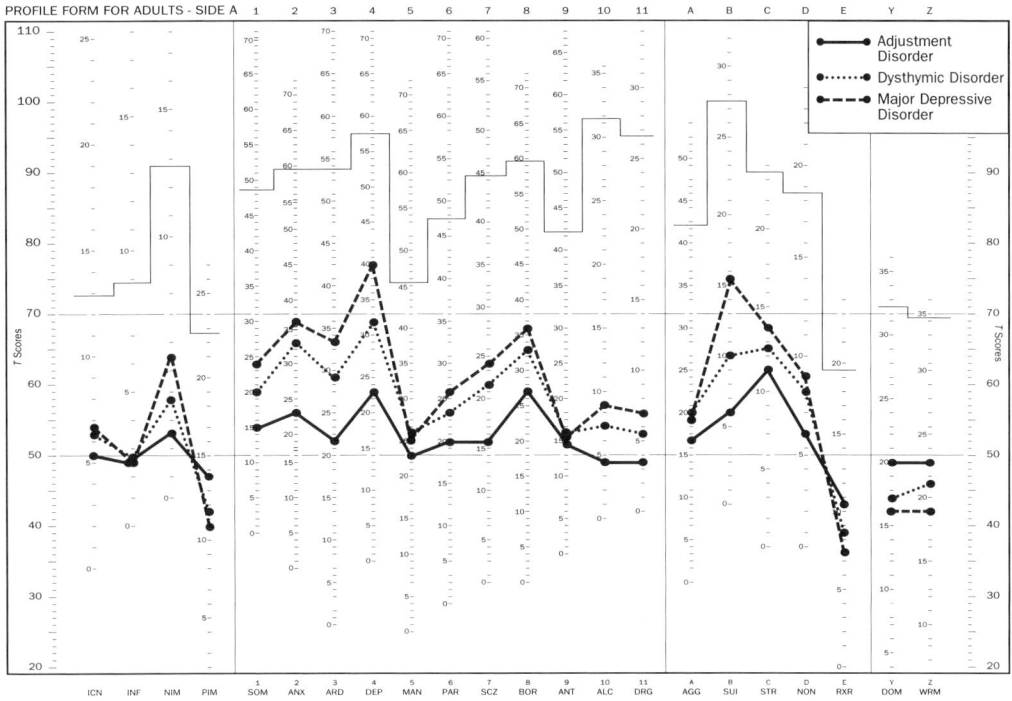

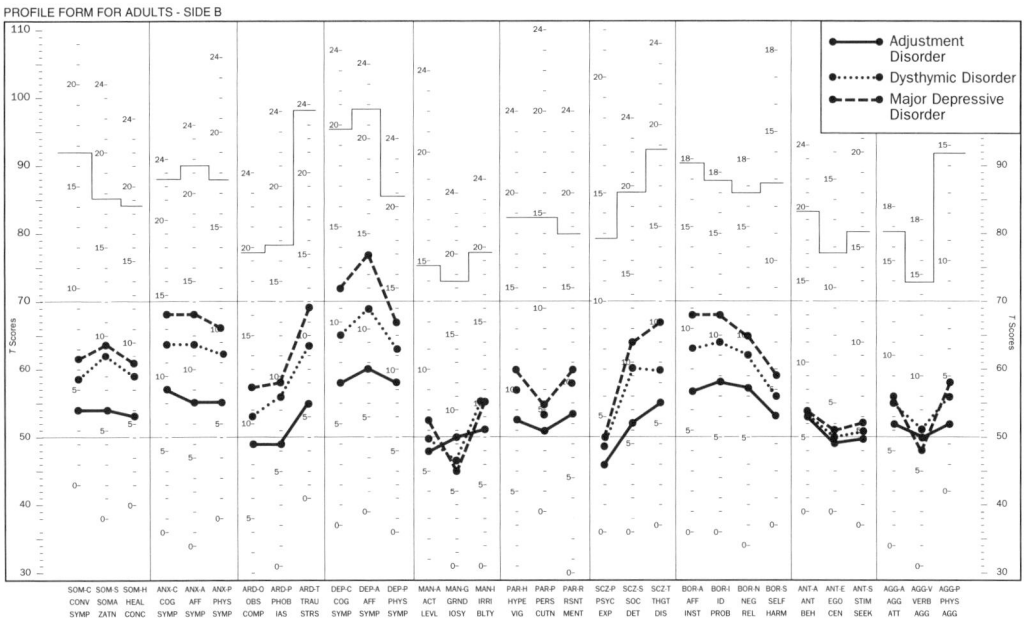

Figure 6-1. Mean profiles for Adjustment Disorder, Dysthymic Disorder, and Major Depressive Disorder samples on the PAI (Morey, 1991).

Adjustment Disorder

The cardinal feature of an Adjustment Disorder is the development of clinical symptoms (typically involving neurotic spectrum features of depression and/or anxiety) in response to some psychosocial stressor or stressors. On the PAI, the adjustment reaction profile presented in Figure 6-1 demonstrates some elevation on the "neurotic" scales, including *DEP*, yet the greatest single elevation on the profile is the *STR* scale. This comparison of *STR* to the clinical scales is a useful means to explore the possibility of an adjustment disorder. If the primary problem that the person seems to be identifying involves aspects of his or her environment (represented by *STR* elevations), this suggests that the respondent's primary concerns are external and, perhaps, crisis related; the lack of suppression on *MAN-G* supports the conclusion that self-esteem has not suffered in the face of these environmental events.

One distinguishing feature of Adjustment Disorders is that they are acute in nature; the *DSM-IV* specifies that symptomatology begins within 3 months of the onset of the stressor and lasts no longer than 6 months after the stressor or its consequences have ceased. In contrast to Adjustment Disorders, Posttraumatic Stress Disorder can have a delayed onset and a far more enduring course. Adjustment Disorders can have elevations on *ARD-T* if the recent stressor was extremely severe. However, Adjustment Disorders can develop in response to a wide array of stressors, and it is more typical that *STR* is elevated to a greater extent than *ARD-T* in this diagnostic group. Also, posttraumatic stress conditions have a particular constellation of features (described in a later section), whereas the psychological sequelae of Adjustment Disorders are typically limited to the first four clinical scales: *SOM*, *ANX*, *ARD*, and *DEP*.

The *DSM-IV* lists a variety of subtypes of adjustment disorder, subdivided according to the symptomatic reactions to the stressors experienced. The primary subtypes include the following:

Adjustment Disorder With Depressed Mood, used when the predominant manifestations are unhappiness, tearfulness, or feelings of hopelessness. Primary PAI indicators would include moderate elevations on *DEP-A* and *DEP-C*.

Adjustment Disorder With Anxiety, used when symptoms such as nervousness, worry, or fearfulness are predominant. On the PAI, such features would be indicated by moderate *ANX-A* and *ANX-C* elevations.

Adjustment Disorder With Disturbance of Conduct, where features involving violations of norms and rules, or of the rights of others, are seen. Elevations on *ANT-A* and *AGG-P* would be expected to accompany such behaviors.

The *DSM-III-R* listed an additional category where the primary symptomatic reactions to the stressors involved physical complaints; this pattern has been relegated to a residual ("Unspecified") category in *DSM-IV*. If observed, the PAI equivalent of such features would be most likely to involve *SOM-S*. However, if some repression of psychological involvement with the stressors is occurring, *ANX-P* and/or *DEP-P* also might display moderate elevations in this constellation.

Dysthymic Disorder

The hallmark feature of Dysthymic Disorder is a chronically depressed mood occurring most days over a 2-year period. It can be distinguished from Major Depressive Disorder by a relatively milder severity of symptomatology, the stability and chronicity of its course, and by its early and insidious onset (often in adolescence, or even in childhood). Because of the centrality of depressed mood and its chronic nature (rather than being a reaction to external events), *DEP* plays a more prominent role than *STR* in identifying dysthymia as compared with adjustment disorders. This can be seen from the mean profile for Dysthymic Disorder in Figure 6-1; the *DEP* scale (as well as the neurotic level scales such as *ANX*, *ARD*, and *SOM*) are all at elevations comparable to or beyond that of *STR*. Also, *SUI* has begun to elevate, as the issues are beginning to become more internal than external in focus.

Although depressed mood is central in Dysthymic Disorder, this group does not typically meet the full criteria for Major Depressive Disorder. Indeed, the dysthymia must be present for 2 years in the absence of meeting the Major Depressive Disorder criteria in order for the diagnosis to be assigned. Most typically, the physiological features of depression are the symptoms absent in dysthymia; because the depressed mood is central to the disorder, *DEP-A* is invariably elevated. Thus, a difference between *DEP-A* and *DEP-P*, with the former 10*T* or more above the latter, is often an indicator of Dysthymic Disorder.

Major Depressive Disorder

The diagnosis of Major Depressive Disorder reflects a constellation of depressed mood, vegetative signs and symptoms, and low self-esteem and helplessness. This disorder is one of the more common psychological conditions, with lifetime prevalence rates estimated from 10% to 20% of the general population. It is a serious emotional condition; up to 15% of patients with severe depression commit suicide, and it is also associated with dramatically increased death rates among older individuals. The seriousness of the mental state is reflected in the major depression profile in Figure 6-1, which displays an overall elevation higher than that of either of the previously mentioned disorders. The profile is character-ized by marked elevations on *DEP* and *SUI*; these two scales emerge consistent with the greater prominence of depressive symptoms over the more general neu-rosis and personality features typical of the lower grade, more chronic dysthymic condition. Also noted with the Major Depressive Disorder diagnosis is greater involvement of social withdrawal and greater indifference (*SCZ-S*) and cognitive inefficiency (*SCZ-T*) than is found in the milder conditions.

The LOGIT function for the diagnosis of Major Depressive Disorder (as con-trasted with other clinical categories) reveals empirical confirmation of many of these indicators. This function (presented primarily for illustration purposes, rather than for routine clinical use) is as follows:

$$.016(DEP\text{-}A) + .011(DEP\text{-}P) + .007(SUI) + .002(DEP\text{-}C) - .015(MAN\text{-}G) + 2.564$$

This function highlights the central role of the aforementioned scales in arriving at the diagnosis of Major Depressive Disorder. The weight for *DEP-C* is relatively low primarily because of that scale's high correlation with *DEP-A*, sug-gesting that the two scales contribute considerable overlapping information in the identification of depression. However, the relatively large negative loading of *MAN-G* demonstrates that low scores on this scale contribute important diagnos-tic information independent of scores on any of the *DEP* subscales. Finally, the large constant at the end of the function serves as a reminder that this is a high base-rate diagnosis, and the odds that any given patient has a diagnosis of Major Depressive Disorder are relatively high.

The profile distinctions between Adjustment Disorders and Dysthymic Disor-ders that were made earlier also can help to distinguish between endogenous and exogenous forms of depression. Differences may be found in the nature of the symptomatology and also search for evidence of marked external stressors. In endogenous depression, one often finds a preponderance of vegetative signs of depression, including sleep and appetite problems, lack of energy, and apathy and indifference. Telltale features here would involve marked elevations on *DEP-P* (with *T* scores at least equal to, if not higher than, the full *DEP* score) and the sup-pression of *MAN-A*, with a *T*-score here expected to be below 40*T*. For exogenous depression, indicators of external stressors should predominate. For example, elevations on *STR* or *ARD-T*, or both, would be indicators. It is worth noting that global elevations on these two scales are very common among individuals pre-senting for treatment. As such, the focus should be on the relative elevation of these scales, relative to the full *DEP* *T*-score. In exogenous depression it would be expected that these scores would be at least as high as *DEP*.

Table 6-1
Summary of Key PAI Diagnostic Indicators for Depressive Disorders

Diagnostic consideration	Elevation indicators	Suppression indicators
Adjustment Disorder	*STR* and/or *ARD-T* > 60*T* Check *SOM, ANX, DEP* for nature of symptoms	Full clinical scales < 70*T*
Dysthymic Disorder	*DEP-A, DEP-C* > 70*T* *BOR* > 65*T* with *BOR-A* predominant	*DEP-P* < 70*T* *SCZ-T* < 70*T*
Major Depressive Disorder	*DEP-A, DEP-P, DEP-C, SUI* all typically > 70*T* *SCZ-T, SCZ-S* often elevated in severe depression	*MAN-G* < 45*T* *MAN-A* often low, can be moderately elevated with agitation

Mean profiles for two additional relevant samples are presented in Figure 6-2: a sample of 47 women patients with "primary affective disorder" (Major Depressive Disorder or Dysthymic Disorder) reported by Cherepon and Prinzhorn (1994) and a sample of 28 women patients in treatment for depression who had Beck Depression Inventory scores above 14 and MMPI-2 Scale 2 scores above 64*T* (Gaies, 1993). The profiles from these two studies are quite similar and reflect the mixed composition of the sample, as both studies apparently included patients with Major Depressive Disorder as well as patients with Dysthymic Disorder. However, the configural similarities of these profiles to those presented in Figure 6-1 reveals that the respondents were clearly demonstrating complaints within the affective realm.

Anxiety Disorders

Nearly all clinical disorders share anxiety as a feature, and the group of conditions known as "anxiety disorders" span such diverse conditions as panic attacks, compulsive hand washing, and posttraumatic reactions to intense life stress. At the level of individual scales, *ANX* and *ARD* (described in detail in chapter 2) both provide critical information about these conditions. *ANX* is generally a nonspecific, global measure of anxiety that, as is the case with the construct in question, could be prominent in a number of different clinical conditions. *ARD*, on the other hand, presents behavioral information that is more closely tied to specific anxiety conditions. The following paragraphs provide suggestions for using these and other scales in identifying particular anxiety-related conditions.

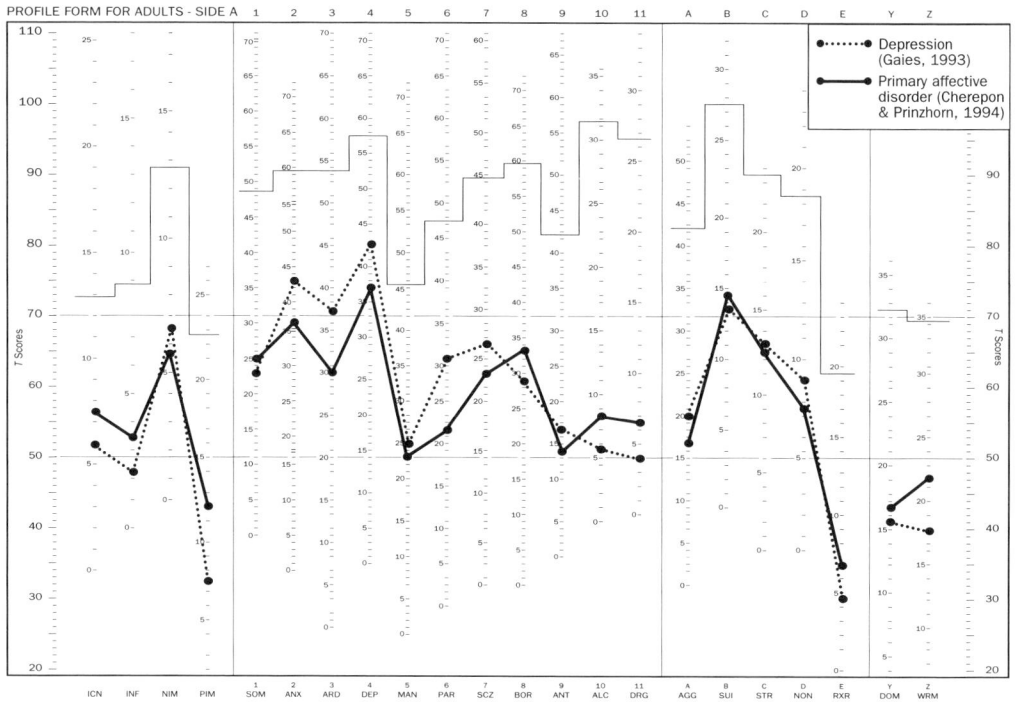

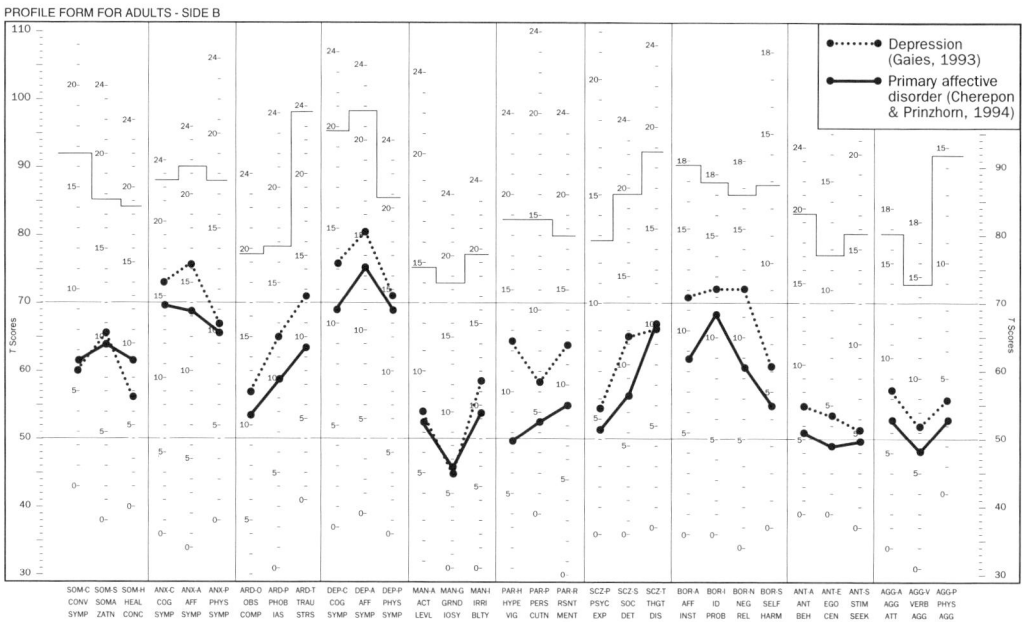

Figure 6-2. Mean PAI profiles for depression and primary affective disorder samples.

Phobias

The essential characteristic of a phobia is an intense and persisting fear of clearly identifiable objects or situations, or both. The individual generally recognizes that the fear is excessive relative to the actual threat, although this recognition does little to circumvent his or her anxiety. The fear will generally appear immediately on exposure to the situation, or it can emerge in anticipation of such an encounter; such fear can be sufficient to precipitate a panic attack in severe cases. In order to be a diagnosable condition, the fear and associated avoidance behaviors must interfere with functioning or cause marked distress.

The *DSM-IV* lists a variety of types of phobias, subdivided according to the particular objects or situations that precipitate the anxiety. Two major subtypes include the following:

Specific Phobia

This disorder (known as "Simple Phobia" in *DSM-III*) involves marked anxiety reactions to circumscribed objects or situations. Among the most common of these phobias are those involving animals (e.g., snakes, insects), natural environment (e.g., storms, heights), blood/injection/injuries (often accompanied by fainting), or situations (e.g., enclosed spaces, flying, public transportation). Obviously, the first place to look for elevations with these conditions is *ARD-P*, which inquires directly about some of these situations. However, in order to be a diagnosable condition, there must be sufficient impairment or distress associated with the situation or its avoidance, and other scales should be examined for indicators of this distress. The most typical elevations will involve *ANX-A*, a sign that the anxiety has become debilitating and somewhat generalized, and *ANX-C*, a sign that the fear has become somewhat of a ruminative preoccupation.

Social Phobia

The critical feature of this disorder is an intense and persistent fear of social or performance situations that might result in embarrassment or humiliation. Fears of certain social situations, such as public speaking, are quite common in the general population, but the anxiety must be interfering with social-role functioning or causing marked distress in order to receive the diagnosis. Nonetheless, this is perhaps the most prevalent phobia, with prevalence estimates ranging from 5% to 10% of the general population. Again, the starting point for identifying social phobias is with *ARD-P*, which inquires directly about such anxieties. However, other sources of information about social impairment are also useful. Low scores on *WRM* are often observed, demonstrating a lack of effectiveness in social situations; *DOM* also is generally low, because serving in a leadership role subjects an individual to a great deal of public scrutiny. As with the specific phobias, signs of impairment and distress are likely to appear on *ANX-A* and *ANX-C*. The *DSM-IV* includes an additional specifier of a "Generalized" form of social phobia, where the fears are related to most forms of social interactions. Such persons are particularly likely to show deficits in social skills and to have resulting social and occupational impairments. In addition to the features noted above, this more generalized form may be expected to show elevations on *SCZ-S*, documenting the lack of interpersonal skills, accompanied by *ANX-A*, showing that the interpersonal withdrawal is due more to anxiety than to a lack of interest in relationships.

Panic Disorder

The defining feature of this disorder is the presence of recurrent panic attacks not tied to some situational trigger. A panic attack is a discrete period of very intense fear with a variety of autonomic nervous system features, such as heart palpitations, sweating, chest pain, dizziness, numbness or tingling, shortness of breath, and chills or hot flashes. Cognitive signs also may be present and typically involve fears of dying, losing control, or going crazy during the attack. Following the attacks, such individuals have persistent concerns about the implications of having another such attack and may show significant behavioral change in order to prevent or control such a possibility.

The features of the panic attacks are largely physiological in nature. Therefore, the *ANX-P* scale is particularly useful in identifying this condition, as it inquires directly about a number of panic symptoms; marked elevations on *ANX-P* are particularly suggestive of disorders with panic attacks. However, elevations on the other two subscales of *ANX* are also likely; *ANX-C* will elevate as the person begins to ruminate about the recurrence of panic attacks, whereas *ANX-A* will reflect the apprehension surrounding the unpredictability of their occurrence. *DEP* elevations also are common, as over half of individuals with Panic Disorder will experience a major depressive episode at some point in their lives. Some patients fear that the attacks may indicate the presence of an undiagnosed, life-threatening illness, such as a heart condition or a seizure disorder. These beliefs often will lead to elevations on *SOM-H*, but not necessarily on *SOM-S* or *SOM-C*, as the panic symptoms are not directly consistent with the physical complaints reflected on those scales.

Panic Disorder can often lead to generalized avoidance behaviors known as agoraphobia. The *DSM-IV* outlines a subtype known as Panic Disorder with Agoraphobia. The agoraphobia involves anxiety about being in places or situations from which escape might be difficult or where help may not be available should the person experience a panic attack. This results in a pervasive avoidance of any place in which the person does not feel safe, and, in its most extreme form, the person will not leave his or her home, and even then may refuse to remain home alone. The presence of agoraphobic features adds a number of elements to the PAI profile, in addition to those described earlier for panic disorder. First, *ARD-P* is typically highly elevated, because the person is fearful of a wide array of situations. Also, the person is extremely apprehensive about novelty and unpredictability in life, and, as such, tends to obtain scores on *ANT-S* that are considerably below the mean. Finally, such people often rely heavily on companions to help them deal with feared situations. The agoraphobic's dependence on such companions is reflected in low *DOM* scores, with *WRM* scores more likely to be in the average-to-high-average range.

Obsessive-Compulsive Disorder

The Axis I diagnosis of Obsessive-Compulsive Disorder is characterized by recurrent or intrusive thoughts, impulses, images, and behaviors that are time consuming or a source of distress for the individual, or both. By definition, the person realizes (or has realized at some point) that the obsessions and/or compulsions are excessive, inappropriate, or unreasonable, although the level of insight varies. Impairments can be identified in many areas; the obsessions can interfere with cognitive tasks, and the disorder can lead to avoidance of situations that provoke the intrusive thoughts or compulsive behaviors. For example, a person with obsessions about germs will avoid public restrooms or shaking hands with strangers.

The *ARD-O* scale is the beginning point for an investigation of this diagnosis, as many of the questions on this scale inquire directly about obsessions and compulsions. Because the disorder is generally a source of marked distress, the *ANX* scale is typically elevated as well. Among the *ANX* subscales, *ANX-C* is the most characteristic of the disorder, as it captures the rumination and uneasiness of the obsessional individual. Other elevations may be seen as a function of some of the problems often associated with this disorder. *SOM* elevations may be obtained, as obsessive-compulsive individuals often have hypochondriacal concerns. Because patients with this diagnosis often have overwhelming guilt and sleep disturbances, *DEP* elevations are fairly common as well.

Posttraumatic Stress Disorder

This disorder (abbreviated PTSD) involves characteristic symptoms that sometimes emerge following the experience of an extreme traumatic stressor that leaves the person intensely afraid, horrified, or helpless. Such events might include military combat, violent personal assaults, severe automobile accidents, or witnessing an event that involves death or injury to another person. The symptoms typically begin within 3 months of the trauma, although there may be a delay of months or even years before symptoms appear. It appears that the severity, duration, and proximity of the patient's exposure to the trauma play the largest role in the development of the disorder and in the severity of the resulting symptomatology.

The mean profile of a group of patients diagnosed with PTSD (originally presented in the *PAI Professional Manual* [Morey, 1991]) is presented in Figure 6-3. As would be expected, the most striking aspect of the profile involves the marked elevation on *ARD-T*, which makes direct inquires about the existence of traumatic stressors. Although many clinical groups demonstrate *ARD-T* scores above 70*T*, *PTSD* patients will typically score at least 80*T* on this scale, and elevations above 90*T* are not uncommon in this group. However, the diagnosis of PTSD should not be based solely on an *ARD-T* elevation; there are a number of other features of the profile in Figure 6-3 that are consistent with the characteristic symptomatology of PTSD. For example, the *DEP* scale reflects a variety of symptoms associated with PTSD. Individuals with PTSD often describe painful guilt feelings associated with the experience, leading to *DEP-C* elevations. Also, recurrent distressing dreams of the event are diagnostic, leading to sleep disturbance and subsequent *DEP-P* elevations. Finally, diminished interest in significant activities are associated with elevated *DEP-A* scores.

Figure 6-3 also includes the mean profile for 44 women psychiatric patients who reported a history of childhood abuse (physical or sexual), adapted from a study by Cherepon and Prinzhorn (1994). This profile is quite similar to the one obtained by Morey (1991), with a few interesting differences. In particular, the Cherepon and Prinzhorn profile displays a greater elevation on the *SUI* scale, and *WRM* is greater than *DOM* (unlike the profile from Morey). These differences may suggest differences in the manifestation of PTSD related to gender; all of the Cherepon and Prinzhorn respondents were women, whereas many of the patients obtained by Morey (1991) were male veterans with combat-related PTSD. Nonetheless, the similarities between the profiles obtained from these two very different samples are striking.

A variety of other features of the PTSD syndrome are also directly reflected in PAI scales. *DSM-IV* symptoms of PTSD include (a) physiological anxiety reactivity, reflected on *ANX-P*; (b) feelings of detachment or estrangement from others, manifest on *SCZ-S* and low *WRM*; (c) hypervigilance, evidenced in *PAR-H* elevations; and (d) irritability, which can be gauged using *MAN-I*. Difficulty in concentration and hazy recall surrounding the event often lead to prominent *SCZ-T* elevations, as seen in Figure 6-3, and, at the full scale level, *SCZ* elevations are far more likely

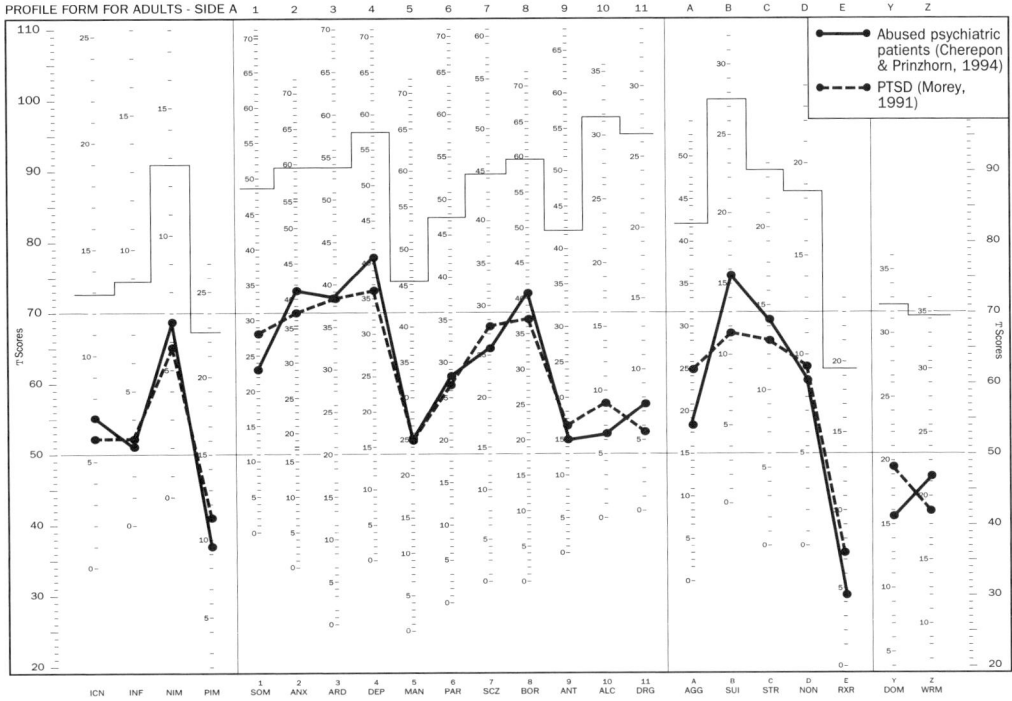

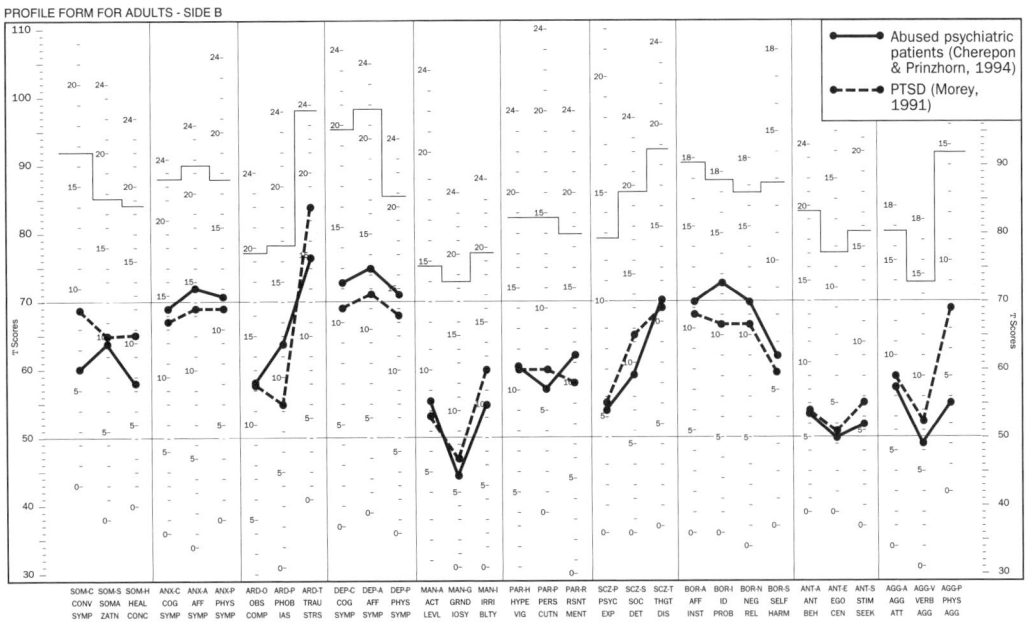

Figure 6-3. Mean PAI profiles for psychiatric patients reporting childhood abuse and patients diagnosed with PTSD.

to be seen in PTSD than in any other anxiety disorder. Finally, outbursts of anger are also diagnostic, and the V-shaped pattern on the *AGG* subscales (i.e., *AGG-A* and *AGG-P* elevated and *AGG-V* low) shown in Figure 6-3 reflects both the underlying anger and the tendency for it to be expressed as "outbursts" (i.e., anger is expressed suddenly and explosively).

The LOGIT function for the diagnosis of PTSD (as contrasted with other clinical categories) provides additional support for many of these observations. This function (presented primarily for illustration purposes, rather than for routine clinical use) included the following weights for PAI variables:

$$.051(ARD\text{-}T) + .001(ANX\text{-}P) + .001(DEP\text{-}P) + .006(SCZ\text{-}T) - .010(BOR\text{-}A) + .245$$

This function highlights the central role of the previously mentioned scales in arriving at the diagnosis of PTSD, particularly the central role of *ARD-T*. The inclusion of the physiological features of depression and anxiety and the cognitive inefficiency reflected in *SCZ-T* demonstrate unique contributions beyond their association with *ARD-T*. The negative weighting of *BOR-A* shows it to be a suppressor variable, as the scale itself tends to be elevated in individuals with PTSD, as seen in Figure 6-3. However, the finding of suppression suggests that many individuals display PTSD-like symptoms associated with personality pathology, and that obtaining the PTSD constellation of features in the absence of such pathology is particularly informative to the diagnosis.

Generalized Anxiety Disorder

The defining feature of this disorder is excessive anxiety and worry that is persistent, is generalized across situations, and lasts for at least 6 months. The diagnosis is somewhat of a residual category, as anxiety of a more specific nature (e.g., phobias, posttraumatic stress, or obsessions) results in the corresponding diagnosis; Generalized Anxiety Disorder is only to be used if a person is anxious, but does not meet criteria for such specific disorders. Despite this exclusion criterion, the disorder is apparently fairly common, with a lifetime prevalence of roughly 5% in the community.

Because the disorder involves rather nonspecific anxiety, the *ANX* scale is central in establishing the Generalized Anxiety Disorder diagnosis, as it is a measure of this type of anxiety. In particular, the *ANX-A* subscale captures the free-floating nervousness and *ANX-C* taps the apprehensive expectation that characterize this disorder. As an illustration, Figure 6-4 presents the profile of a group of 28 patients diagnosed with Generalized Anxiety Disorder; these patients were a subset of a group diagnosed with various anxiety disorders that was originally presented in

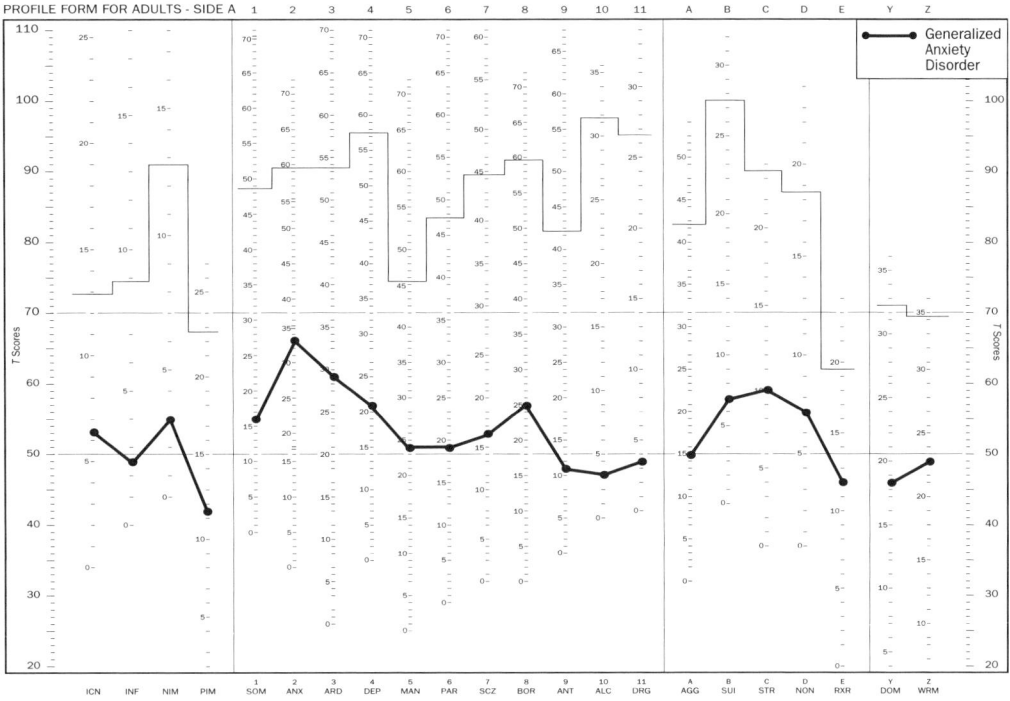

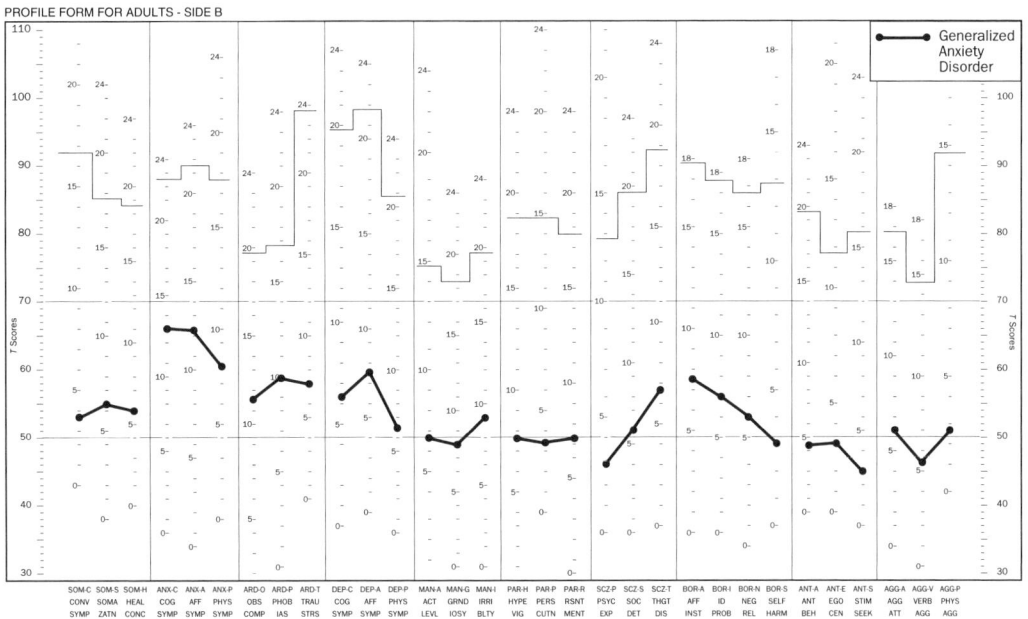

Figure 6-4. Mean PAI profile for patients with Generalized Anxiety Disorder (Morey, 1991).

Table 6-2
Summary of Key PAI Diagnostic Indicators for Anxiety Disorders

Diagnostic consideration	Elevation indicators	Suppression indicators
Specific Phobia	*ARD-P* *ANX-C* and/or *ANX-A*	
Social Phobia	*ARD-P* *ANX* *SCZ-S* if "Generalized"	*WRM* < 45*T* *DOM* < 45*T*
Obsessive-Compulsive Disorder	*ARD-O* *ANX*, particularly *ANX-C* *DEP* often elevated *SOM-H* often elevated	*BOR-S*
Posttraumatic Stress Disorder	*ARD-T*, typically > 80*T* *ANX*, particularly *ANX-P* *DEP*, all *DEP* subscales *SCZ-T, SCZ-S* *MAN-I* *PAR-H* *AGG-P*	*BOR-A* at least 10*T* < *ARD-T*
Generalized Anxiety Disorder	*ANX*, particularly *ANX-A*	*ARD* < *ANX* *SCZ* at least 10*T* < *ANX-A*
Panic Disorder	*ANX*, particularly *ANX-P* *DEP* often elevated	*ANT-S* < 50*T* *SOM-S, SOM-C* < *ANX-P*
Panic Disorder with Agoraphobia	*ARD-P* *ANX*, particularly *ANX-A*	*ANT-S* < 45*T* *DOM* < 45*T*

the *PAI Professional Manual* (Morey, 1991). This figure highlights the prominence of *ANX* relative to other scales when this disorder is present. Although the Generalized Anxiety Disorder profile, in general, is not characterized by marked elevations, there are other features incorporated into the *DSM-IV* diagnostic criteria that might be elevated in particular patients. Among these are (a) sleep disturbances and low energy levels that would manifest in the form of *DEP-P* elevations; (b) irritability, evidenced on *MAN-I*; and (c) difficulty concentrating that might take the form of a moderate *SCZ-T* elevation (i.e., approximately 60*T*).

Somatoform Disorders

The common characteristic of the group of conditions known as Somatoform Disorders is the presence of physical symptoms that suggest some type of medical problem but which are not fully explained by any diagnosable medical condition. The physical symptoms are a significant source of distress and are not intentional or under voluntary control (i.e., they are not malingered physical symptoms). The disorders are often encountered in general medical settings as well as mental health settings.

At the outset, it should be noted that no self-report test can adequately distinguish between "functional" and "organic" foundations of somatic complaints; such distinctions, themselves, may have little meaning. What instruments such as the PAI can do is present a picture of the role of somatic complaints in the overall psychological makeup of the individual. In any instance where somatic concerns are a prominent part of the clinical picture, a complete medical evaluation is far preferable to a personality test in ruling out various organic bases for the conditions. Such a ruling-out process is inherent in the diagnostic criteria for Somatoform Disorders: for example, "After appropriate investigation, the symptoms cannot be fully explained by a known general medical condition or the direct effects of a substance" (*DSM-IV*, p. 451). Any diagnostic guidelines for the PAI presented in the following sections are predicated on the assumption that such appropriate medical evaluation has been performed.

The overall discriminant validity of the PAI does make the test useful in assessing emotional conditions within a general medical population. For example, Osborne (1994) reported data on 105 general medical patients (73 women and 32 men) who were seen by internists within a multispecialty group practice. Patients completed the computer-administered version of the PAI without difficulty. Mean profiles for men and women medical patients are presented in Figure 6-5. This figure reveals that the *SOM* scale was generally the highest point of the PAI profile in this population, although the average score on this scale was below 70*T* (Osborne, 1994). In fact, with the exception of *SOM* and mild indications of negative affect among the women patients on *DEP* and *ANX*, no PAI scales obtained even a mean score of 60*T* in the medical patients. Such results support the conclusion that medical problems alone will not produce significant elevations on the PAI, and that, when such elevations are noted, they most likely reflect associated emotional issues rather than physical symptoms per se.

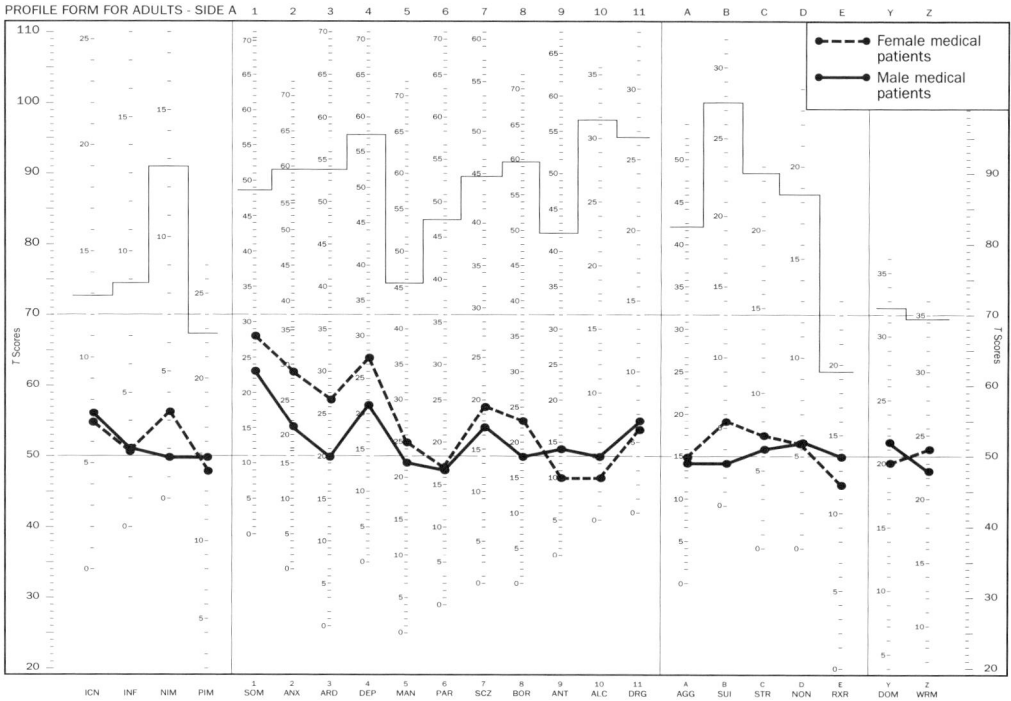

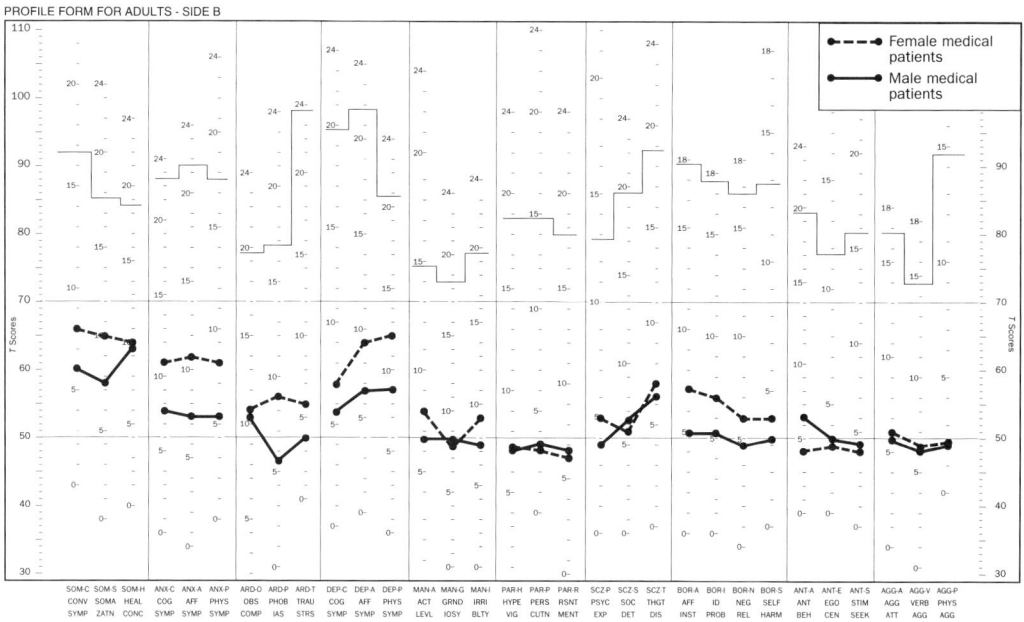

Figure 6-5. Mean PAI profiles for male and female general medical patients who completed the computer-administered version of the PAI (Osborn, 1994).

Conversion Disorder

The distinguishing feature of Conversion Disorders is the presence of symptoms or deficits that involve voluntary sensory or motor functioning and, hence, are suggestive of some neurological disorder. Motor deficits might include paralysis or localized weakness, loss of coordination, or inability to speak; sensory symptoms could include blindness, deafness, or loss of feeling or pain sensations. As with all Somatoform Disorders, these symptoms cannot be explained by any general medical conditions. Such features typically emerge during periods of conflict or stress and are thought to be psychological in origin, although they are not intentionally produced.

The characteristic sensory–motor disturbances in Conversion Disorders are directly addressed by the *SOM-C* scale. However, recall that *SOM-C* also will elevate with actual neurological disorders, and interpretation of elevations as indicating Conversion Disorder should be advanced only after such general medical disorders have been ruled out. There are a number of other features associated with Conversion Disorders that can be identified using the PAI scale configuration. For example, the feature known as *la belle indifference* involves a relative lack of concern or distress about the symptoms and their implications; such indifference might be reflected in a *DEP-A* score considerably below the level of health concerns indicated by *SOM-H*. A certain degree of dependency and adaptation to the "sick role" also may accompany conversion symptoms, resulting in low scores on *DOM* and moderate-to-high scores on *WRM*. Often such individuals tend to minimize both personal distress and interpersonal conflict; in addition to *WRM* scores that are generally above average, they tend to have low *AGG* scores and often are above average on *PIM*.

Somatization Disorder

The central characteristic of Somatization Disorders is the recurrence of multiple somatic complaints, with no known medical origin, over a period of several years. The complaints typically involve multiple organ systems, such as gastrointestinal, sexual–reproductive, sensory-motor, and chronic pain, and the description of the symptoms can be quite dramatic, but vague and lacking in specific factual information. The somatic complaints have an onset prior to age 30 and continue for several years, although no overt physical signs or structural abnormalities become apparent.

The items of the *SOM-S* scale directly tap the vague and diverse nature of somatic symptoms in Somatization Disorder, and, as such, the scale represents the starting point for establishing the diagnosis. Other associated features of the

Table 6-3
Summary of Key PAI Diagnostic Indicators
for Somatoform Disorders

Diagnostic consideration	Elevation indicators	Suppression indicators
Conversion Disorder	*SOM-C* *WRM > 50T* *PIM > 50T*	*DEP-A* at least 10*T* < *SOM-H* *DOM* < 45*T* *AGG* < 50*T*
Somatization Disorder	*SOM-S* *DEP-A* and/or *ANX-A* *BOR-N* and/or *NON*	

disorder also can be investigated from the profile configuration. Prominent depression and anxiety are common, and these affects, in particular, can lead to elevations on *DEP-A* and *ANX-A*. The somatic complaints often seem to play a functional role for the individual with this disorder, particularly in the interpersonal domain. For example, a patient may receive some secondary gain by controlling a spouse through repeated complaints of fatigue, illness, or malaise. However, the chronicity of this behavior invariably leads to conflict with and/or resentment by family or friends. Such a pattern can manifest in elevations on *BOR-N* or *NON*, or both.

Psychotic Disorders

The term *psychosis* involves a number of different aspects of mental status. In the *DSM* manual, the term is used primarily to refer to conditions that involve delusions, hallucinations, or grossly disorganized behavior. The term also has been used variously to describe gross distortions in reality testing, or even any severe impairment that severely interferes with life functioning. In the *DSM-IV*, the term refers to Schizophrenia and related conditions, such as Schizoaffective Disorder and Delusional Disorder. However, the following section also will discuss the diagnosis of Mania (although this is officially a mood disorder), because it is generally more difficult to distinguish Mania from Psychotic Disorders than it is to distinguish it from other mood disorders, such as depression.

Mania

A Manic Episode is distinguished by a distinct period of unusually elevated, expansive, or irritable mood. The mood can involve indiscriminate enthusiasm for interactions with others, but irritability is perhaps even more common, particularly when the person's wishes are thwarted. Inflated self-esteem also is typical, with grandiosity that can reach delusional proportions. The person will report heightened energy and activity, with decreased need for sleep and excessive planning and participation in multiple ventures. The thoughts and speech may race faster than can be successfully articulated. Unwarranted optimism, self-aggrandizement, and poor judgment often lead to unwise involvements in precarious situations involving spending money, sex, or physical danger.

These diagnostic features are represented on the *MAN* scale. The pressured speech, flight of ideas, and overinvolvement in activities lead to *MAN-A* elevations; the grandiosity, expansiveness, and unrealistic self-appraisal are captured by *MAN-G*; and the instability of mood and propensity for abrupt irritability when thwarted is manifest in *MAN-I* elevations. Other scales can provide confirmation and additional refinement of manic indications. The unwarranted optimism typical during a Manic Episode tends to suppress *DEP-C* such that it often is considerably below the mean of community respondents. The *DOM* scale often is elevated, although this does not necessarily indicate that the person is actually effective in controlling others; rather, it reflects a *belief* (probably unrealistic) that he or she is quite effective in a leadership role. The individual's interest in and uninhibited interactions with others means that *WRM* is usually at or above the mean. Lack of insight into the nature and severity of problems often leads *RXR* scores to be at or above 50T. Impulsivity, lack of inhibition, and poor judgment often result in elevations on *BOR-S* and *ANT-S*. Finally, individuals in a Manic Episode often feel that large forces are working to thwart their efforts toward greatness; hence, elevations on *PAR-P* are fairly common, although this sense of persecution does not seem to be accompanied by the bitterness characteristic of the more purely paranoid individual. As such, *PAR-R* tends to be considerably lower than *PAR-P*.

Individuals who have had one or more Manic Episodes are assigned a diagnosis of Bipolar I Disorder, regardless of whether or not they have ever experienced a depressive episode (although most of these individuals do). When an individual has recurrent depressive episodes with at least one "hypomanic" episode (similar to a full Manic Episode, but briefer in duration), the diagnosis of Bipolar II Disorder is assigned. In either instance, such individuals may present on the PAI with the unique combination of elevations on both *DEP* and *MAN*; generally, one of these elevations is caused primarily by historical experiences, although mixed-mood episodes can occur. It is unusual to find both *MAN* and *DEP* at 60T or above; when this pattern is obtained, particularly with *BOR-A* also elevated, the diagnosis of Bipolar Disorder should receive careful consideration.

As a final note, it should be recognized that many individuals in the midst of a severe, acute Manic Episode are not compliant with, or are too agitated for, psychological testing. In such instances when the examinee is too distracted or uncooperative in completing the full administration of the test, the examiner may find the 160-item short form of the PAI useful.

Schizophrenia

The diagnosis of Schizophrenia results from the presence of a number of diverse features that have persisted for a duration of at least 6 months. These features include positive symptoms that reflect an excess or distortion of normal functions, as well as negative symptoms that involve a reduction or loss of different functions. Other features central in establishing the diagnosis include grossly disorganized speech or behavior, or both.

The most prominent positive symptoms of Schizophrenia are delusions and hallucinations. These aspects are assessed by the *SCZ-P* subscale, although other scales are useful in supplementing *SCZ-P* to give a more precise picture of the specific symptoms involved. Delusions involve a distortion of inferential thinking that results in the misinterpretation of experiences and perceptions. The most common forms of delusion in Schizophrenia are persecutory delusions, where respondents believe that they are being followed, deceived, spied on, or harassed. Ideas of reference are often associated with such experiences, where individuals believe that certain events in the environment (e.g., comments on television, song lyrics, or newspaper stories) convey specific information for them. Such persecutory and referential beliefs result in elevations on *PAR-P*. Somatic delusions also can occur, (e.g., believing that someone has surreptitiously removed various internal organs). These delusions, when present, are most likely to appear in the form of *SOM-C* elevations. Hallucinations are typically auditory and are generally experienced as voices that are distinct from the person's own thoughts. Hallucinations in other sensory modalities can occur, although they are less common. Items inquiring about hallucinations appear solely on *SCZ-P*; a few highly unusual hallucinations are referenced in *NIM* items, but these experiences are not typical of schizophrenic symptoms.

The negative symptoms of Schizophrenia tend to be the most stable and unremitting feature of the disorder. Among these features, flattened affect is particularly common and refers to a restricted range of emotional expressiveness. Another prominent negative symptom is decreased productivity of speech and interaction with others. The combination of these features leads to impoverished relationships and poor rapport, behaviors that are ascertained with *SCZ-S* items. Other PAI scales also can be used to gauge the severity of negative symptoms. The social isolation leads to low scores on *WRM*. Avolition, which refers to deficits in initiating and persisting in goal-directed behaviors, can lead to low scores on *DOM* and *MAN-A*, scales which indicate a degree of initiative in interpersonal (*DOM*) and behavioral (*MAN-A*) realms. The diminution and emptiness of affect associated with schizophrenia can lead to scores on *BOR-A* that are low in relation to other aspects of the profile.

Disorganized thinking is another characteristic of Schizophrenia that does not fit neatly into the positive–negative symptoms distinction, yet it has been singled out by some (e.g., Bleuler, 1950, who coined the term *schizophrenia*) as perhaps the core defining feature of the disorder. The associations and speech of such individuals tend to drift off topic, with difficulties in focusing answers to questions and problems in the logical sequencing of ideas. In the extreme, the person may be incoherent or the thought process may be completely blocked, often experienced as if some external force was obstructing or removing thoughts from the person's head. The *SCZ-T* subscale includes items relevant to these experiences. Such individuals also may demonstrate idiosyncrasies in responding to PAI questions, with distorted inferences about the questions interfering with their ability to respond to the question as written. In such instances, the *INF* score may be elevated in a profile that otherwise appears to accurately capture the clinical picture.

The diagnosis of Schizophrenia has a variety of additional specifiers that refer to different patterns, courses, and phases of the disorder. Some of these specifiers and the PAI profile information relevant to their identification are described in the following sections.

Schizophrenia, Paranoid Type. The paranoid subtype is distinguished by the presence of prominent auditory hallucinations and/or paranoid delusions, with a relative preservation of cognitive functions and affective responsiveness. The delusions may be multiple, but they often are organized around some coherent theme. Relative to other subtypes, the paranoid schizophrenic displays deeper affect, most notably anxiety, but also anger and hostility. The psychotic features of this disorder would be expected to elevate *SCZ-P* relative to *SCZ-S* and *SCZ-T*, as well as all three subscales of *PAR*. During acute phases of the disorder, *ANX* elevations would be anticipated. Another possible elevation would involve *MAN-I*, to capture the haughtiness and superior manner that such individuals often display.

Schizophrenia, Disorganized Type. The disorganized subtype is characterized by a lack of goal orientation, flat and/or inappropriate affect, and disruptions in thought process and communication. Such a pattern would be expected to lead to marked elevations on *SCZ-T* as well as *SCZ-S*, with *SCZ-P* considerably lower than those subscales.

Schizophrenia, Catatonic Type. Catatonic schizophrenia is characterized by motor abnormalities, such as catatonic stupor, or by purposeless motor excitement and/or stereotyped movements. In either instance, such patients are not likely to complete the PAI.

Schizophrenia, Residual Type. The residual form of schizophrenia refers to the lingering features of the disorder that remain after the active psychotic symptoms have resolved. These features are predominantly negative symptoms, such as flat affect and poverty of interactions. Such features would be likely to result in *SCZ-S* elevations without accompanying elevations on *SCZ-P*. In addition, the *SCZ-S* elevation should occur in the absence of other noteworthy elevations on the PAI, such as on *DEP* or *ANX*, since these more neurotic spectrum features can lead to *SCZ-S* elevations. The impoverished affect characteristic of residual schizophrenia should result in low scores on these scales relative to *SCZ-S* scores.

Schizophrenia, Undifferentiated Type. This qualifier is added to the diagnosis if prominent negative symptoms are present during or between active phases of the disorder. As noted earlier, *SCZ-S* items are directly pertinent to these symptoms, and marked elevations (i.e., ≥ 80*T*) might merit this additional specification. Other PAI indicators would include low scores on *WRM*, *DOM*, and *MAN-A*, indicating a lack of interest and initiative in interpersonal (*WRM*, *DOM*) and behavioral (*MAN-A*) domains. Also, affective blunting may suppress scores on *BOR-A* relative to other aspects of the profile.

The mean profile of a group of patients diagnosed with Schizophrenia (originally presented in the *PAI Professional Manual* [Morey, 1991]) is presented in Figure 6-6. Unfortunately, this sample was small (32 patients) and the respondents were not in acute phases of the disorder; most were outpatients in a medication maintenance clinic at the time of assessment. Patients were excluded from the sample if their scores on any of the validity scales exceeded 2 standard deviations above the mean of the total clinical sample. As can be seen in the figure, the Schizophrenia group mean profile had no elevations that exceeded 70*T*; the *SCZ* and *PAR* scales were above 60*T*, as were all of the neurotic scales. This pattern should be considered to reflect the residual phase of the disorder, given the characteristics of the sample. The most significant aspect of the profile involves the elevation of the *SCZ* scale to a degree comparable to *DEP* and *ANX*; this is not typical of individuals with milder clinical conditions (e.g., see the Adjustment Disorder profile in Figure 6-1).

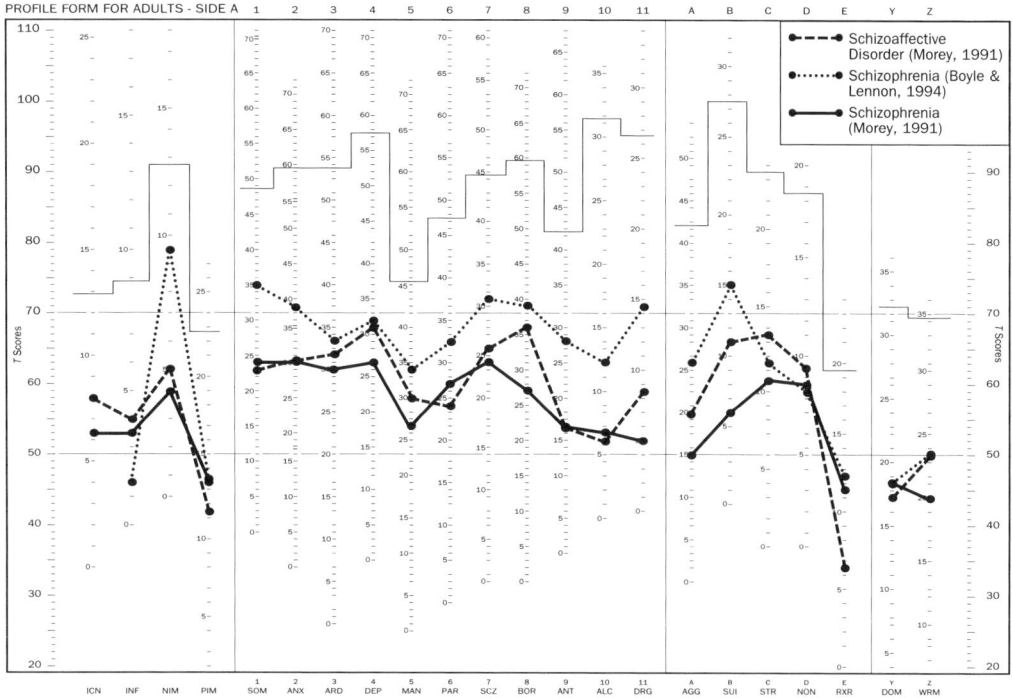

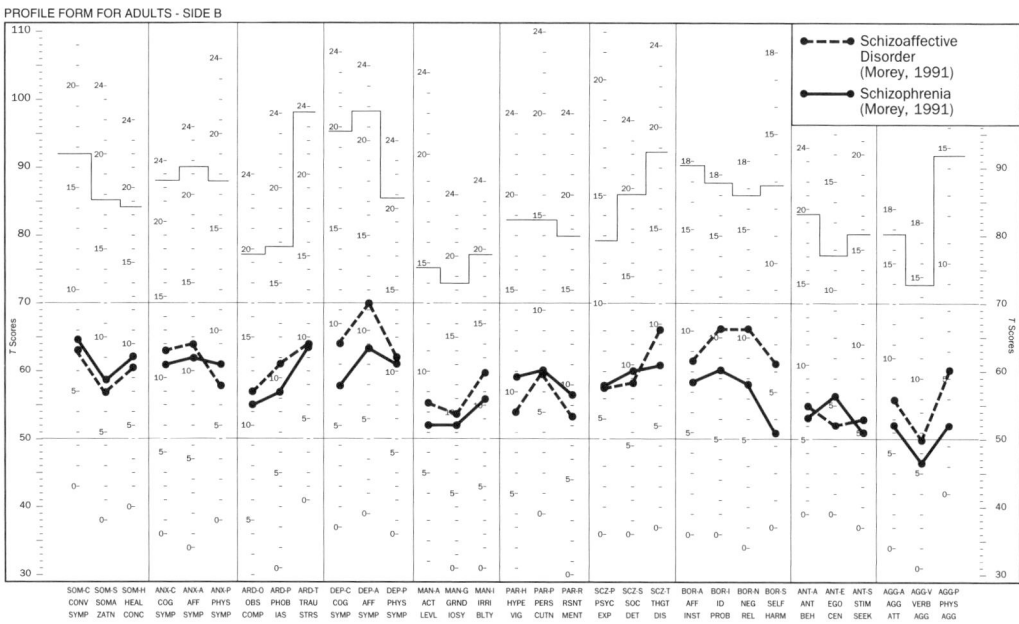

Figure 6-6. Mean PAI profiles for patients diagnosed with Schizoaffective Disorder and Schizophrenia. Boyle & Lennon (1994) did not score the ICN scale or report subscale scores.

Figure 6-6 also includes the mean full scale profile of a sample of 30 patients diagnosed as schizophrenic using *DSM-III-R* criteria, adapted from a study by Boyle and Lennon (1994). This profile demonstrates an elevation on *SCZ* that exceeds 70*T*, but it resembles the Morey (1991) profile in that the clinical scales show little differentiation. The stage of illness for these patients is not known, but such a profile could represent a mixture of patients in acute stages (i.e., elevations on *SCZ* and *PAR*) with patients in more residual stages (i.e., elevations on *DEP* and *ANX*).

Because of the limited nature of these schizophrenia samples, additional groups of patients were identified from the clinical standardization sample on the basis of three characteristics: presence of auditory hallucinations, presence of persecutory delusions, and current treatment with antipsychotic medications. These groups of patients (originally described in the *PAI Professional Manual* [Morey, 1991]) yielded the mean profiles displayed in Figure 6-7. All three of these groups tended to obtain scores on *SCZ* that were elevated relative to most other populations. The group experiencing auditory hallucinations displayed the most elevated profile, with mean scores above 70*T* on *DEP* and *ANX* as well as *SCZ*, and this sample was notably higher than other groups on the psychotic experiences (*SCZ-P*) and thought disorder (*SCZ-T*) indicators. The consistent elevations on each of the *ANX* subscales most likely supports the conclusion that these hallucinating patients were in an acute phase of the disorder; as the disorder shifts into a residual phase or is successfully treated, the *ANX* scale and its subscales appear to drop along with *SCZ-P*. The group with persecutory delusions demonstrated a similar profile configuration, but it was slightly more elevated on *PAR*; as seen in Figure 6-7, the primary source of this elevation was from the persecution subscale (*PAR-P*). Finally, the group receiving antipsychotic medication differed from the other groups on the more "positive symptoms" of Schizophrenia (e.g., psychotic experiences, paranoid beliefs), but not on the more "negative symptoms" (e.g., social detachment); interestingly, this is consistent with the established therapeutic profile of antipsychotic medication.

Figure 6-6 also presents the mean profile for a group of patients diagnosed with Schizoaffective Disorder. This disorder involves the co-occurrence of the active phase of Schizophrenia with a major depressive or manic episode. The profile for the schizoaffective group was somewhat more elevated than that of the schizophrenic group; this was probably a result of a more acute symptomatic picture, as the former were primary inpatients whereas the latter were primarily outpatients, but it may also have resulted from the greater number of symptoms (i.e., from two different disorders) required to meet the diagnosis. The highest clinical scale elevations for the schizoaffective group were *DEP*, *BOR*, and *SCZ*, suggesting that this

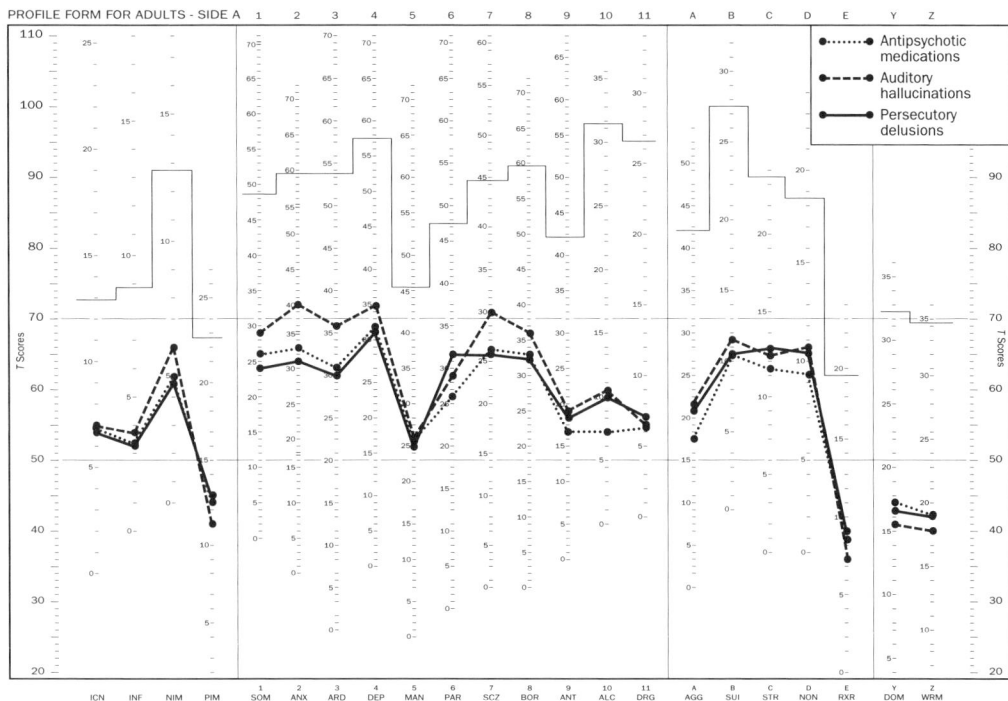

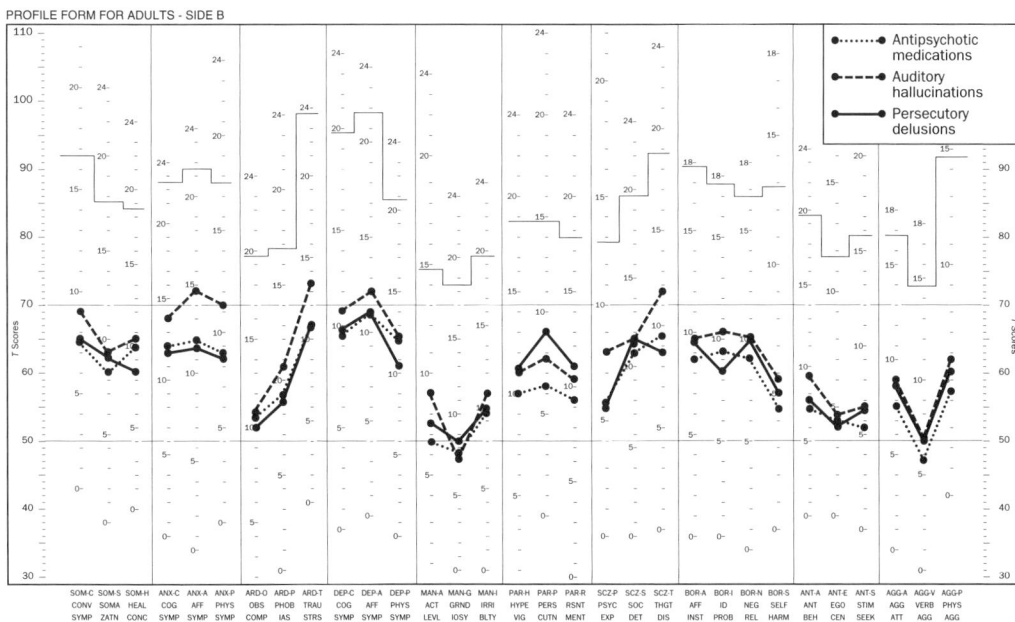

Figure 6-7. Mean PAI profiles for current antipsychotic medication, auditory hallucinations, and persecutory delusions samples (Morey, 1991).

Table 6-4
Summary of Key PAI Diagnostic Indicators for
Psychotic Spectrum Disorders

Diagnostic consideration	Elevation indicators	Suppression indicators
Bipolar Disorder	*MAN-G, MAN-A* *MAN-I* usually up, can vary *DEP-P* can be moderate *BOR-A* above average *ANT-S, DOM, PAR-P*	*DEP-C* *PAR-R* relative to *PAR-P*
Schizophrenia	*SCZ* (all three subscales) *ANX* during acute episodes *PAR-P* for Paranoid subtype If *MAN* and *DEP*, consider Schizoaffective	*WRM* *DOM* *MAN-A*
Delusional Disorder	*SCZ-P* with *PAR-P, MAN-G*, or *SOM-C*	*SCZ-T* relative to *SCZ-P*

group was displaying a wide array of symptoms consistent with the "mixed" diagnosis they received. *DEP* elevations are not uncommon among schizophrenics, and simultaneous elevations on *DEP* and *SCZ* should not automatically be interpreted as an indication of Schizoaffective Disorder. However, the joint elevation of *SCZ* and *MAN* (often with *DEP* also elevated) is rare and points with greater specificity to the possibility of a Schizoaffective Disorder diagnosis.

Delusional Disorder

The defining feature of the Delusional Disorder (formerly known as Paranoid Psychosis) is a relatively circumscribed, nonbizarre delusion, with relative intactness of functions unrelated to the delusional belief. The delusion can take many forms, including persecutory, somatic, jealous, grandiose, or erotomanic (where the person imagines that another person is in love with him or her). The nature of the delusion is distinguished from those typical of Schizophrenia in that it involves situations that could conceivably occur (e.g., being followed, infidelity).

On the PAI, the most likely markers of Delusional Disorder would involve some elevation on *SCZ-P*, accompanied by other scales that would give some indication of the nature of the preoccupation (e.g., *PAR-P* for persecutory beliefs, *MAN-G* for delusional grandiosity, or *SOM-C* or *SOM-H* for somatic delusions). To assign the diagnosis, it would be important that *SCZ-T* and *SCZ-S* be within normal limits, because this disorder does not involve impairments in affective responsivity or cognitive function. Although some distress may occur, depressive symptoms are typically mild; marked elevations on *DEP* should be rare and, when observed, would tend to be less enduring than the indicators of delusional beliefs.

Personality Disorders

The diagnosis of personality disorders, as a group, may be one of the most complicated tasks from the PAI protocol, because the disorders themselves tend to be ill-defined. The *DSM* definition refers to personality *traits* that are inflexible and maladaptive and that cause distress or impairment. In 1937, Allport identified 17,953 nonobsolete trait names in the unabridged Webster's dictionary, a number constituting 4.5% of the total English vocabulary (the number of words in Webster's has grown by about 12% since Allport's study, suggesting that a few additional traits have probably appeared). The PAI is bound to leave a few of these traits uncovered. In fact, of the 10 primary personality disorders defined in the *DSM-IV*, the PAI includes scales directly assessing only 2: Borderline Personality and Antisocial Personality. This decision was made for a number of reasons. First, the two disorders account for the majority of research on personality disorders; Borderline Personality, alone, accounts for over half of all studies on Axis II (Blashfield & McElroy, 1985). Second, the focus on discriminant validity in the construction of the PAI was at odds with the well documented lack of discriminant validity among the personality disorders; for example, individuals meeting criteria for only one personality disorder (as opposed to two or more) are a small minority of personality-disordered patients (Morey, 1988). Given such marked diagnostic overlap, the task of constructing conceptually independent scales is greatly hampered. Under such circumstances, it seemed more useful to focus on only those personality constructs that were empirically supported and clinically relevant (e.g., the interpersonal dimensions) and to use these constructs to supplement Axis II diagnosis.

The *DSM* approach to this area is most notably deficient in its efforts to provide a coherent definition of this class of phenomena. The *DSM-IV* goes beyond previous versions by specifying enduring difficulties in cognition, affectivity, interpersonal functioning, and/or impulse control, although these guidelines are described at a level of generality that would make them difficult to use clinically. Many investigators have a different view of what precisely constitutes Personality Disorder and how it differs from both Axis I disorders and normal personality. There is a need to spell out certain assumptions about the nature of these disorders; with each specified assumption, the concept will become more manageable and less ephemeral. The following sections provide some candidate concepts for defining personality disorder as a whole and suggest some PAI indicators that might be useful in identifying these concepts.

Manifestations of personality disorder are evident early in life. The DSM-IV notes that the manifestations of personality disorders are often recognized by adolescence or earlier, although it suggests that caution is warranted in using these diagnoses with children or adolescents. Relatively little is known about the developmental precursors of personality disorder. Although adult antisocial behaviors can be predicted with some success by behaviors such as aggressiveness and stealing in children as young as 6 to 9 years of age (Loeber & Dishion, 1983; Robins, 1966), other candidates for childhood markers of future personality disorder (e.g., shyness) seem to have little predictive value for later adjustment (Kagan & Moss, 1962; Parker & Asher, 1987). This suggests that scales such as *ANT-A*, *ANT-E*, and *AGG-P* are likely to reflect enduring traits and, when elevated, to suggest the possibility of personality disorder. However, PAI scales pointing to dependency, shyness, or withdrawal (e.g., low scores on *DOM* or *WRM*, or elevations on *ANX-P* or *SCZ-S*) should not automatically be assumed to reflect enduring characteristics. Such indicators can be considerably influenced by mood state, and, as such, concomitant elevations on *DEP* suggest that additional inquiry may be needed to establish the persistence of the withdrawal and dependency.

Manifestations of personality disorder are stable over time. The DSM description of Personality Disorder refers to enduring traits that are characteristic of long-term functioning. This assumption has been the focus of some debate, beginning in 1968 with Mischel's critique of trait psychology. One result of this debate has been the recognition that some "traits" are more stable over the lifespan than others; for certain traits, personality stability is evident well into older age (e.g., McCrae & Costa, 1984). If stability over time is a core feature of personality disorder, then the extreme manifestations of these traits should be particularly promising candidates for study (although probably not for treatment). Because the PAI scales tap most facets of these dimensions reasonably well (Costa & McCrae, 1991) the test should be useful in providing an assessment of these more enduring personality aspects. It should be noted that although the limited evidence confirms that certain personality disorder diagnoses, particularly Borderline Personality Disorder, are stable over time (McGlashan, 1983; Pope et al., 1983), it is not clear that this represents stability of traits. For example, McGlashan's (1986) work suggests that the prominent traits of the borderline personality tend to vary across the life span; the anger and impulsivity seem to diminish, whereas identity disturbances and relational deficits continue. This pattern suggests that *BOR-I* and *BOR-N* may be useful diagnostic features across the lifespan, but *BOR-A* and *BOR-S* elevations may be more characteristic of borderline individuals in their 20s than those in their 50s.

Manifestations of personality disorder are stable across different situations. In his controversial 1968 book, Mischel pointed out that much psychological research has not supported the contention that individual differences in behavior are very stable across different situations. As a result, Mischel and others have argued that the situation in which the person finds himself or herself may be a stronger determinant of behavior than internal personality dispositions. Although the person-situation controversy generated more heat than light, two important points of consensus have emerged (Epstein & O'Brien, 1985; Kenrick & Funder, 1988). First, the stability of personality across situations is most evident when one considers *aggregates* of behavior rather than single behavioral instances; our ability to predict behavior from trait information at a particular point in time is quite limited. In the personality disorders, where the need to make predictions concerning specific behaviors is often salient (e.g., immediate threat to self or others), this limitation has grave implications. The second point of consensus emerging from this literature is that the *interaction* effect between trait and situation is more likely to enhance our ability to predict specific behaviors than a single-minded focus on either traits or situations (Endler & Edwards, 1988). We need to address the question: What types of people perform what behaviors in what types of situations? As an example, we know that suicidal gestures are a hallmark feature of borderline personality (Morey & Ochoa, 1989), but this also seems to be the borderline criterion with the lowest prevalence. Recently, research has begun to focus on the situations most likely to interact with borderline personality features to bring about serious suicidal behaviors, identifying interpersonal rejection as a particularly sensitive situation for these people (Kullgren, 1985; Linehan, 1986). This would predict that people with *BOR* elevations will be at particular risk for suicidal behavior when scales indicative of interpersonal rejection (e.g., *NON*) also are elevated.

Personality disorders are largely ego-syntonic conditions. The early psychoanalytic writers assumed that personality disorders involve character traits that are an essential part of the personality, rather than symptoms that are experienced by the individual as alien to the personality. This distinction is of clear utility in distinguishing certain Axis I and Axis II disorders, such as the obsessive-compulsive disorders. However, because the key problems in personality disorder are experienced as a fundamental part of the personality rather than as a distressing symptom, this allows for limited insight into the nature of the person's difficulty. For example, the presenting complaint for many personality disorders is likely to involve marked depression, anxiety, or interpersonal conflict; it is rare that such people will complain of identity diffusion or lack of empathy. People with personality disorders are likely to present for treatment only during times of crisis, even though their core deficits are there much of the time. For such people, careful attention should be paid to indicators of character (e.g., *BOR*, *ANT*, or *PAR* elevations). These indicators can sometimes be overlooked in the context of extreme elevations on *DEP*, *ANX*, or *SUI* that are associated with the immediate crisis.

Personality disorders are largely interpersonal in nature. Over the past several decades, a number of writers have identified interpersonal behavior as an important focus for the study of personality and psychopathology (Adams, 1964; Horney, 1945; Kiesler, 1983; Leary, 1957; McLemore & Benjamin, 1979; Sullivan, 1953; Wiggins, 1982). One focus of such attention has concerned the utility of the interpersonal approach as a foundation for the diagnosis and classification of personality disorders. It is clear that most personality disorder diagnoses are based on reports or observations of interpersonal behavior, although this does not necessarily imply that personality disorders are distinct from Axis I disorder, in that they are dysfunctional primarily through their expression in the social milieu. Writing from the interpersonal perspective, McLemore and Brokaw (1987) suggest that personality disorders are "disturbances" in the sense that the behavior of such people is disturbing to someone else, implying that a person stranded alone on a desert island cannot have a personality disorder. This implies that nearly all personality disorders will have characteristic patterns on the interpersonal scales *DOM* and *WRM*.

Personality disorders differ quantitatively from normal personality variation. This assumption bears upon the "categorical versus dimensional" debate; the assumption is that individuals with personality disorders and those with "normal" personalities differ in degree rather than in kind. This implies that having a personality disorder is not an "either–or" type of distinction; rather, personality issues can play a role for the person to a greater or a lesser extent. Perhaps the closest operationalization of this "degree" of personality disturbance on the PAI is the *BOR* full scale: The greater the elevation on *BOR*, the more likely it is that personality problems are playing a role in the person's presenting complaints.

Each of these assumptions represents an area of controversy within psychology and psychiatry, but without such assumptions there is no explicit boundary to the domain of phenomena denoted by the concept of "personality disorder." The *DSM* does, however, provide explicit definitions for various specific personality disorders. These disorders, and the PAI indicators relevant to establishing the diagnoses, are described in the following sections.

Borderline Personality Disorder

This disorder is characterized by instability across multiple behavioral domains, including self-image, mood and affect, interpersonal relationships, and impulse control. Individuals with this personality disorder are highly reactive to interpersonal events; they are both distrustful of those closest to them and also fearful that these others will abandon them. Their self-image can fluctuate dramatically and is heavily dependent on the people around them. They are very impulsive in ways that are self-damaging, including spending money, driving, sexual activity, and other reckless behaviors; they often display a pattern of undermining themselves when things appear to be going well. Their mood is very reactive to external events and often fluctuates rapidly between anger, panic, and despair; mood disorders are often comorbid with Borderline Personality.

The mean profile for a group of patients (including both inpatients and outpatients) diagnosed with Borderline Personality Disorder is presented in Figure 6-8. These data were originally presented in the *PAI Professional Manual* (Morey, 1991). This profile demonstrates a prominent elevation on *BOR* as well as a marked elevation on *DEP*. This group also had a mean *SUI* score that approached 80*T*; this elevation is consistent with the repeated suicidal gestures that are pathognomonic for this diagnostic group. Unlike other clinical groups, the borderline group shows elevations on all four borderline subscales; although many individuals with other forms of personality problems may show elevations on one or two subscales, thus perhaps elevating the *BOR* full scale, few respondents who are elevated on all four *BOR* subscales will fail to meet *DSM-IV* criteria for the disorder.

A study of 22 women inpatients diagnosed with Borderline Personality Disorder was reported by Bell-Pringle (1994); the mean profile obtained in that study is also presented in Figure 6-8. The patterns for the two groups are quite similar; the greater elevation on *DEP* observed in the Bell-Pringle sample is likely the result of the sample being restricted to inpatients. If so, the relationship between the two patterns suggests that the absolute elevation of *DEP* is more likely than that of *BOR* to be associated with hospitalization for borderline patients; the level of *BOR* is relatively similar in the inpatient sample and the general sample. This may reflect the sensitivity of *DEP* to the precipitating crisis, whereas *BOR* indicates more stable and enduring pathology that may well continue after discharge.

Other aspects of these profiles are informative as to the characteristics of the disorder. For example, borderline individuals tend to have prominent elevations on *ARD-T*, indicative of a past history of traumatic stress. This is consistent with reports in the literature that the rates of physical and sexual abuse in the developmental history of such patients is extremely high (Herman, Perry, & Van der Kolk,

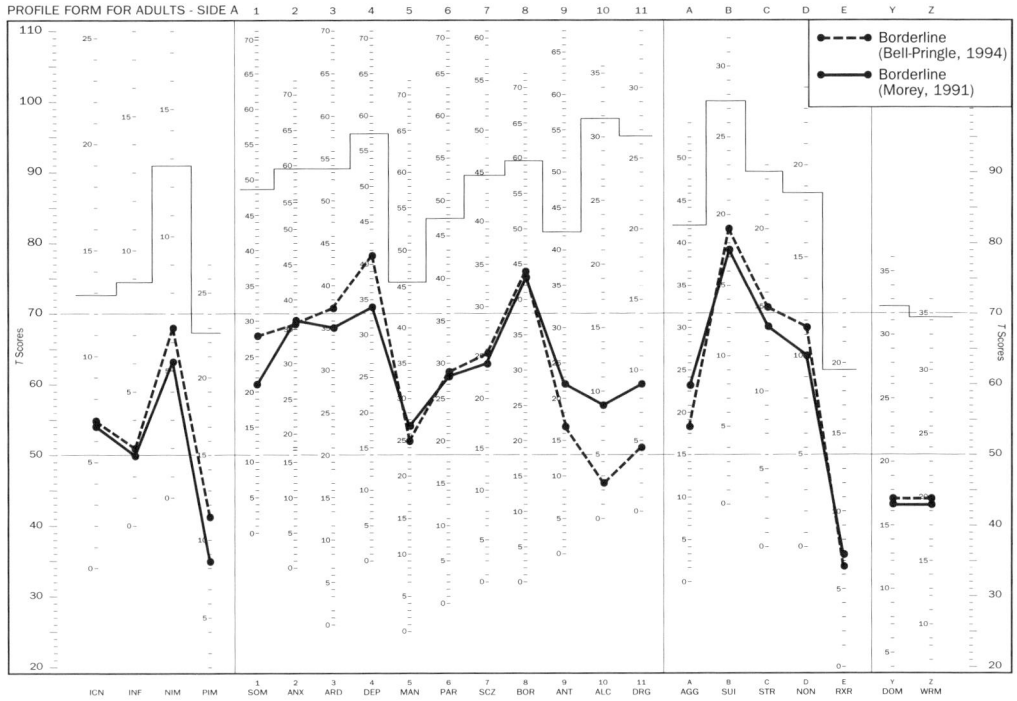

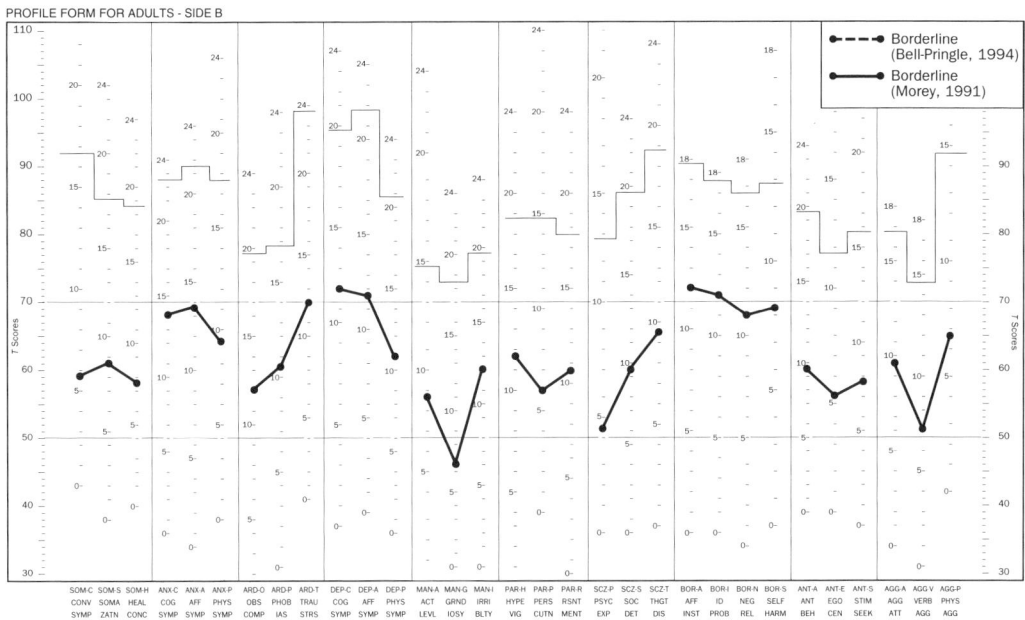

Figure 6-8. Mean PAI profiles for two groups diagnosed with Borderline Personality Disorder. No data were provided by Bell-Pringle (1994) for the PAI subscales.

1989). The elevation on *DEP* reveals borderline individuals to be quite pessimistic and hopeless, but *DEP-P* is not particularly elevated, suggesting the absence of physiological signs of depression. This also is consistent with the research literature that indicates that borderline individuals are not responsive to traditional antidepressant medication; in fact, such medication may actually worsen their symptoms (Soloff et al., 1989). Other features of the disorder that are often reflected on the PAI include marked anxiety, resulting in *ANX* elevations; impulsive substance abuse, manifest on *ALC* and/or *DRG*; very low self-esteem, resulting in low scores on *MAN-G*; and a broadly negative evaluative set that can elevate scores on *NIM*.

The LOGIT function for the diagnosis of Borderline Personality Disorder (as contrasted with other clinical diagnoses) supports many of these observations. The function (presented for illustration purposes rather than for use in routine clinical situations) included the following weights for PAI variables:

$$.020(BOR\text{-}A) + .001(BOR\text{-}I) + .014(BOR\text{-}S) + .005(DEP\text{-}C) - .007(BOR\text{-}N) - .006(PIM) + .245$$

This function highlights the significance of *BOR-A* and *BOR-S* in determining whether a person receives a Borderline Personality Disorder diagnosis. This is probably due to the fact that these elements of the disorder are, perhaps the most dramatic in presentation and the most difficult for the clinician to manage. The *BOR-I* component makes a small independent contribution to the diagnosis, whereas *BOR-N* operates as a suppressor variable, demonstrating that volatile interpersonal relationships are often associated with other disorders and are not necessarily specific to Borderline Personality Disorder. The negative loading for *PIM* is not a suppressor, however; borderline individuals tend to obtain very low scores on *PIM*, reflecting a very negative self-image. Another facet of this self-image is reflected in the *DEP-C* loading, indicating that borderline individuals see themselves as ineffectual and shameful people.

A similar actuarial study, based on a discriminant analysis contrasting 22 borderline inpatients with 22 student controls, was conducted by Bell-Pringle (1994). In this study, the greatest correlations with the discriminant function (which was based only upon the 11 clinical scales) were found with *DEP* ($r = .73$), followed by *BOR* ($r = .59$), *ARD* ($r = .57$), and *SOM* ($r = .51$). With respect to mean comparisons, large group effect differences were also seen on *SUI*, *STR*, and *RXR* among the treatment scales, with diagnostic group differences accounting for at least 40% of the variation on these scales. For all scales mentioned, borderline individuals were elevated relative to controls, with the exception of *RXR*, where the borderline patients had lower mean scores.

Antisocial Personality Disorder

The diagnostic criteria for Antisocial Personality Disorder specify an enduring pattern of disregard for the rights of others, including illegal activities, aggressive acts, and deceit and manipulation of others. Such people tend to be extremely undependable and irresponsible; impulsive decisions and reckless actions are common. Although the antisocial routine exploits others, these individuals experience no remorse, being either indifferent to the plight of others or providing some superficial rationalization for their actions.

The *DSM* diagnostic criteria bear some relationship to the construct of *psychopathy*, but, because the criteria tend to focus on antisocial behavior rather than personality traits, the psychopathy concept is less inclusive than that of Antisocial Personality. The PAI features that are most directly related to the *DSM* concept are *ANT-A*, which captures the acting-out behaviors, and *AGG-P*, which captures the aggressiveness and history of physical confrontation that are represented in the diagnostic criteria. The concept of psychopathy includes a host of additional aspects: lack of empathy, egocentricity, an inflated self-appraisal, and glib, superficial charm are all elements of psychopathy. These aspects are most likely to be reflected in elevations on *ANT-E*. Finally, the recklessness and impulsive gratification-seeking are captured in the items of *ANT-S*; although such features are not necessary to receive the diagnosis of Antisocial Personality, they are invariably present in the narrower constellation of the psychopath.

The mean profile for a group of patients diagnosed with Antisocial Personality Disorder (originally presented in the *PAI Professional Manual* [Morey, 1991]) is presented in Figure 6-9. The prominent elevations on this mean profile include *DRG* and *ANT*. The former elevation is probably artifactually inflated due to the large number of incarcerated respondents in the antisocial group, although drug abuse is reasonably common in antisocial personality. Among the subscales, antisocial behaviors (*ANT-A*) was the most prominently elevated, a pattern consistent with the fact that these diagnoses were based on *DSM* definitions that place a great deal of weight on behavioral features. Other aspects of the profile that bear upon the antisocial constellation are the relative lack of neurotic manifestations and suicidal ideation; these scores tend to be lower than comparable scores from almost any other diagnostic clinical group. Thus, the profile for Antisocial Personality invariably is more elevated on the "right-hand" side of the clinical scales (i.e., *BOR*, *ANT*, *ALC*, *DRG*) than on the "left-hand" side (i.e., *SOM*, *ANX*, *ARD*, *DEP*). The difference between the antisocial and the borderline individual on *MAN-G* is noteworthy and points to the arrogant self-appraisal of the antisocial individual that is maintained in the face of life circumstances that suggest otherwise. Finally, the

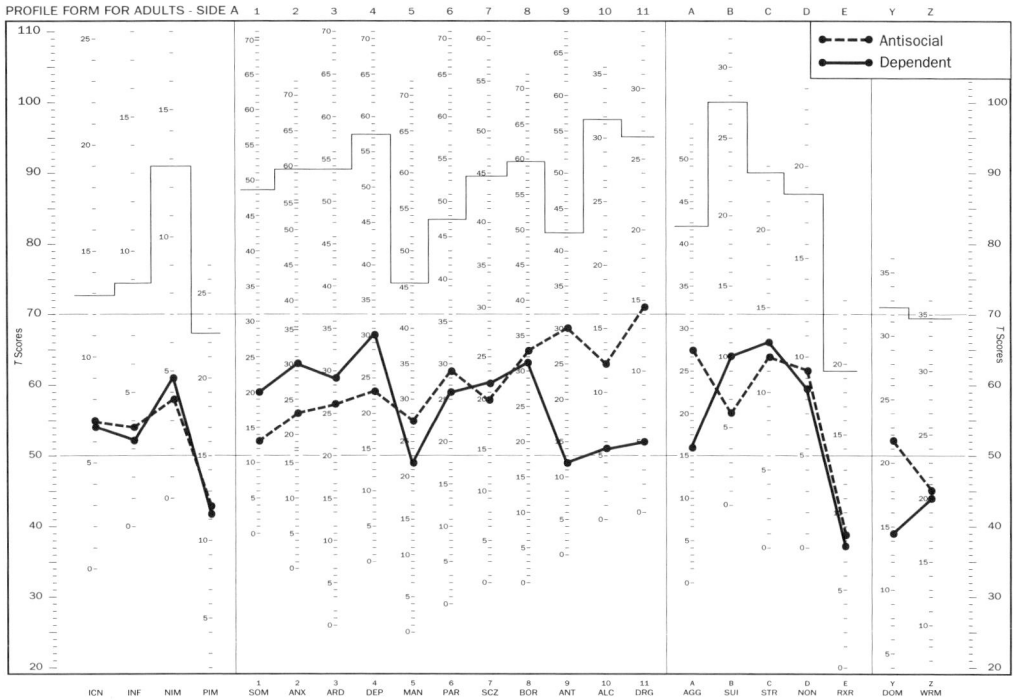

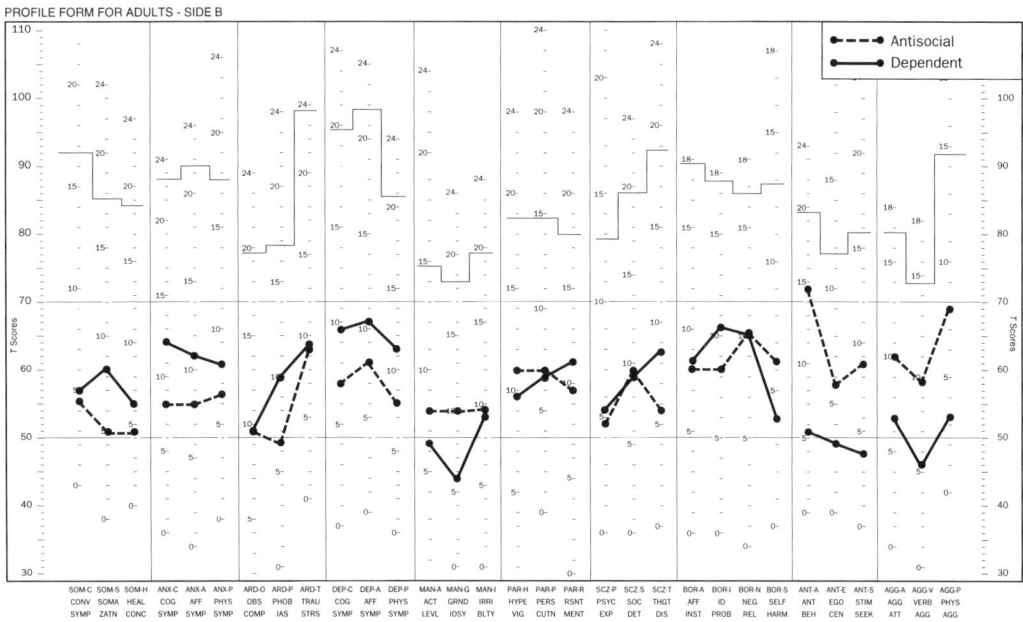

Figure 6-9. Mean PAI profiles for patients diagnosed with Antisocial and Dependent Personality Disorders (Morey, 1991).

downward slope of the interpersonal scales (i.e., with *DOM* considerably higher than *WRM*) is also representative of the cold, controlling interpersonal style of individuals with this personality disorder.

The LOGIT function for the diagnosis of Antisocial Personality (as contrasted with other clinical diagnoses) provides further understanding of the scales that are critical in assigning the diagnosis. The function (presented for illustration purposes, rather than for use in routine clinical situations) included the following weights for PAI scales:

$$.044(ANT\text{-}A) + .017(AGG\text{-}P) - .008(ANT\text{-}E) - .002(ANT\text{-}S) - .028(ANX\text{-}A) + 1.85$$

This function highlights the centrality of *ANT-A* and *AGG-P* in determining whether a person receives a *DSM* Antisocial Personality diagnosis. This is consistent with the way the disorder is portrayed in the *DSM* criteria. The *ANT-S* and *ANT-E* scales act as suppressor variables, but the negative loading for *ANX-A* is not a suppressor; rather, it reflects the fact that this scale is typically lower for antisocial than it is for most other clinical groups.

Narcissistic Personality Disorder

The defining feature of the narcissistic personality is a pattern of inflated self-esteem, demand for admiration, egocentricity, and lack of empathy. Such people overvalue their ideas and accomplishments, appearing self-important and pretentious to the people around them. They believe that their special talents and abilities can only be fully appreciated by others of equal talents and superior status, and they devalue others who fail to admire them or who otherwise disappoint them. Although inflated, their self-esteem is fragile and vulnerable to insult, which can cause them to become depressed, humiliated, and/or furious with those who have not granted them their entitlements.

The haughty and arrogant self-appraisal of the narcissistic individual suggests that *MAN-G* is a logical starting point for identification, with elevations of at least 60T being typical. However, because the self-esteem can be fragile, *MAN-I* can be elevated as well, particularly if there has been a recent narcissistic injury. In contrast to an individual in a manic episode, elevations on *MAN-A* are unusual; whereas the manic can be involved in a great many activities, the narcissist is more selective, participating only in those impressive tasks that merit his or her self-evaluated special talents and unique abilities. *ANT-E* is often elevated in Narcissistic Personality, as it captures the lack of empathy and profound egocentricity specified in the diagnostic criteria. On the interpersonal scales, the narcissistic individuals are invariably above average on *DOM*, because they feel entitled to be in control of almost any interpersonal situation. However, in contrast to anti-social individuals, their elevation on *WRM* is generally within normal limits, as it is more important to the narcissist to maintain relationships (if only to assure a steady supply of admirers).

Histrionic Personality Disorder

The core feature of the histrionic personality style is a pattern of excessive and superficial emotionality and attention-seeking behavior. Such individuals demand to be the center of attention and attempt to attract such attention through dramatic behavior and flirtatiousness. They are overly concerned with physical appearance, often dressing in a provocative manner and attempting to draw compliments from others. They tend to express their emotions in an exaggerated and rapidly shifting way, leading others to feel that the emotions are superficial or even faked. Individuals with this personality style tend to have difficulty establishing and maintaining intimate relationships, often controlling their partners with emotional manipulation. At the same time, relationships with friends also are impaired because of the histrionic's competitive and provocative nature.

The excessive and superficial emotionality of the histrionic personality suggests that *BOR-A* represents an important facet in identifying individuals with this style. The egocentricity and manipulativeness of such people should result in an elevation on *ANT-E*. However, unlike other, more malignant, personality disorders, histrionics place a premium on interpersonal relationships, and the quality of these relationships (at least their superficial quality) is quite important to them. Thus, *WRM* is typically above the mean for this group and, in fact, may be quite elevated. Also prominent in the histrionic character is the repression of anger and other disturbing affects; thus, *AGG-V* is typically quite low, as anger tends to be indirectly expressed. More comfortable with the expression of physical than psychological symptoms, this personality style is associated with various somatoform disorders, and *SOM-S* would be expected to be particularly elevated for this group.

Paranoid Personality Disorder

This disorder is characterized by an enduring pattern of distrust and suspiciousness of others. Such individuals assume that others are malevolent, and they expect harm or deceit from others. In the absence of any objective evidence, they feel that they have been treated unfairly and feel deeply injured by the people around them. They are reluctant to confide in others and feel that any personal information that might be divulged will be used against them. Such people bear grudges against others, are quick to feel attacked or threatened, and react to minor slights with dramatic hostility.

The *PAR* scale is the obvious beginning point for the investigation of Paranoid Personality. Because these individuals are generally not delusional, it is typical to find *PAR-P* to be considerably below *PAR-R* and *PAR-H*, thus forming a V-shaped profile for the three *PAR* subscales. The interpersonal distrust reflected in *PAR-H* and the bitterness and hostility captured by *PAR-R* combine to provide a reasonably complete coverage of the features of the disorder. Other features of the profile can supplement this information. For example, *SCZ-S* may be elevated, reflecting the tendency to keep relationships distant and superficial; *AGG-A* is often high, indicating the extent of the anger underlying the mistrust; and *WRM* scores are typically below average, because the paranoid character places little premium on close relationships.

Schizoid Personality Disorder

The diagnosis of Schizoid Personality Disorder is characterized by an indifference to and detachment from social relationships, as well as a constricted experience and expression of affect. Such individuals neither enjoy nor desire relationships, preferring to be alone in both occupational and leisure time pursuits. They may appear emotionally cold to others, but they are unconcerned about the way that they are regarded and are unaffected by either positive or negative comments from others. The emotional constriction includes anger, which they rarely express, even when directly provoked. Lacking social skills and disinterested in sexual relations, such individuals have few acquaintances and seldom marry successfully.

The social detachment and affective constriction of the schizoid individual are directly captured by *SCZ-S*, and it is unlikely that individuals with this diagnosis would not demonstrate some elevation on this scale. Also, the *WRM* scale is likely to be quite low, given the marked lack of interest in attachment relationships. The affective constriction of the schizoid individual would also lead to suppression of *BOR-A*, which can help to distinguish the disorder from many other personality disorders with prominent social isolation (e.g., Avoidant Personality Disorder); other neurotic spectrum indicators such as *ANX* and *DEP* may also be low, particularly if the individual is not in an occupational situation that is taxing the limited social skills. Finally, the disorder should not be diagnosed if these conditions occur solely during the course of Schizophrenia (including the residual phase), suggesting that *SCZ-P* elevations are likely to be counterindicative of this diagnosis.

Schizotypal Personality

The Schizotypal Personality is distinguished by interpersonal deficits as well as cognitive and behavioral eccentricities suggestive of problems within the

Schizophrenia spectrum. Although not of the severity that would merit a diagnosis of Schizophrenia, the person may admit to mild ideas of reference, magical thinking, or paranoid ideation. Such individuals are not comfortable in social situations, more typically experiencing tension and anxiety (often associated with suspiciousness concerning the intentions of others). Expression of affect is typically constricted, and the individual may also experience mild signs of inefficiency and confusion in thought process.

Because of the similarity of this disorder to the residual phase of Schizophrenia (distinguished primarily by a past episode of active schizophrenic psychosis), the PAI indicators for schizotypal personality are similar to those for the residual diagnosis. The disorder includes many negative symptoms (e.g., flat affect and poverty of interactions); such features would be likely to result in *SCZ-S* elevations that are more prominent than any accompanying elevation on *SCZ-P*. However, it is unlikely that *SCZ-P* would be below 50*T* in such individuals, due to their eccentricity and peculiar beliefs. *SCZ-T* and *PAR-P* also would be expected to display moderate elevations, reflecting the cognitive distortions and mild paranoid ideation characteristic of the disorder. The social awkwardness and anxiety would be reflected in a number of different PAI domains; suppressed scores on *WRM* with elevations on *ARD-P* (driven by the social anxiety items) would be expected. In contrast to Schizoid personality, the schizotypal individual experiences considerable anxiety in social situations, and this latter disorder is more likely to demonstrate *ANX* elevations than is the schizoid individual.

Avoidant Personality Disorder

The defining features of Avoidant Personality Disorder involve marked social inhibition, feelings of inadequacy, and intense sensitivity to negative evaluation. Such individuals typically demonstrate impairment in occupational settings because of their anxiety concerning interpersonal contact that might lead to criticism or disapproval. They are most fearful of new interpersonal situations (i.e., interactions involving strangers, whom they are afraid will reject them as inadequate). Low self-esteem is a core feature of the disorder; they believe themselves to be socially inept, unappealing, and inferior to others. As a result, they will exaggerate the dangers inherent in novel situations and use this as an excuse to minimize interactions with others they do not know well.

Avoidant Personality Disorder overlaps a great deal with the Generalized type of Social Phobia, to the extent that the two diagnoses may be alternative names for the same condition. Thus, the PAI indicators for the disorders are similar, with the core indicator for Avoidant Personality Disorder involving elevations on *ARD-P*.

The social anxiety indicated by that scale leads to interpersonal withdrawal and avoidance, (i.e., scores on *WRM* are typically suppressed). Also, scores on *DOM* tend to be quite low, because the avoidant personality is particularly uncomfortable in leadership roles where there is a great deal of public scrutiny and where any failures are likely to be widely known. Finally, the desire to avoid any novel social situations tends to suppress scores on *ANT-S*, as the avoidant individual seeks to avoid the stimulation associated with unpredictable interactions.

Obsessive-Compulsive Personality Disorder

The obsessive-compulsive personality is preoccupied with orderliness, perfectionism, and a rigid need for internal and interpersonal control. The preoccupation with trivial detail is generally at the expense of a grasp of the overall situation; thus, projects often are not finished because of the attention paid to preventing minor or irrelevant mistakes. However, productivity is far more important than leisure to these individuals, who tend to regard leisure activities as wasted time. Such people are inflexible about matters of morality and rigid in their conviction that others should adhere to their beliefs and values. Miserly in their handling of finances, money is hoarded in order to deal with any future misfortunes. Emotional expression is typically constricted, with the exceptional outburst of righteous indignation. The quality of their relationships with others, even intimates, is stilted and formal.

The *ARD-O* scale includes items that capture these personality elements of the obsessive-compulsive. Whereas the Axis I manifestation of Obsessive-Compulsive Disorder involves a marked distress (appearing on *ANX* and *DEP*) associated with intrusive obsessions and compulsions, the affectively constricted personality disorder may display no such elevations, aside from a moderate elevation on *ANX-C*. Also, as a further indicator of this affective constriction, *BOR-A* may be quite low in the personality disorder variant. These individuals do not like to submit to others' ways of doing things, and, as such, low scores on *DOM* are rare. However, often the obsessive simply will refuse to work with others, rather than experience the failure of others to cooperate, and, thus, *DOM* will not necessarily be elevated. The disinterest in the affective quality of relationships as well as the formal and somewhat stilted style of relating to others are typically expressed by low scores on *WRM*.

Dependent Personality Disorder

The defining trait for this disorder is dependency; an enduring pattern of submissiveness, neediness, and clinging behavior. Such people have great difficulty making independent decisions, preferring to have others make important decisions for them. They feel incapable and helpless on their own, fearing that they will be left alone should their current dependency relationship end. If the relationship does end, they urgently seek another that will meet their needs for care and support. In such relationships, they may suppress their own objective best interests in order to ensure that they will not be abandoned.

The mean profile for a group of 56 patients in the clinical normative sample who were diagnosed with Dependent Personality Disorder is presented in Figure 6-9. One important feature of this profile is the low score on *DOM*, demonstrating the interpersonal submissiveness characteristic of this group. Other suppressed scales are also noteworthy. *WRM* scores will invariably be higher than *DOM* scores, because interpersonal relationships are of such importance to the dependent personality. *MAN-G* scores are typically low, pointing to the poor self-esteem and feelings of inadequacy that drive these individuals to depend on others. Low scores on *AGG-V* are typical, as expressions of anger would be inhibited to avoid endangering all-important relationships. Among the *BOR* subscales, *BOR-I* is particularly salient, as these individuals tend to submerge their sense of identity within the context of a dependency relationship, leading to moderate elevations on this subscale.

The LOGIT function for the diagnosis of Dependent Personality Disorder (as contrasted with other clinical diagnoses) provides further understanding of scales critical in assigning the diagnosis. The function (presented for illustration purposes, rather than for use in routine clinical situations) included the following weights for PAI scales:

$$.001(WRM) - .014(AGG\text{-}V) - .017(DOM) - .012(MAN\text{-}G) + 5.693$$

This function highlights the centrality of low scores on *DOM*, *AGG-V*, and *MAN-G* in determining whether a person receives a Dependent Personality Disorder diagnosis; these negative loadings are reflective of the inverse relationships of these scales to the diagnosis, rather than indicating variance suppression. The small positive loading on *WRM* supports the conclusion that relationships are important to the dependent, although the remaining scales in the function point out the lengths to which this group, as opposed to other clinical groups, will go to maintain these relationships.

Other Personality Disorders

Two personality disorders are described in an appendix to the *DSM-IV* manual: Passive-Aggressive (Negativistic) Personality Disorder, and Depressive Personality Disorder. Although officially classified as "Personality Disorder Not Otherwise

Specified," these two disorders have either been in the nomenclature for many years (i.e., Passive-Aggressive personality) or have been the focus of considerable research (i.e., Depressive personality). Thus, some mention of the PAI indicators for these disorders is warranted.

In the *DSM-IV*, Passive-Aggressive Personality Disorder has been relegated to an appendix of "criteria sets provided for further study." This disorder is characterized by passive resistance and negativistic attitudes toward others who place demands on the person. These demands are resented and opposed indirectly, through procrastination, stubbornness, intentional inefficiency and memory lapses. Such individuals tend to be sullen, irritable, and cynical, and they chronically complain of being underappreciated and cheated. On the PAI, the hallmark combination is one of elevated *PAR-R*, signifying the hostility and resentment, combined with low scores on *DOM*, indicative of the passivity element of the disorder. Scores on *WRM* also are typically low, as such people tend to be unsuccessful in interpersonal relationships because of their capacity to evoke hostility and negative responses from others. Also, any elevation on *AGG-P* would contraindicate the disorder, as it suggests that anger and resentment are likely to be expressed in a direct and overt manner; such elevations would not be typical of the passive-aggressive individual.

Depressive Personality Disorder is also included in the appendix of criteria sets for further study. This disorder is characterized by enduring depressive cognitions and behaviors; some have proposed that this is essentially the same concept as Dysthymic Disorder. Certainly, the PAI indicators for the two disorders would be the same, as the primary distinction seems to be one of duration rather than quality of symptoms. Because of the centrality of depressed mood, *DEP* would be critical in identifying this disorder. The proposed criteria emphasize mood quality and related cognitions, rather than the more somatic features of depression; thus, *DEP-C* and *DEP-A* should be more prominent than *DEP-P*, with the former two scales 10*T* or more above the latter. Because the depression is chronic in nature, rather than a reaction to external events, the *DEP* elevation should be somewhat higher than *STR*, which might indicate more situational mood disruptions. Also, some elevation on *SUI* would be expected, related to the chronic pessimism and brooding nature of these individuals.

Table 6-5
Summary of Key Diagnostic Indicators for Personality Disorders

Diagnostic consideration	Elevation indicators	Suppression indicators
Borderline Personality Disorder	*BOR* (all four subscales) *DEP*, particularly *DEP-C* *ARD*, particularly *ARD-T* *SUI, STR, SOM*	*PIM, RXR*
Antisocial Personality Disorder	*ANT-A* (esp. for *DSM*), *AGG-P, DRG*	*ANX-A, ARD-P*
Narcissistic Personality Disorder	*MAN-G, DOM, ANT-E*	
Histrionic Personality Disorder	*WRM, SOM-S, ANT-E, BOR-A, PIM*	*AGG-V*
Paranoid Personality Disorder	*PAR-R, PAR-H, SCZ-S, AGG-A*	*WRM*
Dependent Personality Disorder	*WRM*	*DOM, AGG-V, MAN-G*
Passive-Aggressive Personality Disorder	*PAR-R*	*DOM, WRM, AGG-P*
Schizoid Personality Disorder	*SCZ-S*	*WRM, BOR-A*
Avoidant Personality Disorder	*ARD-P*	*DOM, WRM, ANT-S*
Schizotypal Personality Disorder	*SCZ-S, PAR-P, ARD-P, SCZ-T*	*WRM*
Obsessive-Compulsive Personality Disorder	*ARD-O*	*WRM, BOR-A*

Substance Abuse Disorders

The key features of substance abuse and dependence involve the continuing use of the substance despite significant problems associated with this use. The diagnostic symptoms presented in the *DSM-IV* are similar across alcohol and the different classes of drugs of abuse, although, for some substances, certain criteria are less relevant (e.g., there is no known withdrawal symptom from LSD). These symptoms include tolerance, withdrawal, failure to cut down despite repeated efforts, social-role impairment, and continued use in the face of significant problems associated with the substance. Because these diagnoses are based heavily on historical life event information rather than on present mental status, it is necessary to establish that the difficulties have occurred within the preceding 12 months in order to assign a diagnosis.

On the PAI, the obvious beginning points in considering a substance-abuse diagnosis are the *ALC* and *DRG* scales; these scales are described in detail in chapter 2. It should be remembered that a good deal of the information gathered on these scales is historical (i.e., inquiries are made about events that may have happened in the past). As such, *ALC* or *DRG*, or both, can be elevated in people who have had a substance-abuse problem in the past, but who are not currently drinking or using drugs. It is certainly possible for a person to score in the vicinity of 70*T* on either scale largely through historical information; however, a person who has a current substance-abuse problem will tend to have scores that are quite elevated.

Because both *ALC* and *DRG* items directly address substance use, the scales are susceptible to denial, a problem of concern to many in the substance abuse field. Although the research literature supports the use of such a direct questioning method, chapter 2 addresses in detail the issue of assessing substance abuse denial. However, such indirect methods have limited ability to circumvent denial issues, and asking directly about substance use is the most straightforward manner of obtaining such information. If there is reason to suspect that marked denial of substance abuse may be occurring, supplementing the PAI with information from collateral informants (e.g., spouse or family member) is recommended.

The mean profiles for alcohol and drug abuse samples (Morey, 1991) are presented in Figure 6-10. The alcoholic mean profile was markedly elevated on *ALC* (i.e., 84*T*) and also was rather elevated on *DRG*, reflective of the prevalence of polysubstance abuse among alcohol abusers. The highest clinical scale elevation for the drug-abuse sample was on *DRG* (i.e., 80*T*). *ALC* approached 70*T* in this group as well, consistent with the relatively high prevalence of alcoholism among drug abusers. Other than the differences reflecting the primary substance of abuse, the alcoholic and drug abuser profiles are quite similar, with the drug abuser sample displaying a slightly more elevated score on *ANT* that seems to reflect a greater likelihood of antisocial behaviors among drug abusers. However, the relative specificity of the *ALC-DRG* elevations demonstrates that other scales will not necessarily be elevated in these respondents; thus, a *DEP* elevation in a person with alcohol problems is not merely an artifact of the alcohol-related issues; instead, it indicates a likely comorbid condition.

Figure 6-11 presents the mean profile from a sample of 229 methadone maintenance patients as reported by Alterman et al. (1995), and the mean profile of a group of 30 alcoholics described by Boyle and Lennon (1994). The methadone patients demonstrated a profile pattern similar to that of the general drug abuser sample, with some differences. Alterman and colleagues found that their methadone patients were significantly higher on *DRG* and *RXR* than the drug patients, whereas their scores were significantly lower on *NIM, BOR, ANT, ALC, SUI, DOM,*

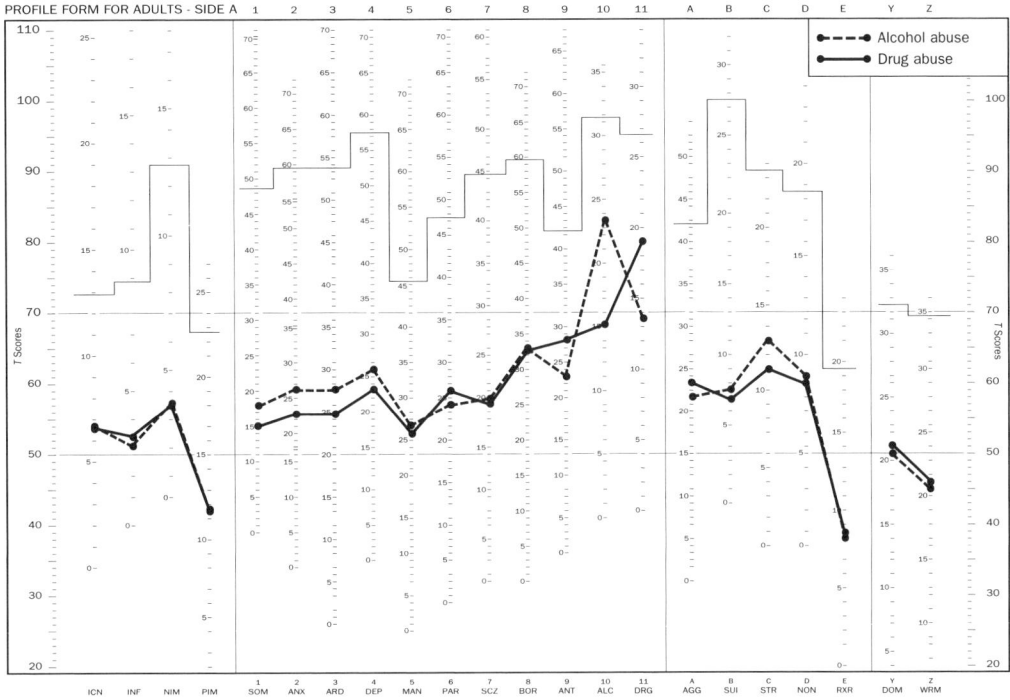

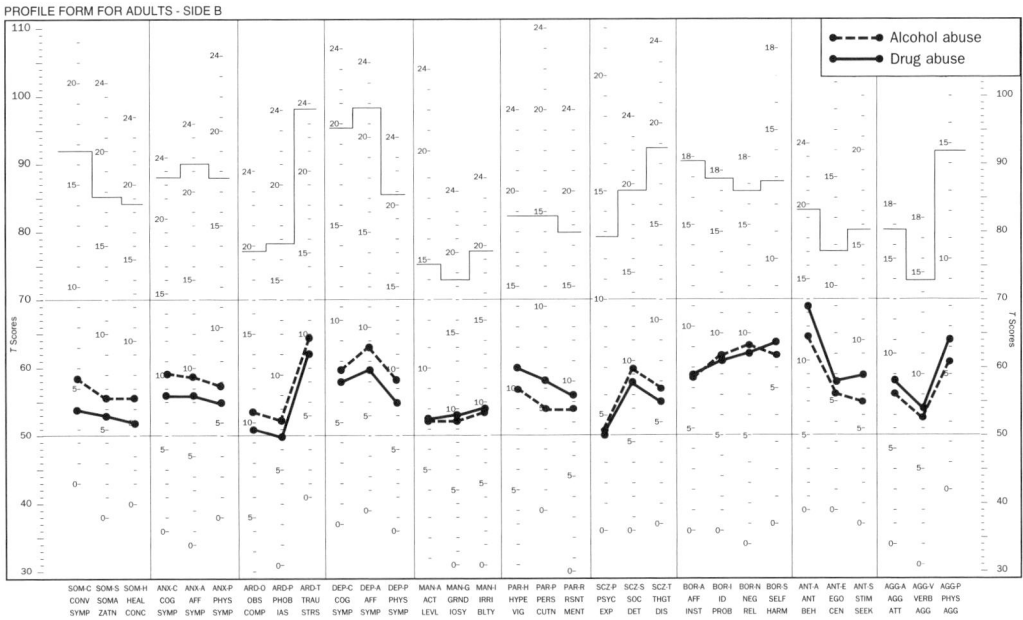

Figure 6-10. Mean PAI profiles for alcohol and drug abuse samples (Morey, 1991).

and *WRM*. Although the greater elevation on *DRG* (i.e., signifying a greater degree of drug related dysfunction) is likely to be a true reflection of a unique aspect of the methadone sample, methodological variation may account for other observed differences. In particular, Alterman et al. used a *NIM* cutoff of 92*T* to establish profile validity, which resulted in 30% of the methadone patients being excluded from further analyses; hence, they are not included in the mean profile presented in Figure 6-11. The drug abuser profile presented in Figure 6-10 did not exclude any respondents based on PAI-derived indicators, including the *NIM* scale. Thus, the greater elevations on scales such as *BOR* and *SUI* in the drug abuser samples may reflect profile distortion of the type measured by *NIM*. The Alterman study is important in that it indicates that marked elevations on *NIM* are relatively common among severely drug-dependent individuals. The results also suggest that among their sample of methadone patients, alcohol problems were relatively infrequent. This may be a result of screening practices (i.e., opiate addicts are poor risks for methadone programs if they are also alcoholics), or it may reflect a narrowing of the drug-taking repertoire among this type of addict.

The mean profile of alcoholics obtained by Boyle and Lennon (1994) (presented in Figure 6-11) displayed far more psychopathology than the alcoholic mean profile reported in the *PAI Professional Manual* (Morey, 1991; shown in Figure 6-10). Although the *ALC* scale was markedly elevated in the Boyle and Lennon sample (i.e., *M* = 88*T*), so was nearly every other clinical scale. The mean score of *NIM* was 100*T*, which is above the recommended cutoff for profile validity. This finding is apparently consistent with the results of Alterman et al. (1995) in documenting frequent *NIM* elevations among this population. These results may reflect the point in treatment at which the PAI was administered; the elevated *NIM* scores may result from having the test completed during detoxification, which could hamper the straightforward interpretation of the profile information. These findings indicate that extreme *NIM* elevations when the PAI is given during detoxification should be evaluated carefully; a readministration of the test following completion of detox is recommended.

LOGIT functions derived for the alcohol and drug dependence diagnoses (as contrasted with other clinical diagnoses) illustrate other elements of the substance abuser profile. The function for alcohol dependence (presented for illustration purposes, rather than for use in routine clinical situations) was as follows:

$$.052(ALC) + .004(ANT\text{-}A) - .011(BOR\text{-}S) + 1.321$$

The substantial contribution of *ALC* is not surprising, as this scale directly taps signs and symptoms of alcohol dependence. The *ANT-A* loading reflects the behavioral impairment often associated with alcohol problems. *BOR-S* appears to act as

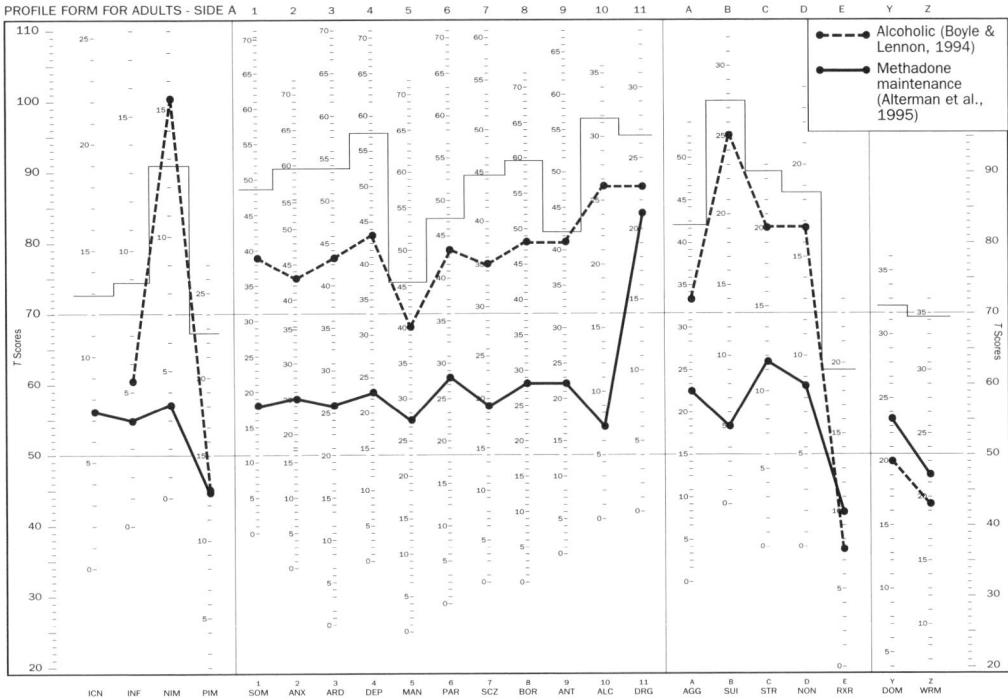

Figure 6-11. Mean PAI profiles for alcoholic and methadone maintenance samples. Boyle and Lennon (1994) did not score the ICN scale.

a suppressor variable, indicating that *ALC* elevations in the absence of prominent scores on *BOR-S* suggest that alcohol problems (as opposed to characterological difficulties) are prominent. This function differs somewhat from the LOGIT function for drug dependence diagnoses, which was the following (presented for illustration purposes, rather than for use in routine clinical situations):

$$.032(DRG) + .022(ANT\text{-}A) + .001(ANT\text{-}E) - .014(BOR\text{-}S) - .013(SOM\text{-}H) + 1.999$$

There are some similarities between this function and the alcoholism function just described. The large contribution of the relevant substance abuse scale, the significance of *ANT-A*, and the suppressor variable of *BOR-S* all replicate the pattern seen in the alcoholism equation. However, the *ANT-A* loading is even larger for the drug dependence group, indicating that it plays a larger role in discriminating drug abusers from other clinical respondents. Also, the more psychopathic elements of *ANT-E* play some role in the drug dependence function, but they are not useful in identifying alcoholics. Finally, the negative loading on *SOM-H* appears to signify a disregard for health among drug-dependent individuals.

Other Diagnoses

There are a number of other diagnoses for which particular PAI configurations are suggestive. For most of the following, additional information would be necessary to supplement the PAI data for diagnostic purposes.

Intermittent Explosive Disorder

This disorder is officially an "impulse-control disorder not elsewhere classified." It is characterized by discrete episodes of aggression that result in serious assaults or destruction of property. The outbursts may be experienced as a "spell" which is immediately followed by relief, but these individuals may later feel upset, remorseful, or embarrassed by their behavior. On the PAI, the *AGG* scale includes information directly relevant to such outbursts. The most typical configuration for this diagnosis would involve a deep V-shaped pattern on *AGG-A*, *AGG-V*, and *AGG-P*. Such individuals are temperamentally quite angry (*AGG-A*), and, when they lose their temper, they have the potential for violence (*AGG-P*). However, anger is typically not expressed verbally (*AGG-V*); rather, it tends to be suppressed and then released in episodic explosions. Individuals who alternate between violent outbursts and extreme remorse over their behavior often will have *DEP-C* scores at a comparable level to the *AGG-P* score.

Dissociative Identity Disorder (Multiple Personality)

The Dissociative Disorders are characterized by disruptions in normally integrated areas of consciousness, including memory, identity, or perception of the environment. The most dramatic manifestation of a dissociative disorder is multiple personality (named Dissociative Identity Disorder in *DSM-IV*), which involves the presence of two or more distinct identities residing within one individual. Switches between these identities result in the individual forgetting important personal information associated with the other personalities.

The dramatic nature of these disorders makes them particular targets for malingering, especially in situations where there may be financial or forensic gain. Indeed, the few cases of multiple personality observed in the standardization of the PAI tended to have elevated *NIM* scores, and a few of the *NIM* items are relevant to dissociative phenomena. Alpher (1995) reported a study of 21 dissociative disorder patients, who obtained a mean score on *NIM* of 75T. However, these patients did not display any noteworthy elevation on the Malingering Index (*M* score = 1.6 items), which suggests that a *NIM* elevation with the Malingering Index within normal limits may signify a dissociative disorder. Alpher also noted marked elevations on *ARD-T* (i.e., 80*T*), which is consistent with theoretical etiology of these conditions. Finally, an elevation on *BOR-I* in the absence of elevations on the other *BOR* subscales can also indicate unstable identity of the type seen in dissociative disorders.

Organic Mental Disorders/Cognitive Disorders

The *DSM-IV* uses the term *cognitive disorder* to refer to conditions that lead to significant changes in cognitive ability or memory, including dementia or delirium. The presence of this type of dysfunction is best established by tests that tap cognitive abilities, and the PAI does not do this. However, the discriminant validity of the PAI makes it particularly useful in assessing the emotional and personological aspects of an individual with suspected or confirmed cognitive impairment, and such considerations are vitally important in diagnosis and treatment planning. On the PAI, a person with central nervous system compromise will not obtain scale elevations merely as a function of the organicity; in fact, over 40% of such patients obtain no clinical scale elevations above 70*T* (Morey, 1991). Similarly, Schinka and Vanderploeg (1995) found that scores on the PAI were largely unrelated to measures of cognitive function from the Neuropsychological Screening Test in a sample of 309 alcohol- and drug-dependent patients. Such findings indicate that the PAI can be of particular help in differential diagnosis of emotional problems (e.g., depression, impulsivity, or paranoia) that are commonly seen in this population.

The pattern of impairment seen in individuals with organic problems will vary as a function of many factors, including the locus and extent of any damage as well as the individual's premorbid functioning. This pattern is as true for the person's emotional status as it is for cognitive status. However, some scales seem to elevate with some regularity in these populations and, when observed, suggest the consideration of organic impairment. The *SOM* scale is a relatively common elevation among individuals with such disorders, with the *SOM-C* subscale often elevated above the other two subscales. *SOM-C* elevations that are accompanied by high scores on *ALC* are common among chronic alcoholics who are experiencing symptoms of Korsakoff's syndrome or an alcoholic dementia; in fact, the *SOM* scale has been found to be inversely related to verbal fluency in a sample of alcoholics (Schinka & Vanderploeg, 1995). *SCZ-T* is another common elevation among the cognitively impaired, as it can reflect the concentration and memory problems that accompany clouded mental status. Finally, *DEP* scale elevations are seen with some frequency in this group, which may reflect either a reaction to their impairment or fatigue, sleep, or appetite problems associated with their organic disorder.

Family/Marital Difficulties

Although not considered to be formal diagnoses, relationships between partners or family members can often be a major focus of clinical attention. On the PAI, marital and family issues are most evident on *NON* and, to a lesser extent, on *STR*. Elevations on *NON* that are 10*T* points above other scales are particularly indicative that the respondent views the primary concerns as existing within the marriage and/or the family. The clinician should pay particular attention to elevations on *PAR* or *BOR*, or both before interpreting the *NON* elevation in this manner. These scales can indicate a generalized pattern of interpersonal bitterness, of which the reported family difficulties are simply an example.

No Diagnosis

Finally, consideration should be given to the absence of diagnosable emotional conditions as well as to their presence. What are the prerequisites of a "clean bill of health" on the PAI? Several factors must be considered. First, there should be no indication that defensiveness is playing a factor in suppressing the profile. Thus, *PIM* scores should be low and there should be few, if any, items from the Defensiveness Index that are positive; establishing these indicators is described in detail in chapter 5. Second, there should be no indications of problems on the clinical scales. In general, this means that all clinical scales and their subscales should be below 60*T*. Similarly, the treatment consideration scales (with the exception of *RXR*) should also be below 60*T*. On the interpersonal scales, *DOM* scores should be within 1 standard deviation of the mean (i.e., 40*T* to 60*T*), indicating that the person is unlikely to be either overcontrolling or overly submissive in relationships. *WRM*, on the other hand, should be above 40*T* although no maximum is given, as there is no indication that marked elevations on *WRM* in isolation can lead to difficulties.

CHAPTER 7
EVALUATING SUICIDE POTENTIAL

The assessment of suicide potential is one of the most critical of all clinical evaluation tasks. Unfortunately, it is also one of the most difficult tasks. Although suicide is the eighth leading cause of death in the United States (National Center for Health Statistics, 1992), it paradoxically is still a relatively rare event, involving 12.2 of every 100,000 people. Thus, it is a low base-rate condition, and such conditions are extremely difficult for instruments with anything short of perfect validity (Meehl & Rosen, 1955). The guidelines offered in this chapter reflect a beginning point for identifying suicidal potential, but, given the difficulty of the task and the critical nature of the issue, it is particularly critical to supplement the PAI with additional information for clinical decisions in this area.

One source of information on the PAI that can be useful in evaluating suicide potential, but which is likely to be overlooked, involves the demographic information gathered on the answer sheet. Information such as gender, marital status, age, and ethnic background provide actuarial information that, in turn, provides a context for the available clinical information on the rest of the instrument. For example, suicide *attempt* rates are roughly three times higher for women than for men, but the rates of completed suicides are three to four times higher for men than for women (Clark & Fawcett, 1992). Widowed individuals, particularly younger ones, demonstrate the highest suicide rates with respect to marital status, whereas married individuals, particularly those with children under the age of 18, show the lowest rates. In general, suicide is more common among the elderly, and this continues to be the trend, although rates have been increasing among adolescents and young adults over the past few decades. Finally, suicide rates tend be about twice as high for Whites as for non-Whites (National Center for Health Statistics, 1992). Each of these factors provides important information to consider when interpreting the PAI test results.

Suicidal Ideation (*SUI*)

The obvious starting point on the PAI for evaluating suicide potential is the *SUI* scale. As with the other scales of the PAI, *SUI* includes items that range in severity from "thinking about death," to "ever having contemplated suicide," to "a current serious consideration of suicide." The latter item is placed near the end of the test as a sort of *sign out* response, a final opportunity to alert caregivers to the desperateness of the person's need for help. Like other scales on the PAI, the content of the *SUI* items is directly related to thoughts of suicide and related behaviors, and individuals who wish to disguise suicidal intents can do so easily. However, the large majority of individuals who completed suicide communicate their intent (Shneidman, 1989), and the *SUI* scale offers an in-depth probe of any such intention.

It must be kept in mind that *SUI* is a suicidal ideation scale, rather than a suicide prediction scale. As such, high scores indicate that a person has thought about and is thinking about suicide; such scores do not necessarily mean that the person will actually commit suicide or even attempt it. *Ideation* (in contrast to completion) is fairly common in clinical settings, and, in fact, the raw score in the general population is not zero, implying that the average individual in the community is likely, at some time, to have thought about suicide. Nonetheless, as suicide rates are fairly low, it is clear that thinking about suicide and actually committing suicide are quite different matters. There are obviously a host of other factors in addition to ideation that determine whether or not a person will attempt suicide. However, ideation still has a central role, as it is a necessary, but usually not sufficient, condition for a completed suicide.

Scores on *SUI* in the average range are those below 60T, and these scores indicate that the respondent is not reporting being disturbed by thoughts of self-harm. It is fairly unusual for individuals in clinical settings to score below 45T. If such scores are accompanied by other risk factors described later in this chapter, the possibility of denial and masked ideation should be considered. Scores from 60T to 69T are typical of clinical respondents. Scores in this range suggest that the person is experiencing periodic, and perhaps transient, thoughts of self-harm. Such people are pessimistic and unhappy about their prospects for the future. Although such scores are common in clinical settings, specific follow-up regarding the details of any suicidal thoughts and the potential for suicidal behavior is warranted.

SUI scores from 70T to 84T suggest recurrent thoughts related to suicide. Although only a small percentage of individuals who entertain suicidal thoughts actually act on them, a score in this range should be considered a significant warning sign of the potential for suicide. The presence of additional risk factors is of particular concern for scores in this range, as such scores still reflect significant ambivalence about suicide. For such individuals, an evaluation of their life circumstances and available support systems is critical. As scores get higher, (i.e., 85T to 99T) this ambivalence lessens, and the thoughts of suicide are intense and recurrent. Such scores are typical of individuals placed on suicide precautions. As *SUI* scores become extreme (i.e., > 100T), the person is likely to be morbidly preoccupied with death and suicide, and many of the steps toward suicide (e.g., giving away belongings, writing a note, formulating a specific plan) are likely to have been completed. In such cases, the potential for suicide should be evaluated immediately, and appropriate interventions should be implemented without delay. Scores at these levels must be considered a significant warning sign of the potential for suicide, regardless of the levels of elevation on other scales.

PAI Profile Configurations and Suicidal Behavior

The mean PAI profiles for three clinical groups with various types of suicidal behavior are presented in Figure 7-1. The three groups, taken from Morey (1991), include (a) patients on suicide precautions at the time of testing, (b) patients with a suicidal gesture-attempt in the preceding 6 months, and (c) patients with a history of self-mutilating behavior. These three profiles are shaped quite similarly and share a pronounced elevation on *SUI*; for each group, this scale is the highest on the instrument. However, there are subtle differences between the profiles that exemplify differences between the groups. The "current precautions" group displays the greatest elevations on *SUI*, but there are also elevations on many of the neurotic spectrum scales (e.g., *DEP* and *SOM*). The scales in this group that would suggest impulsivity and acting-out (e.g., *BOR*, *ANT*, *ALC*, *DRG*) are lower than those for the groups with a history of parasuicidal or self-damaging behavior. The "suicide history" group has a slightly lower score on *SUI*, consistent with the notion that suicide risk, although heightened, is less imminent in this group. The mean profile for a sample of patients with self-mutilating behavior, although generally resembling the other two profiles, is quite similar to the mean profile of patients diagnosed with borderline personality (Morey, 1991). This result is not surprising, as self-mutilation is considered by some to be a pathognomonic sign of borderline personality. Although there is a certain artifactual contribution to this resemblance (i.e., roughly half of the self-mutilating group received a diagnosis of borderline personality), this pattern was also consistent in those self-mutilating respondents who did not receive a borderline diagnosis. It is worth noting that of the three groups portrayed in Figure 7-1, the self-mutilating group has the lowest ratio of *SUI* to *BOR* (i.e., *BOR* is nearly as high as *SUI*).

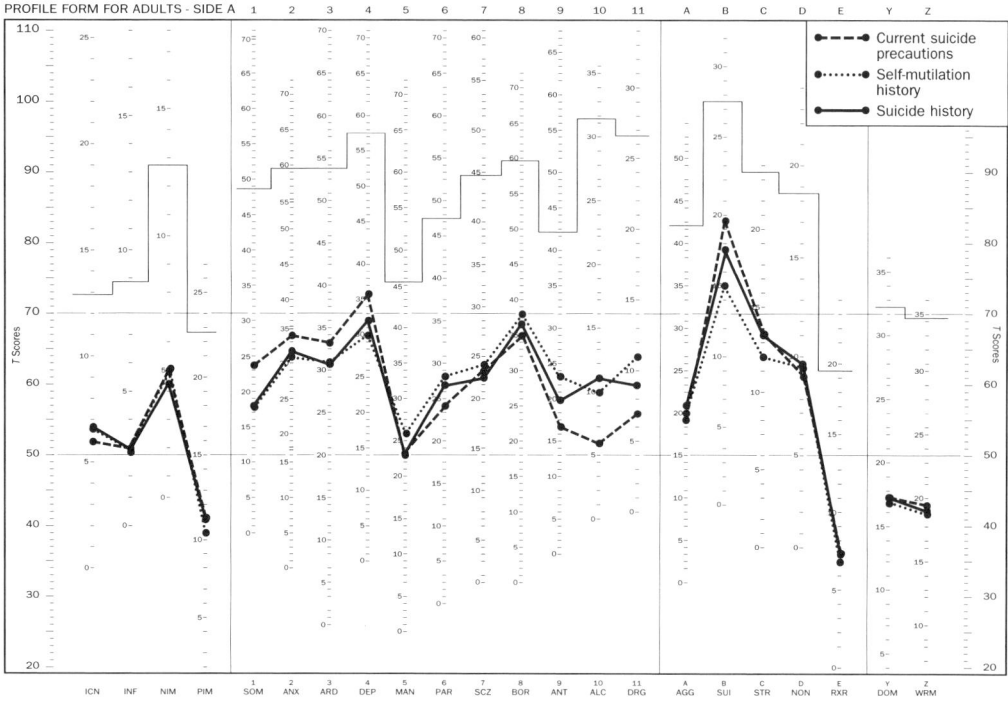

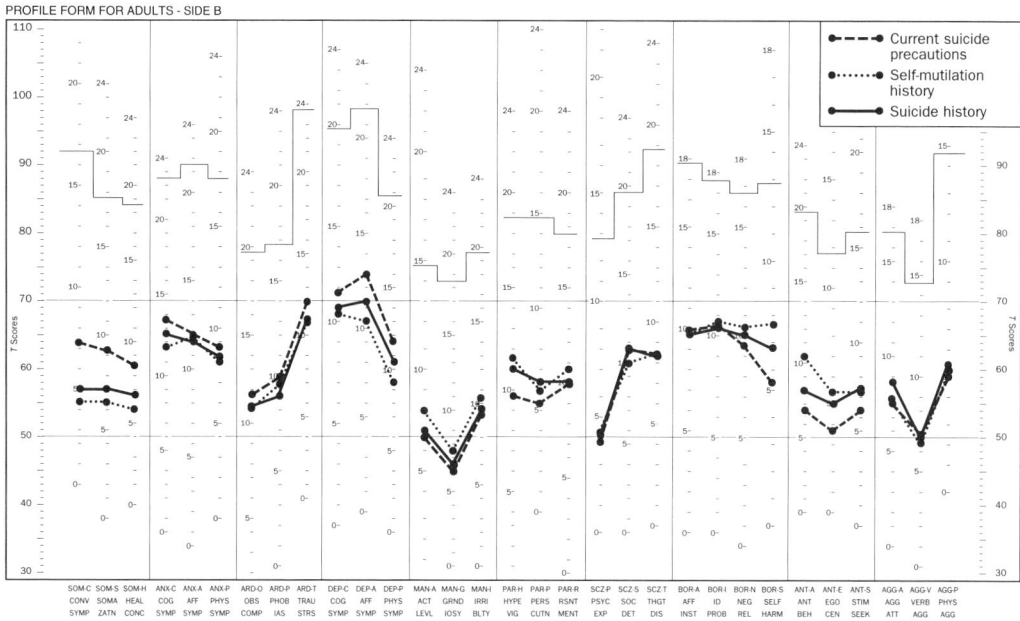

Figure 7-1. Mean PAI profiles for patients with a suicide history, patients on current suicide precautions, and patients with a history of self-mutilation (Morey, 1991).

The PAI Suicide Potential Index (SPI)

Suicidal ideation, although a central component in the evaluation of suicidality, is only one factor needed to assess acute risk. The fact is that suicidal ideation is quite common among individuals presenting for treatment, yet the number of completed suicides is far lower. Thus, ideation may be thought of as a "necessary but not sufficient condition" for suicide; obviously, other variables are needed to account for the differences between those who think about suicide but do not act on it and those who make a serious suicide attempt.

The research literature suggests several risk factors for completed suicide that can be assessed with the PAI. These features, incorporated from research investigating completed suicide by Bongar (1991), Maris et al. (1992), Motto (1989) and others, represent an attempt to form a risk constellation from PAI factors. A listing of these features and their markers is provided in Table 7-1. This constellation, the PAI Suicide Potential Index (SPI), consists of 20 features of the PAI profile that are congruent with the research literature on risk factors for completed suicide. Some evidence for the validity of this index can be obtained from Table 7-2, which compares the means of the community and clinical samples with the three groups presented in Figure 7-1 (i.e., individuals with a history of suicidal behavior, patients currently on suicide precautions, and individuals with self-mutilating behavior).

The features on the Suicide Potential Index (SPI) tap a wide array of different psychological problems, and, in general, respondents with globally elevated profiles will obtain high scores. The literature supports this approach, as completed suicide in the absence of some form of emotional, physical, or behavioral problem is quite rare (Beskow, 1979, Rich, Young, & Fowler, 1986; Robins et al, 1959). The diagnoses noted most often are depression, alcoholism, and schizophrenia, although most of these studies have not done an adequate job of assessing personality disorders. Although the index includes information pertinent to these diagnoses, it also focuses on key behaviors or environmental circumstances that contributed to elevated suicide risk. For example, impulsivity (operationalized by *BOR-S*) heightens risk, because suicidal intent tends to be a transitional phenomenon. This is not to say that individuals completing suicide do so without thinking about it; on the contrary, most have thought of little else for some time. However, the intent itself will vary; a person may be very suicidal one day, and then, the next day, reconsider this intent. Unfortunately, the tendency to act while the feelings or impulses are strong will preclude the personal reflection that could lead to a reduction in intent.

Table 7-1
The PAI Suicide Potential Index (SPI)

Suicide risk factor	PAI markers	Frequency in clinical sample[a]
Severe psychic anxiety	*ANX-C* > 60*T*	49%
Severe anhedonia, degree of depression	*DEP-A* > 65*T*	44%
Global insomnia	*DEP-P* > 60*T*	44%
Diminished concentration	*SCZ-T* > 60*T*	39%
Indecision, OCD features, rigidity, perfectionism	*ARD-O* > 55*T*	42%
Acute overuse of alcohol	*ALC* > 60*T*	36%
Panic attacks	*ANX-P* > 60*T*	36%
Cycling affective disorder	*MAN-A* > 55*T*	33%
No children in home, little chance of rescue or interruption	*NON* > 60*T*	44%
Concomitant drug abuse	*DRG* > 60*T*	35%
Acute interpersonal disruption	*BOR-N* > 65*T*	34%
Intensity of current stress	*STR* > 65*T*	45%
Poor impulse control	*BOR-S* > 60*T*	34%
Anger, held in	*AGG-P* minus *AGG-V* > 10*T*	24%
Hopelessness	*DEP-C* > 65*T*	38%
Mistrust	*PAR-H* > 60*T*	34%
Withdrawn, isolated	*WRM* < 45*T*	44%
Worthlessness	*MAN-G* < 45*T*	40%
Mood fluctuations	*BOR-A* > 65*T*	38%
Somatic problems	*SOM-H* > 55*T*	42%

[a] *N* = 1,246.

A host of other factors can indicate heightened risk for suicide: confusion and indecision, hopelessness, feelings of worthlessness, significant health concerns, and drug abuse. The SPI also includes various environmental features that heighten suicide risk. Social stresses, interpersonal loss, and a lack of social support will both heighten the acuteness of the distress and also diminish the possibility of intervening factors. Each of these factors is incorporated within the index.

The Suicide Potential Index (SPI) is scored by counting the number of positive endorsements on the factors presented in Table 7-1. As the table demonstrates, each feature in isolation is seen with some frequency in a general clinical population. Nonetheless, Table 7-2 reveals that the mean number of positive SPI items in

Table 7-2
PAI Suicide Potential Index (SPI) Means and
Standard Deviations in Relevant Samples

Sample	n	M	SD
Suicide precautions	46	10.35	5.13
Suicide attempt	95	9.90	5.34
Self-mutilating behavior	77	9.84	5.46
Clinical sample	1,246	7.74	5.30
Community sample	1,000	3.14	3.22

patients presenting with self-destructive concerns are all significantly elevated in comparison to community respondents as well as to clinical respondents as a whole. Using 1- and 2-standard deviation points above the mean of clinical respondents as thresholds, Suicide Potential Index (SPI) scores at or above 13 items and 18 items would suggest moderate and marked numbers of suicide risk factors, respectively. Such scores, particularly in combination with elevated scores on *SUI*, should alert the clinician to acute situational as well as ideational factors related to suicide, and a prompt further evaluation of suicide risk is merited. For convenience, Table 7-3 provides transformations of SPI scores to *T* scores, based on the means and standard deviations of both the community standardization sample and the clinical standardization sample (Morey, 1991).

Not surprisingly, scores on the Suicide Potential Index (SPI) are related to *SUI* ($r = .65$ in the clinical sample, $r = .63$ in community respondents) even though the Index includes no items directly tapping suicidal behavior or intent. However, it is interesting to note that *NIM* serves as a mediator of this relationship. The index demonstrates a substantially larger association with *SUI* ($r = .60$ in clinical respondents) for individuals with *NIM* scores below 75*T* than it does for those with *NIM* scores above 75*T* ($r = .35$). Although not conclusive, this interaction suggests that the SPI will be affected by the global profile elevations typical with inflated *NIM* scores; thus, the SPI should be interpreted with caution when *NIM* is elevated. However, future research is needed to further explore the potential interactive relationships between these direct and indirect measures of suicide risk.

To further refine an understanding of this index, a factor analysis (principal axis extraction, followed by varimax rotation) was performed on the items comprising the index, using the data from the clinical standardization sample (Morey,

Table 7-3
T-Score Equivalents for the PAI Suicide Potential Index (SPI)
Standardized Against Community and Clinical Normative Samples

SPI score	*T*-score equivalent community norms[a]	*T*-score equivalent clinical norms[b]
0	40	35
1	43	37
2	46	39
3	50	41
4	53	43
5	56	45
6	59	47
7	62	49
8	65	50
9	68	52
10	71	54
11	74	56
12	78	58
13	81	60
14	84	62
15	87	64
16	90	66
17	93	67
18	96	69
19	99	71
20	102	73

[a]$N = 1,000.$ [b]$N = 1,246.$

1991). Four factors achieved an eigenvalue greater than one; Table 7-4 presents noteworthy (i.e., above .30) loadings on these factors. Factor 1 appears to involve a general distress factor associated with marked anxiety and depression (i.e., high negative affect); Factor 2 involves moodiness, hostility, and interpersonal disruption (i.e., volatility); Factor 3 is marked by poor impulse control and substance misuse (i.e., acting-out); and Factor 4 involves listlessness, apathy, and withdrawal (i.e., low positive affect).

Simplified factor scores may be obtained for each index factor by summing the number of items exceeding the cutoffs listed in Table 7-1 for those items that load on each factor (as listed in Table 7-4). Thus, a total of 10 items are relevant to Factor 1, 11 for Factor 2, and so forth. On Factor 4, 1 point is *deducted* if *MAN-A*

Table 7-4
Factors of the PAI Suicide Potential Index (SPI)

Suicide risk factor	Factor 1	Factor 2	Factor 3	Factor 4
Severe psychic anxiety	.70	.31		
Severe anhedonia, degree of depression	.57	.42		.32
Global insomnia	.61			
Diminished concentration	.64	.30		
Indecision, OCD features, rigidity, perfectionism	.51			
Acute overuse of alcohol			.61	
Panic attacks	.72			
Cycling affective disorder				(−.39)
No children in home, little chance of rescue or interruption		.60		
Concomitant drug abuse			.78	
Acute interpersonal disruption		.59		
Intensity of current stress		.48		
Poor impulse control		.42	.33	
Anger, held in	.32			
Hopelessness	.49	.46		.36
Mistrust		.62		
Withdrawn, isolated		.35		.41
Worthlessness				.54
Mood fluctuations	.47	.51		
Somatic problems	.50			
% variance	32.4%	9.4%	6.9%	5.2%

Note. Factor 1 = High Negative Affect; Factor 2 = Volatility; Factor 3 = Acting-Out; Factor 4 = Low Positive Affect.

exceeds 55*T*, as this item relates inversely to this factor. Table 7-5 presents a number of characteristics of these simplified factor scores. First, individuals identified as at imminent risk for suicide tend to be most prominently elevated on features of high negative affect, low positive affect, and volatility; acting-out behaviors appear more related to parasuicidal gestures and self-mutilating behaviors. Second, although the distress represented by the negative affect and volatility factors is highly related to *NIM*, the feature of low positive affect is relatively independent of *NIM*. Although not conclusive, this suggests that low positive affect may be of particular use in distinguishing between severity of suicidal potential when both *NIM* and *SUI* are elevated. For example, an elevation on *NIM* might lead the clinician to discount an elevated *SUI* score, believing that it may reflect a tendency to over-dramatize personal misery. However, should the low positive affect features of

Table 7-5
Characteristics of the PAI Suicide Potential Index (SPI) Factor Scores

Suicide risk factor	Factor 1	Factor 2	Factor 3	Factor 4
Maximum score	10.0	11.0	3.0	4.0
Clinical sample, M (SD)	3.9 (3.3)	4.4 (3.6)	1.0 (1.1)	1.3 (1.5)
Community sample, M (SD)	1.5 (1.9)	1.4 (2.0)	0.4 (0.7)	0.5 (1.0)
Current suicide precautions, M (SD)	5.9 (3.3)	6.4 (3.3)	0.9 (1.1)	2.3 (1.5)
Recent suicide attempt, M (SD)	5.3 (3.3)	6.0 (3.5)	1.2 (1.1)	2.1 (1.5)
Self-mutilating behavior, M (SD)	4.9 (3.5)	6.0 (3.8)	1.5 (1.1)	1.7 (1.7)
Correlation with SUI (r)	.63	.65	.26	.49
Correlation with NIM (r)	.70	.70	.33	.35

Note. Factor 1 = High Negative Affect; Factor 2 = Volatility; Factor 3 = Acting-Out; Factor 4 = Low Positive Affect.

Factor 4 also be elevated, there may be an increased threat that the ideation may unfold into action.

Using a 1-standard deviation cutoff above the mean scores for clinical respondents may serve as a convenient shorthand to determine whether these factors are elevated. Individuals obtaining these scores thus fall at or above the 84th percentile with respect to individuals presenting for treatment in a wide variety of clinical settings. Application of this strategy would result in cutoffs of eight or more items from Factor 1, eight or more items from Factor 2, three items from Factor 3, and three or more items from Factor 4. Individuals exceeding these cutoffs on several of the factors, particularly with an elevation on SUI, and no elevation on NIM, raise serious concerns about the risk for self-harm.

The Appendix details numerous correlates for the Suicide Potential Index (SPI), of which selected results are presented in Table 7-6. This table reveals that the Index is positively correlated with indicators of distress, depression, and poor morale. On the PAI, the SPI displays association with BOR, DEP, and ANX, which should be expected as these scales comprise part of the Index. However, the correlations with comparable indicators from other instruments are nearly as high. The SPI correlates highly with the total score and most subscales of the Suicide Probability Scale (Cull & Gill, 1982), with Wiggins (1966) Depression and Poor Morale content scales from the MMPI, and with the Beck Depression Inventory (Beck & Steer, 1987).

The Suicide Potential Index (SPI) is also associated with various measures of profile distortion. Because the SPI is highly associated with (and indeed, comprised of) various measures of distress, it is affected by the overall degree of

Table 7-6
Selected Correlates of the
PAI Suicide Potential Index (SPI) Total Score

Variable description	Correlation with SPI score
PAI *NIM*	.69
MMPI *F*	.63
Rogers Discriminant Function score (clinical sample)	.12
PAI *PIM*	−.67
MMPI *K*	−.59
Marlowe-Crowne Social Desirability Scale	−.36
Cashel Discriminant Function score (clinical sample)	.10
PAI *BOR*	.83
PAI *DEP*	.82
PAI *ANX*	.82
MMPI *Sc*	.61
MMPI *D*	.53
Wiggins MMPI Depression	.83
Wiggins MMPI Poor Morale	.77
Beck Depression Inventory	.63
Beck Hopelessness Scale	.49
Suicide Probability Scale, Hopelessness	.64
Suicide Probability Scale, Suicidal Ideation	.65
Suicide Probability Scale, Negative Self-Evaluation	.48
Suicide Probability Scale, Hostility	.39
Suicide Probability Scale, Total Score	.63

Note. MMPI = Minnesota Multiphasic Personality Inventory.

pathology represented by the profile. Thus, factors that produce distortion in a pathological direction will inflate SPI scores, whereas factors that suppress presentation of pathology, such as defensiveness, will also suppress SPI scores. Thus, the SPI score displays high positive correlations with *NIM* and MMPI *F*, and large negative associations with *PIM* and MMPI *K*. However, indices of profile distortion such as the Cashel Discriminant Function (described in chapter 5) and the Rogers Discriminant Function (described in chapter 4) that are more independent of global pathology are less correlated with the Suicide Potential Index (SPI). The implication of this pattern of results is that *NIM* elevations will be common when the SPI reaches critical levels. In such instances, the SPI score should not reflexively be discounted, because the catastrophic cognitions typical of the suicidal individual can also give rise to NIM elevations. An inspection of the Rogers Discriminant Function (RDF) score can provide further information with which to investigate this hypothesis. If the RDF score is also elevated, then the profile may contain noteworthy exaggeration. However, if the RDF score is within normal limits, then the SPI elevation merits serious consideration irrespective of the score on *NIM*.

CHAPTER 8
EVALUATING POTENTIAL FOR AGGRESSION

One of the most important needs, yet one of the most daunting tasks, in clinical assessment involves the prediction of aggression and violent behavior. Decisions about aggressive potential are commonplace in many settings where the PAI is administered; it is a critical consideration in treatment modality and hospitalization decisions, parole and inmate classification decisions, fitness for duty evaluations, custody examinations, and a variety of other core assessment tasks. Unfortunately, this is a very difficult task; in general, psychological measures have limited success in making predictions about highly specific behaviors at highly specific points in time. This is particularly true of the prediction of aggressive behavior (e.g., Megargee, 1970; Werner, Rose, Yesavage, & Seeman, 1984), where judgments about *imminent* dangerousness often need to be made.

The assessment of aggressive behavior is complicated by the number of different ways in which this construct is represented. Although a number of existing conceptualizations of the construct are multidimensional, many of the dimensions within these conceptualization are different. Predictably, empirical studies often find that different measures of aggression correlate minimally with one another (e.g., Govia & Velicer, 1985). In an effort to clarify distinct elements of the construct, Spielberger et al. (1985) have delineated differences between *anger*, which is an emotion; *hostility*, which involves a set of attitudes; and *aggression*, which refers to destructive behavior directed toward other persons or objects. Although anger and hostility both contribute to aggressive behavior, ultimately it is this behavior that clinicians are asked to identify and predict.

One study of several multidimensional measures of aggression is particularly informative about the nature of convergence on the major elements of this construct. Riley and Treiber (1989) examined data from the Buss-Durkee Hostility Inventory (Buss & Durkee, 1957), the Multidimensional Anger Inventory (Siegel, 1985), the Framingham Anger In/Out scales (Haynes et al., 1978), the Anger Self-Report scale (Zelin, Adler, & Myerson, 1972), and the State-Trait Anger Scale (Spielberger et al., 1983). The results of a combined factor analysis of scores from these instruments yielded three factors: one general factor tapping the experience of anger and hostility; and two factors identifying different modes of behavioral expression: one factor involving verbal expression of anger, and another involving physical, maladaptive forms of anger expression (e.g., fighting or smashing things).

The PAI can be useful as part of a comprehensive evaluation of aggressive potential, anger, and hostility. The obvious starting point for the assessment of aggression with the PAI is the *AGG* scale. Thus, this chapter describes the *AGG* scale and its subscale configurations. However, there are additional indicators on the PAI that can supplement the *AGG* scale in assessing aggressive potential, and preliminary work in combining these indicators into an aggregated index is described at the end of the chapter.

Aggression (*AGG*)

The *AGG* scale is a "treatment consideration" scale; it has no direct correspondence to any *DSM* diagnostic category, but, instead, taps fundamental affects and behaviors involved in many categories. Indeed, the *DSM* has been criticized for failing to include any reasonable classification of problems related to anger, aggression, and their management (Deffenbacher, 1992). There are a variety of diagnostic groups for whom anger control is central. Many of these groups are personality disorders: Antisocial, Borderline, and Passive-Aggressive diagnoses all have significant issues surrounding anger management. Intermittent Explosive Disorder is classified as an impulse control disorder, but failure to control anger is central. Physical abuse of adults or children is an "other condition that may be a focus of clinical attention" where anger management problems are involved. Thus, the *AGG* scale provides useful information for a wide array of diagnoses, as is demonstrated in the different configural guidelines described in chapter 6.

The PAI *AGG* scale was assembled to assess the three elements of aggression identified by Riley and Treiber (1989) described earlier. One subscale is devoted to a general assessment of temperamental anger and hostility, whereas the remaining two assess the typical behavioral mode through which anger and hostility are expressed. This combination of subscales permits assessment of a number of different aspects of aggression and its control (or lack of control). For example, strong inhibition and suppression of anger (e.g., an individual who turns anger "inward") might be reflected in positive indications of the experience of anger, but suppression of scales suggesting that this anger might somehow be expressed. The composition and interpretation of these subscales is described in the following sections.

Aggressive Attitude (AGG-A)

The Aggressive Attitude subscale was conceptualized to include general affects and attitudes conducive to aggressive behavior (e.g., having a quick temper, or a belief in the instrumental utility of aggression). The concept is distinct from the expression of anger, in that individuals can be quite angry and yet not express it, but, instead, suppress it or perhaps turn it inward. This concept resembles one of anger-proneness: the tendency to become easily frustrated or irritated, to react angrily when criticized or treated poorly by others.

Low scorers on *AGG-A* would be described as calm and placid individuals, very slow to anger and quite tolerant and forgiving of others. Moderate elevations (i.e., 60T to 70T) suggest individuals who are easily angered and frustrated. Others may perceive them as hostile and readily provoked. Scores exceeding 70T suggest persons who are very prone to anger, often losing their temper with little provocation. Such people may use anger to intimidate or control others and become furious when others criticize or obstruct them in some way. However, such anger may not be readily expressed; if *AGG-A* is elevated in this range and *AGG-V* and *AGG-P* both lie at or below the mean, the individual is apparently suppressing anger (look for low scores on *DOM*) or may be turning it inward (suggested with *DEP-C* elevated and *MAN-G* low).

Verbal Aggression (AGG-V)

The Verbal Aggression subscale included items indicating a readiness to display anger verbally in a milder form, perhaps through sarcasm or criticism, and in a more extreme form through yelling or abusive language. The critical aspect of this mode of anger expression is its visibility; high scorers will display their anger readily when it is experienced, rather than attempting to suppress or hide it. Of the three subscales, *AGG-V* is probably most (but inversely) related to efforts to control anger; low scorers make an effort to hide their anger from others, whereas high scorers make little or no effort to control their outward expression of anger. Thus, the ease with which one can tell that a person is angry is related to this subscale.

Low scores on *AGG-V* suggest individuals who prefer not to express their anger when it is experienced; rather, such people tend to overcontrol their anger, keeping it in to the best of their ability. Although control of anger is desirable, excessive control can lead to passivity and withdrawal (look for low *DOM* scores), intropunitive attitudes (suggested by *DEP-C* elevations or *MAN-G* suppression), or episodic, poorly controlled outbursts of anger when it is released (suggested if *AGG-P* is elevated). Scores on *AGG-V* that are moderately elevated (i.e., 60T to

70T) reflect individuals who are assertive and not intimidated by confrontation; toward the upper end of this range they may be verbally aggressive (e.g., critical, insulting, or verbally threatening) with little provocation. Elevations above 70T suggest that these verbal outbursts are likely to be abusive; such people are generally not popular with others and are viewed as extremely hostile. It is likely that others perceive such people as being angrier than they themselves acknowledge, or of which they are even aware.

Physical Aggression (AGG-P)

The Physical Aggression subscale addresses past history and present attitudes toward physically aggressive behavior. The questions inquire about a history of fighting and physical violence during adulthood; it is unlikely that significant elevations would result from conduct problems during adolescence in the absence of problems during adulthood. This scale has a relatively hard floor (i.e., community adults typically obtain low raw scores). However, elevations in clinical samples are relatively common.

Average scores on *AGG-P* indicate a person who reports being generally in control of angry feelings and impulses and who rarely expresses an angry outburst. Moderate elevations suggest that losses of temper are more common and that the person is prone to more physical displays of anger, perhaps breaking objects or engaging in physical confrontations; such people probably attempt to maintain close control over their anger, preferring to brood rather than risk expressing anger in potentially destructive ways. As scores elevate above 70T, this control often lapses, resulting in more extreme displays including damage to property and threats to assault others. Some of these displays may be sudden and unexpected, as such individuals may not display their anger readily when it is experienced, particularly if *AGG-V* is below the mean. It is likely that others are intimidated by their temper and the potential for physical violence and go to great lengths to avoid provoking them.

AGG Full Scale Interpretation

As a full scale, *AGG* provides a global assessment of attitudinal and behavioral features relevant to aggression, anger, and hostility. The item content ranges from indicators of verbal assertiveness and poor anger control to violent and assaultive behaviors. Average scores on *AGG* (i.e., < 60T) reflect a reasonable control over the expression of anger and hostility; scores below 40T may indicate very meek and unassertive individuals who have difficulty standing up for themselves, even when assertiveness is called for. Scores between 60T and 70T are indicative of individuals who may be seen as impatient, irritable, and quick-tempered when frustrated or crossed. Toward the upper end of this range such people may be increasingly angry and easily provoked by the actions of others around them.

Respondents with scores above 70T are likely to be chronically angry and will freely express their anger and hostility. In this range, at least one subscale is likely to be elevated and these scores should be examined to determine the typical modality (e.g., verbal or physical) through which the anger is expressed. *AGG* scores that are markedly elevated (i.e., > 82T) are typically associated with considerable anger and potential for aggression. Such individuals are easily provoked, and they may explode when frustrated; if *AGG-V* is low and *AGG-P* is elevated, this explosion may come with little warning. Others are likely to be afraid of the respondent's temper, and close relationships will suffer as a result. There is probably a history of fights and other episodes where anger has clouded the respondent's judgment, often leading to legal or occupational difficulties. Aggressive behaviors are likely to play a prominent role in the clinical picture; such behaviors represent a potential treatment complication that should receive careful attention in treatment planning.

AGG Subscale Configurations

The particular configuration of subscales that drive *AGG* elevations is very informative in determining the nature and severity of any aggressive behaviors that may occur. The following sections describe some of the implications of different combinations of elevations on the three subscales. A "high" score generally refers to scores above 70T; however, it should be recognized that *AGG-P* scores are more likely to be elevated than *AGG-V* scores in clinical samples.

AGG-A high, AGG-V high, AGG-P high

This pattern of responses suggests a person who is easily angered and who is probably perceived by others as having a hostile, angry temperament. Such people have difficulty controlling the expression of their anger, often making little effort to control it and displaying it readily when it is experienced. They are likely to be belligerent at relatively low levels of provocation and are not intimidated by confrontation. They tend to escalate to more extreme displays of anger, which might include damage to property and threats to assault others. It is likely that those around such people are intimidated by their temper and the potential for verbal abuse or displays of physical violence.

AGG-A high, AGG-V high, AGG-P average

This pattern of responses suggests an individual who is seen as hostile and angry, with marked difficulty controlling the expression of anger. When angry, such people tend to display the anger immediately, rather than brood about the perceived affront. They are unafraid of verbal confrontation, and they will tend to be verbally aggressive at relatively low levels of provocation. More extreme displays of anger, including damage to property and threats to assault others, are possible, but they do not appear to be a significant part of the clinical picture; this pattern suggests a person whose "bark is worse than their bite." It is possible that the more frequent venting of anger suggested by this pattern serves to prevent a more dramatic and overwhelming loss of control over temper.

AGG-A high, AGG-V average, AGG-P high

This pattern reflects a very angry individual who struggles to maintain control over his or her temper, but who tends to lose this control easily. When this happens, the person is likely to respond with more extreme displays of anger, including damage to property and threats to assault others. When the difference between *AGG-P* and *AGG-V* is substantial (i.e., $\geq 20T$), these displays may be sudden and unexpected, as anger may not be displayed readily when it is experienced. Such people attempt to hold their anger in, but lose control suddenly and explosively. It is likely that those around such people are afraid of their unpredictability, their potentially explosive temper, and the potential for physical violence.

AGG-A average, AGG-V high, AGG-P high

This is an unusual pattern of subscales. It suggests a person who believes that he or she is assertive but generally in control of angry feelings and impulses, expressing an angry outburst relatively infrequently. Nevertheless, the behavior of such individuals suggests that the control over temper is nowhere near as complete as they seem to believe. It is likely that the people who have experienced one of the respondent's angry verbal outbursts regard him or her with considerable wariness; they are likely to view the respondent as being more hostile and angry than the respondent believes is true of himself or herself. Anger is expressed readily when it is experienced, and this may involve more extreme displays of anger, including damage to property and threats to assault others.

PAI Profile Configuration and Aggressive Potential

Although *AGG* is the natural starting point for a determination of aggressive potential, there are many other elements of the PAI profile that are informative in this regard. To illustrate some of these elements, mean PAI profiles for a number of different groups who share problems with anger management are presented in Figures 8-1 and 8-2. These groups, taken from the *PAI Professional Manual* (Morey, 1991), include (a) psychiatric patients with a history of assaultive behavior, (b) patients on precautions for assaultiveness at the time of testing, (c) inmates incarcerated for rape, and (d) men court-ordered for treatment because of spouse abuse. These profiles share a number of features that are unique by comparison to many other clinical groups. For example, all groups tend to have scores on *SUI* that are lower than scores on *AGG*; this configuration is unusual in most clinical settings and suggests that anger is more likely to be directed outward than inward. A similar downward slope is seen in the relationship between *DOM* and *WRM*; these individuals seek to control relationships through hostile means. Scores on *MAN-G* are all above the mean, an unusual finding in clinical groups. Patterns of failure and discomfort in social relationships (e.g., *BOR-N, SCZ-S*) and a history of victimization (e.g., *ARD-T*) are also highlights of these configurations.

The PAI Violence Potential Index (VPI)

It is very difficult to estimate the short-term risk of violence in a given individual, and the research literature has, thus far, provided a meager empirical base for making such estimations. Often, the better predictors are demographic factors such as age and gender, or a past history of violence, as opposed to clinical signs or symptoms of the type measured by instruments such as the PAI. Nonetheless, the PAI does address a variety of factors that have been shown to be of promise in these type of assessments, including hostility and suspiciousness, agitation, or social withdrawal (McNiel & Binder, 1994; Shaffer, Waters, & Adams, 1994). Such studies, in combination with the profile configurations presented in Figures 8-1 and 8-2, suggest a variety of risk factors for violence that can be combined into a risk constellation using PAI configuration information. This constellation, the PAI Violence Potential Index (VPI), consists of 20 features of the PAI profile that are congruent with the available evidence on the prediction of dangerousness. These features and their operationalization are described in Table 8-1. Some preliminary evidence for the validity of this index can be obtained from Table 8-2, which compares the means of the community and clinical samples with a variety of relevant groups for whom dangerousness is a consideration.

The features on the Violence Potential Index (VPI) tap a wide array of psychological problems, but none of the features involve a reference to the absolute elevation of *AGG*, as the index is designed to supplement *AGG* scores in assessing dangerousness. The VPI is scored by counting the number of positive risk factor endorsements in Table 8-1. As the table demonstrates, each risk factor in isolation

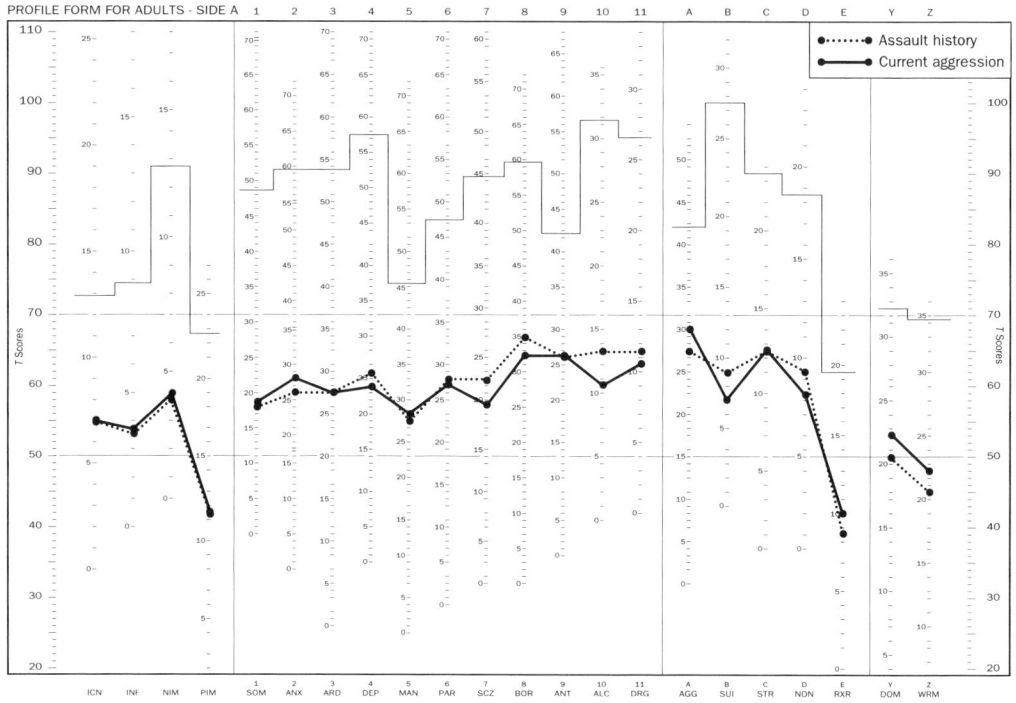

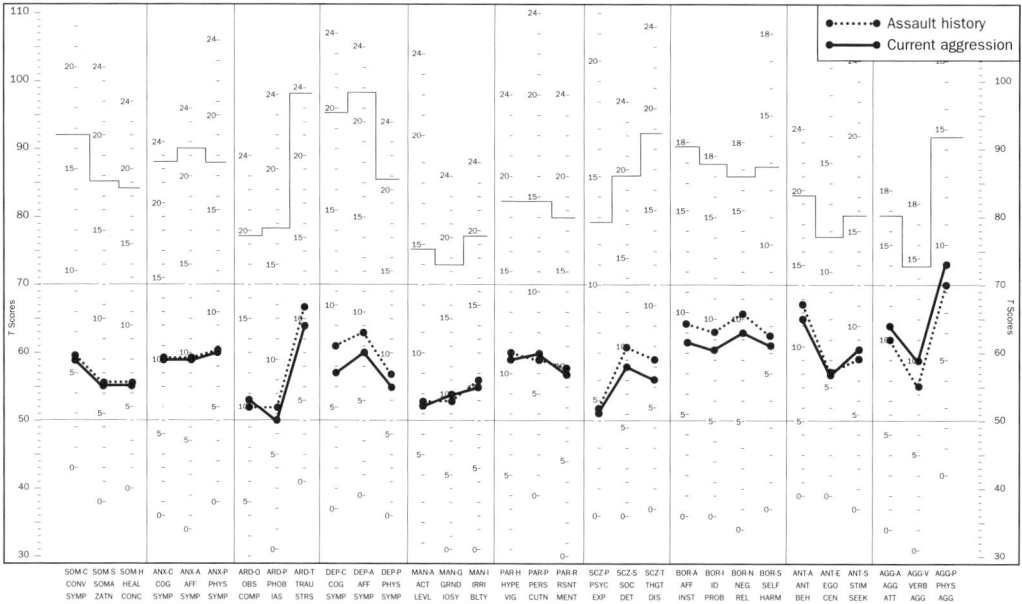

Figure 8-1. Mean PAI profiles for patients on current assault precautions and patients with a history of assaultive behavior (Morey, 1991).

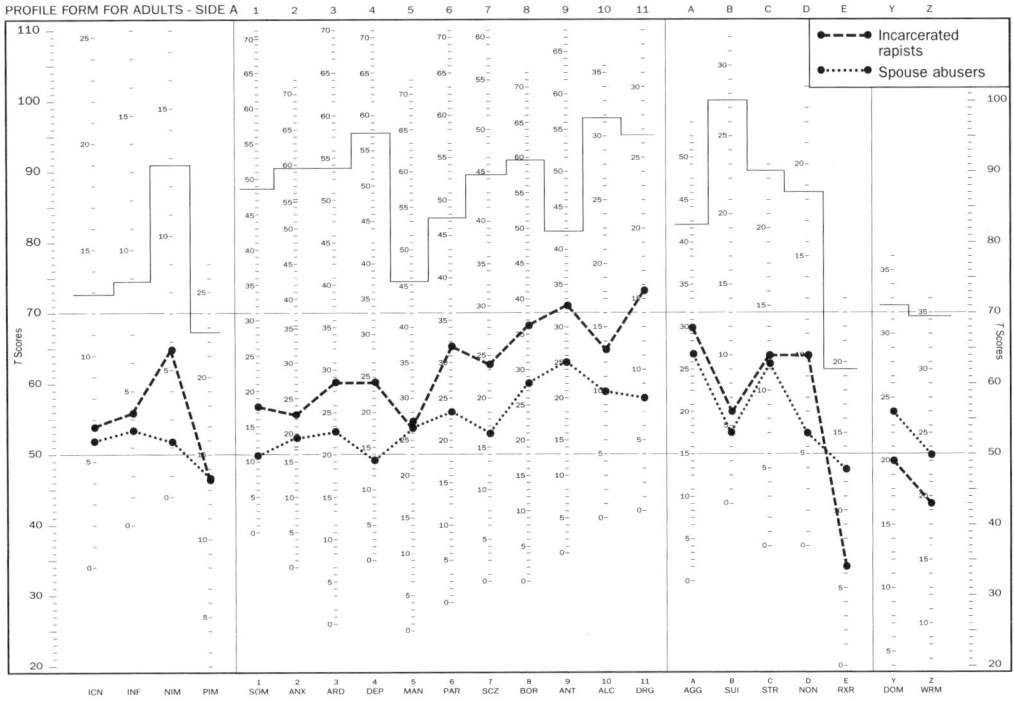

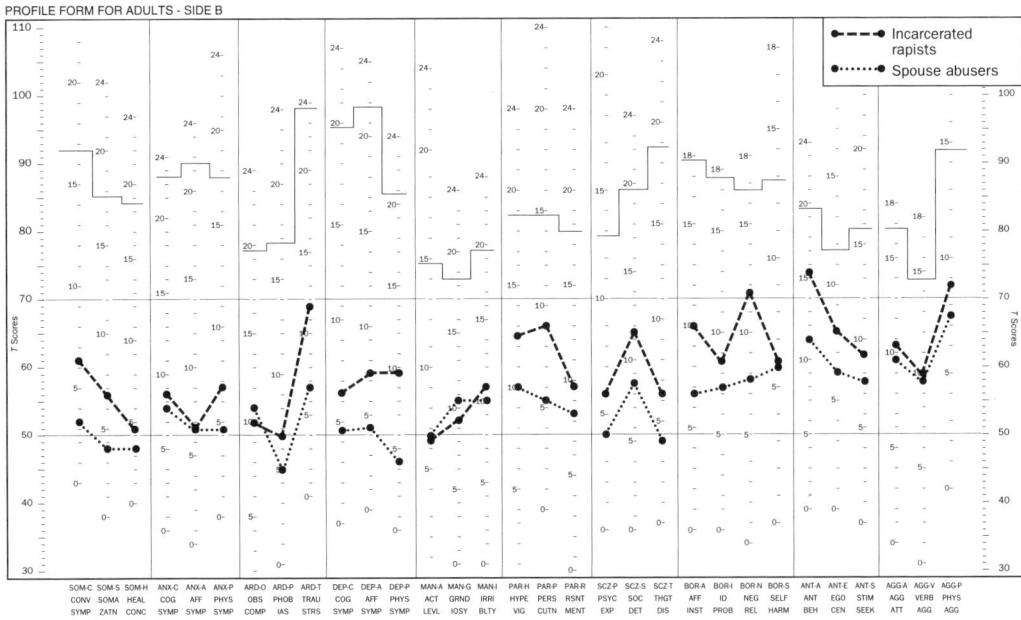

Figure 8-2. Mean PAI profiles for incarcerated rapists and spouse abusers in treatment (Morey, 1991).

Table 8-1
The PAI Violence Potential Index (VPI)

Violence risk factor	PAI markers	Frequency in clinical sample[a]
Explosive expression of anger	AGG-P 15T higher than AGG-V	26%
Anger directed outward	AGG 10T higher than SUI	18%
Hostile control in relationships	DOM 10T higher than WRM	26%
History of trauma without fearfulness	ARD-T 15T higher than ARD-P	33%
History of antisocial behavior	ANT-A > 70T	22%
Limited capacity for empathy	ANT-E > 60T	24%
Sensation seeking	ANT-S > 60T	25%
Rapid mood changes	BOR-A > 70T	26%
Troubled close relationships	BOR-N > 70T	27%
Impulsivity	BOR-S > 70T	21%
Agitation	MAN-A > 60T	24%
Self-centered	MAN-G > 60T	19%
Negative world view	NIM > 70T	19%
Hostile suspiciousness	PAR-H > 70T	17%
Sense of persecution	PAR-P > 70T	14%
Psychotic symptoms	SCZ-P > 70T	8%
Social alienation	SCZ-S > 70T	20%
Alcohol as disinhibitor	ALC > 70T	27%
Drug abuse as disinhibitor	DRG > 70T	24%
Estrangement from support system	NON > 70T	22%

[a] $N = 1,246$.

is seen with some frequency in a general clinical population. Nonetheless, Table 8-2 reveals that the mean numbers of positive index items in patients presenting with issues that raise concerns of dangerousness are all elevated in comparison to community respondents as well as to clinical respondents as a whole.

T-score conversions for the Violence Potential Index (VPI) are presented in Table 8-3, using the community and clinical samples as standardization referents. Using 1- and 2-standard deviation points above the mean of clinical respondents as thresholds, VPI scores at or above 9 items and 17 items would suggest moderate and marked risk of violent behavior, respectively. Such scores, particularly in combination with elevated scores on AGG, should alert the clinician to both historical and personality factors related to dangerousness, and further evaluation of the potential for assault is warranted. However, these scores are dramatically above the mean of community respondents (84T and 121T, respectively),

Table 8-2
PAI Violence Potential Index (VPI) Means and
Standard Deviations in Relevant Samples

Sample	*n*	*M*	*SD*
Current assault precautions	73	6.63	4.52
Current antisocial behaviors	102	6.87	4.83
History of assault or violence	231	6.95	4.54
Convicted for assault	124	7.29	4.61
Convicted for rape	14	6.50	5.40
Clinical sample	1,246	4.40	3.98
Community sample	1,000	1.58	2.18

and, as shown in Table 8-2, samples with a history of violence obtain mean scores above 6 items (70*T*). Thus, even scores in this range raise the possibility that potential for aggression might be a complicating factor in treatment planning.

The Appendix details numerous correlates for the Violence Potential Index (VPI), of which selected results are presented in Table 8-4. This table reveals that the VPI is positively correlated with indicators of anger, hostility, and poor judgment. On the PAI, the Violence Potential Index displays its greatest associations at the full scale level with *BOR* and *ANT*, which are both included as part of the VPI. However, at the subscale level, the greatest association is with *AGG-P*, and this latter score is not directly included in the VPI score, as the Violence Potential Index is intended to independently supplement the information provided by the *AGG* scale and subscales. The VPI also correlates highly with indicators of hostility and poor judgment on the MMPI, with Hare's (1985) self-report measure of psychopathic features, and with a diagnosis of Antisocial Personality Disorder arrived at through structured interview.

The Violence Potential Index (VPI) is also associated with various measures of profile distortion. Because the VPI is highly associated with (and indeed, comprised of) various measures of symptoms and character issues, it is affected by the overall degree of pathology represented by the profile. Thus, factors (e.g., malingering) that produce distortion in a pathological direction will inflate VPI scores, whereas factors that suppress presentation of pathology (e.g., defensiveness) will also suppress VPI scores. Thus, the VPI score displays high positive correlations with *NIM* and MMPI *F*, and substantial negative associations with *PIM* and MMPI *K*. However, the discriminant function-based indices of profile distortion that are more independent of global pathology, such as the Cashel Discriminant Function (described in chapter 5) and the Rogers Discriminant Function (described in

Table 8-3
***T*-Score Equivalents for the PAI Violence Potential Index (VPI) Standardized Against Community and Clinical Normative Samples**

VPI score	*T*-score equivalent community norms[a]	*T*-score equivalent clinical norms[b]
0	43	39
1	47	42
2	52	44
3	57	46
4	61	49
5	66	51
6	70	54
7	75	57
8	79	59
9	84	62
10	89	64
11	93	67
12	98	69
13	102	72
14	107	74
15	111	77
16	116	79
17	121	82
18	125	84
19	130	87
20	134	89

[a] $N = 1,000$. [b] $N = 1,246$.

chapter 4), are less correlated with the VPI. In the assessment of potential for violence, the guarded or defensive individual is typically of greater concern than the exaggerating or malingering individual. The implication of this pattern of results is that guarded responding of the type leading to elevations on *PIM* or the MMPI *K* scale will also lead to the suppression of the VPI score. However, more subtle indicators of defensiveness such as the Cashel Discriminant Function (CDF) score or the Defensiveness Index (DEF) seem largely unrelated to VPI scores, suggesting that the types of intentional positive dissimulation reflected by those indices will not necessarily suppress VPI scores. Thus, for example, an individual with a markedly elevated CDF score and a very low VPI total should not necessarily be assumed to be concealing features of potential violence, particularly in the absence of an elevation on *PIM*.

Table 8-4
Selected Correlates of the
PAI Violence Potential Index (VPI) Total Score

Variable description	Correlation with VPI score
PAI *NIM*	.66
MMPI *F*	.52
Rogers Discriminant Function score (clinical sample)	.21
PAI *PIM*	−.54
Defensiveness Index (clinical sample)	.04
MMPI *K*	−.49
Marlowe-Crowne Social Desirability Scale	−.40
Cashel Discriminant Function score (clinical sample)	.19
PAI *BOR*	.74
PAI *ANT*	.74
PAI *AGG*	.65
PAI *AGG-P*	.72
Wiggins MMPI Psychoticism	.65
Wiggins MMPI Hostility	.63
Hare Self-Report Psychopathy (clinical sample)	.67
Diagnostic Interview for Personality Disorders, Antisocial Personality	.68

Note. MMPI = Minnesota Multiphasic Personality Inventory.

CHAPTER 9
EVALUATING SPECIFIC PSYCHOLOGICAL ISSUES

In addition to the many clinical issues that have been discussed in previous chapters, there are a number of issues of importance in personality assessment that fall within the more normative range of personality and behavior. This chapter explores three specific areas where the PAI can provide valuable information: the domains of self-concept, interpersonal style, and perception of the environment.

Assessment of Self-Concept

The view that people have of themselves can play a critical role in determining their behavior. On the PAI, three clinical subscales are central in assessing three important facets of the self-concept. One facet, *self-esteem*, reflects the evaluative component of self-perception: Do people like themselves, or do they dislike themselves? Are they the way they want to be, or would they prefer to be very different? The most direct measure of this self-facet on the PAI is the *MAN-G* subscale, with high scorers manifesting high, perhaps even inflated, self-esteem. A second facet, *self-efficacy*, reflects a sense of personal competence and perceived control (Bandura, 1977). The *DEP-C* scale provides information relevant to the person's perceived effectiveness: High scorers see themselves as ineffective in controlling the environment to meet their needs. The third facet involves the *stability* of the self-concept: Is it fixed and enduring, or is it unstable and highly vulnerable to environmental events? For example, two people who each have quite high self esteem may differ substantially in the secureness of this esteem; one person may be capable of maintaining high self-esteem in the face of considerable evidence to the contrary, whereas the other's self-esteem may be quite vulnerable to even the slightest "blow to the ego." *BOR-I* provides a measure of the stability of self-esteem, with high scorers having the more variable and more vulnerable self-concepts.

The following sections discuss some of the implications for the self-concept related to different configurations of these three scales. As the implications of the individual scales in isolation have been discussed previously in chapter 2, these implications will not be reviewed here; rather, the following descriptions address the implications of 27 different configurations (e.g., high, average, or low scores for each scale) for the self-concept of the respondent. In dividing the scales into high, average, or low scorers, the distinctions are drawn in reference to a clinical population rather than a community population; because certain self-related issues (e.g., low self-esteem and doubts about self-efficacy) are so common in clinical groups, it was thought that basing the differentiation on expected scores within clinical samples would yield finer discriminations when these rules are applied to such samples. Thus, the ranges differ somewhat across the three scales. For *DEP-C* and *BOR*-I, the high range is considered to be 75*T* or above, whereas for *MAN-G* the high range refers to 70*T* or above. The average range is between 51*T* and 74*T* (inclusive) for *DEP-C* and *BOR*-I, whereas for *MAN-G* this range is between 41*T* and 69*T*. Thus, the low range for *DEP-C* and *BOR-I* involves scores of 50*T* or below, whereas the low range for *MAN-G* includes scores 40*T* or lower.

MAN-G high, BOR-I high, DEP-C high

The self-concept of individuals with this pattern may be poorly established (i.e., their attitudes about themselves are likely to fluctuate wildly in response to situational triggers). The self-perception will vary from states of very poor self-esteem and severe self-doubt to periods of exaggerated confidence and overvalued accomplishments. The episodes of positive self-esteem, when they occur, may be defensive in response to feelings of emptiness and a lack of a sense of purpose. As a result, this self-esteem will be quite fragile and is likely to plummet in response to slights or oversights by other people. Associated with this instability in self-esteem are corresponding shifts in identity and attitudes about major life issues. Because of the normally inverse relationship between *MAN-G* and the other two scales, such a pattern should be quite rare; normatively, it was observed in 0.1% of clinical respondents and was never obtained in the community sample.

MAN-G high, BOR-I high, DEP-C average

This pattern suggests that the self-concept of the respondent appears to be poorly established and is likely to fluctuate in response to the situation. For such individuals, the self-perception will vary from states of poor self-esteem and uncertainty to periods of exaggerated self-assurance and overvalued accomplishments. The episodes of positive self-esteem may be a defense against marked feelings of emptiness; overvaluing their everyday accomplishments may help give such individuals a sense of purpose that they would otherwise lack. However, such feelings of self-importance are likely to be tenuous, and self-esteem during these times may plummet dramatically in response to slights or oversights by other people. Corresponding shifts in identity and attitudes about goals and values are likely to be associated with this instability in self-esteem. Whereas this pattern was never observed in the community normative sample, it was obtained in 0.9% of clinical respondents.

MAN-G high, BOR-I high, DEP-C low

This pattern suggests that the self-concept is poorly established and highly responsive to the nature of external events. Most likely, the self-perception will vary from states of inflated self-esteem and overvalued accomplishments to times of intense uncertainty, resentment, and anger. The generally positive self-esteem may be a defense against marked feelings of superficiality and emptiness and a lack of a sense of purpose. One would anticipate that the favorable self-evaluation is likely to be quite fragile and may internally plummet in response to slights or over-sights by other people; overtly this might take the form of considerable anger directed at these people. Corresponding shifts in goals, values, and attitudes about major life issues may be associated with these evaluative swings. Generally, this is a very rare configuration, occurring in 0.1% of clinical respondents and never observed in the PAI normative community sample.

MAN-G high, BOR-I average, DEP-C high

This unusual pattern suggests a self-concept involving a generally positive self-evaluation, but there are doubts about personal effectiveness in many situations and a pessimistic view of future prospects. It is possible that the positive self-esteem may be defensive in response to these feelings of pessimism and a sense of inadequacy, and these feelings may alternate as a function of the current situation. As a result, self-esteem will tend to be fragile and very reactive to the quality of the individual's interactions with other people. The pessimism may result from a sense that the external environment consistently provides obstacles to the accomplishment of aims and goals. Responsibility for any setbacks is, thus, likely to be attributed externally. The pattern is uncommon, obtained in 0.2% of clinical respondents and never obtained in the community normative sample.

MAN-G high, BOR-I average, DEP-C average

The self-concept of such individuals appears to involve a generally positive, but probably fluctuating, self-evaluation. The positive self-esteem may be a defense against feelings of uncertainty and self-doubt. Thus, the self-perception is likely to be vulnerable and may drop dramatically in response to scrutiny or criticism by other people. Self-esteem may be maintained in such situations through attributing responsibility for setbacks to some external cause, rather than to personal failings.

This pattern is more common in clinical populations (1.0% of respondents) than in normal populations (0.2%).

MAN-G high, BOR-I average, DEP-C low

This self-concept is likely to involve a generally positive and, at times, perhaps uncritical self-evaluation. There may be some variability and uncertainty associated with this self-concept, particularly in the face of scrutiny or criticism from others. Nonetheless, self-esteem is likely to be maintained in such situations through attributing responsibility for setbacks to some external cause, rather than to personal failings. At such times, anger directed at the source is a more likely result of such criticism than inner self-doubt. This pattern is somewhat more common in clinical respondents (1.3%) than in normal respondents (0.6%).

MAN-G high, BOR-I low, DEP-C high

This pattern is a contradiction in terms: a highly positive self-evaluation in combination with a pessimistic view of the personal prospects for the future and doubts about efficacy in dealing with the challenges of the future. Because *BOR-I* denotes a stable sense of self-worth, this pessimism must result from a sense that the external environment consistently provides exceptional obstacles to the accomplishment of personal aims and goals. Responsibility for any setbacks is, thus, likely to be attributed externally. Because of the inherent contradictions in this pattern, it is not surprising that it was never obtained in either the normative clinical or the community samples.

MAN-G high, BOR-I low, DEP-C average

This self-concept pattern appears to involve a generally positive self-evaluation, which may be occasionally punctuated by periods of pessimism. Such individuals describe approaching life with a clear sense of purpose and distinct convictions. The generally stable positive self-evaluation may be vulnerable during times when the external environment is perceived as providing obstacles to the accomplishment of personal aims and goals. However, given the reasonably stable sense of self-worth implied by the low *BOR-I*, responsibility for any setbacks is more likely to be attributed externally than to personal failings. Because of the contradictions between the stability of the self-concept and its positive and negative elements, the pattern is unusual; it was obtained in only 0.2% of clinical respondents and 0.1% of community respondents.

MAN-G high, BOR-I low, DEP-C low

This self-concept pattern appears to involve a highly positive and, at times, perhaps uncritical self-evaluation. Such people describe themselves as effective and competent in most domains, including having a well established sense of purpose in life and distinct convictions. The high self-esteem is probably quite robust in the face of insults, given the reasonably stable sense of self-worth implied by the low *BOR-I*. To maintain this self-esteem, responsibility for any setbacks may be more likely to be attributed externally than to personal failings. This pattern is obtained in about the same proportions in community samples (1.9%) and clinical samples (1.5%).

MAN-G average, BOR-I high, DEP-C high

This pattern implies a self-concept that is poorly established and likely to fluctuate. The self-perception will vary from states of harsh self-criticism and severe self-doubt to periods of relative self-confidence and intact self-esteem. It also will probably vary most as a function of the current status of close relationships; apart from a sense of identity established from these relationships, such people are likely to feel ineffectual, unfulfilled and inadequate. As a result, self-esteem is quite fragile and is likely to plummet in response to slights or oversights by other people. Corresponding shifts in identity and attitudes about major life issues are likely to be associated with these drops in self-esteem. Although uncommon in the community sample (0.2%), this pattern was fairly common in clinical respondents (5.7%).

MAN-G average, BOR-I high, DEP-C average

This pattern suggests that the self-concept is imperfectly established, with considerable uncertainty about major life issues and goals. Although outwardly such individuals may appear to have adequate self-esteem, this self-esteem is likely to be fragile, and the individuals may be inwardly self-critical and self-doubting. Self-esteem may be particularly vulnerable to slights or oversights by other people, arising from a self-image that depends unduly on the current status of close relationships. This pattern is nearly six times more common in clinical samples (4.7%) than in the normative community sample (0.8%).

MAN-G average, BOR-I high, DEP-C low

This configuration, like the preceding pattern, reflects a self-concept that is imperfectly established, with considerable uncertainty about major life issues and goals. On the surface, such individuals are likely to appear to be optimistic and to have adequate self-esteem; however, this self-esteem may be fragile and particularly vulnerable to interpersonal disruption. In part, this vulnerability may arise from a self-image that depends on the current status of close relationships. The blame for any interpersonal problems may be repeatedly attributed outwardly in an effort to preserve self-esteem. This pattern is uncommon in both clinical (0.7%) and community (0.2%) samples.

MAN-G average, BOR-I average, DEP-C high

This pattern suggests a self-concept that involves a generally negative self-evaluation, which may vary from states of harsh self-criticism and self-doubt to periods of relative self-confidence and intact self esteem. This fluctuation is likely to vary as a function of current circumstances, with pessimism and self-doubt predominating at the present time. Under stress, such persons are prone to be self-critical, dwelling on past failures and lost opportunities and having considerable uncertainty and indecision about their plans and goals for the future. Given this self-doubt, they tend to blame themselves for setbacks and to see prospects for future success as dependent on the actions of others. This is a relatively common pattern, although roughly six times more prevalent in clinical (5.9%) than in community (1.0%) samples.

MAN-G average, BOR-I average, DEP-C average

This configuration, representing as it does the average ranges for all three scales in clinical populations, is not surprisingly the most common configuration among clinical respondents. The self-concept of such respondents involves a self-evaluation that has both positive and negative aspects. Their attitudes about themselves may vary from states of pessimism and self-doubt to periods of relative self-confidence and self-satisfaction. Some fluctuation in self-esteem may be observed as a function of current circumstances; during stressful times, in particular, such individuals may be prone to be self-critical, uncertain, and indecisive. However, these fluctuations would not be as extreme as those noted in many clients in clinical settings; in fact, such instability is experienced by most adults. As noted, this is the most common configuration in clinical respondents (26.2%), but also the second most common in community adults (15.4%).

MAN-G average, BOR-I average, DEP-C low

This pattern suggests a self-concept involving a generally positive self-evaluation. Such people are typically confident, resilient, and optimistic, although the self-esteem may be fairly sensitive to changes in current circumstances. During times of stress, these people inwardly may be troubled by more self-doubt and misgivings about adequacy and competence than is readily apparent to others. Reactive changes in self-esteem may be accompanied by uncertainty about goals, values, and important life decisions. This is a common pattern, although obtained somewhat more frequently in community samples (11.0%) than in clinical samples (9.1%).

MAN-G average, BOR-I low, DEP-C high

The self-concept of such respondents appears to involve a fixed, rather negative self-evaluation. People with this pattern are likely to be pessimistic and self-critical and to dwell on past failures and lost opportunities. They may tend to attribute blame for any setbacks internally, rather than externally, but their self-esteem is still likely to be responsive to positive feedback from others. This is a very uncommon pattern in both clinical (0.2%) and community (0.1%) samples, perhaps due to the inherent contradictions given the picture of stable self-concept, combined with very low self-efficacy, yet average self-esteem.

MAN-G average, BOR-I low, DEP-C average

This pattern suggests a self-concept that involves a reasonably stable and positive self-evaluation which, as is the case with most individuals, may be occasionally punctuated by brief periods of self-doubt or pessimism. Such people describe approaching life with a clear sense of purpose and distinct convictions, with a well articulated sense of who they are and what their goals are. This identity should be robust even in the face of significant stresses in their environment. This positive and sturdy self-view is more than twice as common in community (9.6%) as in clinical (3.9%) populations.

MAN-G average, BOR-I low, DEP-C low

This pattern reflects the "picture of health" with respect to self-concept, indicating a stable positive self-evaluation. It reflects a confident and optimistic person who approaches life with a clear sense of purpose and distinct convictions. These characteristics are valuable in that they allow the person to be resilient and adaptive in the face of most stressors. Such people are reasonably self-satisfied, with a well articulated sense of who they are and what their goals are. This is the most common pattern among community adults (39.2%), where it is roughly three times more frequent than in clinical populations (13.1%).

MAN-G low, BOR-I high, DEP-C high

This pattern suggests a self-concept that is poorly established, although harsh self-criticism and severe self-doubt seem to predominate. The self-perception will tend to vary as a function of the current status of close relationships; apart from a sense of identity established from such relationships, the respondent is likely to feel incomplete, unfulfilled and inadequate. As a result, self-esteem is quite fragile and is likely to plummet in response to slights or oversights by other people. Corresponding shifts in identity and attitudes about major life issues, which will largely be derived from those held by important others, are associated with this instability in self-esteem. This pattern is relatively common in clinical respondents (4.7%), although is is uncommon in the general population (0.6%).

MAN-G low, BOR-I high, DEP-C average

The self-concept represented by this pattern appears to be poorly established, and self-criticism and adequacy concerns seem characteristic. Although low self-esteem may not be obvious to others, the self-perception will tend to depend greatly on the current status of close relationships. Apart from a sense of identity derived from such relationships, such people are likely to feel uncertain and unfulfilled. Self-esteem is probably generally low and particularly sensitive to slights or oversights by other people. Corresponding shifts in identity and attitudes about major life issues are associated with any such shifts in self-esteem. This relatively uncommon pattern is seen more in clinical respondents (1.3%) than in community adults (0.3%).

MAN-G low, BOR-I high, DEP-C low

This very unusual pattern suggests a self-concept that is imperfectly established, with considerable uncertainty about major life issues and goals. Although outwardly such people may appear to have adequate self-esteem, inwardly they are likely to be troubled by self-doubt and misgivings about adequacy. Some of the self-image may be derived through close relationships; although this strategy may be working for the respondent at present, the self-esteem may be quite fragile and vulnerable to slights or oversights by other people. This pattern is very infrequent in both clinical (0.1%) and community (0.1%) populations, as it is unusual for people to maintain optimism in the face of marked identity confusion.

MAN-G low, BOR-I average, DEP-C high

This self-concept pattern involves a generally harsh, negative self-evaluation. Such people are prone to be self-critical and pessimistic, dwelling on past failures and lost opportunities with considerable uncertainty and indecision about plans and goals for the future. Given this self-doubt, they tend to blame themselves for setbacks and to see any prospects for future success as dependent on the actions of others. This pattern is fairly common in clinical populations (6.3%), although rare in the general population (0.7%).

MAN-G low, BOR-I average, DEP-C average

This self-concept pattern involves a rather negative self-evaluation. Such people are likely to be self-critical, not handling setbacks very well and blaming themselves for past failures and lost opportunities. They may inwardly be more troubled by self-doubt and misgivings about their adequacy than is apparent on the surface. They may tend to play down their successes as a result, and probably see such accomplishments as heavily dependent on the efforts or good will of others.

This is a relatively common pattern in clinical groups (7.0%), although not uncommon in the general population (4.7%).

MAN-G low, BOR-I average, DEP-C low

This pattern suggests an individual who is reasonably comfortable with himself or herself, although self-esteem may be rather reactive to changes in current circumstances. Such a person may inwardly be troubled by more self-doubt and misgivings about adequacy than is readily apparent to others, but be relatively effective in masking these doubts. This person may tend to discount personal successes, seeing such accomplishments as heavily dependent on the efforts or good will of others. This is a configuration more commonly observed in clinical groups (1.2%) than in community samples (0.3%).

MAN-G low, BOR-I low, DEP-C high

The self-concept suggested by this pattern involves a fixed, negative self-evaluation. Such people are likely to be harshly self-critical and to dwell on past failures and lost opportunities. Plagued by self-doubt, they are likely to attribute blame for any setbacks internally and any successes are dismissed as either good fortune or as the result of actions by others more competent than themselves. Self-concepts with such low self-efficacy and such stability are rare, constituting 0.1% of clinical respondents; this pattern was never observed in the normative sample.

MAN-G low, BOR-I low, DEP-C average

The self-concept of these respondents appears to involve a fixed, rather negative self-evaluation. Such people are likely to be self-critical and to focus on their shortcomings and failures. Similar to those in the preceding group, these individuals may be inwardly troubled by self-doubt and misgivings about adequacy to a greater extent than is apparent to others. They may dismiss their successes as either good fortune or as the result of the efforts of others, being unwilling to give themselves credit for their accomplishments. This pattern is not uncommon in either normative (3.2%) or clinical (2.7%) samples.

MAN-G low, BOR-I low, DEP-C low

The self-concept described by this pattern involves a generally stable, unassuming self-evaluation; such people report approaching life with a clear convictions and distinct (but likely modest) ambitions. Although outwardly such people will appear to have reasonable self-esteem, inwardly they may be troubled by self-doubt and misgivings about personal competence. Although optimistic about the future, they may tend to minimize their role in any anticipated successes, tending to view achievements as either good fortune or as the result of the efforts of others. Fairly common in the general population (9.8%), this configuration is less common in clinical respondents (2.2%).

Assessment of Interpersonal Style

An individual's interpersonal style constitutes a significant portion of his or her personality. The way that a person relates to others is certainly associated with overall adjustment; however, there are a variety of ways in which people interact with one another, and there is no one "healthy" style that is necessary for personal effectiveness. Nonetheless, a person's style can interact with aspects of the situation to produce outcomes both desirable and undesirable; for example, a person who is aloof and retiring may do quite well in a job that requires computer programming skills, but the same person may be uncomfortable and ineffective at cocktail parties. In a clinical context, this person might respond quite differently to some therapies or therapists than another individual who is more outgoing. The interpersonal style thus represents a significant aspect of the personality that can mediate a number of clinical concerns.

On the PAI, the two interpersonal scales, *DOM* and *WRM*, represent the core of the interpersonal style assessment. The selection of these two dimensions was based on the interpersonal circumplex model originally formulated by Leary (1957) and elaborated upon by many others (e.g., Benjamin, 1973; Kiesler, 1983; Wiggins, 1982). The basic circumplex model of interpersonal behavior involves two orthogonal dimensions that, when considered in combination, characterize one's preferred manner of interacting with others. Combining these two scales forms four quadrants: a warm, dominating quadrant; a cold, dominating quadrant; a cold, submitting quadrant; and a warm, submitting quadrant. For each of the quadrants, stereotypic behaviors can be described. A prototype for the "warm control" quadrant would be parenting behavior, which is an example of controlling others while being interested in maintaining the attachment relationship. An impersonal, superordinate–subordinate relationship would characterize the "cold control" quadrant, whereas "cold submission" would be characterized by a person who is submitting to others unwillingly, perhaps a passive-aggressive reaction. Finally, the prototype for the "warm submission" style would be dependency, a person who is very interested in maintaining the attachment relationship and willing to submit in the context of that relationship in order to maintain it.

A particularly interesting aspect of the theory surrounding the interpersonal circumplex is the principle of *complementarity*. This principle governs the expected nature of interpersonal transactions within the circumplex; every interpersonal behavior has a complement, which is the natural interpersonal reaction to a given event or transaction. Complementary behaviors are the same on the warmth dimension and on the opposing end of the dominance dimension. For example, if a person controls people (dominance) in a friendly (warmth) way, as in a parenting relationship, the complementary reaction would be for people to submit in a friendly way. On the other hand, if a person controls others in a hostile and uncaring way, the complementary reaction would be to submit, but in a hostile manner. This property of the interpersonal dimensions is useful in allowing one to predict the types of interpersonal behavior a person is likely to evoke in others.

The *DOM* and *WRM* scales have nearly identical distributions in clinical and normal respondents. This supports the conclusion that the two scales capture variation across a normal personality trait, and that variability on these dimensions exists as widely within normal populations as it does within individuals presenting for treatment. On these scales, high scores may be problematic, and low scores may also reflect problems; the interpersonal scales are probably the most bipolar of all the PAI scales, in that the low and high extremes are equally interpretable and have equal potential for problems. Generally, it appears that obtaining higher scores on *WRM* is preferable, as this scale is typically positively correlated with indicators of favorable adjustment. However, high scores on *WRM* could well reflect a person who is sacrificing too much to maintain attachment relationships and is, thus, ineffective in interpersonal relationships in many ways.

The following sections discuss some of the implications for the assessment of interpersonal style related to different configurations of *DOM* and *WRM*. Five score ranges are provided for these scales: Very low (< 35*T*), Low (35*T* to 44*T*), Average (45*T* to 55*T*), High (56*T* to 65*T*), and Very high (> 65*T*). Because of the similar distributions for the two groups, these ranges are applicable to both clinical populations and community populations. Interpretations for these scales are sometimes supplemented with references to *BOR-N*, which can shed further light on the nature of any difficulties that may be suggested by the interpersonal scales. In addition, there are several other sources of interpersonal information on the PAI, most notably *SCZ-S* (i.e., social disinterest), *ARD-P* (i.e., social anxiety), *ANT-E* (i.e., capacity for empathy), *PAR-R* (i.e., interpersonal bitterness), and *PAR-P* (i.e., suspiciousness and touchiness).

DOM very high, WRM very high

This interpersonal style seems best characterized as involving very strong needs for affiliation and attention. This may result in rather extreme behavior, such as controlling and interfering with the social interactions of others in order to meet the respondent's own needs. Such people may be seen by others as being attention-seeking and dramatic. The needs for attention and affiliation can be so strong that the quality of social interactions may be relatively unimportant as compared to their quantity. As a result, such people may be uninhibited in seeking any opportunity to interact with others, as long as the interaction permits them to maintain some control over the relationship. This control, perhaps intended as a protective measure by the respondent, may be viewed as smothering by others.

DOM very high, WRM high

This interpersonal style seems best characterized as involving very strong needs for attention and affiliation. These needs may result in the respondent being perceived by others as controlling; this may take the form of interfering with the social interactions of others in order to meet personal needs. The need for attention may be sufficiently strong that any opportunity to interact with others will be acted on, as long as the interaction permits the respondent some control over the relationship. This control, perhaps intended as helpful by the respondent, may be viewed less positively by others. If *PAR* is below average, this type of individual may be willing to relinquish some control in the relationship for the sake of maintaining the attachment; however, elevations on *PAR* suggest that such flexibility is unlikely.

DOM very high, WRM average

This configuration suggests an interpersonal style best characterized as being domineering and overcontrolling. Such people have strong needs to control others, and they expect respect and admiration in return. They may be driven to appear competent and authoritative and are likely to have little tolerance for those who disagree with their plans and desires. Others probably view them as being rather overbearing and dictatorial. Although able to express some degree of warmth, the need to be in control in relationships probably taxes the endurance of those close to them. Although they are interested in relationships with others, they are probably quite uncomfortable about the prospect of appearing weak, submissive, or passive in these relationships.

DOM very high, WRM low

People displaying this pattern report an interpersonal style best characterized as being controlling and rather egocentric. They are likely to view relationships more as an opportunity for self-enhancement, rather than as a source of enjoyment. As a result, their relationships are likely to be impersonal and pragmatic. They tend to be quite ambitious and, hence, competitive in relationships; they tend to be skeptical of close attachments, perhaps viewing them as a sign of dependency or weakness. Such people place a high premium on loyalty in others (particularly if *PAR* is above average) and they are not likely to forgive transgressions or slights.

DOM very high, WRM very low

This interpersonal style may be characterized as being egocentric and suspicious. Such people are likely to demand more from relationships than they are willing to give, using relationships for self-enhancement. As a result, their interactions with others are likely to be coldly pragmatic and, perhaps, exploitative. Such people may be quite competitive in relationships, being skeptical of close relationships and avoiding commitment and any signs of dependency or weakness. They will tend to remember any social slight and may have a reputation for nurturing a grudge.

DOM high, WRM very high

This interpersonal style is best characterized as involving strong needs for affiliation and positive regard from others. This may result in rather uninhibited social behavior that may be seen by others as being attention-seeking and dramatic. These needs for attention and affiliation can be so strong that the quality of social interactions may be relatively unimportant as compared to their quantity. These behaviors, perhaps intended as friendly and sociable by the respondent, might be viewed as somewhat controlling and overbearing by others. Eager to be seen by others as popular and socially effective, such people may have little patience with those who do not view them this way, particularly if *MAN-I* is above average.

DOM high, WRM high

This pattern suggests an interpersonal style best characterized as friendly and extraverted. Such people will typically present a cheerful and positive picture in the presence of others. They are generally able to communicate their interests and wants to others in an open and straightforward manner, although, if *AGG-V* is below average, they may have difficulty expressing displeasure with others. They usually prefer activities that bring them into contact with others rather than solitary pursuits, and they are quick to offer help to those in need of it. Such an individual sees himself or herself as a person who has many friends and as a person who is comfortable and effective in most social situations.

DOM high, WRM average

This interpersonal style suggests a person who is self-assured, confident, and dominant. Although they are not unfriendly, such people are likely to be described by others as ambitious and having a leader-like demeanor. Although they are comfortable in social settings, they are not likely to mix indiscriminately, preferring to interact with others in situations over which they can exercise some measure of control.

DOM high, WRM low

This pattern represents a pragmatic and independent interpersonal style. Interactions with others are likely to be practical rather than sentimental, and relationships may be viewed as a means to an end, rather than as a source of satisfaction. Such individuals are not likely to be perceived by others as being warm and friendly, although they are not necessarily lacking in social skills and they can be reasonably effective in social interactions. Others will probably view such individuals as being shrewd, competitive, and self-confident.

DOM high, WRM very low

This interpersonal style seems best characterized as being remote and, perhaps, somewhat egocentric. Such people are not likely to be very interested or invested in social relationships, and they may take more from relationships than they are willing to give emotionally. As a result, their relationships are likely to be pragmatic and to be viewed in terms of their potential benefit, rather than as a source of enjoyment. Others are likely to view such people as harsh and punitive. Such people are probably skeptical of close relationships and will avoid commitment if possible. Above average scores on *MAN-I* accompanying this pattern heighten the probability that such people will be impatient and demanding of others.

DOM average, WRM very high

This interpersonal style is characterized by an exceptionally strong need to be accepted by others. This need for acceptance is likely to dominate the interactions of such people. They may be seen by others as being too caring, trusting, and supportive for their own good. They are at risk for being so committed to acceptance that they lose all individuality or creativity. Such people attempt to avoid any conflict in relationships, and they are reluctant to accept any hint of hostility in themselves, particularly if *AGG-V* and *MAN-I* are below average. Others are likely to take advantage of their strong need to be liked, which may be seen as an invitation to exploit their trust.

DOM average, WRM high

Such an interpersonal style can be characterized as being warm, friendly, and sympathetic. These individuals particularly value harmonious relationships and derive much of their satisfaction from these relationships. Because of the premium placed on harmony, they may be uncomfortable with interpersonal confrontation or conflict and will tend to shun controversy. Such people are probably quick to forgive others and will readily give others a second chance.

DOM average, WRM average

This interpersonal style is best characterized as one of autonomy and balance. Such a person probably has the capacity to adapt to a wide range of interpersonal situations, able to both lead and follow, and able to balance practicality and sentiment. With both interpersonal scales scoring in the average range, their assertiveness, friendliness, and concern for others is typical of that for normal adults.

DOM average, WRM low

This pattern suggests a person who may be somewhat distant in personal relationships. Such people may not appear to place a high premium on close, lasting relationships, and they may well view most social interactions without much enthusiasm. Others may view them as reserved and possibly aloof and unsympathetic. However, they may view themselves as independent, practical, and less preoccupied with the opinions of others than most people.

DOM average, WRM very low

The interpersonal style suggested by this pattern is one characterized as being cold and unfeeling. Others are likely to see such individuals as being stern, impersonal, and unable to either display affection or make a commitment to personal relationships. At times, they may appear almost devoid of warmth and friendliness, and they may make others uncomfortable and uneasy. There are probably few people who consider such people to be anything more than an acquaintance.

DOM low, WRM very high

This interpersonal style is other-oriented to a degree that might be considered naive, conforming, or gullible. Such people have a strong need to be liked by others, and fear of rejection by others (particularly if *ARD-P* is above average) likely makes it difficult to be assertive or to display any anger in relationships. A lack of confidence in relationships (look for a low *MAN-G*) may make these people somewhat dependent, and they may tend to feel helpless and overwhelmed when under pressure. Concerns about being well liked and not offending others may provide situations where others could take advantage.

DOM low, WRM high (with BOR-N < 60T)

This interpersonal style is best characterized as being open, genuine, and conforming. Such people are likely to be somewhat unassuming individuals who prefer to avoid the leadership role in social interactions and relationships. Although not necessarily shy or socially avoidant, they are typically most comfortable in the background of a social setting. Despite this rather unobtrusive stance in social interactions, such people tend to be reasonably effective in their interactions. They often are seen by others as warm, quiet individuals who are fairly eager to please.

DOM low, WRM high (with BOR-N ≥ 60T)

This type of individual is generally interested and rather conforming in relationships. Such a person is likely to be rather unassuming and will prefer to avoid being the center of attention in social interactions, particularly if *MAN-G* is below average. Such people are quite interested in maintaining relationships, and these efforts have probably been a significant source of stress at various times. Given their rather unobtrusive stance in social interactions, such people often value their relationships more than is readily apparent to those around them. They are likely to be seen by others as someone who is fairly eager to please but, at times, overly sensitive in relating to others.

DOM low, WRM average (with BOR-N < 60T)

This interpersonal style is best characterized as being modest, unpretentious, and retiring. Such people are likely to be self-conscious in social interactions, and they are probably not skilled or comfortable in asserting themselves. Others probably view such a person as passive, humble, and unassuming. If *ARD-P* is above average, it is likely that the person is shy and somewhat anxious about social interactions.

DOM low, WRM average (with BOR-N ≥ 60T)

This pattern suggests an interpersonal style that is generally unassuming and self-effacing. Such people are likely to be self-conscious in social interactions and they tend not to be skilled or comfortable in asserting themselves; previous efforts may have led to conflicts that they did not handle well and would prefer to avoid repeating. Others probably view such a person as rather passive, modest, yet fairly sensitive to the appraisals of others.

DOM low, WRM low

This pattern suggests a person who is withdrawn and introverted. Such individuals are likely to appear to others as if they have little interest in socializing. In fact, such people tend not to invite social interaction with others and make little special effort to appear friendly. They may derive little enjoyment from such interactions (particularly if *SCZ-S* is above average) and, as such, it would not be expected that they would have an extensive social network. They are likely to be rather passive and distant in those relationships that are maintained.

DOM low, WRM very low

This interpersonal style characterizes a person who is very uncomfortable in social situations. Such individuals appear to have little interest or need for interacting with others (if *SCZ-S* is above average) and/or are very anxious when interacting with others (if *ARD-P* is above average). In either case, such a person is likely to take a passive, submissive stance when dealing with others. This lack of interest and initiative may result in their being socially isolated, avoiding most social interactions rather than run the risk of being forced to make an active engagement and commitment to a relationship.

DOM very low, WRM very high

This interpersonal style suggests a person likely to be conforming, needy, and gullible. Such a person is likely to have a strong fear of rejection by others and, as a result, he or she finds it difficult to be assertive or to display any anger (particularly if *AGG-V* is below average). Such people will tend to feel helpless and overwhelmed under relatively mild pressure and dependently seek the assistance of others. Marked concerns about offending others can provide many situations where others take advantage of the respondent. An investigation of the self-esteem indicators may reveal that the dependency needs arise from a poor self-image.

DOM very low, WRM high (with BOR-N < 60T)

This pattern represents an interpersonal style best characterized as being submissive, conforming, and perhaps naive. Such people find it difficult to assert themselves or to display any anger in relationships; this may be driven by anxiety about potential rejection by others, particularly if *ARD-P* is above average. They will tend to feel helpless and overwhelmed under relatively mild pressure and dependently seek the assistance of others. Their concerns about offending others may potentially provide situations where others could take advantage of their eagerness to avoid interpersonal conflict.

DOM very low, WRM high (with BOR-N ≥ 60T)

This interpersonal style involves behavior that is generally submissive and conforming. Such people have difficulty with assertiveness or with effectively displaying anger in relationships; past experiences in this regard have likely led to conflicts that these individuals are probably very motivated to avoid. This submissive style may be driven by anxiety about potential rejection or abandonment by others. Such people will tend to feel helpless and overwhelmed under relatively mild pressure and dependently seek the assistance of others, but they may feel that others are not doing enough to meet their needs, particularly if *PAR-R* is above average. The motivation to maintain relationships may potentially provide situations where these individuals feel that others are taking advantage of or exploiting them.

DOM very low, WRM average (with BOR-N < 60T)

This interpersonal style can be described as being self-effacing and lacking confidence in social interactions. These characteristics make it difficult for such people to have their needs met in personal relationships; instead, they tend to subordinate their own interests to those of others in a manner that may seem self-punitive. This failure to assert oneself may result in mistreatment or exploitation by others, although the average score on WRM and the lack of elevation on BOR-N suggests that, to some extent, this strategy has been effective in maintaining important relationships. An inspection of the self-esteem indicators may reveal that this submissiveness could have taken a toll on the respondent's self-image.

DOM very low, WRM average (with BOR-N ≥ 60T)

A person displaying this pattern can be characterized as self-effacing and lacking confidence in social interactions. Such people tend to have difficulty having their needs met in personal relationships and, instead, will subordinate their own interests to those of others in a manner that may seem self-punitive. This failure to assert oneself may result in mistreatment or exploitation by others, and the elevation on BOR-N suggests that this interpersonal strategy has not been effective in maintaining the person's most important relationships.

DOM very low, WRM low

A person displaying this interpersonal style is passive and somewhat uncomfortable in social situations. Such people tend to take a submissive, withdrawn stance when dealing with others; they may feel little interest in or need for interacting with others (particularly with SCZ-S above average), and they are unlikely to initiate most relationships. This passivity may be accompanied by some feelings of resentment when others request cooperation in some matter that the person does not fully support (especially with PAR-R above average). It would be expected that such people might attempt to avoid social interactions, rather than take certain risks that are implicit in relationships.

DOM very low, WRM very low

This is an interpersonal style characterized by marked discomfort in social situations. Such people have little interest or desire for interacting with others and, for the most, part they take a passive, submissive stance when dealing with others. If PAR-R is above average, this passivity probably leads to feelings of resentment when others attempt to secure cooperation. It would be expected that they would attempt to avoid or flee from most social interactions, rather than risk being forced to make an active commitment to a relationship.

Assessment of Perception of Environment

Personality assessment instruments have typically focused on identifying internal aspects of the individual, yet it is clear that a person's behavior is substantially influenced by aspects of the environment. Unfortunately, assessment of the situational environment is very difficult, as situations can vary in nearly infinite ways. The constructs underlying the two PAI scales assessing environmental influences were selected on the basis of the research literature studying these influences on physical and mental health, as well as examining the factor structure of the relatively few scales available for the assessment of the environment. Two aspects of environment emerged from these investigations. One aspect involved the predictability, organization, and structure of the person's surroundings, ranging from fairly predictable environments to highly changeable and very stressful kinds of environments. The second aspect involved the availability and quality of supports in the environment.

The *STR* and *NON* scales provide an assessment of respondents' perception of their environment. The following sections provide a description of these two scales individually, followed by a consideration of the scales in combination for the assessment of the respondents' view of their environment.

Stress (STR)

The *STR* scale provides an assessment of life stressors that respondents are currently experiencing or have recently experienced. Item content includes problems in family relationships, financial hardships, difficulties related to the nature or status of their employment, or major changes that have recently occurred or are about to occur in their lives. The stress scale correlates moderately well with life events checklists such as the Holmes and Rahe (1967) Schedule of Recent Events. However, unlike these checklists, the PAI items are not specific about the precise nature of the stressors; they merely indicate the presence of many changes (i.e., day-to-day circumstances in the person's life are not predictable). Although item content is not specific, it appears that the majority of these changes have not been perceived as being for the better, as correlations between *STR* and most indicators of depression are quite high.

Average scores on *STR* (i.e., < 60*T*) reflect a person who describes life as stable, predictable, and uneventful. Scores between 60*T* and 70*T* are indicative of a person who may be experiencing a moderate degree of stress as a result of difficulties in some major life area. With scores above 70*T*, these difficulties are likely to be having a significant impact on the respondent; a review of current work situation, family and close relationships, or financial status will probably reveal circumstances that are a source of worry, rumination, and unhappiness. Such individuals are at risk for development of a number of adjustment or reactive disorders; scores on the clinical scales should be reviewed to determine the severity and nature of any such symptomatology.

STR scores that are markedly elevated (i.e., > 85*T*) indicate that respondents perceive themselves as surrounded by crises; nearly all major life areas are reported to be in turmoil. They feel that they are powerless to control a series of undesirable events that are happening to them. They see themselves as ineffectual, dependent, and at the mercy of those around them, a situation that may lead to some bitterness. Levels of stress in this range make the respondent vulnerable to many different clinical disorders, and scores on the clinical scales should be examined to determine the precise nature of the individual's reactions to stresses of this magnitude.

Nonsupport (NON)

The *NON* scale provides a measure of a perceived lack of social support, tapping both the availability and quality of the respondent's social relationships. Item content addresses the level and nature of interactions with acquaintances, friends, and family members. The scaling of *NON* is such that low scores reflect high perceived social support, whereas elevations indicate a perception of the social environment as unsupportive. The scale is a measure of the perception of social support, rather than an objective measure (e.g., a count of frequency of contact with family members). This is because one's perception tends to be more important, in terms of looking at the impact of social support as a moderator of stress, than the actual amount of support received.

Average scores on *NON* (i.e., < 60*T*) reflect a person who reports close, generally supportive connections with family and friends. Scores between 60*T* and 70*T* are indicative of a person who may have few close interpersonal relationships, or one who is perhaps dissatisfied with the nature of these relationships. With scores above 70*T*, the respondent is reporting that social relationships offer little support; family relationships may be either distant or combative, whereas friends are generally seen as unavailable or not helpful when needed.

NON scores that are markedly elevated (i.e., > 88*T*) indicate that respondents perceive that they have little or no social support system to help them through significant events in their lives. They tend to be highly critical of themselves as well as of other people, whom they perceive as uncaring and rejecting. Such individuals have few emotional resources for dealing with crises and are particularly prone to severe reactions to stress.

Configurations of STR and NON

The following sections discuss some of the implications for the assessment of the environment related to different configurations of *STR* and *NON*. Four score ranges are presented for *STR*: Low (< 44*T*), Average (45*T* to 59*T*), Moderate (60 to 69*T*), and High (≥ 70*T*). Five ranges are provided for *NON*: Low (< 44*T*), Average (45*T* to 59*T*), Moderate (60*T* to 69*T*), High (70*T* to 84*T*), and Very high (≥ 85*T*). Interpretations for these scales are sometimes supplemented with references to other scales that can shed further light on the nature of any problems suggested by the environmental scales.

STR average, NON average

Such individuals report that their recent level of stress and perceived level of social support are about average in comparison to normal adults. For individuals in a clinical setting, the reasonably low stress environment and the intact social support system are both favorable prognostic signs for future adjustment. However, any problems noted on the clinical scales are most likely enduring rather than the result of situational influences.

STR low, NON average

This pattern involves a person who reports having experienced very few stressful events in the recent past. The perceived level of social support is about average in comparison to normal adults. The combination of a stable and relatively stress-free environment with the reasonably intact social support system is a favorable prognostic sign for future adjustment.

STR average, NON low

This pattern represents a level of stress comparable to that of normal adults, combined with the presence of many individuals to whom the person can turn for support when needed. This highly developed system of social supports has likely been quite effective in buffering the demands of the environment, and this combination is a favorable prognostic sign for future adjustment. However, if scores on *DOM* are low, there is the possibility that the person is somewhat too reliant on the social support system and may be sacrificing autonomy to maintain these supports.

STR low, NON low

This pattern involves a report of very few stressful events in the recent past. Furthermore, the person also describes having a large number of individuals to whom he or she can turn for support when needed. The combination of a stable and relatively stress-free environment with the extensive social support system is a quite favorable prognostic sign for future adjustment. However, when accompanied by difficulties manifested on the clinical scales (particularly on *DEP* or *ANX*), this pattern may suggest a person with a strong tendency to internalize blame for problems.

STR moderate, NON average or low

This pattern suggests a mild degree of stress as a result of difficulties in some major life area. However, there appear to be a number of supportive relationships that are serving as some buffer against the effects of this stress. The relatively intact social support system is a favorable prognostic sign for future adjustment, and difficulties observed on the clinical scales (particularly *DEP* and *ANX*) are likely to be related to these situational stressors, rather than reflecting more enduring patterns.

STR high, NON average or low

This pattern suggests notable stress and turmoil in a number of major life areas. A review of the current employment situation, financial status, and family and close relationships will clarify the importance of these in the overall clinical picture, although the latter are less likely to be a major source of turmoil. Fortunately, the person is reporting a number of supportive relationships that serve as a buffer against the effects of this stress. The intact and committed social support system is a favorable prognostic sign for future adjustment, and difficulties observed on the clinical scales (particularly *DEP* and *ANX*) are likely to be related to situational pressures, rather than reflecting a more enduring pattern.

STR average or low, NON moderate

This pattern represents an individual who experiences his or her level of social support as being somewhat lower than that of the average adult. Such people may have relatively few close relationships (look for *SCZ-S* scores that are above average) or they may be dissatisfied with the quality of these relationships (indicated by above average scores on *BOR-N* or *PAR-R*, or both). However, there appears to be relatively little stress arising from this or other major life areas.

STR average or low, NON high

This pattern reflects a person who believes that social relationships offer little support; family relationships may be somewhat distant, and friends may not be available when needed. Despite the lack of social support, the environment is viewed as reasonably stable and predictable, with relatively little stress arising from this or other major life areas. Low scores on *WRM* may suggest that withdrawal is used as a satisfactory means of coping with the unsupportive social environment. An accompanying elevation on *PAR* indicates that this is part of a more pervasive pattern of dissatisfaction with the behavior and intentions of others.

STR average or low, NON very high

This pattern suggests individuals who believe that they have little or no social support system to help them through difficult events in their lives. Such people see others as rejecting and uncaring, and they believe that there is hardly anyone in their environment to whom they can turn for help. Remarkably, despite their lack of social support, they describe their environment as reasonably stable and predictable, with relatively little stress arising from this or other major life areas. This unusual combination suggests that this pattern of dissatisfaction may be enduring and a facet of their typical interactions with others, particularly if *PAR* or *BOR-N* show elevations.

STR moderate, NON moderate

This pattern reflects a mild degree of stress as a result of difficulties in some major life area, or areas. Some of these stressors may involve relationship issues, because they experience their level of social support as being somewhat lower than that of the average adult. Such people may have relatively few close relationships, or they may be dissatisfied with the quality of these relationships. Interventions directed at any problematic relationships (e.g., those involving family or marital problems) may be of some use in alleviating one potential source of dissatisfaction.

STR moderate, NON high

This pattern represents an individual who reports that social relationships offer little support; family relationships may be somewhat distant or ridden with conflict, and friends are not seen as available when needed. These relationship issues are likely to be a major source of stress for the respondent. Interventions directed at any problematic relationships (e.g., those involving family or marital problems) may be of some use in alleviating other reported problems; however, if there are elevations on *PAR* or *BOR-N*, this dissatisfaction with social relationships may be more enduring and generalized than situational.

STR moderate, NON very high

Such individuals report they have little or no social support system to help them through difficult events in their lives. They see others as rejecting and uncaring and believe that there is hardly anyone in their environment to whom they can turn for help. These relationship issues appear to be a major source of stress and concern. Interventions directed at these problematic relationships (e.g., those involving family or marital problems) may be of some use in alleviating a major source of current stress. However, elevations on *PAR* or *BOR-N* (if present) could suggest that this dissatisfaction with social relationships may be chronic and related to personality problems.

STR high, NON moderate

This pattern involves a report of notable stress and turmoil in a number of major life areas. A review of current employment situation, financial status, and family and close relationships will clarify the importance of these in the overall clinical picture. Some of these stressors may involve relationship issues, because the level of social support is described as being somewhat lower than that of the average adult. Such people may have relatively few close relationships, or they may be dissatisfied with the quality of these relationships. Interventions directed at any problematic relationships (e.g., those involving family or marital problems) may be of some use in alleviating one potential source of dissatisfaction, although additional sources of stress are likely.

STR high, NON high

Individuals with this combination of elevations are likely to be experiencing notable stress, chaos, and turmoil in a number of major life areas. A review of current employment situation, financial status, and family and close relationships will clarify the importance of these in the overall clinical picture. A primary source of stress may involve relationship issues, because social relationships are described as unsupportive; family relationships may be somewhat distant or ridden with conflict, and friends are not seen as available when needed. Interventions directed at key problematic relationships (e.g., those involving family or marital problems) may be of some use in alleviating what may be a major source of dissatisfaction.

STR high, NON very high

This pattern reflects individuals who believe that they have virtually no support system to help with the difficult life events that are besetting them. Such people see others as rejecting and uncaring, and they believe that there is nobody they can turn to for help. These relationship issues are part of a general life situation that is viewed as unstable and unpredictable; a review of the current employment situation, financial status, and family and close relationships will probably reveal that all are areas of concern. Interventions directed at attempting to rebuild problematic relationships (e.g., those involving family or marital problems) may be of some use in alleviating a major source of current stress. However, elevations on *PAR* or *BOR-N* (if present) suggest that this dissatisfaction with social relationships may be chronic and related to personality problems.

CHAPTER 10
TREATMENT PLANNING AND MONITORING

Treatment planning is a critical issue for psychological assessment, yet it is a challenging one, because there is little empirical evidence to definitively support specific treatments for specific problems or patient types. However, the PAI has particular promise for refining treatment-related decision-making (Morey & Henry, 1994), as it provides important information relevant to the treatment process: choice of setting, need for medications, suitability for psychotherapy, selection of therapeutic targets, and assessment of change. This chapter offers guidelines to help the clinician use PAI data to make many commonly faced treatment-related decisions. Because of the subscale structure of the PAI and its articulation with current diagnostic nomenclature, the PAI is also useful in answering many common referral questions in the context of psychological testing.

This chapter is organized into three sections. First, a description of the *RXR* scale is provided, as this scale represents a variable critical at the entry point of treatment. Then, specific issues related to determining prognosis, identifying treatment obstacles, and considering differential treatment strategies are discussed. The final section addresses issues involved in using the PAI in the assessment of change.

Treatment Rejection (*RXR*)

For many years, it has been presumed that one of the most important determinants of treatment outcome is the person's motivation for treatment. Although different authors have somewhat differing views on the nature of this motivation, it is generally agreed that a dissatisfaction with current behavior patterns and a willingness to make an effort to change these patterns are important components of treatment motivation (Sifneos, 1987; Strupp & Binder, 1984). These components can serve as important determinants of treatment outcome, no matter what specific type of treatment is involved. Sifneos identified seven criteria for the evaluation of treatment motivation for his studies of short-term psychotherapy:

1. A willingness to participate actively in the diagnostic evaluation.

2. Honesty in reporting about oneself and one's difficulties.

3. Ability to recognize that the symptoms experienced are psychological in nature.

4. Introspectiveness and curiosity about one's own behavior and motives.

5. Openness to new ideas, with a willingness to consider different attitudes.

6. Realistic expectations for the results of treatment.

7. Willingness to make a reasonable sacrifice in order to achieve a successful outcome.

RXR items were written to indicate attitudes that were not consistent with these characteristics of treatment motivation. In other words, they were designed to identify individuals who would not be motivated for treatment, but rather would be at risk for noncompliance and early termination. Items were written to be applicable across different therapeutic modalities. Broad content areas that were sampled included (a) a refusal to acknowledge problems, (b) a lack of introspectiveness, (c) an unwillingness to participate actively in treatment, and (d) an unwillingness to accept responsibility for change in one's life.

In interpreting scores on *RXR*, it must be remembered that *T* scores are referenced against a community sample, not a treatment sample; hence, scores that are typical of normal respondents actually represent little motivation for treatment. Thus, even *T* scores that appear to be within the average range can have quite negative implications for treatment motivation when working within a clinical setting. If working in other, nonclinical settings (e.g., a preemployment screening) scores of 50*T* may be typical, but they are not typical when working with clinical populations. In the clinical standardization sample, the mean score on *RXR* was 40*T*.

Another aspect of *RXR* that is critical in its interpretation is that it is related to treatment motivation, not prognosis. Motivation is a perhaps necessary, but certainly not sufficient, condition for successful treatment. Merely because a person recognizes the need to make changes does not mean that accomplishing those changes will be easy. In fact, very low scores on *RXR* are often somewhat of a "cry for help," indicative of overwhelming distress and beseeching mental health professionals to do something to alleviate the individual's suffering. For example, individuals with Borderline Personality Disorder who are in acute distress will often score quite low on this scale, presumably indicating very high motivation for treatment. And, in fact, such patients are experiencing so much turmoil that they truly do desperately want their lives to change. However, because such patients are extremely difficult to work with for other reasons, the prognosis for treatment is not necessarily favorable.

The scaling of *RXR* is such that low scores reflect high motivation for treatment, whereas elevations indicate little motivation for treatment. Low scores on *RXR* (i.e., < 43*T*) suggest a person who acknowledges major difficulties in his or her functioning and who perceives an acute need for help in dealing with these problems; scores below 20*T* indicate a desperate quality to these needs. Average scores on *RXR* (i.e., 43*T* to 53*T*) reflect a person who acknowledges the need to make some changes, has a positive attitude toward the possibility of personal change, and accepts the importance of personal responsibility. However, scores in the upper portion of this range are higher than expected in respondents where available information (e.g., from the history or from other PAI scales) suggests some impairment; in such circumstances, the possibility of defensiveness, rigidity, or lack of insight must be considered. Scores between 53*T* and 63*T* are indicative of people who are generally satisfied with themselves as they are and see little need for major changes in their behavior. Individuals scoring in this range would generally have little motivation to enter into psychotherapy and might be at risk for early termination if they did enter treatment. *RXR* scores above 63*T* reflect individuals who admit to few difficulties and who have no desire to change the status quo. Such individuals are not likely to seek therapy on their own initiative and will likely be resistant if they do begin treatment; they will probably dispute the value of therapy and have little, if any, involvement in any therapeutic attempts.

Predicting Treatment Process: Impediments and Assets

Although motivation for treatment is an important factor in determining treatment outcome, it is certainly not sufficient by itself to insure that the treatment will be successful. There are countless patient, treatment, and interaction variables that can potentially affect treatment outcome (Beutler, 1991). Patient predisposing variables, in isolation, will have a limited ability to predict outcome, because different types of patients can and do respond differently to diverse forms of treatment (Frances, Clarkin, & Perry, 1984). Some of these interactions and their implications for PAI interpretation will be discussed in a later section. Nonetheless, there are a number of patient features that suggest a difficult treatment process, regardless of the type of treatment offered.

For example, a number of theorists have offered suggestions about factors influencing amenability to various types of therapeutic approaches. Table 10-1

Table 10-1
Indicators of Suitability for Exploratory Therapy

Characteristic	Low suitability	High suitability
1. Friendliness	Hostile	Amiable
2. Likability	Unlikable	Likable
3. Intelligence	Low	High
4. Motivation	Indifferent	Motivated
5. Psychological-minded	Low	High
6. Conscience factors	Deceitful	Moral sense
7. Self-discipline	Chaotic	Disciplined
8. Impulse control	Impulsive	Self-control
9. Defensive style	Autoplastic	Alloplastic
10. Internalization	Projecting	Admits fault
11. Empathy	Entitlement	Empathy
12. Parental factors	Abusive/Indifferent	Supportive
13. Social supports	Few	Many

presents a list of variables offered as predictors of suitability for exploratory therapy (Stone, 1985; Strupp & Binder, 1984; Waldinger & Gunderson, 1987). However, a close examination of these features reveals that patients with numerous indicators of "low suitability" for exploratory therapy probably are less likely to respond to *any* form of intervention than patients who would be considered of "high suitability" according to this table. For example, deceitful, impulsive, hostile patients from an unsupportive and abusive environment are less than ideal candidates for any treatment; they are unlikely to comply with pharmacotherapy, behavior therapy, or group therapy, as well as exploratory therapy. Thus, this list of indicators is a reasonable starting point for estimating the degree of difficulty likely to be encountered as part of the treatment process. With the exception of "Intelligence," each of these indicators can be assessed using PAI profile information. The following sections describe the assessment of these indicators of treatment difficulty.

Friendliness. Individuals who are reasonably effective interpersonally are better able to make use of any form of helping relationship, regardless of the techniques used to achieve change. Individuals who are hostile are unlikely to cooperate with treatment; the process of treatment is constantly at risk for deteriorating into a struggle for control. For any individual to be considered amiable, some degree of warmth is essential. Hence, extremely low scores on *WRM* (i.e., < 30T) would be a negative indicator of friendliness. Similarly, overt indicators of hostility are also negative signs, and are probably most directly gauged by *PAR-R* or *AGG-A* elevations above 70T.

Likability. Although friendliness and likability are likely to be empirically related, they are separate constructs. Some people can be friendly in an overbearing or ingenuine way and, hence, are not well liked; others can be rather hostile, but (perhaps because, for example, their hostility is expressed in a humorous way) still can be reasonably likable. In general, individuals with personality disorders (particularly those in "Cluster B") are the least likable of individuals presenting for treatment; they tend to be manipulative, disagreeable, and egocentric. Thus, scores on *BOR* and *ANT*, which tap the features of two of these disorders, are probably the best indicators of likability on the test; individuals scoring above 70T on either of these scales are typically not likely to be well liked by many other people.

Intelligence. The PAI is not an intelligence test, and, for this reason, intelligence is the only item in Table 10-1 that cannot be estimated from the PAI profile. However, if the individual has at least the requisite fourth-grade education and cognitive and/or intellectual impairment appears to be interfering with the valid completion of the PAI, this is likely to be a negative indicator for a smooth treatment process.

Motivation. As discussed previously, motivation for treatment is perhaps a necessary, although not sufficient, condition for successful interventions. The *RXR* scale was constructed to yield information relevant to this construct, and scores greater than 60T are a sign of very low motivation for treatment. However, elevated scores on *PIM* can also indicate a level of rigidity and defensiveness that suggests that motivation for personal change will be lacking; scores above 60T on this scale should also be considered an indicator of inadequate interest in treatment.

Psychological-minded. For most forms of psychological therapy, the patient must be willing to consider the psychological origin of problems, if only to allow the individual to participate willingly in such treatments. Even in pharmacotherapy, some capacity to self-monitor is necessary to enable the person to comply with the medication regimen. Several PAI scales are suggestive of difficulties with introspection and self-awareness. Marked impulsivity and acting-out tendencies are negative indicators of introspection; thus, scores above 70T on *BOR-S* or *ANT-A* suggest little capacity for reflection. If *SOM* exceeds 70T, a patient's underlying conflicts are prone to be expressed somatically, and such individuals may be resistant to considering themselves in need of psychological intervention. If *ANT-E* is above 70T the patient may not have sufficient empathic capacity to consider others' experiences or viewpoints. Any of these features suggests limited psychological-mindedness.

Conscience factors. In general, a clearly established system of values and a good moral sense are assets that are favorable prognostic features for therapy. In contrast, deceitful, vengeful, or antisocial types of individuals are likely to have considerable difficulties working within a therapy relationship. Scores on *ANT-E* that exceed 70T indicate a willingness to deceive others for personal gain, a characteristic that portends an arduous treatment process.

Self-discipline. Individuals with the capacity for order and discipline tend to have smoother courses of treatment than those who have little discipline, who act-out behaviorally, and who lead chaotic and uncontrolled lives. These problems may lie in the realm of substance abuse (*ALC* or *DRG* above 70T), behavioral indiscretions (*BOR* or *ANT* above 70T), or in a chaotic approach to life (*NIM* above 70T).

Impulse control. Most psychosocial treatments require some capacity for reflection and delay. Individuals who act-out, rather than reflect on, their emotional experience tend to have more difficulty with treatment in general. Impulsivity can lead to compliance problems, even with treatments in which insight and introspection are minimally important. On the PAI, elevations on *BOR-S*, *ANT-A*, *ANT-S*, or *AGG* are signs of poor capacity for delay and heightened impulsivity, both of which make treatment difficult.

Defensive style. Stone (1985) uses Alexander's terms of alloplastic as opposed to autoplastic defensive styles to refer to the nature of the patient's approach to his or her symptoms and problems. This concept refers to whether the core problems experienced by the person are central to the self-structure and part of the ingrained personality (autoplastic), as opposed to problems that are viewed as ego-alien and seen as a change from the person's normal functioning (alloplastic). Individuals with an autoplastic defensive style are often unable to identify the aspects of their lives that cause them repeated difficulties, because these aspects are, in their own minds, simply "the way they are," rather than a disorder that they have. The characterological aspects of personality represented by *BOR* and *ANT* represent the essence of this defensive style. Similar defensive strategies are often found among substance abusers as well, leading to concerns when *ALC* or *DRG* are elevated.

Internalization. In many clients, the internalization of blame and fault is often both excessive and a source of distress. However, it is generally considered to be a favorable prognostic sign within the context of psychotherapy. Individuals who externalize blame for all their troubles, projecting responsibility outwards rather than accepting some role in their problems, often are unwilling to make the personal changes needed in therapy. The pattern of externalization is likely to repeat in the context of therapy, with the patient eventually coming to blame the therapist for treatment impasses due to the clinician's unwillingness to accept the patient's world view. Such individuals often do not place sufficient trust in others to establish a helping relationship; eventually, they have difficulty with the treating professional as an authority figure, and they may react to the therapist in a hostile or derogating manner. Scores above 70T on *PAR* are generally a sign that marked externalization is part of the clinical picture.

Empathy. The establishment of an alliance with the treating professional is a critical ingredient in therapeutic success, regardless of treatment modality, and the ability to care about and establish rapport with others is central in forging this alliance. Individuals who approach relationships with an entitled, exploitative, and contemptuous attitude tend to have difficulty working within the therapy context. Elevated scores on *MAN-G* or *ANT-E* are particularly related to problems in the empathic realm. If *DOM* is greater than 70T, the patient's need for control over the therapist may also make collaboration difficult.

Parental factors. Individuals who come from a background where caretakers have been abusive, indifferent, or exploitative tend to have great difficulty placing trust in helping professionals. In particular, they will become resistant and may terminate treatment as issues become increasingly sensitive. Elevations on *ARD-T* or *NON*, or both, can serve as cues to difficulties in this area.

Social supports. Research has shown that patients who have an adequate social support network tend to make better and more rapid progress in psychotherapy. *NON* scores below 70T indicate that a patient's perceived social supports are generally within normal limits, and *STR* scores in that range suggest that the support system is reasonably stable and predictable. An adequate and predictable support system is considered a favorable sign, whereas elevations on *NON* or *STR*, or both, reflect problem areas that can serve as both an obstacle and a target for treatment.

The PAI Treatment Process Index (TPI)

Table 10-2 presents the operationalization of these predictors of treatment amenability into a cumulative index known as the Treatment Process Index (TPI). Each feature of the TPI is considered present if *any* of its indicators (listed in the second column of Table 10-2) are present. The features on the TPI tap a wide array of different psychological problems, and, in general, respondents with globally elevated profiles will obtain high scores. However, certain PAI scales appear repeatedly in the calculation of the TPI, and in general the greater the degree of characterological problems, the higher the predicted degree of disruptions in treatment process.

Table 10-2
Operationalization of the Items of the
PAI Treatment Process Index (TPI)

Characteristic	PAI problem indicators	Frequency in community sample[a]	Frequency in clinical sample[b]
1. Friendliness	PAR-$R > 70T$ AGG-$A > 70T$ $WRM < 30T$	7%	27%
2. Likability	$BOR > 70T$ $ANT > 70T$	7%	36%
3. Motivation	$RXR > 60T$ $PIM > 60T$	23%	12%
4. Psychological-minded	BOR-$S > 70T$ ANT-$E > 70T$ $SOM > 70T$ ANT-$A > 70T$	13%	46%
5. Conscience factors	ANT-$E > 70T$	5%	9%
6. Self-discipline	$BOR > 70T$ $ANT > 70T$ $ALC > 70T$ $DRG > 70T$ $NIM > 70T$	12%	55%
7. Impulse control	BOR-$S > 70T$ $AGG > 70T$ ANT-$A > 70T$ ANT-$S > 70T$	10%	37%
8. Defensive style	$BOR > 70T$ $ANT > 70T$ $ALC > 70T$ $DRG > 70T$	10%	52%
9. Internalization	$PAR > 70T$	3%	18%
10. Empathy	MAN-$G > 70T$ $DOM > 70T$ ANT-$E > 70T$	8%	13%
11. Parental factors	ARD-$T > 70T$ $NON > 70T$	7%	40%
12. Social supports	$NON > 70T$ $STR > 70T$	7%	41%
Total score M		1.12	3.86
Total score SD		1.90	3.22

[a]$N = 1,000.$ [b]$N = 1,246.$

The PAI Treatment Process Index (TPI) is scored by counting the number of positive features in Table 10-2. As the table demonstrates, each feature in isolation is seen with reasonable frequency in a general clinical population. Table 10-3

Table 10-3
_T_-Score Equivalents for the PAI Treatment Process Index (TPI)
Standardized Against Community and Clinical Normative Samples

TPI score	_T_-score equivalent, community norms[a]	_T_-score equivalent, clinical norms[b]
0	44	38
1	49	41
2	55	44
3	60	47
4	65	50
5	70	54
6	76	57
7	81	60
8	86	63
9	91	66
10	97	69
11	102	72
12	107	75

[a]$N = 1,000.$ [b]$N = 1,246.$

presents *T*-score conversions for the Treatment Process Index (TPI), standardized against the means for the community and clinical samples. Scores on the TPI will be elevated in individuals who have refractory problems that will tend to complicate treatment process, regardless of the specific modality used. TPI scores below 4 indicate the presence of numerous personal assets that may assist the treatment process. If presenting for treatment, such people may be experiencing transient distress, perhaps associated with current circumstances, rather than chronic difficulties. As the TPI begins to elevate (i.e., 7-10 items positive), there are many and varied obstacles to a smooth treatment process. Problems tend to be more refractory and chronic in nature, and therapy will likely be difficult and have many reversals. Marked elevations (i.e., 11 or 12 items positive) suggest a very difficult treatment process. Because of the complexity of these problems and their enduring nature, considerable efforts will be needed to establish any form of alliance needed to maintain the person in treatment. Such individuals are likely to be among the most challenging of any patients to treat.

Numerous correlates for the PAI Treatment Process Index (TPI) are listed in the Appendix, of which selected results are presented in Table 10-4. This table reveals that the TPI is positively correlated with various indicators of character pathology and of an alienated, hostile detachment and withdrawal from others. It

Table 10-4
Selected Correlates of the
PAI Treatment Process Index (TPI) Total Score

Variable description	Correlation with TPI score
PAI *BOR*	.77
PAI *ANT*	.68
PAI *PAR*	.66
PAI *RXR*	−.46
MMPI *Sc*	.56
Mississippi PTSD scale	.72
Diagnostic Interview for Personality Disorder–Antisocial personality	.46
Diagnostic Interview for Personality Disorder–Schizotypal personality	.40
Hare Self-report Psychopathy	.67

Note. MMPI = Minnesota Multiphasic Personality Inventory; PTSD = Posttraumatic Stress Disorder.

is important to point out that the TPI displays a moderate *negative* correlation with *RXR*. This serves to underscore the observation that low *RXR* scores should NOT be considered to be a predictor of a smooth treatment process. Although it is true that individuals with high scores on *RXR* would be expected to refuse or reject treatment, many individuals with very low *RXR* scores tend to have problems of the sort reflected on the TPI, which can be very disruptive to treatment for different reasons. The following sections describe how these two attributes in combination can be helpful in evaluating prognosis and in anticipating obstacles that may arise in treatment.

The Interaction of Treatment Motivation and Difficulty

As mentioned earlier, the motivation of an individual for psychological treatment and his or her suitability for treatment are somewhat independent issues that are likely to interact to influence outcome. The following sections provide interpretations on various combinations of these factors, using *RXR* scores to gauge treatment motivation and the Treatment Process Index to assess treatment suitability. Motivation is divided according to four levels of *RXR*: Scores above 62*T* are markedly elevated, indicating likely treatment rejection; scores between 53*T* and 62*T* are moderately elevated, indicating probable treatment resistance; scores between 43*T* and 52*T* are in the high average range for clinical groups, raising the question of some resistance to treatment; and scores below 43*T* indicate acceptance of a need for treatment. With respect to treatment difficulty, Treatment Process Index scores above 8 indicate many and varied obstacles to a smooth treatment process, with a degree of difficulty placing them among the top 10% of clinical patients; scores between 4 and 8 are typical for clinical groups; and index scores below 4 indicate the presence of numerous personal assets that may assist the treatment process. The following sections make reference to these ranges of scores.

Treatment Process Index high, RXR markedly elevated

This pattern suggests a level of interest and motivation for treatment that is below average in comparison to adults who are not being seen in a therapeutic setting, and the treatment motivation is substantially lower than is typical of individuals being seen in treatment settings. Such a pattern suggests that the individual is not willing to take responsibility for the many difficulties in his or her life, and there appears to be no desire to make personal changes, despite the fact that several life areas do not seem to be going well at this time. Such people are very unlikely to seek therapy on their own initiative, and they are likely to be highly resistant if they do begin treatment. If treatment were to begin, the combination of problems that is being described suggests that treatment would be an uphill struggle and that the treatment process is likely to be arduous, with numerous reversals. Given the level of resistance to treatment, the respondent is not likely to weather many of these reversals before attempting to terminate treatment.

Treatment Process Index high, RXR moderately elevated

This level of interest and motivation for treatment is somewhat below average in comparison to adults who are not being seen in a therapeutic setting. Furthermore, the treatment motivation is substantially lower than is typical of individuals being seen in treatment settings. Such responses suggest persons who are satisfied with themselves as they are and who see little need for changes in their behavior, despite the recognition that several life areas are not going well at this time. The combination of problems being reported suggests that treatment would be quite challenging and that the treatment process is likely to be marked by significant turmoil.

Treatment Process Index high, RXR high average

The respondent's interest in and motivation for treatment is comparable to that of adults who are not being seen in a therapeutic setting, although they are somewhat lower than is typical of individuals being seen in treatment settings. Despite the recognition that several life areas are not going well at this time, there may be resistance to the idea that personal changes are needed; problems may be blamed on external circumstances, rather than recognized as personal issues in need of improvement. The combination of problems that are reported suggests a difficult treatment process; after the precipitating crisis resolves, it is likely that greater resistance to treatment will emerge and the client may then be at risk for premature termination.

Treatment Process Index high, RXR below average

This pattern suggests an individual who appears to have substantial interest in making changes in life, with satisfactory motivation for treatment. Such responses indicate an acknowledgement of important problems, a perception of a need for help in dealing with these problems, and a positive attitude toward personal responsibility in pursuing treatment. Despite these favorable signs, the combination of problems that are reported suggests that treatment is likely to be difficult, with numerous character and environmental obstacles to a smooth treatment process. The current level of motivation will be a valuable asset in working through the many reversals in treatment that are likely to occur.

Treatment Process Index average, RXR markedly elevated

This level of interest and motivation for treatment is below average in comparison to adults who are not being seen in a therapeutic setting and markedly lower than is typical of individuals being seen in treatment settings. These responses are typical of individuals who are quite satisfied with themselves as they are at present, and who see little need for changes in their behavior. They are acknowledging that a number of life areas are not going well at this time, although the blame for these problems appears to be placed externally. Treatment is not likely to be sought voluntarily. The nature of some of these problems suggests that treatment would be fairly challenging even if a commitment to treatment were made, and that the treatment process is likely to be difficult. Setbacks in treatment are likely and should be anticipated, with the respondent likely to attempt to terminate treatment during such times.

Treatment Process Index average, RXR moderately elevated

This level of treatment motivation, which is somewhat below average in comparison to adults who are not being seen in a therapeutic setting, is substantially lower than is typical of individuals being seen in treatment settings. Such people are generally self-satisfied and see no need for major changes in their approach to life, even though they acknowledge that certain life areas are not going well at this time. Responsibility for most of these problems appear to be attributed externally, and much of the initial treatment phases may need to focus on what role the respondent has played in these difficulties. The nature of the clinical problems presented suggests that treatment would be fairly challenging, with the treatment process likely to be hampered by the respondent's ambivalent commitment to treatment.

Treatment Process Index average, RXR high average

This level of interest and motivation for treatment is comparable to that of community adults, although somewhat lower than is typical of individuals being seen in treatment settings. Despite a recognition that a number of life areas are not going well at this time, the pattern suggests possible resistance to the idea that personal changes are needed to address these problems. Individuals presenting such a pattern may accept treatment in an effort to cope with an immediate crisis, but their commitment to treatment may wane as the crisis resolves, and there may be resistance to dealing with longer-term issues. The nature of some of the presenting problems suggests that the treatment process may be difficult, and reversals should be expected.

Treatment Process Index average, RXR below average

The respondent's interest in and motivation for treatment is comparable to or stronger than that of most individuals being seen in treatment settings. There is an acknowledgement of important problems and a perception of a need for help in dealing with these problems. Such people report a positive attitude toward the possibility of personal change, the value of therapy, and the importance of personal responsibility. However, the nature of some of the presenting problems suggests that treatment will involve some challenges, with a number of character issues that must be addressed if long-term changes are to be realized. The current level of motivation should be an important asset in dealing with the setbacks in treatment that are likely to occur as these issues rise to the surface.

Treatment Process Index low, RXR markedly elevated

The respondent's interest in and motivation for treatment is below average in comparison to adults who are not being seen in a therapeutic setting and a great deal lower than is typical of individuals being seen in treatment settings. Such people are adamant about being satisfied with themselves as they are; they are not experiencing significant distress, and, as a result, they see little need for changes in their behavior. The respondent does report a number of strengths that augur well for a relatively smooth treatment process if he or she were willing to make a commitment to treatment, but it does not appear likely that such a commitment would be made voluntarily at this time.

Treatment Process Index low, RXR moderately elevated

This level of treatment motivation is substantially lower than is typical of individuals being seen in treatment settings and is even below that of adults who are not being seen in a therapeutic setting. These responses suggest a person who is satisfied with his or her approach to life and not interested in making major changes in this approach. Because such people are not experiencing marked distress, they see little need for such changes at this time. However, this pattern does indicate a number of strengths that would predict a relatively smooth treatment process if the person made a commitment to treatment at some future point.

Treatment Process Index low, RXR high average

The respondent's interest in and motivation for treatment is comparable to that of adults who are not being seen in a therapeutic setting, although somewhat lower than is typical of individuals being seen in treatment settings. Because there does not appear to be marked distress at this time, the person does not report needing to make major changes in his or her behavior or approach to life. However, the individual seems responsive to the importance of personal responsibility and self-improvement and reports a number of strengths that are positive indications for a relatively smooth treatment process, should he or she decide that some form of psychological treatment might be needed.

Treatment Process Index low, RXR below average

This level of treatment motivation is comparable to or better than the majority of individuals seen in treatment settings. These responses suggest an acknowledgment of important problems and a perception of the need for help in dealing with these problems. The respondent reports a positive attitude toward the possibility of personal change, the value of therapy, and the importance of personal responsibility. The respondent seems interested and willing to engage in some introspection in order to bring about self-improvement; because there are relatively few clinical problems being reported, this desire appears to be independent of any necessities brought about by immediate crisis. In addition, he or she reports a number of other strengths that are positive indications for a relatively smooth treatment process and a reasonably good prognosis.

Differential Treatment Planning

Treatment selection is a difficult task in the mental health field; among psychosocial interventions alone, there are at least 130 different approaches from which to select (Smith, Glass, & Miller, 1980). There is also frustratingly little evidence to suggest that a specific treatment is unequivocally indicated for a particular disorder. Unfortunately, the realities of clinical practice dictate that many critical treatment selection decisions must be made despite the limited information that can be brought to bear upon these questions. Obviously, making treatment recommendations based upon the PAI results is hampered by this limited database, but some conclusions can be drawn; this section offers some suggestions for this purpose.

Perry, Frances, and Clarkin (1988) have divided mental health treatments according to five intervention parameters:

1. *Setting*, such as inpatient hospitalization, outpatient therapy, or halfway house placements.

2. *Format*, referring to whether treatment should involve individual sessions, group therapy, and/or family or marital therapy.

3. *Time*, involving the length and frequency of sessions, and the total duration of treatment.

4. *Approach*, involving the use of different techniques based upon different theoretical perspectives.

5. *Somatic*, involving the use of psychopharmacologic medications or other somatic forms of treatment.

The following sections are organized according to these five parameters of treatment and the resulting treatment decisions that the clinician often faces related to these parameters. Each common question for which the PAI may provide guidance is followed by a list of topics or areas that are important to assess in answering the question. Each area is, in turn, followed by the specific sources of PAI data most relevant to that area. It should be stressed that these suggestions are to be treated as guidelines to aid in the clinical decision-making process and are not offered as firm rules.

Choice of Treatment Setting

One frequent function of psychological assessment involves determining whether inpatient treatment is required and, if the patient is already in an inpatient setting, to provide recommendations about the continued necessity of such treatment. The following areas should be considered:

Functional Impairment

Is the patient's current level of overall functioning or ability to meet role responsibilities impaired to such an extent that hospitalization is warranted? Such problems can be manifest in a number of areas tapped by the PAI, particularly with extreme scores on the clinical scales that are at or above the profile "skyline" in the absence of any indication of negative distortion of the profile due to malingering or exaggeration. Chronic and severe somatic complaints and accompanying dysfunction or fatigue can compromise functional capacity, and extreme scores on *SOM* can reflect such issues. Anxiety may be so overwhelming that the patient may be unable to meet daily tasks, and mild stressors might precipitate a major crisis in such an individual; *ANX* scores above the skyline would be expected in such respondents. Extreme scores on *DEP* are usually accompanied by a crippling level of fatigue, loss of motivation, social withdrawal, and helplessness that may make outpatient treatment unfeasible. Individuals with extreme *MAN* scores may display a level of impulsivity, inability to delay gratification, and flight of ideas that can render them unable to meet role expectations. With extreme *PAR* scores, particularly elevations on *PAR-P*, the possibility of paranoid delusions that interfere with social and occupational functioning should be explored. Similarly, extreme scores on *SCZ* are typically associated with an active schizophrenic episode requiring hospitalization, and even the more moderate elevations on the *SCZ-P* subscale should be investigated, as this subscale measures psychotic signs unique to schizophrenia.

Potential for Self-Harm

Is the patient an imminent risk to himself or herself due to suicidality or impulsive self-damaging behaviors? Obviously, suicidality is a critical indication of the need for inpatient treatment, and this issue is discussed in detail in chapter 7. The *SUI* scale is an important tool for such assessments; individuals on suicidal precautions display an average score of 84T on that scale. Marked elevations on *SUI* are particularly worrisome when accompanied by the risk factors represented by the Suicide Potential Index. However, impaired judgment and recklessness can place an individual at risk for self-harm in the absence of overt suicidal ideation. Scores above 75T on *MAN* represent a degree of behavioral impulsivity that may increase the risk of self-damaging behaviors. Elevations above 70T on either *BOR-S* or *ANT-S* represent long-standing characterological features that do not necessarily indicate suicidality, but do suggest impulsivity that heightens the risk for self-harm, particularly when combined with other clinical indicators. The *BOR-S* elevation suggests a pattern of impulsive behavior with high potential for negative consequences (e.g., reckless spending, sexual behavior or substance abuse). An *ANT-S* elevation indicates a tendency toward reckless and dangerous behavior and a craving for excitement and stimulation.

Danger to Others

Does the patient require hospitalization because he or she is an immediate danger to others? Obviously, assaultive behavior indicates a need for inpatient treatment; this issue is discussed in detail in chapter 8.

Chemical Dependency

The choice between an inpatient and an outpatient setting for the treatment of chemical dependency is an increasingly common and important decision. Often this decision is based on whether or not the patient has the ability to control substance use on an outpatient basis or can be detoxified safely as an outpatient. If *ALC* is greater than 84*T* or *DRG* is greater than 80*T*, then the patient is increasingly likely to qualify for a diagnosis of substance dependence and may require detoxification in an inpatient setting, particularly if there are emotional complications such as suicidality or danger to others. It should be remembered that the PAI drug and alcohol scales are straightforward measures of what the patient reports; various PAI indicators (as described in chapters 2 and 4) should be checked for evidence of denial.

Traumatic Stress Reaction

Evidence on *ARD-T* of extreme preoccupation with past traumatic events when accompanied by high levels of anxiety (i.e., *ANX* > 90*T*) may indicate the need for crisis hospitalization. In cases where no obvious stressors are known, this pattern has sometimes been observed to indicate the imminent emergence of suppressed memories of childhood abuse. On occasion, the *ARD-T* subscale may be elevated, even in cases where the patient cannot currently report specific traumatic memories. In extreme cases, the patient may be in temporary need of a protected environment. This is particularly true if there is evidence of recent passively self-damaging behaviors, such as car accidents. Signs of thought disturbance also will exacerbate such a clinical picture.

Choice of Treatment Format

Individual treatment remains the most prevalent format for mental health treatment, and it is difficult to imagine situations in which some individual contact with a patient would be contraindicated. Nonetheless, the increasing acknowledgment of interpersonal factors in personal problems has led, in recent years, to a growing use of group and family/marital interventions.

Group-based treatments come in many forms, ranging from self-help groups to psychotherapy groups with heterogeneous members. These different forms share a number of critical mechanisms that emphasize the importance of interpersonal feedback, confrontation, and support within an environment of peers. Such interventions are particularly effective for individuals with poor social skills, distortions in their view of others and themselves, problems with empathy, or social anxiety. A number of PAI scales are global indicators of social ineffectiveness of the type that might be amenable to group intervention, including low scores on *WRM* and high scores on *SCZ-S* (suggesting social awkwardness) and *ARD-P* (potentially indicating social anxiety). Other indicators of problems that may be helped with group interventions include marked distrust (elevated *PAR* scores or any of the *PAR* subscales), rigid needs for interpersonal control (high scores on *DOM*), or failures in empathy (*ANT-E*). Although these latter problems present considerable hurdles for any form of therapy, group-based interventions may be helpful in diffusing the problems with authority (in the form of resistance or hostility toward the therapist) that such people often manifest.

Family and/or marital therapy is particularly effective in ameliorating issues that lie primarily within a family system, and even interventions focused upon particular emotional problems may be more effective if made within a family therapy context. On the PAI, marital and family issues are most evident on *NON* and, to a lesser extent, on *STR*. Elevations on *NON* that are 10*T* points above any of the clinical scales are particularly indicative that the respondent views the primary concerns as existing within the marriage and/or the family. In interpreting the *NON* elevation in this manner, the clinician should pay particular attention to elevations on *PAR* and/or *BOR*, which may indicate a generalized pattern of interpersonal bitterness, of which the reported family difficulties are merely an instance.

Choice of Treatment Length

As cost containment becomes an ever-increasing consideration in health care, efforts to predict and even to limit length of treatment have become important concerns. Unfortunately, in the mental health field it is quite difficult to predict in advance how long treatments should last. Length of treatment also is confounded with treatment approach, with some treatments (e.g., certain behavioral treatments) tending to be briefer, whereas others (e.g., psychoanalysis, or maintenance medication) can last for years. Finally, over the course of treatment, both patient and therapist will reconsider whether the frequency of sessions should change and whether further treatment is necessary.

One rather global guide to the likely duration of treatment is the Treatment Process Index, which will be elevated in individuals who have refractory problems that will require treatments of greater intensity. Persons presenting for treatment with 4 or fewer items on this index are likely to be experiencing transient distress, perhaps associated with current circumstances. A relatively brief intervention with such individuals can have a significant impact, relative to other patients. As the index begins to elevate (i.e., 7-10 items positive), the refractory nature of the problems makes it unlikely that a brief intervention will be effective in ameliorating the issues that are probably driving the observable level of distress, and treatments of greater duration and intensity may be required to effect lasting change. Marked elevations (i.e., 11 or 12 items positive) suggest a need for highly intensive treatments. Because of the complexity of the problems and their enduring nature, brief interventions are likely to involve crisis intervention, and considerable efforts will be needed to establish any form of the alliance needed to maintain the person in more intensive treatment.

In the course of clinical practice, decisions about length of treatment are usually part of the treatment process, rather than fixed at the beginning of treatment. As improvements are noted, the intensity of treatment may be lessened, or formal treatment may be terminated. The scale and subscale structure of the PAI make it particularly useful for charting patient changes and for making decisions about modifications in treatment intensity based on those changes. For example, in the inpatient treatment of severe depression, the relative changes in the affective, cognitive, and physiological components can be measured separately by readministering the test in order to better understand the specific effects of treatment; this will facilitate decisions about the need for continued inpatient care. A reduction in suicidal ideation may be noted, and changes in the patient's openness to treatment (*RXR*), negativity of world view (*NIM*), and perceived balance of external stress (*STR*) versus available support (*NON*) may all be useful for judging the patient's progress and updating treatment plans as needed.

Multiple administrations of the PAI during treatment can be useful in identifying critical elements of the treatment process that might indicate a need for altering the treatment intensity. For example, for clients presenting with *RXR* scores suggestive of treatment rejection, it would be anticipated that initial efforts in treatment might need to be directed at potential resistance. Alternatively, clients receiving an interpersonally-based treatment might be expected to show changes in the interpersonal scales as a prerequisite to addressing any distress that would be evident from the clinical scales. Similarly, clients receiving cognitive therapy for depression might be expected to show the most rapid improvements on *DEP-C*, with improvements in somatic and affective aspects of the syndrome contingent upon this change. If anticipated changes are not observed, revisions in treatment intensity or treatment approach might be needed.

Choice of Differential Treatment Approach

As noted earlier, the research literature provides little evidence to support the selection of specific therapies for specific problems. However, PAI data may be

Table 10-5
Selective Patient Variables for Psychodynamic Therapy

Patient selection variable	PAI indicators
Chronic sense of emptiness and underestimation of self-worth	elevated *BOR-I*, suppressed *MAN-G*
Loss or long separation in childhood	elevated *ARD-T*
Conflicts in past relationships (e.g., with parent or sexual partner)	elevated *STR*, *ARD-T*, *BOR-N*
Capacity for insight	low *RXR*, normal to low *BOR-S*
Ability to modulate regression	normal to low *BOR*, *AGG*
Access to dreams and fantasy	*SCZ* > 45*T*
Little need for direction and guidance	*DOM* > 45*T*
Stable environment	*STR* < 80*T*

coupled with guidelines offered in the literature, as well as with common "clinical wisdom," to provide some general guidance for treatment planning. For example, Karasu (1990a, 1990b) has offered a comparison of psychodynamic, cognitive, and interpersonal approaches along a variety of theoretical and technical dimensions. Using the syndrome of depression as an example, Karasu delimits patient variables that would either call for or contraindicate each of these psychotherapeutic approaches. Although the model is presented in the context of depression, the concepts are equally applicable to many other clinical problems. Tables 10-5, 10-6, and 10-7 present Karasu's selective patient variables for the psychodynamic, cognitive, and interpersonal strategies, respectively, and also list various PAI markers for these selective variables.

The psychodynamic or exploratory approach focuses on insight, understanding, and resolution of internal conflict, taking a developmental approach toward understanding the individual's present difficulties. This approach is particularly suited for individuals with difficulties that are developmental in nature; hence, the issue of conflicts in past relationships is especially salient. However, use of this approach requires the individual to be reasonably psychologically minded, have the capacity for trust, and be able to handle the anxiety resulting from a confrontation of his or her defenses. Karasu (1990b) suggests that individuals with more focused interpersonal problems or social deficits, particularly those pertaining to present-day relationships, might be better treated with an interpersonal

Table 10-6
Selective Patient Variables for Cognitive Therapy

Patient selection variable	PAI indicators
Obvious distorted thoughts about self, world, and future	elevated *DEP-C, ANX-C*
Pragmatic (logical) thinking	*ARD-O* > 55*T, WRM* < 60*T*
Moderate-to-high need for direction and guidance	*DOM* < 45*T*
Responsiveness to behavioral training and self-help (high degree of self-control)	*ARD-O* > 55*T* *BOR-S, ANT-A, AGG-P* < 60*T* *ALC, DRG* < 60*T*

approach. Finally, the cognitive approach is particularly well suited to individuals with negative distortions of the self, because there is less need for introspection and insight during the course of treatment.

There are a variety of other psychosocial approaches in addition to the psychodynamic, cognitive, and interpersonal approaches described by Karasu (1990a, 1990b). For example, many treatments are supportive in nature, aiming to shore up a patient's defenses and restore them to a more functional level. Such treatments are particularly important when there is evidence that the patient is extremely overwhelmed, has highly disorganized thought processes, or is quite vulnerable due to traumatic stress reactions (e.g., Frances et al., 1984). Approaches utilizing behavioral or environmental manipulation procedures may be optimal for difficulties involving circumscribed phobias (look for *ARD-P* elevations), somatization (*SOM-S* or *SOM-H*), assertiveness training, or lack of impulse control (see the following sections below). Conjoint family or marital therapy should be considered in cases of extreme functional impairment, or when the patient reports a marked lack of support by others, as suggested by elevated scores on *NON*.

Choice of Somatic Treatments

In many outpatient settings, the clinician often has to make the important decision of whether or not to refer the patient for a medication consult. In inpatient settings, the test results can help the physician choose between medications based on the relative prominence of depression, anxiety, mania, psychosis, or other symptomatology that is amenable to pharmacologic treatment. For example, Karasu

Table 10-7
Selective Patient Variables for Interpersonal Therapy

Patient selection variable	PAI indicators
Recent, focused dispute with spouse or significant other	elevated *NON, STR, BOR-N*
Social or communication problem	elevated *SCZ-S, ARD-P*; *WRM* < 40*T*
Recent role transition or life change	elevated *STR*
Abnormal grief reaction	elevated *STR*
Modest to moderate need for direction and guidance	*DOM* 40*T*-50*T*
Responsiveness to environmental manipulation (available support network)	*NON* < 75*T*

(1990b), in addition to the indications for different psychotherapy approaches already described, offered a number of indications for pharmacotherapy of depression; these guidelines and related PAI markers are presented in Table 10-8.

In addition to the *DEP* scale and related markers of depression described in Table 10-8, other PAI scales can suggest the possible need for somatic treatment. A variety of scale elevations can serve as general markers for medical evaluation and/or intervention. With respect to anti-anxiety medications, the *ANX* and *ARD* scales are particularly informative. Marked elevations on *ANX* suggest intense preoccupation and rumination that may be intrusive enough to place the patient at risk for inadequate occupational or social functioning and sufficient to interfere with the progress of psychotherapeutic interventions. Also, very high *STR* scores suggest that nearly all major life areas are in turmoil and that the patient feels surrounded by crises. Severe scores on *ARD-P* can indicate multiple phobias, panic disorder, and/or agoraphobia, disorders which may benefit from a combination of medical and psychosocial treatment.

Various PAI markers also can indicate the need to consider antipsychotic medications. Marked elevations on *PAR* (particularly *PAR-P*) indicate a need to evaluate for systematic paranoid delusional systems that may benefit from antipsychotic medication. If the full *SCZ* scale is markedly elevated, or even if the *SCZ-P* subscale displays a more modest elevation, the patient may require neuroleptic medication. Noteworthy elevations on *SCZ-T* indicate marked confusion and concentration

Table 10-8
Indications for Pharmacotherapy of Depression

Patient selection variable	PAI indicators
Marked vegetative signs; extreme or uncontrolled mood	elevated *DEP-P, DEP-A, BOR-A*
Anhedonia; loss of libido; impaired sexual function or performance	elevated *DEP-P*
Significant weight loss, early morning awakening	elevated *DEP-P*
Hyperactivity or motor retardation	elevated *DEP-P*, suppressed *MAN-A*
Depressive stupor	elevated *DEP-P*
Nihilistic or self-deprecatory delusions, self-berating auditory hallucinations	elevated *SCZ-P*
Loss of control over thinking, obsessive rumination, inability to focus or act	elevated *SCZ-T, ARD-O*
Acute, episodic, and uncontrolled suicidal acts or plans	markedly elevated *SUI*
Panic attacks or phobias; persecutory delusions; pseudodementia; physical symptoms or somatic delusions	elevated *ARD-P, ANX-P* elevated *PAR-P, SOM, SOM-C*
Other mental disorders, such as schizophrenia, alcoholism, anorexia	elevated *SCZ, ALC*

problems that may benefit from medication; however, even without elevations on other *SCZ* subscales, *SCZ-T* also may reflect severe depression. Finally, elevations on *MAN* above the profile skyline raise the possibility of a full-blown manic episode (i.e., medication should be considered).

Specifying Therapeutic Targets

The PAI also can be a useful source of data for isolating specific targets for therapeutic work, regardless of approach and/or diagnosis, and may help order the priorities for intervention. Morey and Henry (1994) have described a number of such targets. The following list, derived from the Morey and Henry guidelines, is not exhaustive, but it does cover some commonly observed areas of difficulty that cause people to seek treatment:

Poor Impulse Control

The most obvious priorities for intervention are impulsive and potentially dangerous behaviors, chemical dependency, and maladaptive anger expression. Elevations on any of the following scales and subscales are associated with poor impulse control: *ALC, DRG, MAN, BOR* (particularly *BOR-A* and *BOR-S*), *ANT* (particularly *ANT-S*), and *AGG*. Treatment may involve medical management in the case of a manic episode, or it may require direct limit-setting, therapeutic contracts (conditions under which therapy will or will not proceed), or anger management training. The more numerous the indicators, the greater the problem and the poorer the prognosis. There is some research evidence (e.g., Sloane et al., 1975) to suggest that behavioral approaches may be somewhat more effective with these types of acting-out and antisocial problems.

Anger Repression

Some patients experience problems with overinhibition of impulses (e.g., an inability to appropriately express angry feelings, resulting in maladaptive strategies to contain anger). This may be due to fear of rejection, fear of loss of control, the unacceptability of angry feelings, and so forth. Repressed anger may express itself as timidity and lack of assertion (very low *AGG*), compulsive rigidity (elevated *ARD-O*), or as physical symptoms (*SOM* elevations). Those patients with a history of abuse (observed on *ARD-T*) may also have difficulty expressing anger directly, even though there may be deep underlying anger. In such cases, encouragement of the more direct expression of anger may be a useful first step. It should be noted that the mere expression of anger (e.g., "cathartic" treatment) has not usually been shown to be of lasting benefit in and of itself as the only therapeutic procedure.

Excessive Dependency

Excessive dependency may be a problem for a number of reasons. Patients may be unable to leave abusive relationships, may sacrifice their own needs for those of others, or may be so eager to please and fearful of rejection that they are exploited. Above average emphasis on attachment relationships (high *WRM*), marked submissiveness (low *DOM*), and indications of borderline features (high *BOR*) are often associated with a pathological need for acceptance.

Interpersonal Distrust

Problems related to the ability to trust others, experience and tolerate genuine intimacy, and relinquish some control to others are among the most difficult to address therapeutically. The *PAR* scale is the most obvious indicator of such distrust, but there are many indicators that can be related to a self-protective stance and relational ambivalence or rejection that is based on minimal expectations of others and fears of exploitation. Elevations on *ARD* (particularly *ARD-T*), *SCZ-S*, *BOR* (particularly *BOR-N*), *ANT*, *AGG-A*, and/or *NON* all raise the possibility that establishing trust should be considered to be a treatment goal as well as a treatment obstacle. Group therapy may be of particular benefit as a conjoint therapy for such patients.

Constriction-Rigidity

A rigid, inflexible, perfectionistic, or constricted style, such as those suggested by an elevated *ARD-O*, may cause a host of problems deserving therapeutic attention. These include overreaction or stress response to unexpected events and change in routine, inability to experience pleasure, disrupted interpersonal relationships, fear of loss of impulse control (which may manifest itself in panic disorder symptoms), inefficient work habits, indecisiveness, and so forth. These traits also may indicate the effects of an abusive or traumatic history. Problems related to these obsessional features are exacerbated by a high need for interpersonal control (suggested by an elevated *DOM*) that interferes with the ability to make necessary compromises, and leads others to see the individual as overbearing.

Lack of Self-Confidence–Assertiveness

Lack of self-confidence, difficulty having needs met in relationships, self-doubt, inability to act assertively, excessive preoccupation with pleasing others, submissiveness, and inhibitions concerning expressing negative feelings to others may be associated with any number of pathological conditions. However, if these problems are not extreme and are not accompanied by a complex and polysymptomatic clinical picture, they are quite amenable to therapeutic intervention. Typically a behavioral deficit, rather than a behavioral excess, is involved. Any variety of therapeutic approaches, from behavioral to psychodynamic, might be appropriate, and short-term therapy is often effective. Indicators include elevations on *DEP-C* and *ARD-P* or suppression on *AGG*, *DOM*, or *MAN-G*, particularly when coupled with a relative lack of elevations on other scales.

Cognitive Distortions

Most psychopathology, almost by definition, involves some manifestation of cognitive distortion. However, certain extremely negative evaluations of self, others, and situations might profitably be explored and challenged as an early step in therapy. The PAI contains a number of indicators that suggest a world view that might impede therapeutic efforts. These cognitions could be confronted with straight cognitive or rational-emotive therapy or with cognitive techniques integrated into other theoretical approaches. A high *NIM* score indicates that an individual tends to think in extreme and categorical terms. Substantial *NIM* elevations in the absence of malingering indicate that the patient is reporting a profoundly negative evaluation of self and life. If this elevation is accompanied by elevated *DEP-C* and low *DOM*, the patient likely has a very long-standing, fixed negative self-image that is not likely to yield to brief therapy. *ANX-C* elevations indicate that such respondents are prone to experience considerable tension and worry over events they cannot control, but which they feel they should be able to control. The *DEP-C* scale, when elevated, suggests unrealistic feelings of worthlessness, failure, self-blame, and hopelessness. *PAR*, or any of its subscales, can indicate a fixed belief system involving distorted views and expectations of others. Such respondents may distort their experience in order to attribute their misfortune to the neglect of others, and they may see others' successes as luck or favoritism.

The PAI in the Evaluation of Change

In addition to the applicability of the PAI for treatment planning, the instrument also has many characteristics that make it well suited for the evaluation of treatment efficacy. Newman and Ciarlo (1994) have described 11 criteria for the selection and use of instruments as treatment outcome measures; the following paragraphs discuss these criteria as they pertain to the PAI.

1. *The outcome measure should be relevant to the target group.* The PAI contains a number of scales relevant to a wide variety of clinical conditions, and use of the test as a pre–post measure can provide information about client improvement in several critical areas. However, the utility of the PAI as a treatment outcome measure will obviously vary across different target populations; for example, little information about improvements in eating disorders or sexual dysfunction can be gleaned from the instrument. However, the broad range of symptomatology tapped by the PAI still would provide useful information in studies with such groups, as this information could assist in (a) identifying potentially associated problems in such groups (e.g., depression, anxiety, or anger), and (b) allowing for increased homogeneity for classification in such groups (e.g., differentiating within such groups according to levels of depression, psychotic features, substance abuse, personality problems, etc.).

2. *The method should be simple and teachable.* The implementation of the PAI as a treatment outcome instrument would be quite simple in most settings. The test is self-administered, and it can also be administered by computer. Hand-scoring the test requires no templates, and it can be accomplished by clerical personnel in 10 minutes; optically scanned computer scoring also

is available. It is available for use by both English- and Spanish-speaking individuals. Interpretation of the test is reasonably straightforward for any clinician trained in the basics of psychometric assessment, as well as in descriptive psychopathology. PAI interpretation is aided by the information provided in the Professional Manual, as well as the information presented in this interpretive guide.

3. *The method should have objective referents.* The PAI provides a number of referents against which the clinician can compare a given respondent. The *T* scores are referenced against a census-matched community sample; additional transformations are available based on norms for clinical respondents, college students, African Americans, and older adults. In addition, profile data for many different diagnostic or evaluation groups are presented in this guide or in the *PAI Professional Manual* (Morey, 1991).

4. *Use of multiple respondents is encouraged.* A number of writers have noted that different stake-holders (e.g., patient, therapist, spouse, independent evaluator) can give differing portrayals of treatment outcome. The PAI was designed as a self-report instrument intended to capture the experience of the individual completing it; as such, it is primarily useful in capturing the respondent's perspective. The test includes validity scales that seek to identify any systematic distortions in self-representation, but such scales cannot substitute for the nature of information that can be obtained from collateral informants and from clinical impressions. Thus, self-reported improvements on the PAI, as gauged by reductions of posttreatment clinical scale scores, should be supplemented with information from other sources whenever possible.

5. *Outcome measures should ideally identify the processes by which treatment is producing positive effects.* Newman and Ciarlo (1994) note that this criterion is fairly controversial, as researchers often do not agree on the extent to which treatment processes and treatment outcomes should correspond. However, repeated administrations of the PAI could be useful in documenting the process of change associated with a particular treatment. For example, in treating depression with cognitive therapy, it is assumed that alterations in the attribution system of the respondent will produce effects on other types of depressive symptoms. This theoretically anticipated pattern of change could be mapped by repeated administrations of the *DEP* scale; initial changes on *DEP-C* should be observed, with changes on *DEP-A* and *DEP-P* occurring later in the treatment process. Similarly, efforts at establishing interpersonal trust that might be leading to personal distress

could be mapped by comparing the temporal pattern of changes observed on *PAR* and *ANX*.

6. *The measure should meet minimum criteria of psychometric adequacy.* The psychometric characteristics of the PAI have been described in some detail earlier in this volume, and they reflect one of the primary strengths of the instrument. The reliability of the instrument is very good, leading to standard errors of measurement that are sufficiently small to reliably detect even small changes that might be associated with treatment. The validity of the instrument has been documented with respect to widely used measures of treatment-associated changes, including self-administered (e.g., Beck Depression Inventory, State-Trait Anxiety Inventory) and clinician-rated (e.g., Hamilton Rating Scale for Depression, Brief Psychiatric Rating Scale) instruments.

7. *The measure should have low costs relative to its utility.* The costs associated with a pre–post administration of the PAI for treatment outcome evaluation are relatively minor. As a self-report instrument, it requires no professional time to administer or score the instrument. Scoring can be accomplished by hand in 10 minutes; alternatively, an unlimited-use computer scoring and interpretation program is available at a one-time cost.

8. *The measure should be easily understood by nonprofessional audiences.* The scale names and scaling procedures used in the PAI are easily understood by most individuals. PAI scale names such as Depression or Anxiety, are straightforward descriptions of the types of questions contained on these scales, and the concurrent validity data support the conclusion that the scales measure what their names imply. The linear *T* score is easily interpreted by nonprofessionals, and these scores can also be expressed as percentile scores referenced against a variety of different groups (e.g., census-matched community sample, clinical sample, or various demographic or diagnostic groups). Although the multiple dimensions assessed by the PAI often present a complex picture for a given respondent, the use of profiles in presenting these data often render them comprehensible, even to the client.

9. *The instrument should provide easy feedback and uncomplicated interpretation.* In many respects, this criterion is the result of meeting many of the criteria described previously. In particular, ease of interpretation is precisely what the concept of *psychometric strength* is designed to ensure; a test that is reliable and valid is quite easy to interpret. In particular, the focus on discriminant validity in the construction of the PAI was designed to facilitate interpretation. Many of the difficulties in interpreting measures of

psychopathology stem from inadequate discriminant validity; it can be quite challenging to interpret a scale that was intended to measure schizo-phrenia if there are dozens of other factors that can lead to scale elevations. Thus, interpreting the PAI is more straightforward than interpreting other instruments with lower discriminant validity. In addition, the computer interpretive report and accompanying graphical display of detailed profile information also assists interpretation of the PAI.

10. *The measure should be useful in clinical services.* From its inception, the PAI was designed to be of maximum utility in a wide variety of clinical settings. As a pretreatment measure, the instrument provides a comprehensive assessment of different functional areas, and also provides information crit-ical in making diagnostic assignments. The treatment consideration scales provide information specifically geared to determining treatment intensity (e.g., inpatient vs. outpatient treatment) by providing an assessment of potential for immediate crisis (e.g., suicide or assaultive behavior) as well as the respondent's motivation for treatment and the likelihood of compli-ance with treatment. As a posttreatment measure, the instrument provides empirically defined normal ranges for each scale. Also, scales such as those measuring environmental stress and social support levels provide valuable data for determining the risk of problem relapse.

11. *The instrument should be compatible with clinical theories and practices.* The development of the individual PAI scales was based on a systematic review of the extant theories and supportive empirical research surrounding each construct measured. Key theoretical elements that have received research support were included in scale construction; these elements included aspects from many different theories. Examples include cognitive mecha-nisms in depression (*DEP-C*), identity disturbance in borderline personality (*BOR-I*), or sensation-seeking in antisocial personality (*ANT-S*). Thus, rather than adopting one theoretical approach and applying it to several different disorders, the PAI was constructed to tap specific theoretical elements that have received empirical support as they pertain to specific disorders.

Application of the PAI in Outcome Assessment

At a global level, a successful intervention should have the effect of moving the respondent's PAI scores in the direction of the norm for a community sample (i.e., 50*T*). For most scales, this improvement would be reflected in reductions in scores, although there are exceptions to this rule. For example, *MAN-G* is often abnormally low in clinical samples, revealing very poor self-esteem; thus, increases on *MAN-G* would be desirable if the score fell substantially below 50*T*. Increases on *RXR* would also be expected over the course of a successful treatment, as many of the motivating sources for treatment (e.g., distress or interpersonal difficulties) would be gradually ameliorated.

PAI scores have been found to be quite stable over 1-month periods in non-treatment samples (Morey, 1991); the reliability of the instrument would be expected to be even higher over shorter intervals. It should be noted that most of the scales represent constructs in a way that would not be expected to fluctuate from moment to moment; for example, the *ANX* scale demonstrates a somewhat greater correlation with "trait" anxiety than with "state" anxiety. Thus, researchers interested in measuring momentary mood states would be better served by instruments designed for that purpose. The PAI can profitably be used as a measure of change over periods of longer duration, and the instrument was designed to be able to detect changes that might occur from week to week.

Determining the significance of changes in PAI scores can be accomplished using the standard error of measurement (*SEM*) estimates calculated from various reliability studies. The *SEM* provides an index of variability in measurement that would be expected strictly from random fluctuations in scores; thus, changes in scores that are less than 1 *SEM* cannot be interpreted with any confidence as reflecting true change. For each of the PAI full scales, the *SEM* is 3 to 4 *T*-score points, meaning that the 95% confidence interval for these scale scores is 5 to 6 points. As a result, changes in *T*-scores that are 2 *SEM*s (i.e., 6-8 *T*-score points) in magnitude can serve as a conservative threshold for detecting statistically reliable change *in a given client*. For treatment studies where group comparisons are involved, the statistical significance of any group difference will obviously depend upon sample size, and, with large samples, even quite small differences might attain statistical significance. When the PAI is used for such purposes, any group differences should certainly be larger than the *SEM* for the scale before being interpreted as clinically meaningful.

It should be recognized that although the test-retest reliability of the PAI is high, and, hence, scores tend to be stable, these reliability estimates were derived from *untreated* samples. This does not imply that the PAI is not sensitive to change. This was demonstrated in a study by Friedman (1995), who performed a pre–post administration of the PAI with 22 patients during outpatient psychotherapy that had a median duration of 3 months. Friedman reported that 19 of the 21 scales of the PAI (excluding *ICN*) demonstrated statistically significant changes. However, Friedman's study also is valuable in that it demonstrated that the PAI scales are differentially sensitive to the changes observed in psychotherapy, with some scales

Table 10-9
Pre–Post Changes on PAI Scales

PAI Scale	Effect size (*SD* change)	Direction of change	Significance of change
STR	2.22	reduced	*p* < .0001
BOR	1.74	reduced	*p* < .0001
PIM	1.46	increased	*p* < .0001
RXR	1.46	increased	*p* < .0001
ANX	1.41	reduced	*p* < .0001
DEP	1.39	reduced	*p* < .0001
ARD	1.34	reduced	*p* < .0001
NIM	1.23	reduced	*p* < .0001
WRM	1.17	increased	*p* < .0001
SCZ	1.15	reduced	*p* < .0001
NON	1.08	reduced	*p* < .0001
PAR	1.05	reduced	*p* < .0001
ANT	0.98	reduced	*p* < .001
SOM	0.87	reduced	*p* < .001
AGG	0.74	reduced	*p* < .01
SUI	0.62	reduced	*p* < .01
DOM	0.62	increased	*p* < .01
DRG	0.55	reduced	*p* < .05
ALC	0.50	reduced	*p* < .05
MAN	0.18	reduced	*ns*
INF	0.07	reduced	*ns*

Note. From *Change in Psychotherapy: Foundation for Well Being Research Bulletin 106*, Table 4, by P. H. Friedman, 1995, Plymouth Meeting, PA: Foundation for Well Being. Copyright 1995 by P. H. Friedman. Adapted with permission.

demonstrating changes that were quite substantial and others showing smaller changes. Friedman's results are summarized in Table 10-9, with changes expressed as effect sizes presented in units of standard deviation; thus, on the *STR* scale, the reduction observed following treatment amounted to over 2 standard deviations from the mean of pretreatment scores. This table reveals that most of the PAI scales demonstrated large changes during treatment; generally, effect sizes of greater than .70 are considered large effects, whereas those between .50 and .70 are considered moderate effects (Cohen & Cohen, 1985). The pattern of changes suggests that the largest impact of psychotherapy could be observed in reduction of negative affect (*ANX, DEP, ARD*), improvement of self-esteem (*PIM, RXR, BOR*), and reduction of interpersonal and environmental turmoil (*STR, BOR*). Although the changes in substance abuse scales *ALC* and *DRG* were significant, only moderate effects were observed. This could be expected for two reasons: first, this was not a substance abuse treatment, and there were few significant problems of this nature in the sample; and second, the historical nature of many of the *ALC* and *DRG* items makes these scales somewhat less sensitive to change. For example, if someone has ever lost a job due to alcohol abuse, this item may be endorsed even if the person has not had a drink in 10 years. Nonetheless, the significance of changes on the substance abuse scales demonstrates that *ALC* and *DRG* are sensitive to treatment effects.

In the Friedman (1995) study, the only PAI scale (other than *INF*, which would not be expected to change with treatment) that did not demonstrate a treatment effect was *MAN*. However, this result is somewhat misleading, because, in fact, significant changes on *MAN* subscales *did* take place. The *MAN-G* subscale increased 0.59 standard deviations on average, and *MAN-I* decreased 0.87 standard deviations (no significant changes were observed on *MAN-A*). Thus, the opposing changes in these two subscales canceled each other at the full scale level.

The Friedman (1995) study demonstrates that the PAI can be used to assess improvement in a group of patients. However, the test also has been used in the literature to study change in a particular patient. One interesting application of the PAI as an outcome measure was reported by Saper, Blank, and Chapman (1995), who described the treatment of a patient with visual and auditory hallucinations that were refractory to conventional pharmacotherapy. This patient had continuous auditory hallucinations, including command hallucinations, and intrusive visions occurring roughly 10 times per day. In addition, she reported experiencing flashbacks of traumatic events that included repeated rapes. This patient had been treated unsuccessfully with all classes of neuroleptic medication, as well as tricyclic antidepressants, serotonin reuptake inhibitors, lithium, carbemazepine, and ECT. The authors described a treatment that combined an imaginal exposure (implosion) treatment for the posttraumatic stress symptoms with fluphenazine medication. Saper et al. used the 11 clinical scales of the PAI and two treatment scales, *SUI* and *AGG*, as outcome measures. They reported two measures of treatment success: number of clinical scales reduced below 70*T*, and number of scales that decreased following treatment. Significance testing was conducted in this case study by examining the binomial probability of each of these events occurring. In the study, 12 of the 13 scales examined displayed decreased scores, and none of the 7 scales that had been elevated pretreatment were elevated above 70*T* following the intervention. The binomial probability of either of these outcomes occurring by chance was less than .01. These PAI changes were corroborated by a mental status examination and staff observations at discharge. This use of the PAI is a valuable demonstration of how decisions about outcome and improvement can be made using a solid empirical foundation, even in the context of a case study.

REFERENCES

Abramson, L. Y., Seligman, M. E. P., & Teasdale, J. D. (1978). Learned helplessness in humans: Critique and reformulation. *Journal of Abnormal Psychology, 87,* 49-74.

Adams, H. B. (1964). "Mental illness" or interpersonal behavior? *American Psychologist, 19,* 191-197.

Akiskal, H. S., Hirschfeld, R. M., & Yerevanian, B. I. (1983). The relationship of personality to affective disorders: A critical review. *Archives of General Psychiatry, 40,* 801-810.

Akiskal, H. S., Yerevanian, B. I., Davis, G. C. (1985). The nosological status of borderline personality: Clinical and polysomnographic study. *American Journal of Psychiatry, 142,* 192-198.

Alpher, V. S. (1995). Personality Assessment Inventory and response sets in the assessment of dissociative disorder. Unpublished manuscript.

Alterman, A. I., Zaballero, A. R., Lin, M. M., Siddiqui, N., Brown, L. S., Rutherford, M. J., & McDermott, P. A. (1995). Personality Assessment Inventory (PAI) scores of lower-socioeconomic African American and Latino methadone maintenance patients. *Assessment, 2,* 91-100.

American Psychiatric Association. (1952). *Diagnostic and Statistical Manual of Mental Disorders.* Washington, DC: Author.

American Psychiatric Association. (1968). *Diagnostic and Statistical Manual of Mental Disorders* (2nd ed.). Washington, DC: Author.

American Psychiatric Association. (1980). *Diagnostic and Statistical Manual of Mental Disorders* (3rd ed.). Washington, DC: Author.

American Psychiatric Association. (1987). *Diagnostic and Statistical Manual of Mental Disorders* (3rd ed., Rev.). Washington, DC: Author.

American Psychiatric Association. (1994). *Diagnostic and Statistical Manual of Mental Disorders* (4th ed.). Washington, DC: Author.

Andraesen, N. C. (1985). Positive vs. negative symptoms: a critical evaluation. *Schizophrenia Bulletin, 11,* 380-389.

Angrist, B., Rotrosen, J., & Gershon, S. (1980). Differential effects of amphetamine and neuroleptics on negative vs. positive symptoms in schizophrenia. *Psychopharmacology, 72,* 17-19.

Ban, T. A. (1982). Chronic schizophrenias: A guide to Leonhard's classification. *Comprehensive Psychiatry, 23,* 155-169.

Ban, T. A., Fjetland, O. K., Kutcher, M., & Morey, L. C. (1993). CODE-DD: Development of a diagnostic scale for depressive disorders. In I. Hindmarch & P. Stonier (Eds.), *Human psychopharmacology: Measures and methods.* (Vol. 4, pp. 73-86). Chichester, England: Wiley.

Bandura, A. (1977). Self-efficacy: Toward a unifying theory of behavioral change. *Psychological Review, 84,* 191-215.

Beck, A. T. (1967). *Depression: Clinical, experimental, and theoretical aspects.* New York: Harper & Row.

Beck, A. T., & Emery, G. (1979). *Cognitive therapy of anxiety and phobic disorders.* New York: Guilford.

Beck, A. T., & Steer, R. A. (1987). *Beck Depression Inventory manual.* San Antonio: The Psychological Corporation.

Beck, A. T., & Steer, R. A. (1988). *Beck Hopelessness Scale manual.* San Antonio: The Psychological Corporation.

Beck, A. T., & Steer, R. A. (1990). *Beck Anxiety Inventory manual.* San Antonio: The Psychological Corporation.

Bell, M. J., Billington, R., & Becker, B. (1985). A scale for the assessment of object relations: Reliability, validity, and factorial invariance. *Journal of Clinical Psychology, 42,* 733-741.

Bell, M. J., Billington, R., Cicchetti, D., & Gibbons, J. (1988). Do object relations deficits distinguish BPD from other diagnostic groups? *Journal of Clinical Psychology, 44,* 511-516.

Bell-Pringle, V. J. (1994). *Assessment of borderline personality disorder using the MMPI-2 and the Personality Assessment Inventory.* Unpublished doctoral dissertation, Georgia State University, Atlanta.

Benjamin, L. S. (1974). Structural analysis of social behavior. *Psychological Review, 81,* 392-425.

Bernadt, M. W., Mumford, J., Taylor, C., et al. (1982). Comparison of questionnaire and laboratory tests in the detection of excessive drinking and alcoholism. *Lancet,* 325-328.

Beskow, J. (1979). Suicide and mental disorder in Swedish men. *Acta Psychiatrica Scandinavica Supplementum, 277,* 1-138.

Billings, A. G., & Moos, R. H. (1984). Coping, stress, and social resources among adults with unipolar depression. *Journal of Personality and Social Psychology, 46,* 877-891.

Bishop, E. R., & Holt, A. R. (1980). Pseudopsychosis: A reexamination of the concept of hysterical psychosis. *Comprehensive Psychiatry, 21,* 150-161.

Blashfield, R. K., & McElroy, R. A. (1987). The 1985 journal literature on the personality disorders. *Comprehensive Psychiatry, 28,* 536-546.

Bleuler, E. (1950). *Dementia Praecox or the group of Schizophrenias* (J. Zinkin, Trans.). New York: International Universities Press. (Original work published 1923)

Bongar, B. (1991). *The suicidal patient: Clinical and legal standards of care.* Washington, DC: American Psychological Association.

Boyle, G. J., & Lennon, T. J. (1994). Examination of the reliability and validity of the Personality Assessment Inventory. *Journal of Psychopathology and Behavior Assessment, 16,* 173-188.

Buss, A. H., & Durkee, A. (1957). An inventory for assessing different kinds of hostility. *Journal of Counseling Psychology, 21,* 343-349.

Campbell, D. T., & Fiske, D. W. (1959). Convergent and discriminant validation by the multitrait-multimethod matrix. *Psychological Bulletin, 56*, 81-105.

Carlson, G. A., & Goodwin, F. K. (1973). The stages of mania: A longitudinal analysis of the manic episode. *Archives of General Psychiatry, 28*, 221-228.

Cashel, M. L., Rogers, R., Sewell, K., & Martin-Cannici, C. (1995). The Personality Assessment Inventory and the detection of defensiveness. *Assessment, 2*, 333-342.

Cherepon, J. A., & Prinzhorn, B. (1994). The Personality Assessment Inventory profiles of adult female abuse survivors. *Assessment, 1*, 393-400.

Clark, D. C., & Fawcett, J. (1992). Review of empirical risk factors for evaluation of the suicidal patient. In B. Bongar (Ed.), *Suicide: Guidelines for assessment, management, and treatment* (pp. 16-48). New York: Oxford University Press.

Cleckley, H. (1941). *The mask of sanity*. St Louis, MO: Moseby.

Colligan, R. C. & Offord, K. P. (1990). MacAndrew versus MacAndrew: The relative efficacy of the MAC and SAP scales for the MMPI in screening male adolescents for substance misuse. *Journal of Personality Assessment, 55*, 708-716.

Costa, P. T., & McCrae, R. R. (1985). *The NEO Personality Inventory manual*. Odessa, FL: Psychological Assessment Resources.

Costa, P. T., & McCrae, R. R. (1989). *The NEO-PI/FFI manual supplement*. Odessa, FL: Psychological Assessment Resources.

Costa, P. T., & McCrae, R. R. (1992). Normal personality in clinical practice: The NEO Personality Inventory. *Psychological Assessment: A Journal of Consulting and Clinical Psychology, 4*, 5-13.

Cronbach, L. J. (1951). Coefficient alpha and the internal structure of tests. *Psychometrika, 16*, 297-334.

Crowne, D. P., & Marlowe, D. (1964). *The approval motive: Studies in evaluative dependence*. New York: Wiley.

Cull, J. G., & Gill, W. S. (1982). *Suicide Probability Scale manual*. Los Angeles: Western Psychological Services.

Deffenbacher, J. L. (1992). Trait anger: Theory, findings, and implications. In C. D. Spielberger & J. N. Butcher (Eds.), *Advances in Personality Assessment* (Vol. 9, pp. 177-201). Hillsdale, NJ: Erlbaum.

Deisinger, J. A. (1994). *Relationship between coping style and psychopathology in a community sample*. Doctoral Dissertation, Illinois Institute of Technology, Chicago.

Edwards, G., Arif, A., & Hodgson, R. (1982). Nomenclature and classification of drug- and alcohol-related problems: A shortened version of a WHO memorandum. *British Journal of Addiction, 77*, 259-273.

Edwards, G., & Gross, M. M. (1976). The alcohol dependence syndrome: Provisional description of a clinical syndrome. *British Medical Journal, 1*, 1058-1061.

Endler, N. S., & Edwards, J. M. (1988). Personality disorders from an interactional perspective. *Journal of Personality Disorders, 2*, 326-333.

Epstein, S., & O'Brien, E. J. (1985). The person-situation debate in historical and current perspective. *Psychological Bulletin, 98*, 513-537.

Fals-Stewart, W. (1996). The ability of individuals with psychoactive substance use disorders to escape detection by the Personality Assessment Inventory. *Psychological Assessment, 8*, 60-68.

Faravelli, C., Albanesi, G., & Poli, E. (1986). Assessment of depression: a comparison of rating scales. *Journal of Affective Disorders, 11*, 245-253.

Finney, D. J. (1971). *Probit Analysis.* Cambridge, England: Cambridge University Press.

Frances, A., Clarkin, J., & Perry, S. (1984). *Differential therapeutics in psychiatry: The art and science of treatment selection.* New York: Brunner/Mazel.

Friedman, P. H. (1995). *Change in psychotherapy: Foundation for Well Being Research Bulletin 106.* Foundation for Well Being, Plymouth Meeting, PA.

Fuller, R. K., Lee, K. K., & Gordis, E. (1988). Validity of self-report in alcoholism research: Results of a Veterans Administration cooperative study. *Alcoholism: Clinical and Experimental Research, 12*, 201-205.

Gaies, L. A. (1993). *Malingering of depression on the Personality Assessment Inventory.* Doctoral Dissertation, University of South Florida, Tampa.

Greenstein, D. S. (1993). *Relationship between frequent nightmares, psychopathology, and boundaries among incarcerated male inmates.* Unpublished doctoral dissertation, Adler School of Professional Psychology, Chicago, IL.

Goodwin, F. K., & Jamison, K. R.. (1990). *Manic-depressive illness.* New York: Oxford University Press.

Govia, J. M., & Velicer, W. F. (1985). Comparison of multidimensional measures of aggression. *Psychological Reports, 57*, 207-215.

Grinker, R. R., Werble, B., & Drye, R. C. (1968). *The borderline syndrome.* New York: Basic Books.

Gunderson, J. G., & Elliott, G. R. (1985). The interface between borderline personality disorder and affective disorder. *American Journal of Psychiatry, 142*, 277-288.

Gunderson, J.G., & Singer, M. (1975). Defining borderline patients: An overview. *American Journal of Psychiatry, 132*, 1-10.

Guze, S. B., Woodruff, R. A., & Clayton, P. J. (1971). A study of conversion symptoms in psychiatric outpatients. *American Journal of Psychiatry, 128*, 643-647.

Hamilton, M. (1960). A rating scale for depression. *Journal of Neurology, Neurosurgery, and Psychiatry, 23*, 56-62.

Hare, R. D. (1985). Comparison of procedures for the assessment of psychopathy. *Journal of Consulting and Clinical Psychology, 53*, 7-16.

Harpur, T. J., Hare, R. D., & Hakstian, R. (1989). A two-factor conceptualization of psychopathy: Construct validity and implications for assessment, *Psychological Assessment, 1*, 6-17.

Hart, S. D., Kropp, P. R., & Hare, R. D. (1988). Performance of male psychopaths following conditional release from prison. *Journal of Consulting and Clinical Psychology, 56*, 227-232.

Hathaway, S. R., & McKinley, J. C. (1967). *MMPI manual* (Rev. ed.). New York: Psychological Corporation.

Helmes, E. (1993). A modern instrument for evaluating psychopathology: The Personality Assessment Inventory Professional Manual. *Journal of Personality Assessment, 61,* 414-417.

Herman, J. L., Perry, J. C., & Van der Kolk, B. A. (1989). Childhood trauma in borderline personality disorder. *American Journal of Psychiatry, 146,* 490-495.

Hesselbrock, M. N., Babor, T. F., Hesselbrock, V., Meyer, R. E., & Workman, K. (1983). "Never believe an alcoholic"? On the validity of self-report measures of alcohol dependence and related constructs. *International Journal of the Addictions, 18,* 563-609.

Hollon, S. D., & Mandell, M. (1979). Use of the MMPI in the evaluation of treatment effects. In J. Butcher (Ed.), *New developments in the use of the MMPI.* Minneapolis: University of Minnesota Press.

Holmes, T. H., & Rahe, R. H. (1967). The Social Readjustment Rating Scale. *Journal of Psychosomatic Research, 11,* 213-218.

Horney, K. (1945). *Our Inner Conflicts.* New York: Norton.

Hyler, S. E., Rieder, R. O., Williams, J. B. W., Spitzler, R. L., Hendler, J., & Lyons, M. (1988). The Personality Diagnostic Questionnaire: Development and preliminary results. *Journal of Personality Disorders, 2,* 229-237.

Jackson, D. N. (1970). A sequential system for personality scale development. In C. D. Spielberger (Ed.), *Current topics in clinical and community psychology* (Vol. 2, pp. 62-97). New York: Academic Press.

Jackson, D. N. (1971). The dynamics of structured personality tests. *Psychological Review, 78,* 229-248.

Jellinek, E. M. (1960). *The disease concept of alcoholism.* New Haven, CT: College and University Press.

Kagan, J., & Moss, H. A. (1962). *Birth to maturity: A study in psychological development.* New York: Wiley.

Karasu, T. B. (1990a). Toward a clinical model of psychotherapy for depression: I. Systematic comparison of three psychotherapies. *American Journal of Psychiatry, 147,* 133-147.

Karasu, T. B. (1990b). Toward a clinical model of psychotherapy for depression: II. An integrative and selective treatment approach. *American Journal of Psychiatry, 147,* 269-278.

Keane, T. M., Caddell, J. M., & Taylor, K. L. (1988). Mississippi scale for combat-related posttraumatic stress disorder: Three studies in reliability and validity. *Journal of Consulting and Clinical Psychology, 56,* 85-90.

Kenrick, D. T., & Funder, D. C. (1988). Profiting from controversy: Lessons from the person-situation debate. *American Psychologist, 43,* 23-34.

Kernberg, O. F. (1975). *Borderline conditions and pathological narcissism.* New York: Jason Aronson.

Kiesler, D. J. (1983) The 1982 interpersonal circle: A taxonomy for complementarity in human transactions. *Psychological Review, 90,* 185-214.

Koksal, F., & Power, K. G. (1990). Four systems anxiety questionnaire (FSAQ): A self-report measure of somatic, cognitive, behavioral, and feeling components. *Journal of Personality Assessment, 54*, 534-545.

Kurtz, J. E., Morey, L. C., & Tomarken, A. J. (1993). The concurrent validity of three self-report measures of borderline personality. *Journal of Psychopathology and Behavioral Assessment, 15*, 255-266.

Lambert, M. J. (1991). Introduction to psychotherapy research. In L. E. Beutler & M. Crago (Eds.), *Psychotherapy research: An international review of programmatic studies.* Washington, D.C.: American Psychological Association.

Lang, P. J. (1971). The application of psychophysiological methods. In S. Garfield & A. Bergin (Eds.), *Handbook of psychotherapy and behavior change* (pp. 75-125). New York: Wiley.

Lazarus, R. S., & Cohen, J. P. (1977). Environmental stress. In I. Altman & J. F. Wohlwill (Eds.), *Human behavior and the environment: Current theory and research.* New York: Plenum.

Leary, T. (1957). *Interpersonal Diagnosis of Personality.* New York: Ronald.

Lenzenweger, M. F., Dworkin, R. H., & Wetherington, E. (1989). Models of positive and negative symptoms in schizophrenia: An empirical evaluation of latent structures. *Journal of Abnormal Psychology, 98*, 62-70.

Linehan, M. M., Chiles, J. A., Egan, K. J., & Devine, R. H. (1986). Presenting problems of parasuicides versus suicide ideators and nonsuicidal psychiatric patients. *Journal of Consulting and Clinical Psychology, 54*, 880-881.

Loeber, R. & Dishion, T. (1983). Early predictors of male delinquency: A review. *Psychological Bulletin, 94*, 68-99.

Loevinger, J. (1957). Objective tests as instruments of psychological theory. *Psychological Reports, 3*, 635-694.

Louks, J., Hayne, C., & Smith, J. (1989). Replicated factor structure of the Beck Depression Inventory. *Journal of Nervous and Mental Disease, 177*, 473-479.

MacAndrew, C. (1965). The differentiation of male alcoholic outpatients from non-alcoholic psychiatric patients by means of the MMPI. *Quarterly Journal of Studies on Alcohol, 26*, 238- 246.

Maris, R., Berman, A., Maltsberger, J. T., & Yufit, R. I. (1992). *Assessment and prediction of suicide.* New York: Guilford.

McCrae, R. R., & Costa, P. T. (1984). *Emerging lives, enduring dispositions: Personality in adulthood.* Boston: Little-Brown.

McGlashan, T. H. (1983). The borderline syndrome. I. Testing three diagnostic systems. *Archives of General Psychiatry, 40*, 1311-1318.

McLemore, C. W. & Benjamin, L. S. (1979). Whatever happened to interpersonal diagnosis? A psychosocial alternative to DSM-III. *American Psychologist, 34*, 17-34.

McNiel, D. E., & Binder, R. L. (1994). The relationship between acute psychiatric symptoms, diagnosis, and short-term risk of violence. *Hospital and Community Psychiatry, 45*, 133-137.

Meehl, P. E., & Rosen, A. (1955). Antecedent probability and the efficiency of psychometric signs, patterns, or cutting scores. *Psychological Bulletin, 52,* 194-216.

Megargee, E. I. (1970). The prediction of violence with psychological tests. In C. D. Spielberger (Ed.), *Current topics in clinical and community psychology* (Vol. 2, pp. 98-156). New York: Academic Press.

Montag, I., & Levin, J. (1994). The five factor model and psychopathology in nonclinical samples. *Personality and Individual Differences, 17,* 1-7.

Moran, P. W., & Lambert, M. J. (1983). A review of current assessment tools for monitoring change in depression. In M. J. Lambert, E. R. Christensen, & S. S. DeJulio (Eds.), *The measurement of psychotherapy outcome in research and evaluation* (pp. 263-303). New York: Wiley.

Morey, L. C. (1985). An empirical comparison of interpersonal and DSM-III approaches to classification of personality disorders. *Psychiatry, 48,* 358-364.

Morey, L. C. (1991). *The Personality Assessment Inventory Professional Manual.* Odessa, FL: Psychological Assessment Resources.

Morey, L. C., & Henry, W. (1994). Personality Assessment Inventory. In M. Maruish (Ed.), *The use of psychological testing for treatment planning and outcome assessment* (pp. 185-216). Hillsdale, NJ: Erlbaum.

Morey, L. C., Waugh, M. H., & Blashfield, R. K. (1985). MMPI scales for DSM-III personality disorders: Their derivation and correlates. *Journal of Personality Assessment, 49,* 245-251.

Motto, J. A. (1989). Problems in suicide risk assessment. In D. G. Jacobs & H. N. Brown (Eds.), *Suicide: Understanding and responding. Harvard Medical School perspectives on suicide* (pp. 129-142). Madison, CT: International Universities Press.

National Center for Health Statistics. (1992). Advance report of final mortality statistics, 1989. *NCHS Monthly Vital Statistics Report, 40,* 8 (suppl).

Newman, F. L., & Ciarlo, J. A. (1994). Criteria for selecting psychological instruments for treatment outcome assessment. In M. Maruish (Ed.), *The use of psychological testing for treatment planning and outcome assessment* (pp. 98-110). Hillsdale, NJ: Erlbaum.

Osborne, D. (1994, April). *Use of the Personality Assessment Inventory with a medical population.* Paper presented at the meetings of the Rocky Mountain Psychological Association, Denver, CO.

Overall, J. E., & Gorham, D. R. (1962). The Brief Psychiatric Rating Scale. *Psychological Reports, 10,* 799-812.

Parker, J. G., & Asher, S. R. (1987). Peer relations and later personal adjustment: Are low-accepted children at risk? *Psychological Bulletin, 102,* 357-389.

Perry, S., Frances, A., & Clarkin, J. (1988). *A DSM-III-R casebook of treatment selection.* New York: Brunner-Mazel.

Pinel, P. (1801). *Traite medico-philosophique sur l'alienation mentale, ou la manie.* Paris: Caille et Ravier.

Pope, H. G., Jonas, J. M., Hudson, J. I., Cohen, B. M., & Gunderson, J. G. (1983). The validity of *DSM-III* borderline personality disorder. *Archives of General Psychiatry, 40,* 23-30.

Procidano, M. E., & Heller, K. (1983). Measures of perceived social support from friends and from family: Three validation studies. *American Journal of Community Psychology, 11,* 1-24.

Rachman, S. J., & Hodgson, R. J. (1980). *Obsessions and compulsions.* Englewood Cliffs, NJ: Prentice-Hall.

Reynolds, W. M. (1982). Development of reliable and valid short forms of the Marlowe-Crowne Social Desirability Scale. *Journal of Clinical Psychology, 38,* 119-125.

Rich, C. L., Young, D., & Fowler, R. C. (1986). San Diego suicide study: I. Young vs. old subjects. *Archives of General Psychiatry, 43,* 577-582.

Riley, W. T., & Treiber, F. A. (1989). The validity of multidimensional self-report anger and hostility measures. *Journal of Clinical Psychology, 45,* 397-404.

Robins, E. (1981). *The final months: A study of the lives of 134 persons who committed suicide.* New York: Oxford University Press.

Robins, E., Murphy, G. E., Wilkinson, R. H., Gassner, S., & Kayes, J. (1959). Some clinical considerations in the prevention of suicide based on a study of 134 successful suicides. *American Journal of Public Health, 49,* 888-897.

Robins, L. N. (1966). *Deviant children grown up: A sociological and psychiatric study of sociopathic personality.* Baltimore: Williams & Wilkins.

Rogers, R., Flores, J., Ustad, K., & Sewell, K. W. (1995). Initial validation of the Personality Assessment Inventory-Spanish Version with clients from Mexican American communities. *Journal of Personality Assessment, 64,* 340-348.

Rogers, R., Ornduff, S. R., & Sewell, K. (1993). Feigning specific disorders: A study of the Personality Assessment Inventory (PAI). *Journal of Personality Assessment, 60,* 554-560.

Rogers, R., Sewell, K. W., Morey, L. C., & Ustad, K. L. (in press). Detection of feigned mental disorders on the Personality Assessment Inventory: A discriminant analysis. *Journal of Personality Assessment.*

Saper, Z., Blank, M. K., & Chapman, L. (1995). Implosive therapy as an adjunctive treatment in a psychotic disorder: A case report. *Journal of Behavior Therapy and Experimental Psychiatry, 26,* 157-160.

Schinka, J. A. (1995). Personality Assessment Inventory scale characteristics and factor structure in the assessment of alcohol dependency. *Journal of Personality Assessment, 64,* 101-111.

Schinka, J. A., & Borum, R. (1993). Readability of adult psychopathology inventories. *Psychological Assessment, 5,* 384-386.

Schinka, J. A., & Vanderploeg, R. D. (1995, August). *Validity of the NST in a drug-dependent sample.* Paper presented at the meetings of the American Psychological Association, New York.

Schlosser, B. (1992). Computer assisted practice. *The Independent Practitioner, 12,* 12-15.

Selzer, M. L. (1971). The Michigan Alcoholism Screening Test: The quest for a new diagnostic instrument. *American Journal of Psychiatry, 127,* 1653-1658.

Serin, R., Peters, R. D., & Barbaree, H. E. (1990). Predictors of psychopathy and release outcome in a criminal population. *Psychological Assessment, 2,* 419-422.

Shaffer, C. E., Waters, W. F., & Adams, S. G. (1994). Dangerousness: Assessing the risk of violent behavior. *Journal of Consulting and Clinical Psychology, 62,* 1064-1068.

Shneidman, E. S., Farberow, N. L., & Litman, R. E. (1970). *The psychology of suicide.* New York: Jason Aronson.

Siegel, J. S. (1985). The measurement of anger as a multidimensional construct. In M. A. Chesney & R. H. Rosenman (Eds.), *Anger and hostility in cardiovascular and behavioral disorders.* New York: Hemisphere.

Sifneos, P. E. (1987). *Short-term dynamic psychotherapy: evaluation and technique* (2nd ed.). New York: Plenum.

Skinner, H. A. (1982). The drug abuse screening test. *Addictive Behaviors, 7,* 363-371.

Sloane, R. B., Staples, F. R., Cristol, A. H., Yorkston, N. J., & Whipple, K. (1975). *Short-term analytically-oriented psychotherapy vs. behavior therapy.* Cambridge, MA: Harvard University Press.

Smith, M. L., Glass, G. V., & Miller, T. I. (1980). *The benefits of psychotherapy.* Baltimore: Johns Hopkins University Press.

Sobell, L. C., Sobell, M. B. (1975). Outpatient alcoholics give valid self-reports. *Journal of Nervous and Mental Disease, 161,* 32-42.

Soloff, P. H., George, A., Nathan, R., & Schulz, P. M. (1989). Amitriptyline versus haloperidol in borderlines: Final outcomes and predictors of response. *Journal of Clinical Psychopharmacology, 9,* 238-246.

Spielberger, C. D. (1983). *Manual for the State-Trait Anxiety Inventory.* Palo Alto, CA: Consulting Psychologists Press.

Spielberger, C. D. (1988). *State-Trait Anger Expression Inventory.* Odessa, FL: Psychological Assessment Resources.

Stone, M. H. (1985). Schizotypal personality: Therapeutic aspects. *Schizophrenia Bulletin, 11,* 576-589.

Strupp, H. H., & Binder, J. (1984). *Psychotherapy in a new key.* New York: Basic Books.

Sullivan, H. S. (1953). *The Interpersonal Theory of Psychiatry.* New York: Norton.

Trapnell, P. D., & Wiggins, J. S. (1990). Extension of the Interpersonal Adjective Scale to include the big five dimensions of personality. *Journal of Personality and Social Psychology, 59,* 781-790.

Trull, T. J. (1995). Borderline personality disorder features in nonclinical young adults: 1. Identification and validation. *Psychological Assessment, 7,* 33-41.

Trull, T. J., Useda, J. D., Conforti, K., & Doan, B. T. (1995, August). *Two-year outcome of subjects with borderline features.* Paper presented at the meeting of the American Psychological Association, New York.

Wahler, H. J. (1983). *Wahler Physical Symptoms Inventory.* (1983). Los Angeles: Western Psychological Services.

Waldinger, R. J., & Gunderson, J. G. (1987). *Effective psychotherapy with borderline patients: Case studies.* New York: MacMillan.

Wiggins, J. S. (1966). Substantive dimensions of self-report in the MMPI item pool. *Psychological Monographs, 80,* 22 (whole No. 630).

Wiggins, J. S. (1973). *Personality and prediction: Principles of Personality Assessment.* Reading, MA: Addison-Wesley.

Wiggins, J. S. (1982). Circumplex models of interpersonal behavior in clinical psychology. In P. Kendall & J. Butcher (Eds.), *Handbook of Research Methods in Clinical Psychology.* New York: Wiley.

Wiggins, J. S. (1987, August). *How interpersonal are the MMPI personality disorder scales?* Paper presented at the meeting of the American Psychological Association, New York.

Wiggins, J. S. (1995). *Interpersonal Adjective Scales.* Odessa, FL: Psychological Assessment Resources.

Wiggins, J. S., Trapnell, P., & Phillips, N. (1988). Psychometric and geometric characteristics of the revised Interpersonal Adjective Scales (IAS-R). *Multivariate Behavioral Research, 23,* 517-530.

Wolpe, J., & Lang, P. (1964). A fear survey schedule for use in behavior therapy. *Behavior Research and Therapy, 2,* 27-30.

Zanarini, M. (1987). *Diagnostic Interview for Personality Disorders–Revised.* Belmont, MA: McLean Hospital.

Zelin, M. L., Adler, G., & Myerson, P. G. (1972). Anger self-report: An objective questionnaire for the measurement of aggression. *Journal of Consulting and Clinical Psychology, 39,* 340.

Zung, W. W. (1965). A self-rating depression scale. *Archives of General Psychiatry, 12,* 63-70.

APPENDIX

INDEX CORRELATIONS WITH CLINICAL, PERSONALITY, AND VALIDITY INDICATORS

Table A-1
Index Correlations With PAI Full Scale Scores

PAI scales	MAL	DEF	CDF	SA Est	TPI	VPI	SPI	RDF
ICN	.07	−.23	.01	.16	.18	.19	.15	.28
INF	.00	−.08	.18	.04	.02	.03	.08	.37
NIM	.61	−.18	.26	.48	.64	.66	.69	.09
PIM	−.39	.56	.06	−.50	−.57	−.54	−.67	.10
SOM	.35	−.20	.13	.17	.37	.32	.58	.10
ANX	.46	−.49	.17	.28	.50	.46	.82	.07
ARD	.50	−.30	.22	.38	.60	.58	.80	−.02
DEP	.40	−.47	.11	.25	.50	.42	.82	.18
MAN	.33	.24	.40	.47	.44	.53	.30	−.19
PAR	.55	−.19	.26	.49	.66	.68	.65	.35
SCZ	.51	−.37	.17	.45	.59	.65	.79	.16
BOR	.45	−.48	.28	.67	.77	.74	.83	−.01
ANT	.25	−.06	.07	.94	.68	.74	.37	.02
ALC	−.03	−.06	−.52	.39	.33	.39	.21	−.10
DRG	.05	−.22	−.17	.54	.46	.53	.30	.03
AGG	.31	−.24	.21	.75	.59	.65	.44	.08
SUI	.32	−.34	.19	.38	.47	.44	.65	.06
STR	.33	−.27	−.14	.42	.59	.53	.64	−.11
NON	.34	−.24	.11	.39	.56	.59	.66	.27
RXR	−.21	.52	.26	−.37	−.46	−.41	−.56	.26
DOM	−.09	.49	.10	.06	−.09	.00	−.37	−.23
WRM	−.22	.40	.06	−.20	−.28	−.32	−.51	−.33

Note. Sample of clinical patients, n = 447. MAL = Malingering Index; DEF = Defensiveness Index; CDF = Cashel Discriminant Function; SA Est = estimated Substance Abuse scale scores; TPI = Treatment Process Index; VPI = Violence Potential Index; SPI = Suicide Potential Index; RDF = Rogers Discriminant Function.

Table A-2
Index Correlations With PAI Subscale Scores

PAI subscales	MAL	DEF	CDF	SA Est	TPI	VPI	SPI	RDF
SOM-C	.36	−.13	.15	.23	.39	.38	.52	−.07
SOM-S	.31	−.26	.10	.11	.32	.26	.56	.17
SOM-H	.26	−.15	.10	.11	.27	.23	.47	.16
ANX-C	.43	−.42	.13	.25	.48	.41	.77	.02
ANX-A	.40	−.50	.14	.27	.46	.43	.77	−.01
ANX-P	.45	−.39	.20	.27	.46	.44	.73	.22
ARD-O	.39	.12	.21	.20	.37	.40	.54	−.27
ARD-P	.34	−.45	.11	.17	.36	.25	.61	.28
ARD-T	.44	−.29	.19	.44	.63	.64	.72	−.04
DEP-C	.38	−.51	.11	.30	.50	.42	.77	.29
DEP-A	.38	−.46	.10	.25	.48	.41	.78	.09
DEP-P	.32	−.33	.09	.12	.38	.29	.68	.12
MAN-A	.29	.07	.32	.40	.37	.44	.38	−.18
MAN-G	−.03	.52	.23	.12	.04	.12	−.23	−.21
MAN-I	.54	−.14	.34	.53	.59	.62	.56	−.05
PAR-H	.41	−.11	.19	.48	.61	.65	.60	.22
PAR-P	.65	−.08	.24	.43	.55	.60	.49	.26
PAR-R	.34	−.29	.23	.35	.53	.48	.58	.43
SCZ-P	.46	−.10	.18	.36	.40	.49	.43	.13
SCZ-S	.26	−.36	.05	.30	.45	.48	.64	.30
SCZ-T	.51	−.33	.20	.41	.53	.55	.76	−.06
BOR-A	.42	−.45	.28	.55	.66	.65	.79	.02
BOR-I	.37	−.39	.23	.41	.59	.49	.71	−.09
BOR-N	.35	−.34	.23	.46	.62	.60	.67	.21
BOR-S	.33	−.26	.19	.81	.69	.69	.56	−.18
ANT-A	.08	−.14	−.09	.79	.58	.60	.29	−.04
ANT-E	.35	.10	.08	.70	.53	.55	.24	.11
ANT-S	.25	−.08	.23	.82	.57	.67	.37	.03
AGG-A	.32	−.19	.16	.63	.56	.57	.50	.09
AGG-V	.13	−.17	.20	.48	.31	.36	.07	.06
AGG-P	.34	−.23	.18	.79	.63	.72	.50	.05

Note. Sample of clinical patients, *n* = 447. MAL = Malingering Index; DEF = Defensiveness Index; CDF = Cashel Discriminant Function; SA Est = estimated Substance Abuse scale scores; TPI = Treatment Process Index; VPI = Violence Potential Index; SPI = Suicide Potential Index; RDF = Rogers Discriminant Function.

Table A-3
Index Correlations With MMPI Clinical and Validity Scales

MMPI scales	MAL	DEF	CDF	SA Est	TPI	VPI	SPI	RDF
L	−.08	.55	.04	−.21	−.23	−.17	−.40	.02
F	.39	−.15	.24	.33	.55	.52	.63	.13
K	−.37	.25	−.29	−.42	−.46	−.49	−.59	−.07
Hs	.06	−.10	−.12	−.03	.21	.10	.25	.18
D	.22	−.30	.12	.11	.36	.22	.53	.26
Hy	−.02	−.11	−.05	−.17	.10	−.06	.22	.14
Pd	.08	−.21	−.15	.31	.47	.33	.38	.04
Mf	.21	.25	.00	.40	.26	.29	.01	−.03
Pa	.38	−.20	.14	.18	.45	.39	.53	.05
Pt	.13	−.23	−.09	.28	.41	.33	.49	.00
Sc	.26	−.24	.09	.39	.56	.51	.61	.09
Ma	.19	.20	.17	.41	.40	.45	.32	−.25
Si	.28	−.45	.23	.00	.25	.21	.49	.31

Note. Sample of clinical patients, *n* = 91. MMPI = Minnesota Multiphasic Personality Inventory; MAL = Malingering Index; DEF = Defensiveness Index; CDF = Cashel Discriminant Function; SA Est = estimated Substance Abuse scale scores; TPI = Treatment Process Index; VPI = Violence Potential Index; SPI = Suicide Potential Index; RDF = Rogers Discriminant Function.

Table A-4
Index Correlations With Wiggins MMPI Content Scales[a]

	MAL	DEF	CDF	SA Est	TPI	VPI	SPI	RDF
HEA	.38	−.41	.30	.21	.44	.40	.57	.27
DEP	.39	−.52	.40	.60	.70	.63	.83	.16
ORG	.33	−.31	.36	.12	.36	.36	.49	.12
FAM	.29	−.15	.21	.49	.50	.40	.54	.01
AUT	.42	.14	.57	.43	.39	.42	.47	.12
FEM	.01	−.18	.08	.03	.04	.02	.03	.22
REL	.23	.00	.08	.03	.04	.02	.01	.09
HOS	.40	−.14	.48	.68	.62	.63	.63	−.02
MOR	.43	−.49	.26	.48	.61	.52	.77	.08
PHO	.13	−.31	.33	.03	.19	.18	.30	.19
PSY	.49	−.10	.63	.40	.59	.65	.69	.12
HYP	.27	.29	.61	.40	.31	.40	.39	−.09
SOC	.11	−.28	.09	.02	.12	.15	.28	.26

Note. Sample of clinical patients, *n* = 91. MMPI = Minnesota Multiphasic Personality Inventory; MAL = Malingering Index; DEF = Defensiveness Index; CDF = Cashel Discriminant Function; SA Est = estimated Substance Abuse scale scores; TPI = Treatment Process Index; VPI = Violence Potential Index; SPI = Suicide Potential Index; RDF = Rogers Discriminant Function.
[a]J. S. Wiggins, 1966.

Table A-5
Index Correlations With Indicators of Clinical Symptomatology

	MAL	DEF	CDF	SA Est	TPI	VPI	SPI	RDF
Beck Depression Inventory (BDI)[a]	.39	−.28	−.08	.01	.35	.21	.63	.15
Beck Anxiety Inventory (BAI)[b]	.38	−.26	.01	.10	.30	.25	.52	.09
Hamilton Rating Scale for Depression (HAM-D)[c]	.05	−.47	.19	.04	.30	−.11	.11	.11
Mississippi Combat-related PTSD scale[d]	.46	.32	.48	.49	.72	.63	.56	.12
Self-report Psychopathy scale (SRP)[e]	.25	−.36	.27	.70	.50	.67	.59	−.07
Suicide Probability Scale (SPS),[f] Hopelessness	.24	.19	−.10	.06	.45	.39	.64	−.12
Suicide Probability Scale (SPS),[f] Suicidal Ideation	.14	.01	−.16	.03	.42	.31	.65	−.19
Suicide Probability Scale (SPS),[f] Negative Self-evaluation	.14	−.01	−.19	−.17	.31	.18	.48	−.05
Suicide Probability Scale (SPS),[f] Hostility	.19	.15	−.11	.21	.44	.40	.39	−.08
Suicide Probability Scale (SPS),[f] Total score	.24	.12	−.10	.07	.46	.39	.63	−.10
Wahler Physical Symptoms Inventory (WPSI)[g]	−.16	−.79	−.23	−.07	.22	−.08	.50	.29

Note. Sample of clinical patients, n = 91. MAL = Malingering Index; DEF = Defensiveness Index; CDF = Cashel Discriminant Function; SA Est = estimated Substance Abuse scale scores; TPI = Treatment Process Index; VPI = Violence Potential Index; SPI = Suicide Potential Index; RDF = Rogers Discriminant Function.
[a]A. T. Beck & R. A. Steer, 1987. [b]A. T. Beck & R. A. Steer, 1990. [c]M. Hamilton, 1960. [d]T. M. Keane, J. M. Caddell, & K. L. Taylor, 1988. [e]R. D. Hare, 1985. [f]J. G. Cull & W. S. Gill, 1982. [g]H. J. Wahler, 1983.

Table A-6
Index Correlations With MMPI Personality Disorder Scales[a]

MMPI scale	MAL	DEF	CDF	SA Est	TPI	VPI	SPI	RDF
Histrionic	−.06	.41	.04	.12	−.10	−.12	−.31	−.35
Narcissistic	.01	.45	.20	−.01	−.07	−.06	−.34	−.25
Borderline	.29	−.35	.36	.64	.55	.53	.68	−.07
Antisocial	.16	−.20	.20	.59	.53	.52	.53	−.06
Dependent	.42	−.52	.17	.36	.46	.44	.67	.23
Compulsive	.35	−.15	.34	.23	.40	.44	.57	−.16
Passive-Aggressive	.60	−.07	.33	.49	.57	.60	.81	.06
Paranoid	.58	.00	.51	.39	.56	.59	.66	.17
Schizotypal	.41	−.33	.37	.20	.44	.49	.61	.29
Avoidant	.36	−.41	.21	.15	.37	.39	.63	.29
Schizoid	.14	−.15	.21	−.08	.11	.15	.31	.32

Note. Sample of clinical patients, $n = 91$. MMPI = Minnesota Multiphasic Personality Inventory; MAL = Malingering Index; DEF = Defensiveness Index; CDF = Cashel Discriminant Function; SA Est = estimated Substance Abuse scale scores; TPI = Treatment Process Index; VPI = Violence Potential Index; SPI = Suicide Potential Index; RDF = Rogers Discriminant Function.
[a]L. C. Morey, M H. Waugh, & R. K. Blashfield, 1985.

Table A-7
Index Correlations With Personality Disorder Questionnaire–
Revised[a] *DSM-III-R* Personality Disorder Scale Scores

	MAL	DEF	CDF	SA Est	TPI	VPI	SPI	RDF
Histrionic	.27	.10	.07	.27	.23	.14	.22	.20
Narcissistic	.32	.30	−.16	.45	.45	.28	.19	.17
Borderline	.25	−.37	.06	.36	.49	.24	.19	.15
Antisocial	.03	−.34	−.32	.58	.51	.25	.16	.15
Dependent	.09	−.27	−.03	.05	.17	.01	.05	.12
Obsessive-Compulsive	.25	.20	.10	.33	.28	.28	.17	−.12
Passive-Aggressive	.20	−.33	−.11	.33	.35	.19	.11	.16
Paranoid	.39	−.31	−.17	.10	.35	.22	.20	.27
Schizotypal	.31	−.17	.19	.22	.54	.41	.32	.36
Avoidant	.33	−.34	−.15	.02	.35	.24	.23	.16
Schizoid	.01	−.12	−.08	−.17	.11	.16	.00	−.02
Self-defeating	.30	−.25	.04	.30	.37	.19	.03	.05
Sadistic	.01	.09	−.26	.38	.21	.32	−.12	−.08

Note. Sample of clinical outpatients, *n* = 64. MAL = Malingering Index; DEF = Defensiveness Index; CDF = Cashel Discriminant Function; SA Est = estimated Substance Abuse scale scores; TPI = Treatment Process Index; VPI = Violence Potential Index; SPI = Suicide Potential Index; RDF = Rogers Discriminant Function.

[a]S. E. Hyler, R. O. Rieder, J. B. W. Williams, R. L. Spitzler, J. Hendler, & M. Lyons, 1988.

Table A-8
Index Correlations With Diagnostic Interview for
Personality Disorder[a] *DSM-III-R* **Personality Disorder Diagnoses**

	MAL	DEF	CDF	SA Est	TPI	VPI	SPI	RDF
Histrionic	−.08	.43	.03	.36	.10	.06	−.01	.16
Narcissistic	.00	.01	−.10	.41	.33	.15	.01	.11
Borderline	−.12	−.04	−.10	.23	.06	−.05	.03	.17
Antisocial	.42	−.43	−.09	.27	.46	.68	.37	.24
Dependent	.09	−.28	.17	−.19	.01	.00	.00	.13
Compulsive	.24	.30	−.04	.16	.24	.16	.21	.01
Paranoid	.35	−.39	−.18	−.05	.30	.20	.12	.14
Schizotypal	.24	.00	.14	.11	.40	.18	.16	−.08
Avoidant	.16	−.31	−.25	−.09	.21	.06	.15	.05
Schizoid	−.01	−.13	.08	−.10	.15	.21	.15	.10

Note. Sample of clinical outpatients, *n* = 72. MAL = Malingering Index; DEF = Defensiveness Index; CDF = Cashel Discriminant Function; SA Est = estimated Substance Abuse scale scores; TPI = Treatment Process Index; VPI = Violence Potential Index; SPI = Suicide Potential Index; RDF = Rogers Discriminant Function.
[a] M. Zanarini, 1987.

Table A-9
Index Correlations With Brief Psychiatric
Rating Scale (BPRS)[a] Clinician Ratings

BPRS ratings	MAL	DEF	CDF	SA Est	TPI	VPI	SPI	RDF
Somatic concern	−.10	−.07	−.12	−.18	.00	−.17	−.19	−.02
Anxiety	−.16	−.29	−.09	.20	.25	.03	.11	−.13
Emotional withdrawal	−.03	.03	−.17	−.18	−.23	−.19	−.04	.08
Conceptual Disorganization	.10	.30	.12	−.02	.02	.00	−.12	−.15
Guilt feelings	−.09	−.39	−.20	.14	.20	.10	.23	−.12
Tension	.19	.16	.32	.27	.35	.20	.21	−.01
Mannerisms and posturing	.08	.17	.00	.01	−.01	.02	.05	−.18
Grandiosity	.25	.39	.13	.16	.20	.16	.03	−.11
Depressive mood	−.01	−.49	.01	.13	.22	.02	.16	.19
Hostility	−.09	−.21	.27	.19	.26	−.07	−.12	.07
Suspiciousness	.07	−.20	.19	.13	.25	−.02	−.09	.10
Hallucinatory behavior	−.17	−.08	.14	−.08	.01	−.26	−.33	−.09
Motor retardation	.02	−.34	−.19	−.08	.02	−.04	.15	.22
Uncooperative	−.08	.01	.29	.10	.16	−.15	−.24	.00
Unusual thought content	.08	.18	.10	.10	.07	.01	−.07	.12
Blunted affect	.01	−.06	−.14	−.10	−.22	−.10	.02	.23
Excitement	−.18	.13	.21	−.11	−.02	−.09	−.07	.05
Disorientation	−.15	−.27	−.02	−.16	−.21	−.18	−.17	−.09

Note. Sample of psychiatric inpatients, $n = 72$. MAL = Malingering Index; DEF = Defensiveness Index; CDF = Cashel Discriminant Function; SA Est = estimated Substance Abuse scale scores; TPI = Treatment Process Index; VPI = Violence Potential Index; SPI = Suicide Potential Index; RDF = Rogers Discriminant Function.

[a]J. E. Overall & D. R. Gorman, 1962.

Table A-10
Index Correlations With Indicators of Personality and Environment

	MAL	DEF	CDF	SA Est	TPI	VPI	SPI	RDF
Social Readjustment Rating Scale[a]	.05	.17	.05	.32	.42	.33	.36	−.15
Perceived Social Support Rating Scale−Friends[b]	−.14	.20	−.01	−.25	−.29	−.27	−.44	−.15
Perceived Social Support Rating Scale−Family[b]	−.07	−.15	.13	−.21	−.13	−.12	−.22	.06
Marlowe-Crowne Social Desirability Scale[c]	−.19	.28	.27	−.49	−.27	−.40	−.36	.09
Interpersonal Adjective Scales−Warmth[d]	−.21	−.03	−.09	−.45	−.33	−.44	−.34	.13
Interpersonal Adjective Scales−Dominance[d]	.03	.53	.11	.32	.21	.27	−.19	−.18

Note. Sample of community adults, n = 85. MAL = Malingering Index; DEF = Defensiveness Index; CDF = Cashel Discriminant Function; SA Est = estimated Substance Abuse scale scores; TPI = Treatment Process Index; VPI = Violence Potential Index; SPI = Suicide Potential Index; RDF = Rogers Discriminant Function.
[a]T. H. Holmes & R. H. Rahe, 1967. [b]M. E. Procidiano & K. Heller, 1983. [c]D. P. Crowne & D. Marlowe, 1964. [d]J. S. Wiggins, 1995.

Table A-11
Index Correlations With Indicators of Clinical Symptomatology

	MAL	DEF	CDF	SA Est	TPI	VPI	SPI	RDF
Self-report Psychopathy Scale[a]	.03	−.08	.28	.81	.67	.69	.25	.22
Maudsley Obsessive-Compulsive Index[b]	.20	−.24	.15	−.06	−.06	.17	.60	.00
Fear Survey Schedule[c]	.16	−.14	.19	−.13	−.29	−.26	.20	−.11
Beck Hopelessness Scale[d]	.13	−.12	−.06	.01	.06	.07	.49	.32
State-Trait Anxiety Inventory–State[e]	−.09	−.32	−.06	−.11	.12	−.04	.55	.39
State-Trait Anxiety Inventory–Trait[f]	.24	−.37	−.03	−.05	−.16	−.07	.66	.03
State-Trait Anger Expression Inventory–State Anger[f]	−.07	−.35	.14	.08	.06	.12	.43	.13
State-Trait Anger Expression Inventory–Trait Anger[f]	.07	−.19	.13	.38	.32	.46	.33	.06
State-Trait Anger Expression Inventory–Angry Temperament[f]	.09	.06	.31	.30	.22	.49	.42	.00
State-Trait Anger Expression Inventory–Angry Reaction[f]	.05	−.16	−.12	.18	.24	.24	.19	−.02
State-Trait Anger Expression Inventory–Anger In[f]	.19	−.24	−.04	.22	.08	.27	.35	.05
State-Trait Anger Expression Inventory–Anger Out[f]	−.11	−.16	.00	.46	.18	.37	−.02	.15
State-Trait Anger Expression Inventory–Anger Control[f]	.34	.39	.11	−.19	.06	−.16	−.05	−.26
State-Trait Anger Expression Inventory–Anger Expression[f]	−.09	−.40	−.08	.37	.08	.35	.20	.20

Note. Sample of college students, $n = 42$. MAL = Malingering Index; DEF = Defensiveness Index; CDF = Cashel Discriminant Function; SA Est = estimated Substance Abuse scale scores; TPI = Treatment Process Index; VPI = Violence Potential Index; SPI = Suicide Potential Index; RDF = Rogers Discriminant Function.
[a]R. D. Hare, 1985, [b]S. J. Rachman & R. J. Hodgson, 1980. [c]J. Wolpe & P. Lang, 1964. [d]A. T. Beck & R. A. Steer, 1988. [e]C. D. Spielberger, 1983. [f]C. D. Spielberger, 1988.

Table A-12
Index Intercorrelations in Clinical and Community Samples

	MAL	DEF	CDF	SA Est	TPI	VPI	SPI	RDF
MAL	—	.15	.17	.34	.40	.42	.47	.26
DEF	.10	—	.32	−.07	.08	.04	−.18	−.07
CDF	.24	.17	—	.22	.13	.19	.10	.27
SA Est	.32	−.22	.19	—	.68	.79	.61	.31
TPI	.44	−.22	.16	.78	—	.75	.65	.30
VPI	.48	−.17	.19	.83	.87	—	.65	.21
SPI	.50	−.39	.13	.54	.76	.72	—	.36
RDF	.11	−.06	.19	.07	.10	.09	.12	—

Note. Values above diagonal from community normative sample, *N* = 1,000; values below diagonal from clinical normative sample, *N* = 1,246. MAL = Malingering Index; DEF = Defensiveness Index; CDF = Cashel Discriminant Function; SA Est = estimated Substance Abuse scale scores; TPI = Treatment Process Index; VPI = Violence Potential Index; SPI = Suicide Potential Index; RDF = Rogers Discriminant Function.

INDEX